TAKING CASH OUT OF THE CLOSELY HELD CORPORATION

Tax Opportunities, Strategies, and Techniques

Fourth Edition

LAWRENCE C. SILTON

PRENTICE HALL
Englewood Cliffs, New Jersey 07632

Prentice-Hall International (UK) Limited, *London*
Prentice-Hall of Australia, Pty. Limited, *Sydney*
Prentice-Hall Canada Inc., Toronto
Prentice-Hall Hispanoamericana, S.A., *Mexico*
Prentice-Hall of India Private Limited, *New Delhi*
Prentice-Hall of Japan, Inc., *Tokyo*
Simon & Schuster Asia Pte. Ltd., *Singapore*
Editora Prentice-Hall do Brasil, Ltda., *Rio de Janeiro*

Printed in the United States of America

10   9   8   7   6   5   4   3   2

This publication is designed to provide accurate and
authoritative information in regard to the subject
matter covered. It is sold with the understanding
that the publisher is not engaged in rendering legal,
accounting, or other professional service. If legal
advice or other expert assistance is required, the
services of a competent professional person should be
sought.
*. . . From the Declaration of Principles jointly
adopted by a Committee of the American Bar Association and a Committee of Publishers and Associa-
tions.*

Library of Congress Cataloging-in-Publication Data

Silton, Lawrence C.
 Taking cash out of the closely held corporation.

 Includes index.
 1. Close corporations—Taxation—United States.
I. Title.
KF6484.S54   1988   343.7306'7   87-38499

ISBN 0-13-882713-3   347.30367

ISBN 0-13-882713-3

PRENTICE HALL
BUSINESS & PROFESSIONAL DIVISION
A division of Simon & Schuster
Englewood Cliffs, New Jersey 07632

This book is dedicated
to my wife Susan,
without whose insight and
encouragement it would never
have been written.

What This Guide Will Do for You

The Tax Reform Act of 1986 and the recently passed Budget Reconciliation Act of 1987 have had a significant impact upon the closely held corporation. Many of the planning opportunities in the past are no longer available while whole new opportunities present themselves. There are numerous pitfalls in not reappraising the tax plans which were established prior to the implementation of the Tax Reform Act of 1986. Many of the transitional rules implemented by the Tax Reform Act offer opportunities which if not quickly acted upon will cease to be available. The Fourth Edition of *Taking Cash Out of the Closely Held Corporation* provides you with up-to-date advice for maximizing the cash flow to stockholders in the most tax favored form.

The new Acts have made critical changes in literally hundreds of sections of the Internal Revenue Code, especially in the areas of capital gains, installment sales, fringe benefits, dividend distributions, and loans between corporations and their employees and stockholders. This Fourth Edition explains how the new law affects these and other areas. More important, you are provided with step-by-step instructions for taking maximum advantage of new tax-saving opportunities while minimizing, or in many cases avoiding altogether, the new tax traps.

This Fourth Edition incorporates not only the changes in the Tax Reform Act of 1986 and the Omnibus Budget Reconciliation Act of 1987, but also expands upon the changes made in the Tax Reform Act of 1984 and the Social Security Act of 1983. The Fourth Edition, like the preceding editions, shows you the opportunities and strategic techniques for extracting money from the closely held corporation at minimum tax cost. These techniques, which can be used during all phases of corporate life—incorporation, operation, and termination—provide numerous opportunities both for reducing corporate taxes and for improving the after-tax cash flow to stockholders.

This Guide will show you how to use the tax laws, including the Tax Reform Act of 1986, to meet specific business and personal financial objectives. You will be shown, step by step, how to mold your corporation into a tool which fits your own particular business and personal needs. The closely held corporation allows for a flexibility that major corporations (which must report and justify their actions to their shareholders and governmental agencies) envy. Taking maximum advantage of the opportunities available to the closely held corporation requires careful planning and equally careful implementation. This Guide will provide you with the knowledge of the law and the latest tax planning strategies and techniques to help achieve your own business and personal financial objectives.

Here are a few of the situations for which this Guide offers practical answers, key ideas, and helpful hints:

- ☐ How the Tax Reform Act of 1986 affects your closely held corporation and what changes must be made to accommodate, recategorize, and prepare the corporation to continue to maximize its benefits to you.

- ☐ How to arrange to have tax-free income "pass through" the corporation into the hands of stockholders.

- ☐ How to recategorize some items of income to escape tax.

- ☐ How to set the salary of owner/employees at the best tax level for both the employee and the corporation. The Tax Reform Act of 1986 has completely changed the prior emphasis in this area. Maximum salaries and minimum retention may be the goal.

- ☐ How to shift and divide income to minimize the tax bite while keeping more of the money in the family. Again, the Tax Reform Act of 1986 has provided traps for the unwary and also allowed for positive planning in the future.

- ☐ How to avoid incurring taxes when you set up a new corporation and when it makes the most sense to make incorporation taxable.

- ☐ How to avoid the new tax trap for installment sales.

- ☐ How to avoid having corporate loans to shareholders reclassified as nondeductible dividends, and how to handle interest-free loans between corporations and their shareholders.

- [ ] Why the personal holding company will be a tax saving vehicle in the future.

- [ ] What the corporation can do to justify retained earnings and avoid the accumulated earnings tax penalty.

- [ ] How to increase the basis of property held by the corporation.

- [ ] How to use key tax strategies to gain maximum savings through election of an S corporation.

- [ ] How the owner can take maximum advantage of tax-saving opportunities while minimizing the changes of a challenge by the IRS. How, if challenged, the owner can convince the IRS that salary and other trouble-prone deductions are legitimate business expenses.

- [ ] What the alternatives are to liquidating a corporation, and how they can be used when transferring ownership as well as terminating a corporation.

- [ ] How to determine reasonable compensation if the corporation is owned by a single shareholder and its taxable income has fluctuated a great deal.

- [ ] How to pick a retirement plan that will provide the greatest future benefits at the least cost.

- [ ] In retirement planning, is the 401(k) the instrument of the future? Why will there be less defined benefit and more defined contribution plans utilizing the provisions of 401(k) in the future?

- [ ] Has the Tax Reform Act of 1986 made the spin-off a tax planning opportunity without equal?

- [ ] How has the Omnibus Budget Reconciliation Act of 1987 adversely affected personal service corporations?

This Guide provides a wide range of alternative strategies for extracting cash from the closely held corporation at each stage of corporate existence. It allows you to choose alternatives best suited to your own personal and business needs, and also to weigh opportunities against any risks which may exist for each alternative. You will find detailed explanations of what to do, when to do it and why, and most important, how to do it.

Lawrence C. Silton

Contents

1

How to Achieve the Maximum Benefits from Preincorporation Techniques

[100] WHY THE PREINCORPORATION PERIOD IS SO IMPORTANT

The preincorporation period is one of the most important stages in tax planning. In this stage, it is necessary for you to develop a program that allows for the extraction of funds during the operation or upon termination of the corporation at either no tax cost or at minimum tax cost. Planning during the preincorporation period is dictated in many respects by preexisting conditions. These conditions set parameters on the use of a certain type of planning and may preclude the use of a plan which would provide maximum tax benefits. For instance, if a small family business is being incorporated for estate-planning purposes, the goal will usually be to minimize taxes upon the founder's death so maximum tax planning may be implemented. If, on the other hand, the corporation is being established by unrelated parties to develop a new product or service, different objectives dictate the appropriate planning. Here, taxes play a subordinate role, and the success of the business becomes paramount.

The planning devices which are available for your client for the mimization of taxes are limited in number. These planning devices take different forms at different periods of the corporate existence. In spite of the different forms they may take, they do appear at all stages of the corporate development.

[100.1] Five Key Tax Devices That Can Be Used during the Preincorporation Period

1. *Dividing the income:* Even after the full implementation of the Tax Reform Act of 1986, we still have maintained the progressive nature of the income tax rates. If a married individual filing a joint return earns $130,000 net taxable income, he is going to pay approximately $35,437.50 of federal income tax beginning in 1988. However, if $50,000 is earned by a corporation of which he is the sole shareholder and $80,000 is earned by him individually as salary, the total tax on both the corporation and himself is $26,437.50, resulting in a tax savings of $9,000.

The following is an example of some of the opportunities available for dividing income:

> **Example:** Eli Avery is in a capital-intensive field. His inventory of wooden widgets and receivables has been growing rapidly and is increasing approximately $40,000 a year. Before salary to himself and income taxes, he is netting $110,000 as a sole proprietorship. His wife claims that they are always poor, stating that she can run a house and pay the bills of the family on $60,000 a year before income taxes. Her sister, whose husband is a junior executive in a multinational corporation and makes $60,000, lives better than she does. What are the tax effects of incorporating? (State taxes are disregarded.)

TAX EFFECTS OF INCORPORATION

A. Tax Effects as a Sole Proprietor

Sole Proprietorship Income	$110,000.00
Other Income	5,000.00
Total Income	$115,000.00
Exemptions and Itemized Deductions	5,000.00
Net Taxable Income	$110,000.00
Federal Income Tax	$ 28,837.50

In calculating tax savings, it is also imperative that you look at disposable net income. Disposable net income is total income less taxes and money retained in the business. In analyzing Mrs. Avery's complaint in the previous example, you will notice that in effect her family's disposable net income is really less than her sister's. The reason for this is that while the sole proprietorship produced $110,000 of net income, the cash flow from the sole proprietorship was really $40,000 less since Mr. Avery is in a growing business and his receivables and inventory are growing at about $40,000 a year. Accordingly, the Avery family's disposable cash flow would be as follows:

Sole Proprietorship and Other Income		$115,000.00
LESS:		
Increase in Receivables and Inventory	$40,000.00	
Federal Tax	28,837.50	68,837.50
Net Disposable Income		$ 46,162.50

Mrs. Avery's sister has a disposable income calculated as follows:

Income from Multinational Corporation	$60,000.00
Other Income	5,000.00
Total Income	$65,000.00
LESS: Exemptions and Itemized Deductions	5,000.00
Net Taxable Income	$60,000.00
Federal Income Tax	$12,932.50
Net Disposable Income (total income of $65,000 less federal tax of $12,932.50)	$52,067.50

B. Tax Effects of Incorporating and Paying Eli Avery
$60,000 a Year Salary for His Services

1. Corporate Tax

Income before Salary	$110,000.00
Salary	60,000.00
Net Taxable Income	$ 50,000.00
Corporate Income Tax	$ 7,500.00

2. Individual Tax after Incorporation

Salary	$ 60,000.00
Other	5,000.00
	$ 65,000.00
Deductions and Exemptions	5,000.00
Taxable Income	$ 60,000.00
Personal Income Tax	$ 12,932.50

3. Total Tax after Incorporation

Corporate Tax	$ 7,500.00
Individual Tax	12,932.50
Total Tax	$ 20,432.50
Savings Accomplished by Incorporating	$ 8,405.00

In this instance, incorporation not only produced tax savings, but it also raised the owner's disposable net income from $46,162.50 to $52,067.50, if the liabilities are assumed to remain constant. In calculating the need for disposable income, it is best to determine the change in the net equity of the business, that is, the difference between the total assets over the total liabilities in the beginning of the year from that at the end of the year. A growing business such as Eli Avery's will usually require increased equity. Many times, if there is a significant capital purchase, for example, the purchase of a new building or a major piece of equipment, there will be an offsetting liability so the increased immediate capital needed will not be that great.

Schedule Showing the Impact of Salary When Considering Incorporating

In order to obtain the maximum tax benefits of incorporating, the payment of salary is extremely important. The following schedule will determine the maximum tax benefits available by properly using salary but disregards both the cost of incorporating and any fringe benefits that may be applicable. For example, contributions to qualified deferred compensation plans will not be taken into consideration. If the corporation had established a qualified plan, a higher salary with a lower retention of after tax income by the corporation may provide maximum benefits. Before the Tax Reform Act of 1986, it was appropriate to incorporate a going business, if the sole proprietor was married and had taxable income of $75,000 or more. After the enactment of the Tax Reform Act of 1986 and its full implementation in 1988, the benefits of incorporating have been reduced, and it would appear that this amount has been increased to at least $100,000.

Total Business Income	Married Taxpayer Optimum Practical Salary**	Approximate Tax in Unincorporated Form	Approximate Total Tax (Individual) and Corporate in Incorporated Form with Salary at Optimum Rate	Approximate Tax Savings
$ 50,000	$29,750	$10,132.50	$ 7,500.00	$ 2,632.50
75,000	29,750	17,647.50	11,250.00	6,397.50
100,000	50,000	25,537.50	17,632.50	7,905.00
125,000	71,900	33,787.50	24,539.50	9,248.00
150,000 and up*	75,000 and up*	42,000.00	31,037.50	10,962.50

* After $150,000 of business income, of which $75,000 is retained in the corporation, there is a negative benefit in retaining any further corporate income. Accordingly, even if there is a small possibility that a portion of the salary will be considered unreasonable compensation, it is usually to the best interest of the parties to pay the maximum salary.

** The concept of practical rather than just "optimum" salary applies when corporate and individual rates are approximately the same. In those instances, it is usually advantageous to maximize salary. For example, if the corporation is in the 25 percent marginal tax bracket and the individual is in the 28 percent marginal tax bracket, income should "if feasible" be paid to the shareholder as salary.

For this schedule, assume, as in the previous example, that the unearned income equals the deductions and exemptions which were allowable to the taxpayer (see the charts on pages 8 and 9). The tax rate schedules are those which will take effect in 1988. It is interesting to note that both the Economic Recovery Tax Act of 1981 and the Tax Reform Act of 1986 have discouraged the retention of corporate income.

For example, if an individual had a total business income of $175,000 in 1980 and if he incorporated and retained $100,000 in the corporation for future expansion, his total tax, utilizing the maximum tax planning opportunities in effect prior to the enactment of the Economic Recovery Tax Act of

1981, would have been $54,528. After the Economic Recovery Act of 1981 was completely implemented in 1984, this tax was reduced to $47,218, which is slightly less than a 13 percent reduction. After full implementation of the Tax Reform Act of 1986 in 1988, the tax would have been reduced only to $39,287.50. The expressed intent of the Economic Recovery Tax Act (ERTA), and the implied goal of the Tax Reform Act of 1986 was to provide for the maximum retention of corporate income by small corporations. The actual application to the smaller corporations indicates that both acts may not provide the projected results.

As will be seen in Chapters 2, 3 and 4, the new goals will be maximum salary payments and minimum retention in the corporation. This will definitely adversely affect future expansion through retention of corporate income and will necessitate the increased financing for growth in the future. Not only will smaller corporations be affected, but the larger corporations will also find that the elimination of the favorable tax rates for capital gains will put them under increased pressure to dividends, again diluting the capital base. The actual impact upon the economy at this time is premature. However, the pressures for instant gratification through salary and dividends will increase. Management may not be able to withstand these pressures and justify its position, basing it on the favorable tax structure in the future.

Corporate Tax Chart*

The following chart will not only show the total tax at various levels of taxable income for the corporation but also will show the effective tax rate on all the income earned. It should be noted that the breakpoints on the taxable income beginning in 1988 are as follows:

0–$50,000	15 percent
$50,000–$75,000	25 percent
$75,000–$100,000	34 percent
$100,000–$335,000	39 percent
$335,000 and over	34 percent

* Beginning in 1988, personal service corporations will be taxed at a flat 34 percent. Thus, personal service corporations will lose the benefits of the corporate graduate rates available to other "C" corporations.

NOTE: For both corporate and individual purposes, the 5 percent surcharge included in the above schedule has created an anomaly. For corporate purposes, the large corporation will incur smaller marginal tax cost than the smaller corporations. For example, the large corporation will pay $34,000 in tax on the next $100,000 of income between $335,000 and $435,000. The smaller corporation with the same $100,000 in income increase from $100,000 to $200,000 will incur $39,000 in tax. This runs counter to the historical nature of the progressive tax system and either indicates a harbinger of change or will necessitate a change in the corporate and individual tax structures through some future tax acts.

Accordingly, not only the effective rate must be considered, as shown below, but also the various breakpoints of the change in rates must be analyzed in planning salary and other payments, as follows:

Taxable Income	Amount of Tax Paid	Effective Rate Percent
$ 25,000	$ 3,750	15.00
30,000	4,500	15.00
35,000	5,250	15.00
40,000	6,000	15.00
45,000	6,750	15.00
50,000	7,500	15.00
55,000	8,750	15.91
60,000	10,000	16.67
65,000	11,250	17.31
70,000	12,500	17.86
75,000	13,750	18.33
80,000	15,450	19.31
85,000	17,150	20.18
90,000	18,850	20.94
95,000	20,550	21.63
100,000	22,250	22.25
105,000	24,200	23.05
110,000	26,150	23.77
115,000	28,100	24.43

continued

Taxable Income	Amount of Tax Paid	Effective Rate Percent
120,000	30,050	25.04
125,000	32,000	25.60
130,000	33,950	26.12
135,000	35,900	26.59
140,000	37,850	27.04
145,000	39,800	28.45
150,000	41,750	27.83
155,000*	43,700	28.19

* Note that after $155,000 of corporate income, the effective rate is equivalent to the maximum individual rate without the 5 percent surcharge. Thus, while there may be some benefit in retaining income in a corporation with income of $155,000 or less, it would appear that after that amount there is absolutely no tax benefits for the retention of income in the corporation.

INDIVIDUAL FLAT TAX (EXAMPLE FOR MARRIED TAXPAYERS)

Income	Tax Rate
0–$ 29,750	15 percent
$ 29,750–$ 71,900	28 percent
$ 71,900–$149,250	33 percent
$149,250 and over	28 percent

Key Idea: When a sole proprietorship is generating income in excess of $100,000 and when a good portion of the income must be plowed back into the business for either increased working capital or other assets, it is a good idea to seriously consider incorporating the business and paying the individual officer/shareholder a reasonable salary.

2. *Shifting the income:* This concept is very much akin to the basic idea of dividing income. It is different in the respect that an attempt is made to shift income from higher base taxpayers to lower base taxpayers without creating a new entity. An example of this is our married individual filing a joint return with a net taxable income of $100,000 shifting income to his children who are in a lower tax bracket. If this can be accomplished, the overall tax burden will be significantly reduced. In the above example, if $10,000 can be shifted to each of his

three children for future educational needs, the total burden is reduced from about $25,537.50 to approximately $20,232.50, resulting in a $5,305 tax savings.

The Tax Reform Act of 1986 has had a significant impact upon this planning device. One of the cornerstones of this act was to tax the family unit on the combined income rather than on the income of each individual. However, there is still tax planning for family members with unearned income for children over the age of 14 and for all family members if they have earned income.

> **Key Idea (A):** During the preincorporation period, it is a good idea to consider the election as a Subchapter S Corporation. This could provide the shifting of income to the lower basis taxpayer over the age of 14. (See Chapter 5.)

> **Key Idea (B):** It is also a good idea to consider multiple incorporations, with one corporation being an ordinary corporation and the other being a Subchapter S Corporation. (See Chapter 5.)

> **Key Idea (C):** Salary payments to children will have increased application and utilization in closely held corporations. (See Chapter 3.)

3. *Converting ordinary income into capital gains:* Prior to the Tax Reform Act of 1986, capital gains rates were 40 percent of ordinary income rates with a maximum rate of 20 percent. Therefore, the ability to convert ordinary income into capital gains produced substantial tax savings. The future of this technique is in doubt. The structure has been retained, and there is a favorable tax rate on capital gains through 1987. However, as scheduled, in 1988, all capital gains will be taxed at the same rate as ordinary income. Exactly what Congress will do with capital gains in the future is still open to question, and planning in this area is at best unsettled.

4. *Recategorizing income or properly paying expenses:* This is an area of taxation where an expense, if properly categorized or paid by the corporation, will produce more beneficial results than if paid by the individual taxpayer. An illustration of this can be seen in the fringe benefit area regarding payment of medical expenses.

The Internal Revenue Code is structured so that only extraordinary medical expenses are deductible. The concept of extraordinary has included as deductions all expenses in excess of 7.5 percent of the person's adjusted gross income. Accordingly, when the employee has $50,000 of adjusted gross income, extraordinary medical expenses are only those in excess of $3,750.

On the other hand, if these payments are made by the corporation, pursuant to a nondiscriminatory medical reimbursement plan, the corporation will get a deduction for the payment, and the person will not be taxed for the amount of payment made by his corporation. By designating the corporation as the party to pay the expenditure, an additional $3,750 tax deductible expense has been created.

WARNING: The whole area of fringe benefits is being reappraised. Substantial changes have been scheduled to be implemented in 1988. (See Chapter 2.) It would appear that even more changes are in the offing. Thus, planning should proceed with care.

> **Key Idea:** Beginning in 1987, certain expenses to be deductible must exceed 2 percent of the adjusted gross income. Examples of these are professional dues and business publications. On the other hand, if these expenses are paid by the corporation, no income should result to the employee.

> **Example:** Middle Executive is earning $60,000. Normally it is his obligation to join various professional organizations and purchase a trade magazine. These amount to $600 a year. If he pays these individually, beginning in 1987, there probably will be no tax benefit. If, on the other hand, the corporation pays these expenses, they are deductible to the corporation and will not result in any taxable income to Middle Executive.

5. *Timing of income:* The basic concept here is that if income is bunched in any one year, it will produce a significantly higher tax burden than if it is spread over a period of years. An illustration of this is the installment sale. If real property with a basis of $10,000 sells for $110,000 and the gain is all reported in one year, the tax burden could approach, at capital gains rates in 1987, $28,000. If, on the other hand, five payments of $22,000 each were received, the tax burden could be reduced to as low as $15,000.

CAUTION: For all years after 1986, income averaging, which had the effect of mitigating the need to time the receipt of income, has been repealed by the Tax Reform Act of 1986. The need to time income will therefore be even more important in the future. Beginning in 1988, a timing difference of $10,000 in income can result in a tax savings or cost of $1,800.

The Omnibus Budget Reconciliation Act of 1987 has had an impact on the timing of taxation for installments sales. Before attempting to defer taxable income through an installment sale, this Act should be reviewed.

How Timing the Date of Incorporation and Payment of Salaries Can Maximize Tax Savings

Key Idea: Incorporate during the year and do not pay any salary prior to the following January 1. Close the corporate year on or after January 31 of the following year and have the income taxed at the lower corporate rate.

The following is an example showing the advantage of not paying salary during the first couple of months of incorporation:

Example: A, who operates Jake's Bar & Grill, during the first six months of the year, has realized a $75,000 net taxable income from his business. It is anticipated that during the next six months he will realize an additional $50,000. If all income is reported as a sole proprietor, his total income for the year would be $125,000, on which he would pay approximately $33,787.50 in tax. If he incorporates on July 1, receives no salary during the current year, and has the corporation's year end on January 31, he has reduced his tax burden as follows:

Individual Tax on $75,000	$17,647.50
Corporate Tax on $50,000	$ 7,500.00
TOTAL	$25,147.50
Tax Savings	$ 8,640.00

WARNING: The IRS could allocate a portion of the earnings during the last half of the year to his individual income.

Initially under the Tax Reform Act of 1986, all personal service corporations must elect a calendar year as their fiscal year unless they can satisfy the IRS that there is a business purpose for having a different taxable year. For this purpose, a personal service corporation is a corporation whose principal activity is the performance of personal services that are substantially performed by owner/employees. The Omnibus Budget Reconciliation Act of 1987 permitted these corporations to retain fiscal years; however, the Act requires the deferral of deductions for payments to owner/employees, if disproportionately high salary payments are made toward the end of the year.

[101] HOW TO USE PREINCORPORATION CHECKLISTS TO YOUR MAXIMUM ADVANTAGE

In the preincorporation period, it is imperative that the various financial, accounting, and legal advisors of the client meet with him. This is done to ascertain what the client's objectives are in incorporating the business and also to allow for the accumulation of data.

Before incorporating, the individual businessperson should consider both the nontax and the tax reasons for incorporating. The table on page 15 shows the points to consider prior to incorporation.

Historically, the nontax considerations were the major impetus in determining the benefits of incorporating. However, because of the increase in tax rates since World War II, tax considerations now play a significant role.

Conceptually, the business community can be divided into three separate groups:

1. Manufacturing
2. Merchandising, either wholesale or retail
3. Sales or service organizations

These categories are not exclusive, but they provide for a basic differentiation of the business community and also provide for reflection on the historical basis of incorporating. Historically, virtually all manufacturing businesses were incorporated, and they were among the first to do so. It is difficult to name a single sizable manufacturing firm that does business in the incorporated form. The second group, merchandising, also requires a great deal of capital, and this was the second area of

TAX AND NONTAX REASONS FOR INCORPORATING

Favorable Characteristic $+$ Negative Factor $-$ Neutral Factor or Depends on Fact Situation 0	Sole Proprietor- ship	General Partner- ship	Limited Partner- ship	Corpo- ration
I. Nontax Considerations				
A. Limited Liability	−	−	0	+
B. Continuity of Existence	−	−	0	+
C. Centralization of Management	−	−	+	+
D. Free Transferability of Ownership	−	−	0	+
E. Flexibility and Freedom of Doing Business	+	+	−	−
F. Growth Capital	−	−	−	+
G. State and Local Taxation	+	+	+	0
II. Tax Considerations				
A. Tax Rates—Profitable Corporation	−	−	−	+
B. Double Taxation and Accumulated Earnings	0	0	0	−
C. Nature of Income	+	+	+	−
D. Deferred Compensation	0	0	0	+
E. Nontaxable Fringe Benefits	−	−	−	+
F. Sale or Liquidation of Business	0	0	0	0
G. Estate Planning	−	0	0	+

major mass incorporation. Until recently, major service organizations, stockbrokers, accountants, attorneys, and so on, were still doing business in the partnership form.

The reason that our service-oriented firms have only recently begun incorporating is that the historical nontax considerations have not provided them with sufficient reasons for incorporating. The reasons for the service corporations incorporating now are almost solely tax-oriented. The Tax Equity and Fiscal Responsibility Act (TEFRA) and the newly passed Tax Reform Act of 1986 have attempted to slow the growth of incorporating for tax purposes. Some of the techniques utilized by Congress can be summarized as follows:

1. Increasing the qualified deferred compensation benefits available to the unincorporated entities.

2. Attempting to have all corporations elect a calendar year. This has the effect of reducing the benefits of timing.

3. Changing the individual and corporate rates so that the retention of income is less beneficial than it was in the past.

[101.1] Determining Your Business Objectives

Determining your client's true objectives, priorities, and the nature of the benefits he desires is your first order of business.

> **Key Idea:** You should analyze your client's nontax objectives.

☐ *Is there a need for limiting liability?* First and foremost in the nontax considerations is the ability to limit the client's loss to the amount of money invested in the particular entity. In a sole proprietorship, general partnership, or the general partner in a limited partnership, the liability is unlimited. If the loss in the entity exceeds the amount of the capital contributed, the individual creditors can pursue their claims against each and every one of the participants in the business. On the other hand, in the corporation, the shareholder's liability is usually limited to the amount of his investment. Sometimes his limited liability is illusionary because banks will require the individual guarantee of the shareholders before they will make the loan to a corporation. In certain risky businesses where tort liability is great, incorporation should also be considered. Usually this will protect the shareholders who are not actively involved in the corporation from a judgment in excess of the amount of the insurance which they must purchase.

☐ *What is your client's needs for the continuity of existence?* When a sole proprietor dies, the proprietorship automatically terminates, and the executors or personal representatives must operate the business. If the personal representative or executor is a trust company, there are many businesses that they either do not wish to operate or are incapable of operating. On the other hand, if the entity is a corporation, the sole liability of the trust company is to ensure that the directors and officers of the corporation have sufficient ability to operate the business.

Continuity of existence also includes, within its parameters, the individual problems of the investors in the business. A corporate form should be considered if any of the participants in the business are candidates for divorce, death, or bankruptcy.

The following example will illustrate how the corporate form could have prevented a problem:

Example: A, B, and C had formed a partnership to develop real estate condominiums. A and B were substantial citizens, while C was a promoter with a good deal of knowledge, but extremely unstable. Unfortunately for A and B, C, during this particular venture, had marital problems, and his wife's attorney filed a *Lis Pendens* (a notification of interest in the property) on this project. This held up the sale of the units and caused great financial stress.

Key Idea: In the event that any of the participants in the business is very old, financially shaky, or have family problems, doing business as a corporation (S or C Corporation), has a great deal of merit.

☐ *Does your client wish centralization of management?* In a small business, it is rarely necessary to separate the management of the business from the owners. However, when the business grows, this becomes a factor which would tend to favor incorporation with its structured division of responsibility.

☐ *Is free transferability of interest imperative?* The definition of free transferability of interest is the ability to transfer all right, title, and interest without any restrictions. When doing business as a partnership, this is usually not possible. Partnership law or the agreement may restrict the transfer of an interest and especially the transfer of an interest with the right to management. Stock—unless it is restricted either in the articles of incorporation, bylaws, or by a shareholders agreement—is freely transferable. This is a positive factor for big corporations, such as AT&T and GM. It is not a benefit to a small corporation where the individual participants wish to impose restrictions on the transferability.

☐ *Is flexibility and freedom of doing business essential to your client?* Corporations limit the flexibility of the parties. In the corporate form, it is more difficult to change names, to borrow money, or to change form. Many times any significant change requires filing of documents with the secretary of state, thus incurring additional legal and filing costs. Usually, in the inception of the business when the total scope of the problems and potential is not known, doing business in an unincorporated form, from the flexibility standpoint, is dictated.

☐ *Is growth capital imperative?* If a business will require a great deal of growth capital, the corporate form is usually dictated. Both tax and nontax considerations will dictate this result. It is generally easier to obtain additional capital through the issuance of corporate stock than through the sale of partnership interests. New investors generally prefer the limited liability and the favorable tax treatment of profits available to a corporation.

☐ *Does your client realize that state and local taxation is usually a negative factor in considering incorporating?* Most states impose a different tax rate on corporate businesses. In addition, there is a cost on the continued issuance of the corporate license. This additional cost may range from a nominal fee to a fee that is rather substantial. Both of these factors should be taken into consideration prior to incorporating.

Key Idea: You should analyze your client's tax objectives.

☐ *Is your client aware of the current corporate tax rates?* At the lower levels, corporate tax rates are usually lower than the individual rates of the taxpayers. An individual earning $50,000 in net taxable income will pay just under $10,132.50 of tax. On the other hand, if the corporation earned all this money, the total tax would be $7,500. On the other side of the coin, even after the corporation has paid taxes on its earnings, the stockholder will still have to pay taxes on any distribution of earnings.

The following example will show the approximate tax savings if a sole proprietorship is incorporated and if the optimum practical salary is paid to the sole officer shareholder of the corporation.

Example: It is assumed that the officer/shareholder is married, that his other income equals his exemptions and tax deductions, and that the 1988 tax rates are applicable.

These tax savings do not reflect state taxation or any additional costs that may be occasioned by incorporating. Accordingly, for tax purposes alone, a sole proprietorship earning less than $100,000 probably should not be incorporated. The method of determining total tax savings is the amount by which the tax on sole proprietorship income exceeds the combined tax of the corporation and the individual officer/shareholder. (See ¶100.1 for a full discussion.)

Total Business Income	Approximate Tax Savings
$50,000	$2,632.50
$75,000	$5,882.50
$100,000	$7,905.00
$125,000	$9,248.00
$150,000	$10,962.50

☐ *Is your client aware of the double taxation factor?* Chapter 4 will explore double taxation at greater length. Both the constructive and the actual dividend present problems and are continuing negative factors in incorporating. However, the impact has been reduced by the Tax Reduction Act of 1986.

☐ *Is your client aware of a possible accumulated earnings tax?* This is also a negative factor in incorporating. (See Chapter 8 for a detailed discussion.)

☐ *What is the nature of your client's income?* If the income to be earned by the corporation is tax free or sheltered, part of the benefits can be lost by having the corporation earn it. In the same vein, if the property to be owned may appreciate in value, and is a passive investment, that is vacant land, its ownership by a corporation may cause problems in the future (see ¶103). Therefore, the nature of the income and the nature of the property to be held have a definite impact on whether or not the business should be incorporated.

☐ *Is your client considering deferred compensation?* See Chapter 2 for a complete discussion on deferred compensation plans. In general, the corporation has more freedom to determine the nature of the benefits which it offers to its employees and to offer different benefit packages to different categories of employees. However, the Tax Equity and Fiscal Responsibility Act of 1982 has limited some of the advantages which corporate qualified deferred compensation plans have historically had over those that could be established by a sole proprietorship or partnership. This will not only necessitate a complete review of the advantages and disadvantages for new corporations but will also require existing corporations to reevaluate the plans and benefits that they presently have established and may necessitate revisions in these plans.

☐ *What are your client's goals when it comes to nontaxable fringe benefits?* There are definite advantages to a corporate entity if nontaxable fringe benefits are the primary goals of incorporating (see Chapter 2).

☐ *What are the implications of the sale or liquidation of the business?* The sale or liquidation of the business may be easier or more difficult in the corporate form. The ability to plan is very dependent upon the facts at the particular date. Therefore, eventual liquidation or sale should not be a factor at the time of incorporating.

☐ *What are your client's estate-planning needs?* Usually if the goal of incorporating is estate planning, a corporate vehicle will be the most readily utilized technique. The ability to restructure the business and to eliminate future equity growth in the business for the individuals who are the older generation can be facilitated by the corporate form.

What Can Happen When the Client's Business Is an Established Income Earner

If the client's business is an established income earner and if his objective is purely estate planning, the structure of the corporation will most likely be different from the corporation established to develop a new product.

An example of the former is a successful business being incorporated by the original founder with the intention of shifting not only control from his estate but also eliminating any future appreciation in his estate. If this business was established with one class of stock and if the business had a net equity of $200,000, and 1,000 shares were issued for this stock, each year it would become more difficult to shift control. The reason for this increased difficulty is that as the corporation earned money, the value of the stock would increase. The initial book value was $20 ($200,000 divided by 1,000) per share. This book value would increase each year as the income was retained. On the other hand, if the initial capitalization was $50,000 common stock and $150,000 preferred stock, it is possible for the father to immediately gift away the common stock to the son and retain the preferred stock with all future appreciation in the business being attributed to the common stock. The father may retain the preferred stock for income or, at a later date, have the corporation redeem the preferred stock. There is great flexibility in this dual stock structure. **CAUTION:** The Omnibus Budget Reconciliation Act of 1987 has attempted to eliminate the benefits of estate freezes. Prior to incorporating and using this technique or recapitalizing an existing corporation, the current law should be reviewed.

If, on the other hand, the corporation is established to develop a new product, and if you are dealing with two individuals who are contributing equally, there is no need for differing classes of stock, and each will, in all probability, own 50 percent of the common stock issued.

The variations between these two extremes are infinite; however, the goals remain the same—to allow for maximum flexibility for future extraction of funds without interfering with the current operation of the business.

[101.2] Gathering Information to Avoid Mistakes

Before decisions can be made, it is extremely important that all appropriate information is accumulated in one place. This is why the following checklist is indispensable. The information listed here will indicate the proper planning that can be accomplished in the initial stages. The ultimate goal of this checklist is to ensure that all necessary information is summarized so that appropriate planning methods may be considered. The checklist also helps you avoid missing certain information that could create embarrassing situations or lead to misunderstandings.

Checklist for Gathering the Information

☐ Name:_____ ☐ Incorporator:_____
☐ Business Address:_____ ☐ Telephone No.:_____
☐ Sent to Sec. of State:_____ ☐ Sent to Reg. of Deeds:____
☐ Minute Book Ordered:_____
☐ Incorporation Letter Sent:_____

Names Salary Director No. of Shares

☐ Officers:
☐ President: _____
☐ Vice Pres.: _____
☐ Secretary: _____
☐ Treasurer: _____
☐ Other Shareholders: _____
☐ Date of Initial Meeting of Directors: _____ ☐ Bank: _____
☐ Capital Contribution:
☐ Cash: _____ ☐ Property or Services: _____
☐ Need for Bill of Sale: _____
☐ Number of Shares to Be Issued: _____
☐ Debt Instrument (Terms): _____
☐ Shareholder Agreement: _____
☐ Price: _____ ☐ How Determined: _____
☐ Restrictions on Sale: _____
☐ Mandatory or Optional Buy-Out: _____
☐ Funded by Insurance: _____
☐ Fringe Benefits: _____
☐ Medical Reimbursement: _____
☐ Disability Insurance: _____
☐ Group Term: _____
☐ Other Provisions: _____
_____

☐ Special Provisions:
☐ 1. Professional Corporation: i.e., File with Reg. of Deeds:
_____
☐ 2. Articles of Incorporation: _____
☐ 3. Preincorporation Subscription Agreement: _____
☐ Attorney: _____ ☐ Accountant: _____

The Incorporation Letter and How to Use It

Another tool in ensuring that all the initial incorporation procedures have been adequately undertaken and accomplished is an incorporation letter. This letter indicates those actions that should be taken during the incorporation period. It covers the vast majority of the routine changes that are sometimes overlooked in incorporating the business.

The incorporation letter should be forwarded to the client with a copy to the accountant as soon as the articles of incorporation have been returned. If the initial preincorporation planning meeting precedes the actual incorporation of the corporation by a significant period of time, it may be best not to send the preincorporation letter until just before the actual incorporation date.

Sample Incorporation Letter

Profitable Corporation
1234 West South Street
Appleton, Wisconsin 54911

Dear Sirs:

Upon the receipt of this letter, we will have completed the basic procedures for the incorporation of your new corporation.

This corporation will be a separate entity for both tax and nontax considerations, and I believe that it is best to set forth the general responsibilities of a recently formed corporation.

Accordingly, I have prepared the enclosed memo for your consideration and while the suggestions in the memo are not all-inclusive nor will they all be applicable to your particular corporation, this memo can serve as a broad guideline.

If I can be of any further assistance, please feel free to contact me.

Sincerely,

John Q. Lawyer

Sample Memo upon Incorporation

To: Profitable Corporation
From: John Q. Lawyer
RE: Responsibilities of Recently Formed Corporations

A. Tax Considerations

1. Register with the Wisconsin Department of Revenue and obtain a Wisconsin Employer Identification Number;
2. Apply for a Federal Employer Identification Number (Form SS-4);
3. Obtain the appropriate Federal and State Withholding Tax Forms from the State and your employees;
4. Obtain the Federal and State Unemployment Tax Forms;
5. Obtain forms for filing Estimated Corporate Income Tax;
6. Obtain Sales Tax Forms, if needed;
7. Establish a salary for yourself and your fellow officers. Do not withdraw money as needed. The corporation is a separate entity and transfers between you and the corporation have legal consequences;
8. The enclosed Federal and Wisconsin Employers Tax Guide will be of help in answering the basic tax questions that you may have.

B. Nontax Considerations

1. Since you have incorporated and changed the basic nature of your business, you should take the following action:

    (a) Change all lettering, signs, marquees, and other emblems of the business to indicate the new corporate name;

    (b) Change stationery, business forms, letterheads, invoices, and so on, to indicate the new corporate name;

    (c) Establish banking and checking accounts in the corporate name;

    (d) Complete a corporate resolution designating the appropriate officers to sign for the corporation;

(e) Change your telephone book listing to indicate the change;

(f) Have any and all outstanding insurance policies changed to reflect the new insured or beneficiary;

(g) All leases and contracts should be entered into in the corporate name, and not yourself individually. One of the reasons for establishing the corporation may have been the need to limit personal liability. If you enter into these contracts personally, the corporate entity will be of no benefit to you in this respect;

(h) All utility and similar bills should be transferred to the corporate name;

(i) All expenses incurred before incorporation should be paid individually.

2. Your creditors and other parties that you do business with should be notified of your change in business structure. You may find it worthwhile to send out announcements or put a notice in the paper; otherwise, your billing, invoicing, and correspondence will notify them of this change.

3. It is important that all business papers, leases, and correspondence be signed by you in your corporate capacity. In most instances, you should sign as follows: "XYZ Corporation, by John Smith, President."

4. Review your insurance needs in light of the change to a corporate form.

5. Consider employment contracts for you and your key employees.

6. A new set of accounting records should be established and accounting methods reviewed with your accountants. In particular, consider the following:

   (a) Determine the proper fiscal year;

   (b) Decide whether a change in accounting procedures would be appropriate.

[102] HOW TO WEIGH THE BENEFITS THAT CAN BE DERIVED FROM MAKING THE INCORPORATION EITHER TAXABLE OR TAX FREE

[102.1] Weighing the Requirements for a Tax-Free Incorporation

The first decision that is made before incorporating a business is whether or not this incorporation should be a taxable or a tax-free transaction under Section 351. Most incorporations fall within the requirements of a 351 transaction whether or not planning has preceded the incorporation. Section 351 sets forth the prerequisites for a tax-free incorporation of a business. These requirements may be summarized as follows:

1. The property must be transferred to the corporation.
2. The transfer must be solely in exchange for stock or securities.
3. Immediately after the exchange, the person or persons making the transfer must control at least 80 percent of the voting power of the corporation.

Usually the individuals will want to utilize this section because the minimization of income taxes is normally a primary reason for incorporating the business. Accordingly, the last thing the incorporating individuals desire is to create a taxable transaction and thereby increase their already high income taxes.

[102.2] Deciding If the Incorporation Should Be Taxable

It may be advantageous to increase the basis of the property transferred to the corporation through the utilization of a taxable incorporation. If either the sole proprietor or partners are in a low tax bracket, the income created by a partially taxable transaction could be more than offset by the benefits to be derived by an increase in the tax basis. The reason a taxable transaction is used and may be advantageous is that the new corporation in a tax-free Section 351 transaction will assume the basis of the property previously held in the proprietorship or partnership. However, if it is a taxable event or a partially taxable event, then the basis of the property held by the new corporation will be increased. A chart analyzing the reasons for incorporating and deciding the taxability of the incorporation follows.

There are two methods used to increase the basis of property held by the corporation.

Method 1: You can transfer some of the assets to the new corporation and retain some of these assets individually, as shown in the following example.

> **Example:** X is a land developer who owns several tracts of land. The first tract of land, worth approximately $500,000 is already in the process of being developed and has a loan of approximately $250,000 representing development costs applicable to this tract. Adjacent to this tract is another parcel of land zoned differently from the original tract and on which no development has yet taken place. The cost basis to X of this tract of 50 acres was approximately $1,000 per acre but is currently worth (because of the development taking place on the adjacent tract) $5,000 per acre. Therefore, the adjoining property has increased from a cost basis of $50,000 to a current fair market value of $250,000.

The intended results are severalfold: If X had individually developed this property, there would be a total gain of approximately $325,000 ($200,000 land appreciation plus $125,000 income earned on development). This would be taxed individually as ordinary income to him if he retained it as a sole proprietorship because he is a real estate developer and is in the business of buying and selling lots. In this case, the corporate tax structure may give him a lower effective rate, allow him to divide the income, and provide the positive planning which has previously been discussed. On the other hand, it is not appropriate for him to also transfer the 50 acres that are currently worth $5,000 per acre. It is possible, in the future, that the capital gains rates will be less, and accordingly he may be able to obtain capital gains treatments on this 50 acres. If at a later time it is advantageous for him then to convey the 50 acres to the corporation, this may also at that time qualify for a tax-free treatment under Section 351. However, the flexibility that can be maintained by retaining this 50 acres individually should be preserved. At a later date, it may even be possible to sell these acres to the corporation and receive an installment sale. However, before this planning device is utilized, Section 453 should be thoroughly examined.

How to Tell Whether an Incorporation Should be Taxable or Tax Free

		Recommendation	
		Tax-Free	Taxable
Goal	Consideration	Incorp.	Incorp.
Property to change character	Unimproved real estate which has been previously held for investment is to be subdivided. If a portion of the appreciation and gain to be realized was from the date of acquisition to the current date, this would normally yield capital gains. However, if the property is subdivided, this property will yield all ordinary income. It may be best to sell this property to the new corporation and recognize the appreciation as capital gains rather than having it all taxed as ordinary income upon development. This could provide for positive tax planning. The future of this planning device will be		X

		Recommendation	
continued			
Goal	*Consideration*	*Tax-Free Incorp.*	*Taxable Incorp.*
	dependant upon the action of Congress in either retaining the favorable capital gains rate or discarding it in favor of taxing all income at the same rates.		
Transferor in high tax bracket	Ordinarily, one of the major reasons that a business is incorporated is to allocate business income to the corporation and to avoid the higher individual tax rates. If the incorporation is taxable, this will increase the overall tax burden.	X	
Transferor in low tax bracket	If the business is being incorporated for reasons other than tax, we may find the transferor in a low tax bracket, and it may be beneficial to have him realize a portion of the income currently rather than have the corporation realize this income at a later date.		X
Capital gains property subject to 1245 and 1250 recapture	Usually the transfer of capital gains property, which is subject to recapture, would be inappropriate property	X	

| continued | | Recommendation | |
| | | Tax-Free | Taxable |
Goal	Consideration	Incorp.	Incorp.
	to create a taxable transaction. The reason for this is that the income generated would normally be ordinary income and may spark investment credit recapture and will be taxed at a higher bracket than at corporate rates.		
Recognition of a loss	If the property has declined in value so that its fair market value is less than its basis, it may be possible to recognize a loss and take some current benefits from incorporation.		X
Transferor having a net capital loss carryforward or operating loss carryover			X

Two planning tools have been used for this type of transaction, as follows:

1. The income that was going to be realized is spread over two or more years.

2. A part of the income was shifted from X, a higher base taxpayer, to the corporation, a lower base taxpayer. In addition, if at a later time the undeveloped real estate is sold to the corporation and if the favorable capital gains treatment is retained, we have also converted a portion of the gain (the rise in value before development) as capital gains and only been taxed at the ordinary income rates on

the ordinary income portion, which in essence is the development gain.

This particular transaction is fraught with many tax problems. Three of the most important problems which must be considered are as follows:

1. The corporation may be considered a collapsible corporation (see Chapter 8).

2. If the favorable capital gains rates are retained after 1987, the IRS may attack the conversion of the capital gains into ordinary income.

3. The Installment Sales Revision Act of 1980 established a new set of rules for installment sales of nondepreciable property between related parties. Under the general provisions of the law, if you make an installment sale to a related party, who then resells the property before you have received all the installment payments, then you will be treated as if you had received the proceeds on the date of resale. In other words, a subsequent sale by a related party will accelerate the recognition of gain on the initial installment sale. The law now states that the amount that must be treated as received by the first seller as a result of the resale cannot exceed:

    (a) The amount realized on resale before the close of the tax year or the contract price, whichever is less;

    (b) The total amount of payments received on the original sale before the close of the tax year, plus the amount that was treated as received on the first sale in earlier years.

For the purposes of this act, related parties would not only include the real estate developer and his corporation, but it would also include spouses, children, grandchildren, parents, as well as partnerships, trusts, and estates in which the developer and/or related parties have a controlling interest.

For property other than marketable securities, the resale rule will apply only if the second sale occurs within two years of the first sale. There are certain provisions which will suspend the running of the two-year rule if the risk of loss is not shifted.

For marketable securities, the resale rule applies without time limit to resales made before the entire obligation is satisfied. In our particular case, the question is, when does X realize his gain? If there is no subsequent sale of the property for two years, then X would realize his gain under the normal install-ment sales provisions.

Practically, some portion of the transferred real estate would be developed and sold prior to the two-year period. The question then becomes, how much must be reported by Mr. X? While the exact answer is not evident, the taxable income will at least be the greater of (1) the actual receipt of proceeds by X or (2) the gross profit from the lots sold less any improvements.

While the law is not clear, an example will illustrate the most advantageous application of the act:

Example: X sells real property to a related party on the following terms:

(a) Sales price, $250,000

(b) $50,000 in cash at closing on December 31, 1986

(c) $50,000 plus interest on each anniversary date of the sale until completely amortized

This sale was executed on December 31, 1986, and no sales were made until 1988 when 30 lots were sold. The profit on the sale of each lot would be calculated as fol-lows:

Sales Price per Lot		$10,000
Cost of Sale		1,000
Gross Profit		$ 9,000
LESS:		
Land Cost	$1,000	
Improvement	4,000	5,000
Net Profit		$ 4,000

In this case, at least $150,000 would have to be reported by X by 1988: 30 × ($4,000 profit plus $1,000 land cost). The amount of $100,000 of previously reported receipts could be subtracted from the $150,000 of reportable income. There-fore, only the $50,000 paid would have to be reported in 1988.

It is also possible that the IRS could contend that the entire proceeds from the sale would be considered received. If the IRS could sustain this position, the entire sale of $250,000 would have to be realized by 1988 since there was a subsequent sale of $300,000.

WARNING: If the property to be transferred is depreciable property, a patent application, or 1231 property, then the use of an installment sale may not be appropriate, as follows:

1. If the property to be transferred is depreciable property instead of vacant real estate, it will come within the provisions of Section 1239 of the Internal Revenue Code. This code section converts what would normally be capital gains into ordinary income if it is a sale between a person and his controlled corporation and partnership. Controlled for these purposes is defined as 80 percent ownership either directly or 50 percent through the attribution rules set forth in Section 318.

    Accordingly, if the property to be transferred is depreciable property and if the favorable capital gains rates applicable to 1987 and prior are retained, an unrelated party will have to own at least 21 percent of either the corporation or the partnership.

2. If the property being transferred is depreciable property giving rise to depreciation recapture, the depreciation recapture is fully recognized in the year of the installment sale.

3. If the transferred property is a patent application or 1231 property, the sale which would otherwise have given rise to capital gains will instead produce ordinary income.

Even with the problems created by the Installment Sales Revision Act of 1980 and the other problems listed above, there is still a substantial amount of positive planning opportunities in structuring a transaction such as this.

Method 2: You can increase the basis of the properties in order to convert a tax-free transaction into a partially taxable transaction. Using this method, the corporation issues not only stock and securities (one of the prerequisites of Section 351)

but also short-term notes. The notes are to be treated as boot.
The gain on the transaction is to be taxable to the extent of the
boot received by the shareholder. In other words, if property
with a fair market value of $100,000 and a basis of $10,000 was
transferred to the corporation, the stock received will have a
value of $100,000 and a basis of $10,000. If the new corporation were to issue common stock and demand notes of $30,000,
the Code states that it is taxable to the transferor to the extent
of the boot received, in this instance $30,000. The Internal
Revenue Service has taken the position that it will contest a
good number of these types of transactions, and care must be
utilized if this particular technique is to be successfully de-
fended.

There are two ways in which it may be possible to convert a
tax-free incorporation into a taxable transaction. The following
table illustrates how this can be accomplished.

TWO WAYS TO OBTAIN A TAXABLE TRANSACTION

Transaction	What to Do	Consequence
1. Sale	Sell property for cash or for notes or other debt obligations to the controlled corporation.	IRS may challenge debt characterization by contending that the purported debt is in substance an equity investment (see *Burr Oaks Corp. v. Comr.*, 43 TC 635, [1965], aff'd 365 F.2d 224 [7th Cir. 1966]. *cert. den.* 385 U.S. 1007 [1967]). Even if unsuccessful on debt issue, the IRS may attack and the courts may consider this a security within the meaning of Section 351. The courts have seemingly differentiated between those transferors who have an interest in the stock ownership of the corporation and those who do not. If the person does

continued

TWO WAYS TO OBTAIN A TAXABLE TRANSACTION

Transaction	What to Do	Consequence
		not have a proprietary interest in the corporation, the transaction may be considered taxable (see Rev. Rul. 73-472, 1973-2-CB 114). If, on the other hand, the transferor already has a stock ownership, this may destroy the whole transaction (see *Parkland Place Co. v. U.S.*, 354 F.2d 916 [5th Cir. 1966]. IRS Regulations 1, 385, et al.).
2. Creation of debt (which is not a security)	Issue in addition to stocks and securities, short-term notes.	1. This, like many other problems in the tax law, is basically a fact determination. If the transferor exchanges his property for an interest which can be considered dependent upon the success of the corporation, this would be a proprietary interest and considered stock. On the other hand, if the interest is such that the transferor and transferee expect it to be repaid whether or not the business is a success, this more closely resembles a debt instrument. 2. If the corporation is thinly capitalized (the debt equity ratio is extremely high), the IRS and courts may attack this as a form of equity.

continued

TWO WAYS TO OBTAIN A TAXABLE TRANSACTION

Transaction	What to Do	Consequence
		3. If such things as fixed maturity date, interest rate, manner of determining interest rate, whether it is equivalent to what other lenders would be charging, whether payments are duly made, and whether it is subordinated to other creditors are all duly considered, then the usual characteristics of a debt instrument are present.
		4. Likelihood of repayment. If the indebtedness is issued by a corporation that is solvent and more likely to repay the loan when due, it is more likely to be characterized as debt rather than equity.
		5. The IRS regulations under Section 385 have significant impact on whether the debt would sustain attack by the IRS as disguised equity.

[103] THE PROPER TAX STRATEGY FOR FUNDING A CORPORATION

Too many incorporations are accomplished without a complete analysis of which assets are to be transferred to the corporation. This will have a significant impact on future estate and income tax planning. More frequently than should be the case, the real property in which the business is housed is transferred to the corporation as part and parcel of the initial incorporation.

However, it is seldom necessary or desirable to transfer this real property to the corporation.

What to do: In most instances, the proper planning procedure will be for the transferor to retain the real property in his individual name and lease the building to the corporation at a realistic rental.

Why do it:

1. The rental will probably pay the mortgage payments and offer a small return to the transferor. This rental income in all likelihood will not produce any taxable income to the transferor. The reason that there is little or no taxable income is that the interest, depreciation, insurance, and other deductions will more than offset the rental income, at least in the beginning years.

At a later date, after the mortgage is paid, this income check will provide a significant retirement benefit in the form of a continued monthly income. Because these rental payments are not earned income, they will not directly reduce the social security benefits of the transferor. Earned income can reduce the benefits received by a recipient of social security. If he is over 65 and his earned income is more than $8,160 in 1987, each dollar of earned income in excess of that amount reduces his social security benefits by fifty cents. If he is over 62 but under 65, the applicable amount in 1987 is $6,000, and if he is over the age of 70, there is no reduction for the amount of earned income. In addition to the possibility that the earned income of an individual would reduce the benefits, if his income base (basically adjusted gross income plus one-half of his social security benefits) exceeds $32,000 if married or $25,000 if single, one-half of the excess will be included in his income. If the above procedure is utilized, there will be no need in the future (when he is due to retire) to retain the transferor as a paid employee because his other retirement income is supplemented by the unearned rental income. If, however, he is a paid employee, the income earned from the corporation, would reduce the payments that he would receive under social security.

2. Removing the passive asset of the real estate from the corporate fold will reduce the equity of the business that must be reflected either as stock or as securities. Accordingly, this

would facilitate the current and future transfer of the business via gifts or sales.

3. If this building is subsequently sold, the profit is realized by the individual and not locked in the corporation to be taxed twice upon distribution.

4. If the individual retains the real estate, this allows for additional flexibility. If this asset is needed at a later date as an asset of the corporation, it probably can be transferred without any additional tax. Once it is in the business, it is extremely difficult to return this asset to the individual. This reflects my tax maxim that "it is easy to get an asset into the corporation tax free but harder than (expletive deleted) to get it out."

5. In 1987 and thereafter, it will be possible to use any income generated by the real estate to offset other passive losses.

> **Example:** Joe has previously invested in limited partnerships that are distributing to him $35,000 in passive losses. In 1987 and thereafter, the total amount of these losses will not produce current tax benefits. If he leases the real estate to his closely held corporation and the lease produces $25,000 in taxable income, this will directly offset his other passive losses, and all losses will be able to be utilized. (Beware that the Omnibus Budget Reconciliation Act of 1987 has reduced if not eliminated this technique if the passive losses are derived from publicly traded partnerships. For purposes of the passive loss rules, losses from a publicly traded partnership cannot offset income from a passive activity or income from another publicly traded partnership.)

> **Key Idea:** In the past, there was very little emphasis on realizing the maximum rental income from properties. In the future, the positive benefits of the passive income generated by this rental which if allowed to offset passive losses could provide for positive planning.

> **Key Idea:** Many times it will be worthwhile to pay off the mortgage on the real estate to increase the passive income. If an individual has available financing on his first and second home, it may be worthwhile to borrow against both the first and second home to pay off the mortgage on the rental property. In the above example, Joe was renting his building to the

corporation which paid all of the insurance, taxes, repairs, and so on. The rental schedule for Joe was as follows:

Rental Income		$50,000
Interest	$15,000	
Depreciation	10,000	(25,000)
Net Rental Income		$25,000

If Joe had no mortgage on his house which had a basis of $125,000 and he could borrow $125,000 at 12 percent, this would generate an additional $15,000 of passive income without any personal loss of the interest expense. This would increase the allowable portion of another passive loss to be taken against this income.

BEWARE: The IRS has the ability to redesignate payments if they exceed a reasonable rental. (See Chapter 4.) After 1987, an individual has the ability to obtain an "equity loan," as indicated above, and deduct the interest on said loan as long as the equity loan does not exceed the lesser of $100,000 or the taxpayer's basis in the residence.

Since it seems advantageous to retain certain assets, the question becomes: "Which assets should be retained?" As previously indicated, the property which is most often suitable to be retained by the transferor or tranferors is real estate. As a practical matter, it is very rare that vacant real estate should be transferred to the corporation. Improved real estate has many possibilities for utilization if retained by the transferor.

Another class of property for possible retention by the transferors is equipment. Normally the incorporation of a business will not spark any Section 1245 or investment credit recapture. From time to time in this book, there will be reference to both depreciation recapture under either Section 1245 or 1250 or investment credit recapture. "Recapture" is a term which refers to recategorizing capital gains as ordinary income. For example, an item of personal property subject to depreciation and investment credit had an initial cost of $5,000 and was depreciated on a straight-line basis over five years. After three years, it was sold for $4,000. The $2,000 gain ($4,000 sales price less [$5,000–$3,000]) would have to be reported as ordinary income. In addition, there would be investment credit recapture because the original credit was taken on a five-year basis yielding a 10 percent credit. Since it was held for only three years, 6 percent was allowable. Therefore, 4 percent of the original cost of $5,000, or $200 of the original credit of $500, would have to be repaid to the government (recaptured).

WARNING: If either equipment or real estate is retained by the transferor, it is possible that the investment credit previously taken could be recaptured.

For example, if an existing construction business is being incorporated, the equipment would have been previously utilized in the operation of the business. When the equipment is retained by the transferor rather than included in the corporate assets, the active construction use is converted to a passive lease. This may spark a recapture of the investment credit. In addition, there will be a problem of recapture of investment credit, when the transferor has failed to transfer substantially all of the assets to the corporation.

Revenue Ruling 76-514 indicates the position that the Internal Revenue Service has taken in applying the concept of transferring substantially all of the assets to the corporation. In this ruling, a dentist who had previously operated as a sole proprietorship incorporated his dental practice and transferred to the newly formed corporation dental and office equipment. However, he retained in his own possession the building in which the practice had operated and leased this building to the corporation.

The question presented was whether or not the incorporation was a mere change in form of conducting business? According to the law, a mere change in form does not spark recapture. The IRS concluded that not substantially all of the assets of the active business were transferred, and accordingly a recapture of investment credit should take place. This defintiely indicates the future position of the Internal Revenue Service. Whether or not the courts will concur in this finding is not presently known.

One area of particular concern is the incorporation of the family farm. The reason for this is three fold:

1. A substantial percentage of the total assets transferred is the value of the real estate. Normally, the value of the real estate will be more than one half of the total value of farm assets.

2. The family farm has the potential to spark a great deal of investment credit recapture. Because of the capital-intensive nature of farming, major equipment is usually purchased which generates a substantial investment credit.

3. For general planning purposes, it is very seldom appropriate to transfer the land to the corporation.

With the elimination of the investment credit for all years after 1985, this should become less of a problem. Notwithstanding this fact, in the near future, before any assets are retained and not transferred to the corporation, it is a good idea to review how much investment credit would be recaptured in the event that the Internal Revenue Service prevailed in sustaining an argument that the incorporation was not a mere change in business form. The risk should be balanced with the benefits. In many cases, the retention of the equipment, a portion of the equipment, or real estate may be advisable. This is especially true if it is contemplated that these assets will be placed into a trust. The trust will then lease these assets to the corporation. This will shift the income to a lower basis taxpayer.

The following is an example of benefits of a trust leasing equipment to the corporation:

Example: X is the sole shareholder of ABC Corporation. S is in the 33 percent marginal bracket, and the corporation is in the maximum 39 percent bracket. He has a large family, and it has been exceedingly difficult for him to retain sufficient after-tax income to provide for his children's education. His corporation has utilized several trucks and other transportation vehicles. These vehicles have historically been leased by him to the corporation. He has transferred these vehicles to a trust with an independent trustee and then has the trustee negotiate a lease with the corporation. The lease has provided a sufficient economic return of income on the investment. The corporation could justify this transaction for the reason that they did not need to tie up any of their investment capital in transportation vehicles but could utilize their funds solely in the production of income.

The Tax Reform Act of 1986 has had a substantial negative impact upon this planning. However, if the trust were established (not as a Clifford or spousal remainder trust) and had the proper spray provisions, the income could be distributed to beneficiaries over the age of 14 (this would be complementary to the stated purpose of the trust which is to provide for education). This would produce up to 18 percent in tax savings on the funds distributed. This tax savings is determined as the difference between the 15 percent lower rates taxed to the individual beneficiaries and the 33 percent paid by the parents. On $10,000 of income, the savings would be $1,800 per year.

Probably no decision as to the amount of tax benefits to be derived from a plan such as illustrated above should be made without an analysis of the gift tax consequences on the particular transaction. Because of the unified credit which was enacted pursuant to the Tax Reform Act of 1976, gift and estate taxes play a significant role in the decision-making process of the current income tax savings. However, ERTA has had a significant positive impact upon the adverse effect of the Tax Reform Act of 1976. This positive impact is twofold:

1. The unified credit has been substantially increased.
2. The yearly exemption has been increased from $3,000 to $10,000.

Accordingly, except in major transfers, it is not necessary to weigh the current tax savings with the possible usage of the unified credit or the additional transfer taxes. The reason is that the amount of gift tax incurred will usually be small in relation to the income tax saved. However, in major transfers, it does become necessary to weigh the current income tax savings with the possible additional transfer tax incurred.

Beware of the Tax Trap of Transferring Liabilities in Excess of Basis

The incorporation of a service corporation reporting on the cash basis or a manufacturing corporation that has a real net worth, but whose liabilities exceed the cost basis of the assets, can produce taxable income upon incorporation.

The following example will illustrate how this problem can trap the unwary:

Example: X has operated ABC Company as a sole proprietorship. He has substantial outside income and has been able to utilize the investment credit and losses generated by the start-up expenses to offset his tax liability. Now ABC is about to generate a profit, and X wants to utilize the corporate structure to shelter his future profits. The balance sheet of ABC is as follows:

ASSETS

	Book Value	Fair Market Value
Cash	$ 1,000	$ 1,000
Receivables	50,000	50,000
Machinery and Equipment (net of depreciation)	100,000	150,000
Goodwill	-0-	100,000
TOTAL ASSETS	$151,000	$301,000

LIABILITIES AND EQUITY

	Book Value	Fair Market Value
Accounts Payable	$ 75,000	$ 75,000
Note Payable—Bank	200,000	200,000
Equity	(124,000)	26,000
TOTAL LIABILITIES AND EQUITY	$151,000	$301,000

If X incorporates this business and transfers all the assets subject to all the liabilities to the corporation, he will realize $124,000 of income pursuant to Section 357.

Key Idea: Before incorporating a business whose liabilities exceed the cost basis of assets transferred, consider the following: (1) retain and pay part of the liabilities individually and (2) transfer additional property with a cost basis to the corporation, that is land, building, stocks, and so on.

As indicated before, this particular problem can also appear in a service business utilizing the cash basis method of reporting. However, the problem is usually not as serious because accounts payable do not need to be considered as a liability to a cash basis taxpayer for these purposes (*see* Revenue Ruling 80-199).

> **Key Idea:** Before incorporating any business, prepare a balance sheet listing both the cost and the fair market value of the assets and liabilities to be transferred (see the previous example).

WARNING: With the implementation of the Accelerated Cost Recovery System (ACRS) cost recovery guidelines, this problem has become more and more prevalent. In the past with a longer useful life, straight-line depreciation on equipment often approximated the principal payments on notes. ACRS and its increased depreciation in the beginning years have a tendency to reduce the cost basis of the depreciable property much faster than under the previous law. After the full effect of the longer amortization schedules established by the Tax Reform Act of 1986 has been implemented, this problem should again be reduced. Obviously the changes in the law during the last decade have either aggravated or reduced the scope of this problem.

[104] HOW TO RETURN PART OF YOUR INVESTMENT AT CORPORATE INSTEAD OF INDIVIDUAL TAX RATES

[104.1] Capitalizing with Debt

In preincorporation planning, it is extremely important for you to determine how to correctly categorize the net equity transferred to the corporation. For the purposes of this book, net equity is defined as the net book value of the assets transferred less the liabilities transferred. Without any planning, the ability to return at a later date a portion or all of this equity to the individual shareholder without further taxation is lost without adverse tax considerations.

If the entire net equity is categorized as outstanding stock, all cash distributions will result in ordinary income or capital gains to the stockholder. All too often, when businesses are being incorporated, the possibility of allocating a portion of the net equity in the form of notes to the shareholder and the remainder to him in the form of stock is often overlooked. The advantages of capitalizing a portion of this net equity as debt are threefold:

1. A corporation is entitled to a deduction for the interest paid on the debt. On the other hand, any payments on equity stock are usually considered dividends, not deductible by the corporation, and taxable to the individual shareholder.

2. The payment of principal on indebtedness is almost always tax free.

3. The existence of indebtedness may justify the accumulation of earnings. This offers a reason for avoiding the accumulated earnings tax, a subject which is discussed in more detail in Chapter 8.

If this debt is classified as equity (stock), all the advantages will be lost, and considerable problems will be created.

For the purposes of this chapter, the corporation's debt to equity ratio is the ratio that the corporation's liabilities (excluding trade accounts, accrued operating expenses and taxes, and similar items) bears to the shareholders' equity. The shareholders' equity, sometimes referred in this book as "net equity," is the excess of the adjusted basis of the corporation's assets (less reserve for bad debts and similar asset offsets) over its liabilities (including trade accounts payable, accrued operating expenses and taxes, and similar items).

[104.2] Avoiding the Problems of Having Debt Classified as Equity and Thin Capitalization

It is extremely important that in establishing the corporation, the concept of properly capitalizing a portion of the net equity as indebtedness is not overlooked. Once categorized as indebtedness, it is imperative that this indebtedness withstand any attack as disguised equity.

Checklist for Determining Whether Debt Should Be Treated as Equity (Section 385 of the Internal Revenue Code)

☐ Is there an unconditional promise to pay on demand or at a specified date?

☐ Is the debt subordinated or preferred over any other indebtedness of the corporation?

☐ What is the ratio of debt to equity?

☐ Is the debt convertible into stock of the corporation?

In other words, the questions are: Is this debt "real?" and do the parties consider it "real"? The intent of the parties is extremely important. However, intent is usually lost in the ambiguity of the facts. The moral, if there is any, is twofold: Do not get greedy and treat all indebtedness as "real." For these purposes, "real" means that the indebtedness should have the following characteristics:

1. It should be secured by a note.
2. It should bear interest at a reasonable rate (both principal and interest should be timely paid).
3. It cannot be converted into stock.
4. It is neither secured by property nor subordinated to general creditors.
5. It has a debt equity ratio that is not so great that it invokes the rules relating to thin capitalization.

Thin capitalization is the tax concept that causes even bona fide debt obligations to be treated as stock for tax purposes. This problem occurs if the capitalization of the corporation is too thin to support the debt structure. Stated in the converse, if the ratio of debt to equity is excessive, there is thin capitalization. While historically under Section 385 there have been no clear-cut rules in this matter, it is generally considered that any time the total indebtedness of the corporation (including the debt owed to the shareholder) exceeds three or four times the equity, the corporation runs the risk of being too thinly capitalized.

WARNING: Before capitalizing with both debt and equity, the recently withdrawn regulations should be reviewed. (see ¶104.3).

[104.3] Considering the Impact That the Withdrawn Regulations Would Have Had on the Debt Equity Question

In an attempt to clarify the questions which arise in attempting to apply Section 385, the Internal Revenue Service reviewed this section of the Code and proposed new regulations which were scheduled to go into effect on December 31, 1981. These proposed regulations deviated substantially from the prior law, and in some cases, introduced entirely new concepts. The entire tax community was upset. Implementation of the regulations was repeatedly delayed, and several changes were introduced into the provisions of the proposed regulations. Finally, in June 1983, Assistant Treasury Secretary Chapoten sent a letter to House Ways and Means Committee Chairman Rostenkowski wherein the Treasury Department revoked the outstanding debt equity regulations and stated: "We are continuing to study the general question of the appropriate Treasury response to Section 385, and expect to complete our examination in the near future."

Accordingly, the final chapter in this story has not yet been written, and the future remains cloudy at best in this area of tax planning. Since that time, Congress and the IRS have devoted their efforts in other directions. This has left a void which has yet to be filled.

The proposed regulations which have been withdrawn would have applied to all corporate instruments and to corporate indebtedness. These rules would not generally affect instruments or advances predating the effective date of the regulations. However, if a debt instrument preceding the effective date of the regulations was later modified, or if there was a nonpayment of principal and interest, the rules might apply. The approach of the regulations was logical and straightforward. The withdrawn regulations did the following:

1. Established objective safe harbor standards. If the corporate debt in question complied with the requirements of a safe harbor, then the instrument would be considered as a debt.

2. Established certain other criteria which, if the safe harbor requirements are not complied with, will determine

whether or not the obligation can be considered debt. If these criteria are not met, the instrument will be considered stock for tax purposes.

These regulations introduced a new concept into the law, and that was proportionality. Proportionality implied that overlap existed between the owners of the stock and the holders of the class of supposed debt. If there is no proportionality (that is, if you obtain debt from a nonrelated party), invariably the obligation will be treated as debt.

The first analysis must be of the safe harbor rules. Using these rules, even if the debt is proportionate, it will be considered as debt for tax purposes if the following conditions were met:

1. The obligations must be evidenced by some written document.

2 It must be what is called a straight-debt instrument and should not be convertible into stock and must not be contingent upon payment.

3. Reasonable interest must be paid on the note. The outer limits as to what is considered as reasonable interest are the following:

   (a) The interest currently set by the Internal Revenue Code under Section 6621. After the Tax Reform Act of 1986, the overpayment rate is the federal short-term rate plus two points and the underpayment rate is the federal short-term rate plus three points. The rate is adjusted quarterly. The rate for a calendar quarter beginning January 1, 1987, is 9 percent on underpayments and 8 percent on overpayments.

   (b) The prime rate in effect on the date of issuance at the corporation's local commercial bank or within two points above such rate.

   (c) A rate to be determined periodically by the Internal Revenue Service, taking into account yields of comparable marketable federal obligations.

   (d) The rates in effect at the time of issuance pursuant to Section 482.

4. The obligation must be issued for the face amount.

5. The debt equity ratio of the corporation may not exceed three to one. Debt and equity are two terms created by the regulations and do not correspond to normal usage. First, debt does not include common obligations such as trade accounts payable, accrued operating expenses, and other similar items. Equity, for these purposes, is normal book value equity as set forth above. However, there is an adjustment to determine equity in the event that the corporation is using accelerated depreciation methods. In this event, the difference between straight-line depreciation and accelerated depreciation is added to equity.

6. If a corporation utilizes the cash rather than the accrual method of accounting, its equity will include the face amount of its accounts receivable.

7. There are various other conditions which do not have general applicability to closely held corporations.

8. The debt must be paid when due. The concept of prompt payment is significant in determining whether or not an instrument will be considered debt.

As indicated above, the regulations introduced the concept of proportionality. If your obligation met the above safe harbor requirements, it was immaterial whether the debt of a corporation was held proportionally or not. Normally, in a small corporation, if there is not complete proportionality of debt, at least there will be some proportionality, and thus it would be wise to comply with the safe harbor rules.

To be considered proportional under these regulations, there must be a total overlap with respect to stock indebtedness of over 50 percent. The total overlap for a corporation is equal to the sum of the overlap factors for each person who owns either stock or debt which is under examination. The overlap factor then is the lesser of either the percentage of stock or percentage of debt owned. This concept of proportionality has seemingly been borrowed from the idea of controlled corporations. The following example will help clarify this:

Example: XY Corporation has four unrelated shareholders—A, B, C, and D. A and B have each loaned $50,000 to

XY Corporation in return for five-year, unsecured notes. XY has no other liabilities.

Holder	Percent of Notes	Percent of Stock	Overlap Factor
A	50%	35%	35%
B	50%	25%	25%
C		15%	0%
D		25%	0%
TOTAL			60%

Accordingly, the notes issued to A and B are considered to be held proportionally.

WARNING: If the interest charged on a debt doesn't satisfy the safe harbor rule (110 percent of applicable federal rate), the IRS could categorize the debt as an original discount note subject to unfavorable tax treatment under the Tax Reform Act of 1984.

A more detailed discussion of proportionality is beyond the scope of this book. However, the logical inquiry in this case would be as follows:

1. If the creditor is independent, (that is, completely unrelated to the corporation) and receives a straight-debt instrument (an instrument not convertible into stock or contingent on earnings), this will normally pose no problem.

2. If, on the other hand, you have a proposed debt instrument which is proportional and you comply with the safe harbor rules as set forth above, again the instrument will be considered debt.

3. If a test of proportionality is made and the debt is proportional to stock, and it does not comply with the safe harbor rules, then additional crtieria should be investigated or the debt will be considered stock.

Obviously, this was a very dynamic area of tax planning, and prior to utilizing debt in preincorporation planning or in creating new debt of the corporation, a complete analysis of the area should be made. It is also important to note that the initial regulations attempted to include guaranteed loans within its parameters. The regulations as revised did state that the law governing guaranteed loans would remain as it was before. A discussion of this is contained in ¶104.6. Basically, the regulations as originally proposed introduced new concepts into the old historical framework. With the withdrawal of these regulations, the law is left without any direction as to where the future will lie. Planning in this area, which was never very sharply defined, is now clouded almost beyond belief.

[104.4] Impact of the Tax Reform Act of 1986 on Capitalizing with Debt

The recently passed Tax Reform Act of 1986 will have a definite impact upon all areas of individual and corporate tax planning. It is obviously one of the most pervasive tax acts that have been passed in at least three decades. The question during the preincorporation period becomes: What effect will it have on capitalizing part of the equity as debt? In the past, with the higher personal rates and lower corporate rates (at least on the first $50,000), it behooved most businesses to incorporate and obtain the benefits of dividing the income, which was previously discussed in ¶100.1. With the reduction in individual rates, without the corresponding reduction in corporate rates at the lower level, the benefits of dividing the income, while still substantial, are not as great in the past. For this reason, many planners may not devote the time and energy that they did in the past to properly classify and divide the capital contributed into both capital and debt. It is my belief that this is a mistake for the following two reasons:

1. There are still substantial benefits to be derived from dividing income, as was previously demonstrated in this chapter.

2. In the event that the Tax Reform Act which was expected to be a "revenue neutral act" does not produce the required income, personal income tax rates may again be raised. If this is the case, the proper structuring of a corporation will be tremendously important. It is extremely difficult, if not impossible, to restructure the corporation after it has been incorporated.

[104.5]   Classifying Debt as a Security to Avoid Upsetting Tax-Free Incorporation

In capitalizing with debt, it should be considered that, unless this debt retains the form of a security, the advantages of a tax-free incorporation are lost. One of the previously indicated prerequisites for a tax-free incorporation is that the transferor receives nothing but stock or securities of the corporation. It is generally accepted that "security" for the purpose of tax-free incorporation can refer to an instrument representing a debt obligation. However, not all corporate debt obligations are securities. The classification will depend upon an analysis and a review of the length of time to maturity of the indebtedness. Again, there is no simple answer as to how long the term must be to ensure that this indebtedness is a security. As the length of the term increases beyond five years, the problems of having the IRS sustain a successful attack decreases.

[104.6]   Alternatives to Creating Debt

One of the most common alternatives to the initial creation of a debt interest as a part of the net equity is the use of outside financing guaranteed by the shareholder. This approach can mitigate the problems just discussed.

The following is an example of excessive shareholder debt (thin capitalization):

> **Example:** A family group consisting of A, B, and C intends to buy a resort in another state which is going to be operated by A. The resort has a valuation of $1 million and is going to be sold to A, B, and C via a land contract in the amount of $760,000. It is anticipated that the resort is going to produce a net taxable income of approximately $50,000 a year after A's salary. B and C, the two passive members of this group, have other substantial income, and their net worth is also substantial. As in many instances, A, B, and C, even though they have an appreciable net worth, do not have liquid assets of $80,000 each to establish the corporation. Accordingly, they are going to go to their respective banks, borrow the money, and invest it in the corporation. For repayment, they are looking to

the $50,000 of corporate income to pay their notes to individual banks.

The debt equity ratio, even if they put in the total amount of capital stock, is already in excess of three to one. (Land contract $760,000 equity $240,000).

There is a better way and a way that is virtually safe from attack. Each of the individual shareholders invests $20,000 in cash as stock. The three banks that were going to loan A, B, and C the remainder of the investment loaned the corporation the money directly. Each of the shareholders (A, B, and C) guarantees the payment of the indebtedness. Because the indebtedness is to a nonshareholder, there is no problem of thin capitalization and a lesser problem of having this indebtedness classified as stock. The corporation then repays the debt to the banks without any tax effects to these shareholders.

WARNING: The plan set forth above utilizes a guaranteed loan in place and in lieu of a loan from a shareholder. The concept was subjected to a great deal of scrutiny in a court case decided approximately fifteen years ago. Accordingly, those cases involving a third party loan to a corporation (guaranteed by a stockholder) are governed by the holding in *Plantation Patterns, Inc. v. Commissioner*, 462 F.2d. 712 (5th Cir. 1972), *cert. denied* 404 U.S. 1076 (1972), and this case should be reviewed prior to implementing any plan as set forth above.

[104.7] Using More than One Class of Stock

It is common to have a situation where a father and son convert a partnership into a corporation. The father is now retired, out of state, or has a very inactive interest in the business. If, upon incorporation, this business utilizes two classes of stock, many of its tax planning goals can be satisfied. The father will receive preferred stock for his interest in the partnership. The son will be issued the common stock of the corporation. Preferred stock, which is created upon incorporation, is not Section 306 stock. (Under Section 306 of the Internal Revenue Code, preferred stock, which is issued as a tax-free dividend, can become taxable as ordinary income upon its subsequent redemption or sale.) Since the father's preferred stock is not Section 306 stock, its later sale, disposition, or redemption by the corporation will rarely produce ordinary income. If taxable at all, it will be taxed at the capital gains rates then in effect. In this case, the benefits from the issuance of the preferred stock to the father are as follows:

1. The dividend income received by the father does not directly affect his social security benefits, although if his base income exceeds $25,000 for single payers or $32,000 for joint filers, as much as one-half of his social security benefits can be subject to an income tax under the recently passed Social Security Act.

2. The control of the business interest is shifted to the younger generation.

3. The value of the father's interest in the business is frozen as of the date of incorporation. All future earnings are attributable to the common stock.

4. The payment of dividends may at a future date relieve or alleviate any accumulated earnings tax.

CAUTION: OBRA 1987 attempted to effect a crackdown on estate freezes such as this. Accordingly, not only in the preincorporation period but in addition, all recapitalizations should be implemented only after the law has been carefully reviewed.

[104.8] Basic Objectives in Incorporating the Business

The prior discussion has dealt with the various options available in funding the corporation and also in structuring the new corporate entity. However, it is important not to lose sight of the client's major objectives in incorporating the business. A checklist of these objectives follows, along with suggestions on how to best implement them upon incorporation.

Checklist of Suggestions to Accomplish Your Client's Major Objectives on Incorporation of Business

1. *Clients major objective for incorporating:*
   Limited Liability
   Goal of incorporation: Nontax
   Suggested approaches to accomplish goal:
   ☐ (a) Minimize capitalization

☐ (b) Retain assets individually and lease to corporation

☐ (c) Capitalize with debt and stock

2. *Clients major objective for incorporating:* estate planning
   Goal of incorporation: Tax
   Suggested approaches to accomplish goal:

   ☐ (a) Capitalize with common, preferred stock, and debt

   ☐ (b) Retain some of the assets individually (building, and so forth)

   ☐ (c) Form multiple corporations

3. *Clients major objective for incorporating:* Reduce income tax burden
   Goal of incorporation: Tax
   Suggested Approaches to Accomplish Goal:

   ☐ (a) Capitalize with debt

   ☐ (b) Utilize two corporations—an S Corporation and a C Corporation

   ☐ (c) Maximum fringe benefits:

   (i) Pension and profit-sharing plans/integrate with social security

   (ii) Install group term insurance

   (iii) Install disability insurance

   (iv) Provide for death benefit

   (v) Install medical reimbursement

   (vi) Install other appropriate fringes

[105] HOW TO USE THE INITIAL CORPORATE MINUTES FOR MAXIMUM TAX SAVINGS

In addition to all the active considerations which must be made during the preincorporation period, certain safeguards should be instituted and should either be put into the minutes or the by-laws. As a practical matter, these safeguards can alleviate problems which could occur in the operation of the corporation.

[105.1] Advanced Planning Can Shield the Corporation and Shareholder Officers from Future IRS Attack

The initial minutes of the corporation set the tone for the entire structure and direction which the corporation will take during its corporate existence. You should be absolutely certain to establish these minutes with full and complete review— otherwise disaster may result. Many times, these minutes are established without full and complete review. The disastrous results, which occur from this lack of planning, may not be felt for many years. In the initial stages of establishing the corporation, it is wise to anticipate those problems that may occur during the corporate existence. If the business being incorporated is one that has produced substantial income over many years, and the reason for incorporating is the tax benefits to be derived from dividing the business income, as explained in ¶100.1, initial corporate planning may alleviate the future problems of unreasonable compensation (see ¶301) or the accumulated earnings tax (see ¶801).

The initial corporate minutes, in this instance, should state that the compensation paid to the officers is not sufficient to compensate them for the services they render to the corporation. The minutes should further recite that the reason that reasonable compensation is not paid is that the corporation is currently unable to bear the cost of such a salary. At a later date, the minutes can be supplemented to show that the increase in salary is not reflective of the change in the services rendered, but of inadequate salary that had previously been paid to the individual.

This type of planning provides a twofold benefit. First, it allows for verification and substantiation of reasonable compensation. Second, it allows the corporation to maximize the salary distribution to the individual shareholder/employees at a later date. In addition, this salary maximization can increase the contribution to the pension and profit-sharing plans during these later years. The use of maximum distributions from the corporation as reasonable salary has always been an important planning tool; however, with the enactment of the Economic Recovery Tax Act of 1981 and the Tax Reform Act of 1986, maximizing salary payments will become an even more important tax-planning tool vehicle.

Sample Initial Corporate Minutes

Thereupon, the chairman, Jack Smith, proposed to the meeting that salaries be established for the various officers of the corporation. It was suggested that the compensation be set to reflect the services rendered by the officers to the corporation and accordingly, the two officers who would receive this compensation, the president and the secretary-treasurer, would each be entitled to $50,000 a year in salary. Upon further discussion, it was ascertained that the current cash flow of the corporation would not support a salary payment of $50,000 to each of these officers. After discussion, it was decided that the salary should reflect not only the contribution of the various officers but also the ability of the corporation to pay this salary. It was further suggested that as soon as the corporation is able to pay the difference between the salary compensation actually received and the amount that should have been paid, that this amount be paid as additional compensation.

Thereupon, on motion duly made, seconded, and unanimously carried, the following resolutions were adopted:

RESOLVED: That the salary for the current fiscal year for the president and the secretary-treasurer be established at $30,000 per year.

FURTHER RESOLVED: That this salary is not reflective of the services of these two officers to the corporation, and that the difference between this salary and $50,000, the true value of the services, shall be paid to the officers at a later date when the corporation is able to make these payments.

Sample Minutes That Authorize Additional Compensation

Thereupon, the chairman, Jack Smith, then suggested that the compensation of the officers be established for the current fiscal year. Upon discussion, it was duly established that the reasonable compensation to the two officers of the corporation, the president and the secretary-treasurer, which is reflective of the services rendered to the corporation is $50,000 per year. The meeting was then informed that the corporation had an obligation to pay an amount as salary which is reflected as the difference between the salary payments to these two officers for the first five years of the corporation actually paid and the amount of compensation which would reflect their services. The chairman then informed the meeting that the corporation had sufficient cash flow to begin to pay a portion of this previously unpaid compensation.

Thereupon, on motion duly made, seconded, and unanimously carried, the following resolutions were adopted:

RESOLVED: That the salary for the officers for the current fiscal year be established at $50,000 for the president and $50,000 for the secretary-treasurer. This salary is reflective of the current services of these two officers to the corporation.

FURTHER RESOLVED: That an additional $10,000 be paid to the president and the secretary-treasurer which is reflective of the compensation to which the corporation has an obligation to pay and which is the difference between the value of the services rendered by these officers during the years 1980, 1981, 1982, 1983, and 1984 and the salaries actually paid to them.

WARNING: It is important for accrual basis taxpayers to review the law and ascertain the year in which the deduction can be taken. It may also be better to state in the minutes that there is no legal but only a moral obligation to pay the difference between the actual value of the services and the salary paid. If there is a "legal right" to make these payments, the question arises "What happens if one of the officers leaves the employ prior to being fully compensated. Does he have a right to sue for the back wages?"

The above is an example of a method which anticipates problems that may occur and can be dealt with in your initial planning. Chapter 8 will give you a complete review of other problems that can be encountered by the corporation.

If, in the initial planning stage, some of these problems are anticipated, minutes should be implemented to provide a sound basis for avoiding them in later years. In addition, there are many areas, especially in corporate reorganizations, that, in order to obtain favorable tax treatment, may require a business purpose. An example of this would be a recapitalization (see ¶403.3 and ¶604).

At the inception of the corporation, it is rarely anticipated that within the near future a complete restructuring of the corporation will occur. However, if the newly formed corporation is a closely held family corporation, it does no harm to establish the different roles of the various officer/shareholders and at the same time lay the groundwork for a recapitalization or restructuring of the corporation at a later date.

The final area where the initial minutes can provide planning opportunities is when debt is established. As you will see in Chapter 4, any time that money is repaid to a shareholder/employee, there is always the possiblity of dividend treatment. Accordingly, in the initial minutes it is usually imperative to set up the need to borrow and authorize the officers to borrow from the shareholder. Most incorporations do not transfer from the sole proprietorship to the corporation the cash which was previously held in the proprietorship.

Sample of Minutes Establishing Debt

The chairman, Jack Smith, then discussed with the meeting the necessity for current working capital. He informed the meeting that the corporation's bank is willing to loan money to the corporation on an unsecured open loan at the rate of 12 percent per annum. He further informed the meeting that the two shareholders of the corporation offered to loan money, not to exceed $20,000 on a short-term basis to the corporation, to cover the current operating capital of the corporation. They have further informed the corporation that the interest which they would charge would be only 11 percent on an unsecured open loan.

Thereupon, on motion duly made, seconded, and unanimously carried, the following resolution was adopted:

RESOLVED: That the officers of the corporation are hereby authorized and empowered to execute demand promissory notes to the two shareholders of the corporation in a sum not to exceed $20,000, bearing interest at a rate of 11 percent.

WARNING: Before establishing any debt instrument through the loan of cash to the corporation, a review of Section 385 should be undertaken to ensure that these instruments will be classified as debt and not as stock by the Internal Revenue Service. Before establishing the interest rate, review the impact of Section 7872 on what interest rate should be charged so that there is no imputed interest problem.

[105.2]   Actions to Include in the Annual Minutes

Probably one of the most often asked questions of the corporate attorney is: What should be included in the corporate minutes? It should be understood that corporate minutes have the primary function of recording what has transpired during the prior year as a result of actions taken by the shareholders and directors. In most cases, in a closely held corporation, these actions are not always as the result of formal meetings but more often as the result of informal discussion among the principals. The memorializing in the form of minutes of the oral agreement of the shareholders and directors could have an effect on any of the following situations:

1. Upon an Internal Revenue Service audit to determine whether or not those actions reported to the Internal Revenue Service on the annual income tax return are supported in fact by action taken by the shareholders and/or directors. For example, establishment of salaries, approval of qualified deferred compensation payments, payment of dividends, and so on.

2. In the event of a disagreement involving shareholders, these minutes could conclusively reflect the action taken by the shareholders and directors.

3. There are always special instances when the minutes could be utilized. For example, creditors attempting to assert corporate liability upon individual shareholders may find it to their benefit to review the minutes.

With the above as a basic understanding of what the minutes are trying to accomplish, it is relatively easy to see that while it is important to memorialize in minute form those important actions taken during the year, that to include within those minutes all action discussed by the directors would be inappropriate. For example, there is no doubt that corporate borrowing should be approved by the directors, but the purchase of a duplicating machine may not have significant import to be included. The following letter will give rise to those actions that normally should be included in the minutes:

November 21, 1989

Mr. Joe Smith
Smith Manufacturing, Inc.
Highway 1
Anytown, U.S.A.

Dear Joe:

One of the most common questions I am asked regarding general corporate matters is, "What should be included in the minutes of the corporation?"

The corporation is an inanimate object, and therefore the minute book serves as a record of all actions taken by the shareholders and board of directors during its existence. These minutes have ramifications on various parties. The most significant are the Internal Revenue Service and the group of individuals comprising shareholders, directors and officers.

A list of the most common topics which should be included in the minutes are as follows:

1. Election of directors
2. Election of officers
3. Compensation of directors and/or officers
4. Corporate reorganizations
5. Deferred compensation agreements
6. Officers, employee bonuses
7. Dividends declared
8. Stock redemptions
9. Recapitalizations
10. Authorization of additional stock
11. Accumulation of earnings
12. Loans to:
    (a) Shareholders
    (b) Directors

      (c) Officers

      (d) Employees

      (e) Third parties

13. Loans from:

      (a) Shareholders

      (b) Directors

      (c) Officers

      (d) Employees

      (e) Third parties

14. Changes and adoption of bylaws

15. Bank signature cards

16. Bank resolutions and lines of credit

17. Lease contracts

18. Major purchases:

      (a) Land

      (b) Buildings

      (c) Equipment

      (d) Companies

19. Major sales contracts

20. Major charitable contributions

21. Employee benefit plans and programs

22. Pension and profit-sharing plans and contributions to same

23. Corporate name change

24. Change in articles of incorporation

25. Change in corporate year-end

The above is not inclusive, but it does list those matters that normally are included in either the shareholders' or director's minutes.

In addition, it is usually a good idea to have the minutes set forth contemporaneous reasons for actions being taken or policies adopted, particularly in the following areas:

1. Why were the officers' salaries adjusted?

2. Why wasn't a dividend paid?

3. What were the reasons for creating a deferred compensation package?

4. Why is money being accumulated?
5. Who are the officers and directors?
6. Why wasn't a particular acquisition pursued?
7. Why was a particular piece of property acquired?
8. Why was a division sold or abandoned?
9. Are there any negotiations for the purchase or sale of the business?

This letter serves to remind you that if you are in need of tax planning, you should contact me. If not, at least supply me with the information so that I can draft the year-end minutes.

If you have any questions regarding the substance of this letter, please do not hesitate to contact me.

Sincerely,

Lawrence C. Silton

The above letter was used as a general communication to my clients. It would probably be a good idea to send it out immediately after the execution of the corporate minute book. In addition to this letter, it is my practice to send the following letter during the last month of the corporate client's year. This allows him to meet with you if necessary to discuss tax planning and, if not, at least to ensure that the minute book is kept up to date.

Mr. Joe Smith
Smith Manufacturing, Inc.
Highway 1
Anytown, U.S.A.

Dear Joe:

Our records indicate that the year-end for the above-captioned corporation is April 30, 1987. Tax planning for yourself individually and for the corporation occurs at two separate times during the year. The first is in December, and the second is prior to the end of the corporate year. Accordingly, I would appreciate your reviewing your current year's operation, individually or with your accountant, to ascertain whether or not you believe any action need be accomplished for the current year. Please be aware that the Tax Reform Act of 1986 has had a significant impact on tax planning. The future appears clouded, and particular care in planning should occur this year.

If I can be of any assistance, please do not hesitate to contact me. If, on the other hand, no planning need be accomplished during this year, I would appreciate if either you or your accountant would forward to me a copy of the tax return after it has been prepared so that I can prepare the annual corporate minutes. In addition to the tax return, if substantial developments or occurrences have taken place during the prior fiscal year, I would appreciate your summarizing these so that I can ascertain whether it is appropriate to include the same in the minutes.

Sincerely,

Lawrence C. Silton

[105.3] Providing for Reimbursement of Disallowed Expenses

A problem which must be considered in the initial minutes is how to deal with the possibility that the IRS will disallow reimbursed expenses. The following will help illustrate this problem and the two alternative approaches:

Problem: The company, either in its initial stages or at a later date when it begins to prosper, purchases a car for the use of one of its officer/shareholders for corporate business.

Subsequently, the IRS conducts an audit and ascertains that a portion of the time that the car is being utilized is for personal, not corporate business. Accordingly, the Internal Revenue Service disallows $1,000 of the automobile expense as a personal expense.

Since the officer is also a shareholder, the IRS taxes the individual officer/shareholder, with the $1,000 as dividend income. The public is under the misconception that dividend income must be pro rata to a person's shareholdings in the corporation—for example, $1 per share. In other words, if he owns one-third of the outstanding stock and if the total dividends are $3,000, it appears that he would receive $1,000 in dividends. The IRS has been able to sustain the non-pro rata imposition of dividend income on shareholders. If dividends are imposed, it results in a twofold problem: a disallowed expense (now categorized as dividends) and taxable dividend income.

Alternative: An apparent solution to this problem is to insert in the minutes of the corporation an obligation on behalf of any officer/shareholder to repay any portion of the disallowed expenses. This is sometimes referred to as a hedge agreement. In theory, at least, this obligation then becomes a debt of the officer/shareholder to the corporation, which would not result in dividend income. At a later date, it is anticipated that this debt will be repaid by a bonus or by additional salary. A sample of the minutes or the bylaws that could be placed into the corporate records appears in Appendix A.

Until recently, the IRS had apparently acquiesced to this particular approach. However, their position in several court cases has cast some doubt as to its future position.

Alternative: If you believe that a hedge agreement is not the proper approach, you should insert in the minutes that the agreement was discussed and deemed inappropriate for the corporation. A sample of these minutes follows:

Sample Minutes

The chairman then presented to the meeting a resolution (see Appendix A) which would provide for the reimbursement of disallowed expenses. The meeting then discussed the validity of adopting said resolution. A discussion then occurred, and it was decided that because the compensation paid to the various officers would always be reasonable and that no personal expenses of the individual officers would be paid by the corporation, there was no need to insert this resolution in the minutes or as part of the bylaws of the corporation.

Thereupon, on motion duly made, seconded, and unanimously carried, the following resolution was adopted:

RESOLVED: That the corporation would not adopt Appendix A as a part of the minutes or bylaws of the corporation.

[105.4] Reasons That the 1244 Election Is "Something for Nothing"

The general rule of law is, that when corporate stock is sold at a gain, it will result in either long-term or short-term capital gains, depending upon its holding period. The Tax Reform Act of 1984 has reduced the holding period required to qualify for long-term capital gains treatment from twelve to six months for properties acquired between June 23, 1984, and December 31, 1987. If the property has been held for the necessary period of time and qualifies for the long-term capital gains treatment, at least through the year 1987, it will receive favorable tax benefits. After that period of time, the favorable taxation of long-term capital gains is somewhat in doubt.

If, on the other hand, the property is sold at a loss of $1,000, this $1,000 loss can produce some tax benefits. If the loss occurs from property qualifying for capital gains and loss treatment and was held for six months or less for properties acquired between June 23, 1984, and December 31, 1987 (twelve months or less for properties acquired before June 23, 1984, or after December 31, 1987), the loss qualifies as a short-term capital loss and all $1,000 could be utilized as a loss against other income if there are no other capital transactions. If, on the other hand, the loss results in a long-term capital loss and there are no other capital transactions, the tax benefit could be reduced by 50 percent—(100 percent after January 1, 1987).

Prior to ascertaining the total capital loss applicable to the individual shareholder, all long-term and short-term gains and losses for the year and any carryovers must be offset. The net loss, if it is short-term capital loss, is deductible on a one-to-one basis, but only one-half of the net long-term capital loss is deductible.

The net capital loss deduction is limited to $3,000 a year. The excess is carried forward to subsequent years. A few situations will illustrate how the gains and losses are taxed. The Tax Reform Act of 1986 as previously noted has had a significant impact on the taxation, and currently the effect after 1987 of the taxation is still in doubt. The reason for this is that it appears that Congress eliminated the favorable benefits of the capital gains treatment after 1987 but at the same time still retained in the law the definition of capital gains and losses and the basic structure and definitions for taxation of these. The expressed intent being that at a later date, it may be beneficial to once again have favorable capital gains rates. It should be noted that there is a limitation of the utilization of either short- or long-term capital losses even after the full implementation of the act.

Situation 1: A realizes a capital gain of $2,000 which qualifies for long-term capital gain treatment. He has no other capital gains or losses. In 1987, he would pay a maximum tax at 28 percent.

Situation 2: A sells a piece of property that yields a $3,000 short-term capital gain. He has no other capital gains or losses. This gain will be taxed at his marginal tax bracket.

Situation 3: A has two transactions during the taxable year which would qualify for capital gain or loss treatment. They are a long-term capital gain of $6,000 and a short-term capital loss of $2,000. His net long-term capital gain is $4,000. After 1987, this gain will be taxed at the highest marginal tax bracket which for individuals will be 33 percent including the 5 percent surcharge. As in situation 1 above, the maximum tax rate in 1987 is 28 percent.

Situation 4: A has only one capital transaction during the taxable year which yields a short-term capital loss of $3,000. This can be used to directly offset his other income.

Situation 5: A has a short-term capital loss of $1,000 and a long-term capital loss of $3,000 during the taxable year. He can deduct a loss against his other income as follows:

Short-term capital loss	$1,000
*50% of long-term capital loss	1,500
TOTAL LOSS	$2,500

* Beginning in 1987, long-term capital losses will no longer have to be reduced by 50 percent before they can be utilized against other income. However, the limitation on the utilization of capital losses against other income will be retained.

If the corporate stock qualifies as Section 1244 stock, the individual investor is given the best of both worlds. The Section 1244 stock, if sold at a gain, will result in a capital gain. If it is disposed at a loss, it is treated as an ordinary loss which can be deducted as long as it does not exceed an annual loss limitation of $50,000 for a single individual and $100,000 for a married individual filing a joint return. The remainder of the loss in that year would be a capital loss. The requirements of Section 1244 are relatively easy to satisfy. The basic requirements are as follows:

1. The investor must be an original investor in the corporation and must be an individual and not a corporation or trust.

2. The corporation must be an active corporation (as opposed to a passive holding company) wherein the total stock issue was less than $1 million.

3. Prior to the Tax Reform Act of 1984, the only stock that qualified for 1244 treatment was common stock. The Tax Reform Act of 1984 provided that preferred stock can also qualify.

While a full discussion of the Section 1244 requirements are beyond the scope of this book, it is important to understand the reason behind its enactment. This will provide an understanding as to its utilization by the closely held corporation. The purpose was to provide a partial cure for the discrepancy of the tax treatment of losses which an unincorporated business would sustain and the losses sustained by a business conducted in the corporate form. Ordinarily, a loss by an unincorporated business, be it a partnership or a sole proprietorship, is deductible in full against the ordinary income of the owners. On the other hand, the net operating losses sustained by the corporation are deductible only against the income of the corporation. They are not attributable to the individual shareholders except in the Subchapter S Corporation. It is possible that this loss will be wasted and lost forever if a corporation has never had any income at all. It is true that this loss by the corporation should have an effect on the value of the stock and will produce some tax benefit upon the sale by the shareholder. However, as noted before, the tax impact, because of long-term capital loss treatment, may be less beneficial.

Accordingly, if persons were going to start a new venture whose success was uncertain, it was not at all unusual to commence in an unincorporated form. The goal was to take the ordinary loss against the other income that they may have, even if valid nontax reasons would indicate incorporation. As soon as this venture was a success, they would then incorporate and have the income taxed to the corporation. The purpose of the act was to permit taxpayers under such circumstances to incorporate immediately if general business reasons indicated that this was the proper method. Of course, the total goal of reducing taxes as a consideration has not been reached because the benefit of Section 1244 stock is only realized upon the sale or disposition of that stock.

However, as a planning tool, and as a practical matter, as long as the original stock issue is not going to extend beyond two years from the date of incorporation, there is no reason not to have in the corporate minutes a Section 1244 election. (A sample of the minutes establishing this election is included in Appendix B.) Since there is no tax cost and only taxpayer benefit, there is probably little if any reason that this election should not be inserted in all corporate minutes. The necessity of formally adopting an election was liberalized by the 1978 Revenue Act. The failure to satisfy the requirements of this section would mean only that the loss instead of being an ordinary loss would be a capital loss. Unlike other tax savings plans where the taxpayer becomes committed by the election, this allows taxpayer benefits with none of the responsibility or any future restrictions on operations.

2

How to Take Money Out during the Operation of the Corporation— in a Tax-Protected Form

[200] HOW TO PAY FOR OFFICERS' AND OTHER EMPLOYEES' PERSONAL LIVING EXPENSES WITH TAX DEDUCTIBLE DOLLARS

[200.1] Defining a Pure Fringe Benefit

Widespread publicity has focused much attention on the area of fringe benefits, causing confusion and misunderstanding. Therefore, it is mandatory that we define the term "fringe benefit," also referred to as a "perk." The term "perk" is English in derivation and originates from the word "perquisites." This probably could be traced back to the profits accrued to a lord of a manor by virtue of his position over and above the yearly profits from his land. The term "perk" has evolved to mean those additional rights, privileges, and benefits which accrue to an individual in addition to the salary earned.

The "pure fringe benefit" is defined as follows:

1. A personal living expense that is paid by the employer for the benefit of the employee.
2. The expenditure is currently deductible by the employer.
3. The personal expense is not included in the employee's wages either currently or at a future date.

Fringe benefits, such as group term insurance and qualified medical reimbursements, fall within the terms of this defi-

73

nition. However, some of the more popular fringe benefits (for example, qualified deferred compensation plans), while they are properly categorized as a "fringe benefit" because of the important tax advantages which they render, do not fulfill all the requirements. The reason for this is that the final distribution of the benefit is not tax free. All fringe benefits have one common element—they provide some tax benefit to either the employer or the employee, or to both.

WARNING: The Subchapter S Revision Act of 1982 has curtailed the ability of shareholders owning more than 2 percent of the issued and outstanding stock of Subchapter S Corporations to obtain various fringe benefits. Accordingly, before establishing a fringe benefit for a Subchapter S Corporation or electing Subchapter S status, a complete review of the law's impact should be undertaken. (An explanation of the effects of this act on Subchapter S Corporations is set forth in Chapter 5.)

WARNING: The Tax Reform Act of 1986 has established new uniform rules for statutory fringe benefits. Thus, before implementing either an individual fringe benefit or a whole program of integrated fringe benefits, the impact of the Tax Reform Act of 1986 should be considered. (For a discussion of the general terms and conditions of this new act, see ¶201.1.)

[200.2] Evaluating the Overall Effects of Fringe Benefits

No matter which of the fringe benefits are implemented, it will always be necessary for you to ascertain the actual cost of the plan to determine its advisability. The actual cost is the total cost to the corporation less the tax benefit. This cost is compared with the benefit to the individual officer/shareholder.

The following is an example of how to calculate the cost of a fringe benefit.

Example: B Corporation has three principal shareholder/officers, X, Y, and Z, who wish to implement a group term life insurance program to supplement their personal life insurance. The corporation has a total of 15 employees, including X, Y, and Z. The program which is presented by the insurance company will cost $2,750 a year. This will provide $50,000 of term life insurance for X, Y, and Z. It is also determined that if this plan were not instituted, three insurance policies for X, Y, and Z providing the same benefits as group term insurance could be purchased for a total of $1,600. The remaining twelve employees will be covered by varying amounts of insurance from $5,000 to $20,000. The total cost of the remaining twelve employees is $1,150. Assuming that insurance premiums which are paid by the corporation are part of a qualified plan, they will be deductible to the corporation and not taxable to the employee. On the other hand, if $50,000 of life insurance is purchased by the employee, this premium will have to be paid in after-tax dollars.

In this example, we are assuming that the corporation will either pay the life insurance premiums for the shareholder/officers, or, in lieu thereof, distribute additional salary which will provide the after-tax income for each of the shareholder/officers to purchase $50,000 worth of term life insurance.

The total cost to the corporation if the shareholder/employees purchase and own their own insurance is calculated as follows:

Additional Compensation Needed to Pay Premiums	$2,388.00
LESS: Tax Calculated at 33%	788.00
After-Tax Salary Available to Shareholder/Employee to Pay Premium	$1,600.00

If group term is purchased, the total amount should be fully deductible, and thus the total cost to the corporation is $2,750. Therefore, the establishment of the fringe benefit will cost the corporation $362; however, there will be the intangible benefit of the additional coverage for the employees.

Questions you should ask prior to the establishment of this group term plan in addition to "how much it will cost" are as follows:

1. How will this insurance program affect the total fringe benefits of the other employees?

2. Is this the type of life insurance which is most beneficial to X, Y, and Z?

3. Do the other employees need additional life insurance?

In this example, we have seen that the overall cost to the corporation is slightly more than that which would have been incurred by X, Y, and Z if they had personally paid for the $50,000 term life insurance policies. In addition to this tax analysis, you should also consider the economic consequences. For example, can this fringe be integrated into the general compensation structure of the corporation to reduce the other out-of-pocket costs? Is it possible to provide this fringe instead of an across-the-board wage increase?

There are also alternative methods available to you for increasing the insurance on the individual shareholders/employees. For example, as an alternative to obtaining a group term policy, it may be beneficial to purchase split dollar insurance for the executive. The remainder of this chapter will help you analyze the benefits and costs of fringe benefits.

[201] HOW THE CORPORATION CAN UTILIZE THE MOST COMMON CLASSES OF FRINGE BENEFITS

[201.1] Effect of the Tax Reform Act of 1986 on Statutory Fringe Benefits

The Tax Reform Act of 1986 has had a significant impact upon certain statutory fringe benefits and cafeteria plans. Under the law prior to the effective date of the enactment of the Tax Reform Act of 1986, virtually every type of fringe benefit was governed by its own set of nondiscrimination rules as to eligibility and benefits. The Tax Reform Act of 1986 sets forth a comprehensive set of nondiscrimination laws for certain statutory fringe benefits and cafeteria plans. These tests generally supersede all pre-act tests except as they apply to certain fringe benefits and to employees who own a greater than 5 percent interest in the company.

The original effective date of this law was supposed to be December 31, 1987. However, since regulations have not been issued by that time, the rules are effective for the earlier of the plan years beginning at least three months after the regulations are issued or plan years beginning after December 31, 1988. Accordingly, at least in the near future, it will be necessary not only to understand the new law but also to understand the old law.

The Tax Reform Act of 1986 has had a specific impact upon the following types of statutory fringe benefits:

1. Group term life insurance
2. Accident and health plans whether insured or self-insured
3. Any of the following plans if the employer elects to apply the law as established by the Tax Reform Act of 1986:
    (a) Qualified group legal services
    (b) Dependent care assistant programs
    (c) Educational assistance plans

The method of approach to fully comprehend both the old law and how it is scheduled to be changed by the new law is to discuss the new restrictions placed by the Tax Reform Act of 1986 on all the statutory fringe benefits and then to discuss the old law and see how they will coexist after the effective date of the Tax Reform Act of 1986. It is absolutely necessary now for people who are in personnel or who make decisions as to the future of the fringe benefits within the corporation to be cognizant of both the rules prevailing currently and those that are to be implemented upon the effective date of the tax reform act.

WARNING: The institution of a comprehensive fringe benefit plan for the employees of any corporation should take into consideration not only the law currently in effect but also the changes which will be implemented upon the effective date of the Tax Reform Act of 1986.

Under the new law, the general concept is that all employees will include in income an amount equal to the employer-provided benefits under a statutory fringe benefit plan unless the plan contains the following characteristics:

1. It is in writing.
2. The employer's rights are legally enforceable.
3. Employees are given reasonable notification of the benefits available under the plan.
4. The plan is maintained for the exclusive benefit of the employees.
5. The plan was established with the intention of being maintained indefinitely.

Most of the just-stated provisions other than certain notification provisions should be fairly easy for the employer to meet. The problem comes in determining whether or not the plan was established for the exclusive benefit of the employees (it meets the appropriate nondiscrimination requirements). The definition of an employer-provided benefit is the value of the benefits provided to the employee. If the accident and health plan does not meet the nondiscrimination requirements, then the value of excess benefit, for example $200 or $250 a month, will be included in the employee's wage. The concept is to include the excess benefit in the income of highly compensated individuals who participate in a discriminatory fringe benefit plan. In other words, if there was a general benefit provided, only the amount in excess of that provided to all employees will be included in the wage of the highly compensated employee.

It should be noted that a plan will be considered discriminatory, as will be set forth shortly, unless it passes both the nondiscrimination tests for eligibility and benefits. Obviously, it becomes necessary to understand the impact of the new act by understanding the following terms:

1. Highly compensated employee
2. Discrimination
3. Excess benefit

1. *Who is defined as a highly compensated employee?:* A highly compensated employee will be defined to include the following:

1. The 5 percent owner
2. Earn more than $75,000 in annual compensation
3. Earn more than $50,000 in annual compensation and whose compensation is in the top 20 percent of all the employer's benefits
4. Certain current and prior officers

2. *What are the nondiscrimination provisions under the new act?:* The statutory benefit plan must satisfy the following three tests:

1. The 90 percent test. At least 90 percent of the employer's non-highly compensated employees must be eligible to participate in a plan. In addition, these highly compensated employees must be eligible for a benefit that is at least 50 percent as valuable as the benefit available to the highly compensated employee to whom the most valuable benefits are made available.

2. The 50 percent test. Non-highly compensated employees must constitute at least 50 percent of the group of employees eligible to participate in the plan. A plan will be deemed to have passed this test if the percentage of highly compensated employees are eligible to participate is not greater than the percentage of non-highly compensated employees who are eligible.

   The following example will illustrate how this test operates:

   Example: XYZ Corporation has twenty employees, fifteen of whom are considered highly compensated under the act. Because more than 50 percent of the workforce is highly compensated, this employer could make all employees eligible but still not satisfy the 50 percent test. However, if all employees are eligible, the employer would satisfy the 50 percent test because the percentage of highly compensated employees and non-highly compensated who are eligible are the same (100 percent).

3. The nondiscriminatory provision test. This test requires that the plan not contain any provision on eligibility to participate that by its terms or otherwise discriminates in favor of highly compensated employees.

   The above three tests deal mainly with eligibility. The second set of tests deals with discrimination and benefits. A statutory benefit plan will be discriminatory if it fails to meet the benefits test that compares the benefits received by non-highly compensated employees to benefits received by highly compensated employees. Under this test, the average employer-provided benefit which is received by a non-highly compensated employee under all plans of the employer of the same type must be at least 75 percent of the average employer-provided benefit received by the highly compensated under all plans. The alternative to meeting both of the above tests is that if any plan benefits at least 80 percent of the employer's nonhighly compensated employees during the plan year, it is considered to satisfy both eligiblity and benefits test for this year. There is a caveat, of course, that this test will not apply if the plan contains a provision that by its terms or otherwise discriminates in favor of the highly compensated employees.

The thrust of the act is simple: to provide equality of benefits for all individuals. The question in the small closely held corporation becomes: What effect will this have upon the plan? Obviously, in big corporations that maintain multiple plans at different plants, divisions, and so on, these changes may have a great deal more impact than in a closely held corporation that normally will provide the "same benefits" for all its employees. For example, all qualifying individuals will receive 100 percent health plan coverage and group term life insurance. In the past, especially with group term life insurance, it was not necessary to determine the "value of the benefit." Now, under the new law, this benefit may need to be determined. For example, a $50,000 life insurance policy will have a greater benefit to an individual who is age 55 than to an individual who is age 25. The cost will be determined from the table set forth in Appendix F, and the excess benefit for the highly compensated individuals will need to be reported as income.

3. *What is the concept of excess benefits?:* Basically, an excess benefit which is includable in the gross income of a highly compensated individual is the amount by which the plan benefit received by such employee exceeds the highest permitted benefit. (As indicated above, the excess benefit includable in the income of a highly compensated employee is computed by subtracting the highest permitted benefit under a plan from the general employee-provided benefit received by such employee.) A plan's highest permitted benefit is determined by reducing the nontaxable benefits of highly compensated individuals to a level at which the plan would not be discriminatory. The rules are obviously complex because we are dealing with converting benefits for groups into actual dollar cost for individuals.

While a complete discussion is beyond the scope of this book, the following example will at least describe the general concepts involved:

Example: Under a health plan covered by XYZ Corporation, all employees are entitled to basic hospitalization which provides in-hospital care on a semiprivate room basis. There are two supplementary plans. Supplementary A provides middle and top management with reimbursement for visits to physicians outside of the hospital, and Supplementary B provides reimbursement to top management employees for the additional cost of private hospital rooms.

The basic coverage is $1,500 per year per employee. The value of coverage under Supplementary A is an additional $500 per year and for Supplementary B an additional $750 per year. XYZ Corporation's health benefit plan fails the benefit test since the general employee benefit of $1,500 is less than 75 percent of the average benefit received by highly compensated employees over $2,000. The plan would comply if highly compensated employees received only Supplementary A and consequently an average benefit of $2,000 since this would bring benefits of non-highly compensated employees to 75 percent of the benefits of compensated employees. Consequently, the cost of Supplementary B would be the excess benefit taxed to the highly compensated employees who received it.

[202] HOW THE CORPORATION CAN UTILIZE THE VARIOUS STATUTORY FRINGE BENEFITS BEFORE THE IMPLEMENTATION OF THE TAX REFORM ACT AND HOW THESE WILL BE AFFECTED BY THE TAX REFORM ACT

[202.1] Paying Employees' Personal Medical Bills and Accident Insurance Premiums

Before the implementation of the Tax Reform Act of 1986, it was possible to discriminate without problems as far as insured health and accident policies. For example, a corporation with one hundred employees could pay 100 percent of the officers'

premiums and only 10 percent of all other nonofficer participants. Obviously, the Tax Reform Act has had a definite impact
upon the payment and coverage provisions, and any corporation which has been paying health insurance for any of its
participants will have to review the impact of the new law.

In addition, many corporations had established medical
reimbursement plans which were not insured but were provided by the employer for the employee to cover those medical
costs that were not covered by insurance. With the increased
limits on nondeductibility of the individual imposed by the Tax
Reform Act of 1986 (7.5 percent of the adjusted gross income),
the benefit of these medical reimbursement plans becomes extremely important if they are considered nondiscriminatory.
As previously set forth, the prior nondiscrimination tests continue until the new regulations are promulgated. Accordingly,
until the effective date of the Tax Reform Act of 1986, these
rules remain effective.

How a Medical Reimbursement Plan under the Revenue Act of 1978 Can Benefit All Employees

How It Works: The law on self-insured medical reimbursement plans has undergone a significant revision which became
effective as of January 1, 1980. Prior to its enactment, the plan
need not have covered all employees. It was subject to attack by
the IRS if it appeared to exclusively cover shareholders/em-
ployees and if payments were a form of disguised dividends.
However, under the Revenue Act of 1978, to qualify as a self-
insured plan, it cannot discriminate in favor of highly compensated employees either in eligibility or in the benefits provided
by the plan. If the plan does not satisfy all the requirements of
the Internal Revenue Code Section 105(h) and the employee is
considered highly compensated, he must include in his gross
income amounts designated as excess reimbursement.

What to Watch Out For: Individually, the taxpayer receives a
deduction for expenditures for health care and insurance premiums only to the extent that they exceed 7.5 percent of the
taxpayer's adjusted gross income. For example, if the individual taxpayer has an adjusted gross income of $50,000, the 7.5

percent or $3,750 paid for health and related items is, for tax purposes, lost.

The Way to Prevent the Loss of This Deduction: The corporation adopts a nondiscriminatory self-insured plan. The corporate employer pays the premiums for the accident and health insurance plan to cover all its employees. In addition, the corporation will pay medical expenses not covered by the insurance company. The law now states that the plan must fulfill rather stringent requirements to be considered nondiscriminatory. Basically, the highly compensated employees are defined to include the five highest paid officers; a shareholder who owns, directly or indirectly, 10 percent of the stock; or the highest 25 percent of all employees. These highly compensated employees will be able to exclude from their income only those reimbursements equal to the reimbursement allowable to the lowest paid employee of the company. If the plan is nondiscriminatory, neither the premium payments nor the actual benefits received will be taxable income to the employees.

WARNING: The Subchapter S Revision Act of 1982 has vastly curtailed the ability of shareholders owning more than 2 percent of the issued and outstanding stock of Subchapter S Corporations to obtain the benefits of medical reimbursement plans. (See Chapter 5 for a complete discussion of the impact this act has had on Subchapter S Corporations and their shareholders relative to qualified medical reimbursement plans and other fringe benefits.)

Requirements for Self-Insured Plans

The requirements for medical reimbursement plans are as follows:

1. Only self-insured plans are subject to restrictions. A plan is considered self-insured if the benefits to be paid under the plan are not made from the health and insurance carrier.
2. There can be no discrimination as to eligibility or benefits. Eligibility and participation is determined as follows:
    (a) 70 percent or more of all employees, or
    (b) 80 percent or more of eligible employees if 70 percent or more are eligible to participate

3. Any classification which receives IRS approval.

4. Certain employees may be excluded. The major exclusions are as follows:
   (a) Employees who are under the age of 25 or who have less than three years of service
   (b) Part-time and/or seasonal employees. Part time is less than thirty-five hours, and seasonal is less than nine months
   (c) Employees covered by a collective bargaining agreement
   (d) Nonresident aliens

5. Benefit rules. All benefits provided for the highly compensated individuals must also flow to all other qualified participants.

How the Taxable Reimbursements Are Computed

The participant is taxed on his excess reimbursements. Excess reimbursements are defined to include the following:

1. A benefit available to a highly compensated individual, but not to the lower based employee.

2. All other benefits paid by a self-insured discriminatory plan. Basically, in this instance, the percentage applicable is the percentage that is paid to the prohibited group over the total of the benefits paid to all groups.

For example, a corporation's self-insured plan is considered discriminatory. The corporation, pursuant to the terms of the plan, pays $100,000 in medical reimbursements. Forty thousand dollars of these reimbursements is made to the highly compensated employees. The remainder is made to those employees who would not be defined under the Code as highly compensated. The president of the corporation, during the year, has been paid $3,000 from the plan. He will have to include 40 percent of the $3,000 in his taxable income. (A sample copy of a self-insured discriminatory plan is included in Appendix C.)

Prior to January 1, 1980, the medical reimbursement plan was used as an additional perk for the benefit of a group of highly compensated employees. Many times, this was restricted solely to the officers who may or may not have been shareholders of the corporation. In an attempt to maintain these benefits, several insurance companies offered plans which provided that the premium would be based upon 105 percent to 110 percent of the total benefits actually paid pursuant to the plan. For example, if a plan was designed to cover only officers of the corporation, health insurance would be purchased for these individual parties. The actual premiums charged by the insurance company would be based upon the claims paid plus 5 percent. If the claims during the relevant period were $10,000, the total premiums for that year were $10,500. The Internal Revenue Service in the regulations under Section 105 has indicated that these health insurance plans will be considered self-insured even if reimbursement is provided under an insurance policy or prepaid health plan unless the policy or plan involves shifting of "**risk.**"

WARNING: If the health insurance policy purchased does not involve risk shifting, it will not be considered a health insurance plan but solely a self-insured medical reimbursement plan and will be subject to the regulations regarding medical reimbursement plans. The IRS has taken the position that a plan underwritten by a cost-plus policy will be considered self-insured and therefore subject to reimbursement rules.

> **Key Idea:** Even after the implementation of the Revenue Act of 1978 and the regulations adopted pursuant to said act, there is nothing to prohibit the purchase of health insurance on a discriminatory basis. If the insurance company will write a group term plan on a specific group (that is, all officer/employees or some other defined group), this will not be under the restrictions applicable to medical reimbursement plans. In addition, it is still possible to purchase individual policies for those employees if desired.

An interesting plan of action can be implemented in certain selected cases. The exact tax ramifications are not fully predictable at this time; however, it would appear that a plan such as set forth below would have a reasonable chance of sustaining IRS attack until the implementation of the provisions of the Tax Reform Act of 1986.

Example: A doctor's office employs four doctors, all officers, and eight support personnel. Of these support personnel, some are married and have spouses who are covered by insurance programs at their place of employment, and some are single. The officer/shareholders wish to implement a medical insurance plan and possibly a medical reimbursement plan. The current family coverage costs are $150 per month, while current single coverage costs are $40 per month. No health insurance has previously been purchased for the employees. A plan such as the following could be implemented:

1. The board of directors could enact a plan to purchase and pay for health insurance for all officers. (See Appendix D).

2. A group plan could be purchased for all employees of the corporation. By reason of the prior action of the board of directors, all premiums for the doctors would be paid in full. All other employees, if they wished coverage, would have to pay 100 percent of the premiums.

3. A nondiscriminatory medical reimbursement plan could be implemented covering all employees to a maximum amount of $1,000 per year. This would provide $1,000 of medical coverage to each of the four doctors for unpaid medical expenses. In addition, the married employee whose spouse is not covered by health insurance at work could designate his medical reimbursement of $1,000 to be applied against the $1,800 yearly premium ($150 per month × 12 = $1,800) and, accordingly, would pay $800 of the total premiums. In the event that the spouse has family coverage, this $1,000 would provide the family with reimbursement for uncovered medical costs. The plan provides more benefits than would otherwise be available and implements both corporate and individual needs such as:

    a) If the corporation pays 100 percent of all premiums on all employees, there is usually some double coverage (husband and wife each being covered by health insurance at work).

b) Those families who could have both spouses covered now will have the opportunity to receive actual out-of-pocket benefits, thus producing a real economic benefit to the family unit.

c) The costs of health insurance have vastly escalated in the past ten years. During this period, they have at least doubled. Depending upon the portion of the country and the cost of health care where the person is located, these monthly premiums can cost as much as $250 per month. If the employer pays the full premium, he is absorbing a rapidly increasing cost without the employee realizing the full benefit. Under the structure as set forth above, the employee will be fully aware of the actual benefit he is receiving.

A sample of what would appear to be a qualified medical reimbursement plan is attached as Appendix E. There are certain problems that are occasioned through the enactment of a medical reimbursement plan such as the one outlined above. While the law as enacted allows the employer to exclude any employee who works less than thirty-five hours per week, the final regulations state that in order for an employer to be allowed to utilize this exclusion, there must be employees other than those in the prohibited group who work more than thirty-five hours. If there are no employees, other than those in the prohibited group, doing similar work in the corporation, then employees engaged in "similar work in the same industry and location" must be considered. This is rather confusing and the exact ramifications of the final regulations are not fully known. However, the regulations have provided a safe harbor for excluding part-time employees. The regulations state that an employee is considered part-time if he (1) works twenty-five hours or less per week or (2) is employed less than nine months a year. Accordingly, it may be worthwhile to utilize the "safe harbor" restrictions from the Regulation in the plan rather than those seemingly permitted by the letter of the law.

[202.2]   Group Term Insurance

How It Works: The requirements which are set forth in Section 79 of the Internal Revenue Code state that an employer may provide up to $50,000 in group-term insurance for his employee without the necessity of the employee including any portion of the cost of the insurance premium in his gross income. This must be pure term insurance. There can be no cash surrender value in group term insurance. Section 79 also states that in groups over ten, the insurance carrier cannot require a medical exam. If the group contains fewer than ten participants, there are special requirements which must be met. The Tax Equity and Fiscal Responsibility Act of 1982 and the Subchapter S Revision Act of 1982 has had a serious impact on the use of group term insurance as a fringe benefit. The prior ability of a Subchapter S Corporation to have a tax deductible payment for the benefit of a 2 percent or more shareholder and exclusion from his taxable income has been altered. A full discussion of this impact and the impact of the Subchapter S Revision Act of 1982 is provided in Chapter 5.

In addition, TEFRA has imposed changes on group term insurance for all regular corporations. In order that there be complete exclusion from taxable income to the key employees for all group term insurance under $50,000, the plan must not discriminate in their favor in eligibility, type, or amount of benefits.

While all employees must be covered, they need not be covered by the same amount of insurance. The amount of coverage is stratified in relation to the wage categories. The classifications are fairly complex. However, insurance companies will establish brackets under which no bracket exceeds two-and-one-half times the next lower bracket and the lowest bracket is at least 10 percent of the highest bracket. If the individual wishes protection in excess of $50,000, the tax cost to him for this protection is usually less than if he individually purchased this life insurance. Tables set forth in Regulation 1.79-3 of the Internal Revenue Code (Appendix F) indicate the amount that must be included in the taxable income of the employee. Needless to say, this fringe can be of significant benefit to the employee.

How to Decide If You Are Making the Best Choice: In the final analysis, the decision as to whether or not any insurance in excess of $50,000 should be purchased can be made only after an analysis of the benefits. You must consider the cost of this insurance plus tax costs versus the alternative methods of approach such as an individual purchase of whole or term insurance or the corporate purchase of split dollar insurance.

It is also important to note that the payment of this insurance upon death is also income tax free. Upon his death, the group term policy will normally be included in the gross estate of the individual employee for estate tax purposes. However, if state law permits, the employee may be able to assign his policy to his spouse, his heirs, or to an irrevocable insurance trust, thus excluding the proceeds from his taxable estate.

WARNING: Many persons, upon joining a group plan, tend to cancel some of their long-term whole life insurance. It may become extremely difficult, costly, or impossible to maintain all or any part of the group term coverage if the individual terminates his employment. Before the permanent insurance coverage is canceled, a complete analysis of the person's individual insurance program should be made.

WARNING: Be aware that for all tax years beginning after December 31, 1983, the Section 79 income exclusion for employer-provided group term life insurance will not apply to key employees if the employer's program discriminates in favor of the key employees as to eligibility or benefits. Eligibility requirements are not discriminatory if:

1. At least 70 percent of all employees benefit.
2. At least 85 percent of all participants are not key employees.
3. Participants comprise a classification of employees that the IRS determines is not discriminatory.

Because of the change in the law, previous income exclusions for group term payments may be disallowed. The full impact of this law will not be clear until the IRS has promulgated regulations applying the law.

WARNING: The Tax Reform Act of 1986 has a substantial impact on this fringe benefit. The law will completely change once the effective date of the act takes place. (For the impact of the new law, see ¶201.1.)

[202.3] Using Group Prepaid Legal Service Plans

The Tax Reform Act of 1976 provided a new fringe benefit: group prepaid legal expenses. Group prepaid legal expenses have a great deal of potential, but so far have only been sparingly used.

How It Works: Similar to the medical reimbursement plan in concept, this fringe allows for employees to exclude the value of personal legal expenses or amounts received as reimbursements for such expenses, from taxable income, if provided under a qualified plan. It also supplies the employee's spouses and dependents with personal legal services. The group prepaid legal plan must be established pursuant to a written plan. This plan should be enacted by the board of directors of the corporation. (A sample of this plan is included in Appendix G.)

There are several options available to the employer as to the type of plan he can establish. The employer may pay the contribution to an insurance company, to certain trusts or organizations which are to be a part of the qualified plan, to legal service providers, or to any combination of these. A major deterrent for small closely held corporations in establishing this plan appears to be in the area of nondiscrimination. No more than 25 percent of the annual contributions to this plan may be provided for the benefit of the employee/shareholders who are owners of more than 5 percent of the stock of the corporation. In order to qualify a group prepaid legal services plan, the employer must notify the Internal Revenue Service. The procedure for obtaining approval is set forth in the regulations. The application for qualification is made on Form 1024 to the district director. Originally, the law was to be in effect for a five-year period beginning in 1977 and ending in 1982. The effective date has been extended to all tax years ending before 1988. All indications are that this fringe benefit will have little if any real impact upon closely held corporations. And, in the absence of new legislation extending the effective date these plans are no longer available.

NOTE: After the Tax Reform Act of 1986, the employer is given the option of complying either with the law under the new act (see ¶201.1) or with the prior law.

[202.4] Using the New Exclusion for Dependent Care Assistance

The Economic Recovery Tax Act of 1981 provided a new fringe benefit in the form of dependent care assistance programs. This new fringe excludes from gross income the amount paid by an employer for child care or dependent care assistance. Basically, dependent care assistance is defined as the payment of, or provision for, those services which, if paid by the employee himself, would have been considered employment-related services for the child care credit. In other words, child care expenses which would qualify for the child credit if the employee had paid those expenses himself are within the provisions of this fringe benefit. Basically, the dependent child care deduction is limited to the earnings of the lower income spouse.

For example, if the husband was earning $5,000 and the wife was earning $10,000, the amount that could be excluded would be limited to $5,000. However, if a spouse is a student or is mentally or physically incapable of caring for himself, $200 per month shall be considered his income. Of course, there are no double benefits. In other words, any amount properly excluded as a dependent care expense is not available for the child care credit.

Prerequisites for a Qualified Dependent Care Assistance Program

The requirements for a qualified dependent care assistance program are as follows:

1. It must be in writing in favor of officers, owners, or highly compensated employees, or their dependents.
2. It may not discriminate in favor of officers, owners, or highly compensated employees, or their dependents.

3. No more than 25 percent of the dependent care assistance paid during the year may be provided to officers/share holders or owners (or their spouses or dependents) who own more than 5 percent of the stock of the corporation.

4. It may, but need not, be funded.

5. Reasonable notice of availability and terms of the program must be given to eligible employees.

6. The plan must furnish a written statement to each employee showing the amounts paid for expenses incurred by the employer in providing dependent care assistance to such employee during the calendar year.

Again, because of the discrimination requirements, it would appear that the major utilization of these child care benefits will be in larger corporations or through union-negotiated contracts.

NOTE: After the Tax Reform Act of 1986, the employer is given the option of complying either with the law under the new act (see ¶201.1) or with the prior law.

[202.5] Providing an Exclusion from Income for Employer-Paid Education Assistance

The Revenue Act of 1978 provided an exclusion for employer-provided education assistance for the fiscal years between 1979 and 1985. The Tax Reform Act of 1986 extended the applicability of this provision for all taxable years ending before January 1, 1988. It also increased the maximum amount of assistance to be provided, from $5,000 to $5,250.

In order to qualify, this program had to be a written plan of the employer which operated for the exclusive benefit of the employees. It did not have to be funded. However, all eligible employees must have been given reasonable notice of the availability of benefits and terms of the program. There were stiff nondiscrimination rules. Therefore, a plan could not discriminate in favor of employees who were officer/shareholders or were highly compensated. A plan would be considered discriminatory if more than 5 percent of the amounts paid or incurred for educational assistance in any one year went to shareholders or owners (or their spouses or dependents) who owned more than 5 percent. The plan in and of itself would not be considered discriminatory simply because it was used by one class of employees more than the other or because the benefits depended upon successful completion of a course or attainment of a certain grade.

The expenses that could have been covered included, but were not limited to, tuition and fees of the educational institution. It could also include books, supplies, and equipment related to the course. These educational benefits were not limited to improving one's skills. The courses did not need to be job-related but could not be for courses involving sports, games, or hobbies. Because of the stiff nondiscrimination portion of the act, the full utilization by the closely held corporation was never realized.

NOTE: After the Tax Reform Act of 1986, the employer is given the option of complying either with the law under the new act (see ¶201.1) or with the prior law.

[202.6] Employer Fringe Benefit Program Implemented by the Tax Reform Act of 1984

You must determine whether the business fringe benefits are nontaxable or additional compensation. In 1975, the IRS issued proposed regulations which were to help determine whether or not nonstatutory fringe benefits were taxable as compensation. Between that time and the enactment of the Tax Reform Act of 1984, Congress prohibited the issuance of regulations that would be effective before 1984. The new act defines the various types of employee fringe benefits and whether or not they will be taxable in the employee's wages. The corollary appears to be that any fringe benefits that do not qualify for the exclusion under the new law or any other provision are taxable income and are subject to employment taxes. The amount which normally would be taxable will be the excess of the fringe benefit's fair market value over the amount paid by the employee. The excludable fringes are set forth in the Tax Reform Act of 1984 and are divided into five areas:

1. No additional cost services. This is the type of fringe available to the employee which is generally provided to the

general public. In order to qualify under this particular section, the employer must not incur any substantial additional cost. The term "cost" here does include within its purview the loss of revenue because services are furnished to an employee rather than to the general public. An obvious example of this particular fringe is furnishing excess airline tickets or unused motel rooms. To qualify, this fringe benefit must have the following characteristics:

    (a) It can be made available to the employees, their spouses, and their dependent children.

    (b) The benefit must be available on substantially the same terms to each member of a group of employees. In other words, it must not discriminate in favor of the key employees or shareholders.

    (c) The services must be of the same type that are sold to nonemployee customers in the ordinary course of a line of business. In other words, the airline employees cannot exclude free motel rooms provided by the hotel business and vice versa. The idea here is not to give an undue competitive advantage to large conglomerates over small one-line businesses.

    (d) As noted above, there can be no additional cost.

2. Qualified employee discounts. Basically, this fringe benefit allows employees and their dependents (assuming the appropriate nondiscrimination provisions have been met) to purchase goods or services at a discount from that available to the general public. Again, as in the no additional cost services, the goods or services must be provided in the same line of business. However, in this particular case, all commonly controlled businesses in the same line are treated as one. The amount of the discount for goods cannot exceed the normal selling price multiplied by the employer's gross profit percentage. For example, if an employer has $2 million of gross sales and the cost of goods sold is $1.4 million, the gross profit percentage is 30 percent. If the employee wishes to purchase goods sold by the employer, the maximum amount of the discount cannot exceed 30 percent. On the other hand, if instead of providing goods, the employer provides services, the maximum amount of the discount is 20 percent.

3. Working condition fringe. The new law allows an employee to exclude from his income the fair market value of any employer-related property or services for which he could have taken a deduction as ordinary and necessary business expenses. Probably a good example of this is the insurance salesman who is an employee of the company. He could take an ordinary business deduction for the use of his car. However, his use for personal purposes will not qualify (other than incidental personal use, which may qualify as a de minimus fringe).

Key Idea: The past problems of whether or not employer-provided free parking is a taxable fringe have been eliminated. An employee can now exclude from income as a working condition fringe the fair market value of free or reduced parking provided on or near the employer's business premises.

4. De minimus fringes. The concept here is that the law will exclude the fair market value of any property or services so small that accounting for it is unreasonable and administratively impractical. These fringes, but for this exclusion, would be includable in income. There are probably two very important factors in determining whether or not the fringe benefit will be taxable, and these are cost and frequency. Some examples of these fringes are typing of personal letters by a company secretary, occasional personal use of the company copy machine, occasional cocktail parties or picnics for employees, occasional cab fare for overtime work, holiday turkeys, or coffee and doughnuts furnished to employees.

5. Qualified tuition deduction. This will have little applicability to the owners of a small corporation since the fringe is available only to employees of qualified educational institutions. The Tax Reform Act of 1984 allows employees to exclude qualified tuition deductions including cash grants. This exclusion applies to tuition for education at any educational institution, not only the employer's school. It should be noted that prior to the Tax Reform Act of 1986, this provision was limited to education below the graduate level. The Tax Reform Act of 1986 extends the coverage

to certain graduate level students. For this particular exclusion to be available to officers, owners, and the hightly
paid employees, the tuition reductions must be made
available under classifications which do not discriminate in
their favor.

[202.7] Providing the Full Range of Benefits through a Cafeteria Plan

The Law Prior to the Implementation of the Tax Reform Act of 1986

Cafeteria plans have provoked a lot of discussion and
some actual tax savings for larger corporations, but as yet they
have not had much impact on closely held corporations. The
cafeteria plan is a product of the rapid escalation of the nonsalary costs of employees to their employers. The compensation
package of employees has always been composed of three distinct parts: salary, government-imposed taxes, and voluntary
nonsalary compensation (insurance, deferred compensation,
and so on). Recently the expenses for taxes and voluntary nonsalary compensation have been rising at a considerably more
rapid pace than salary expenses.

The disproportionate rise in nonsalary expenses in conjunction with the typical desire of employers to weigh benefits
in favor of their highly paid employees has encouraged the
development of benefit plans which correlate the amount of
fringe benefits offered to salary levels. In addition, the rise in
the number of couples where both spouses work has led to
expensive duplication of coverage. A perfect example of this is
health insurance, where each spouse's employer provides (and
pays for) coverage for the entire family. When the cost of
health insurance was only $40 a month, overlapping coverage
made little difference. However, as the cost of providing family
coverage for an employee exceeds $250 a month in many cases,
it has become an important consideration. Many employees
would gladly forego duplicate coverage in exchange for extra
direct compensation or for other more needed fringe benefits.
Accordingly, employers and employees share a desire to structure benefit packages in such a way as to maximize the actual
benefits received by the employees for a given expense to the
employer.

The cafeteria plan is a result of these developments. It allows employees to choose their own benefits within the framework of a package developed by the company. The total benefits available to an employee are often based upon some percentage of salary. For example, XYZ Corporation establishes a cafeteria plan providing that an amount equal to 15 percent of each employee's total salary can be spent to purchase a combination of benefits from among those offered by the plan. Any portion of these funds not spent by an employee on the nontaxable fringe benefits will be paid as salary. The employee with a salary of $10,000 will have $1,500 available, and the employee with a salary of $100,000 will have $15,000 available.

There has been considerable confusion with regard to the tax treatment of these plans. However, the Tax Reform Act of 1984 has further clarified the Revenue Act of 1978's provisions with respect to the tax treatment of cafeteria plans. The Tax Reform Act of 1984 provides that employees need only include the cost of benefits in their gross income to the extent to which they have elected taxable benefits. The nontaxable benefits which can be chosen have been restricted by the Tax Reform Act of 1984 to statutory nontaxable benefits such as group term insurance, disability benefits, and accident and health benefits. (Previously it was believed that certain nonstatutory fringe benefits could also be chosen without creating taxable income to the employee.)

Notwithstanding the preceding, amounts contributed to the plan for highly compensated employees will be included in the gross income to the extent the employees could have elected taxable benefits unless the plan satisfies certain antidiscrimination requirements regarding coverage, eligibility, contribution of benefits, and that not more than 25 percent of the plan's statutory nontaxable benefits are provided to key employees. These requirements are divided into health and nonhealth benefits.

The requirements for exclusion of nonhealth benefits are as follows:

1. Coverage and Eligibility:
    (a) The plan must benefit a class of employees that is determined by the Internal Revenue Service as nondiscriminatory.

(b) The plan cannot require more than three years of consecutive employment for plan participation.

2. Contributions of benefits: A plan will not be considered discriminatory as long as the total benefits attributable to the highly compensated parties are not significantly greater than the total of nontaxable benefits to other employees. For these purposes, a percentage of total compensation may be used to determine the amount of benefits which can be elected without being classified as discriminatory. It should be noted that the Tax Reform Act of 1984 added the restriction that a key employee will not be exempt from taxation on the taxable benefits made available to him under a cafeteria plan (whether or not the employee elects those benefits) if more than 25 percent of the plan's statutory nontaxable benefits are provided to key employees. Accordingly, there is both an objective and subjective qualification requirement.

3. A highly compensated employee is defined to include the following:
    (a) An officer (however, an officer who earns less than $45,000 in 1984 unless he has one of the other attributes is excluded from the definition of key employee).
    (b) A shareholder owning more than 5 percent of the common stock.
    (c) One who is highly compensated (obviously some further definition and clarification must be forthcoming).
    (d) A spouse or dependent of an individual who would otherwise be considered as highly compensated.

The requirements for exclusion of health benefits are as follows:

In order for health benefits to be considered nondiscriminatory, a determination must be made on a dollar-for-basis rather than as a percent of compensation. If a plan provides health benefits, it must satisfy two tests to be considered nondiscriminatory.

    (a) i. Total contributions for each participant must include either an amount equal to 100 percent of the health benefit coverage under the plan of the majority of similarly situated highly compensated participants, or

        ii. An amount equal to or greater than 75 percent of the costs of health benefit coverage for similarly situated participants who have the highest health benefit coverage under the plan, and

    (b) Other contributions or benefits under the plan must bear a uniform relationship to compensation.

The question prior to the enactment of the Tax Reform Act of 1984 was: "What are the nontaxable benefits that can be included in a cafeteria plan?" The act answered that by saying that such a plan can offer employees choices to include only cash and statutory nontaxable benefits other than scholarships, fellowships, van pooling, educational assistance, and employer-provided fringe benefits (see ¶201.8). In addition, the cost of group term insurance that is includable in income only because coverage exceeds $50,000 is treated as a nontaxable benefit. Vacation days are also a nontaxable benefit provided that they cannot be cashed in later. Also, medical reimbursement and group legal plans can be eligible.

The final question that is posed is: "How do you determine the amount of benefits or compensation which will be paid under a cafeteria plan?" There are two different methods of approach.

The following example will illustrate the alternatives available:

Example: An employee who does qualify for a cafeteria plan is making $10,000.

1. A plan could be established that would provide that he allocate 10 percent of his total salary to the range of benefits under the plan.

2. The plan could provide that the employer will provide him with 10 percent above his salary, which he would then allocate among the benefits.

Obviously, under the first alternative, it will cost the corporation nothing but administrative costs to establish a plan. Under the second alternative, the cost will initially be borne by the corporation.

In reviewing the above, it is clear that the entire impact of the cafeteria plans has not yet been felt in the tax-planning community. Their future use by the closely held corporation will depend on the regulations and rulings issued by the Internal Revenue Service. The discussion covered above deals only with the tax effects on regular corporations and does not concern Subchapter S Corporations. With the enactment of the Subchapter S Revision Act of 1982, the ability of a corporation to provide benefits for shareholders owning more than 2 percent of the issued stock of the corporation will be adversely affected. Accordingly, before instituting a cafeteria plan in a Subchapter S Corporation, the new rules under this act should be reviewed. (A full discussion of the Subchapter S Revision Act of 1982's impact on fringe benefits for Subchapter S Corporations is contained in Chapter 5.)

The problem that will probably be a detriment to the implementation of these plans in small corporations is that if, for a year, more than 25 percent of the total nontaxable benefits are provided to key employees, they will be taxed as though they had received all taxable benefits under the plan. Therefore, the implementation in the future may be more restricted.

In spite of the continuing uncertainties surrounding certain tax implications of the use of cafeteria plans by the closely held corporation, the almost unlimited possibilities for fulfilling both employer and employee needs are likely to lead more and more companies to utilize cafeteria benefit plans in the future. (A comprehensive article discussing these plans and a sample summary of a flexible benefit plan can be found in Appendix V.) This is a rapidly changing area, and before implementing a plan, you should carefully review the latest regulations regarding fringe benefits.

Changes Wrought by the Tax Reform Act of 1986

The Tax Reform Act of 1986 was to be effective for all plan years after 1987. However, this general effective date was postponed since regulations interpreting these code sections were not issued by September 1987. The law is to be effective for plan years which begin the earlier of the following dates:

1. Three months following the issuance of the regulations, or
2. December 31, 1988.

Because of the changes wrought by the Tax Reform Act of 1986 and the need for comprehensive regulations to be able to interpret these changes, a full discussion is probably inappropriate; however, at the same time, it is absolutely necessary to understand the general thrust of the law to understand where the law is going and what the possibility is of the implementation of these cafeteria plans in small corporations.

One change is in the actual definition of what a cafeteria plan is and what the qualified benefits are. The Tax Reform Act of 1986 defines a cafeteria plan as the following:

1. A plan in which all participants are employees.
2. The plan participants may choose the following:
    (a) Among two or more benefits consisting of cash or qualified benefits.
    (b) Among two or more qualified benefits.

It should be noted that in addition to all the requirements set forth in the cafeteria plan itself, the cafeteria plan must also meet the nondiscrimination requirements, which have previously been described in ¶201.1. The term "qualified benefit" generally means a benefit which is excludable from the employees gross income under a specific code section. Certain benefits are not included within the purview of a qualified benefit for cafeteria plan purposes, that is, scholarships, fellowships, educational assistance, and so on. However, specifically included within the term "qualified benefits" are the following:

1. Group term insurance
2. Any other benefit permitted by regulation

While the pre-1986 Tax Reform Act provided that a plan may not discriminate in favor of highly compensated participants in the eligibility to participate and in contributions or benefits, the post-1986 Tax Reform Act prohibits only discrimination favoring highly compensated employees as to eligibility to participate. A cafeteria plan must be available to a group of employees who qualify under a classification which the employer sets up and which the Treasury Department determines is not discriminating in favor of the highly compensated employees. It should be noted of course that the highly compensated employee test has been changed and an attempt has been made to make it uniform. (The general definition of who is a highly compensated employee is set forth in ¶201.1.)

Since the Tax Reform Act of 1986 deletes the rule prohibiting discrimination in cafeteria plans benefits favoring highly compensated employees but does put in the general plan provisions relative to discrimination, which is described in ¶201.1, each type of benefit available or provided under the plan is subject to its own applicable nondiscrimination rules. For example, the group term life insurance benefits under a cafeteria plan must satisfy the eligibility and plan benefit test available generally. Exactly how this is going to be administered is at this time impossible to determine. It would appear from the way that the law is written that each benefit must be nondiscriminatory. In other words, the plan overall could be nondiscriminatory as to benefits; however, because certain employees choose one form of benefits over the other, certain portions of the plan can provide discriminatory benefits. It should also be noted that the cafeteria plan under the post-1986 regulations will fail the nondiscrimination rules if the qualified benefits provided to key employees under the plan exceed 25 percent of the aggregate benefits provided for all employees under the plan. Does this mean that there is an individual and an aggregate test? If so, how will it be administered? Obviously, there are a number of questions to be answered in the not-too-distant future which will provide some idea as to the future administration of these plans.

It would appear from the manner in which the law is developing that eventually comprehensive cafeteria plans may be the future of the fringe benefit area. The Tax Reform Act of 1986 appears to be the first step in this direction in including an overall rule as to what will qualify for a fringe benefit and then to provide specific provisions for each of the fringe benefits. In other words, there will be a general provision and then specific provisions that will be applicable to each plan benefit. The Tax Reform Act of 1986 seems to be an extension of this particular principal which in essence appears to be started by the Tax Reform Act of 1984 when it attempted to provide certain uniform standards for certain fringe benefits.

The questions raised as to the possibility of implementing such an act and its overall usefulness in society are obviously beyond the scope of this book. However, the initial concept of what a fringe benefit is, where it is, and what it might become is probably appropriate.

A fringe benefit is an additional benefit to be received. The major benefit to the employee is the actual receipt of the compensation. Each class or group of employees may need different benefits and may have different priorities. For example, a young unmarried employee just starting out in business has little if any use for group term insurance and retirement benefits. His immediate needs involve the accumulation of material things, purchasing a car, house, and so on. Thus, his desire for a comprehensive fringe benefit plan is substantially less than for a middle-age married couple with children. They are particularly concerned about life insurance, health insurance, and retirement benefits.

It would appear that, if the goal of Congress is to provide for nontaxable fringe benefits on a nondiscriminatory basis, instead of approaching these benefits on an individual basis (is there discrimination in the group term insurance?), it should be considered in the aggregate. There are two major ways to approach this: The first is that the nontaxable fringe benefits allowable should be on a dollar basis per individual. The second is the approach that is used in the area of qualified deferred compensation where the benefits can be based upon salary. For example, the amount of fringe benefits available is 10 percent of the employee's salary. Neither of these approaches has yet been adopted by Congress in implementing the law; however, with its attempt in 1986 to provide for general nondiscrimination rules, it may not be long before all fringe benefits are within the purview of a general and specific test. Hopefully, Congress will develop a plan unlike the one it implemented in 1986—which is complicated and difficult to administer—which will provide simple but fair application.

[202.8]   Effect of the Tax Reform Act of 1986 upon the Closely Held Corporation

The Tax Reform Act of 1986 has had a direct effect upon the closely held corporation to establish the following more common types of fringe benefit plans:

1. Health and accident
2. Group term
3. Medical reimbursement plans

In the past, the laws were fairly simple. The ability to either satisfy or fail to satisfy the law was subject to individual rules and was therefore relatively easy to determine. The new law adds complications and additional restrictions as to discrimination of eligibility and benefits, the full effects of which cannot be determined until regulations are implemented and understood by the tax community. While the law for a number of years had allowed various statutory fringe benefits, including educational assistance, dependent care, legal, and so on, these have never been generally available for the small corporations. The reasons lie in the prior restrictions as to benefits that can be available to the highly compensated. In these areas, the new law probably provides little planning opportunities; however, there were few planning opportunities available in these areas anyway except in specialized instances.

The overriding concern of the small closely held corporation is the continued core benefits of health and accident, group term, and medical reimbursement which have become so ingrained in the benefit package available to all employees that any tinkering with these benefits, even though it is only to correspond to the new law, will probably cause concern and some distrust among the employees. Thus, the next couple of years are going to be of grave concern to both the small and the large corporations in order to comply with the complex new provisions that have been imposed by the Tax Reform Act of 1986.

While we have currently dealt with those fringe benefits that have been affected by the Tax Reform Act in this section and will shortly discuss the other fringe benefits, a question should be asked: Are the "unified discrimination provisions" going to presage a time when all fringe benefits are going to be under the umbrella of one set of general restrictions instead of a separate set of individual restrictions? Obviously, at this time it is not possible to answer that question. However, in dealing with the other fringe benefits, it should be realized that they are currently under their own set of restrictions, but that in the future they may be covered by the general restrictions contained in this section.

[203] HOW THE CORPORATION CAN UTILIZE OTHER FRINGE BENEFITS TO BENEFIT ITS EMPLOYEES

[203.1] Determining How the Corporation Can Cover Disability Insurance Payments for Its Officers and Directors

Disability Insurance

How It Works: In determining who should pay disability insurance premiums, various factors must be balanced. If the disability insurance is carried individually by the officer, the premiums are paid in after-tax dollars. No tax deduction is allowed for these payments. If the corporation pays the premium, this is a deductible expense to the corporation. This payment is not includable in income to the individual officer when the premium payment is made.

If the individual officer pays the premium and becomes disabled, the payments he receives on his own individual policy are excludable from gross income. If, on the other hand, the corporation pays the premium, the disability payment made to the individual is completely taxable unless it meets very rigid requirements.

[203.2] Getting the Maximum Tax Benefit from the Life Insurance Dollar: Group Term (063), Split Dollar, Retired Lives Reserve, and Universal Life

Split Dollar

Many times it is necessary for a younger executive to carry an unusually large amount of life insurance. One reason for this is that he and his family have a life-style necessitating a large cash flow. Because of his age, he has not accumulated a sizable estate which would support his family's standard of living if he should die prematurely. One type of insurance that will help his family maintain its life-style and provide for an estate upon his death at minimum income tax cost is called "split dollar." This is a whole life policy purchased by the employer, which in essence provides term life insurance for the employee.

How It Works: Under this program, the employer and the employee jointly take out life insurance on the employee's life. The net premium for insurance is split between the employer and the employee. The employer pays the premium equal to the increase in the cash surrender value each year and the employee pays the difference. At death, the proceeds equal to the cash surrender value will be paid to the employer and the balance to the employee's beneficiaries.

A benefit to the employee is that the employer is purchasing term insurance for him. The economic tax cost to the employee is considerably less than if he individually acquired insurance. Another benefit to the employee is that the employer is loaning money to him for insurance premiums interest free. There are many variations to this particular theme, which gives split dollar the flexibility to meet a variety of needs.

Retired Lives Reserve Insurance

The insurance companies have been marketing a product called "retired lives reserve" in the recent past. This product is a response to the disadvantages connected with group term insurance that occur upon an employee's retirement. Normally, group term coverage terminates upon retirement, and the cost of maintaining an equivalent amount of insurance is likely to be prohibitive, especially to an employee who may have a reduced income at that time. This is particularly crucial for the officer/shareholder in a closely held corporation and also for the higher paid executives in public companies. Both of these groups may face liquidity problems for which insurance would normally serve as a partial solution. The retired lives reserve product was designed to fill this gap.

The concept of the retired lives reserve is to have the

employer pay a composite payment, part covering the cost of the current group term insurance and the remainder going into an investment fund to provide for the payment of premiums upon retirement. This investment fund will earn income tax free. In effect, retired lives reserve has converted the group term into a permanent life insurance policy. At the same time, the employer can currently deduct group term premiums and side fund deposits. This deduction is based upon the following prerequisites:

1. The reserve fund must be held solely for the purpose of providing group term life insurance for retired employees covered under the plan as long as any active or retired employee remains alive.
2. The payments are deductible in the tax year paid or accrued if they are made on a level basis.
3. The employer must have no right to recapture any portion of the reserve while any of the employees subject to the plan remains alive. If any portion of a reserve is recaptured by the employer on termination of the retired lives reserve contract, the employer will have to record this return as income.

There are certain negative factors with regard to retired lives reserve, as follows:

1. The current costs are higher than pure group term policy premiums.
2. The Economic Recovery Tax Act of 1981 has significantly reduced the eventual liquidity needs of most estates. Thus, the need for life insurance in this instance may be greatly diminished.
3. The general need for insurance tends to be reduced as a person gets older. A major exception to this general rule is a large estate with a lack of liquidity to pay estate taxes and cost of administration.

In those instances, where there is a need for permanent life insurance to be purchased with tax deductible dollars, the retired lives reserve offers a solution. The retired lives reserve is not limited to $50,000 per employee. However, if policies providing more than this coverage are purchased, there would be current income tax effects to the individual employees. Prior to 1984, the purchase of life insurance was includable in income only while the individual was employed. After retirement, no income need be reported even though the corporation still pays the premium. However, as noted in the section on group term insurance, after 1983 all premiums on retired employees (who are not disabled) on policies in excess of $50,000 will have to be included in taxable income. Therefore, the continued viability of retired lives reserve may be in question.

With proper planning, these policies can be removed from the taxable estate of an individual through either a transfer of ownership to his spouse, his children, or the creation of an irrevocable life insurance trust. Planning has been facilitated by the increase in the annual gift tax exclusion from $3,000 to $10,000 per year per individual recipient.

WARNING: Under the law before the Tax Reform Act of 1984, an employer could cover retired employees with group term insurance in excess of $50,000 without any of the cost of insurance paid by the employer being included in the gross income of the employee. However, effective for the tax years beginning after 1983, the same rules that apply to active employees will apply to retired employees. Therefore, the first $50,000 of group term coverage is tax free. The cost of coverage in excess of $50,000 is taxable in the year of the coverage to the amount of the employer's contributions. The one exception to this is employer-paid premiums for retired "disabled" employees. The payment of these premiums still do not result in any taxation to the employee.

WARNING: The Tax Reform Act of 1986 has included within its general nondiscrimination provisions group term insurance. This indirectly if not directly does have an effect upon the future viability of the retired lives reserve product. At this time, it is unsure as to whether or not the nondiscrimination provisions will provide the death knell for the retired lives reserve product. However, until the final regulations are promulgated and until the insurance industry has an opportunity to respond to the new tax reform act, care should be taken before retired lives reserve is instituted as a fringe benefit for the employees of a closely held corporation.

Universal Life

As any insurance person selling life insurance will tell you, the rising star in the life insurance industry in the last ten years is universal life. Historically, all life insurance except for term policies were investment vehicles as well as insurance policies. The return on investment was small, however, as long as the return on individual investments paid by banks, savings and loans, and mutual funds was also comparatively small; life insurance was an attractive investment vehicle for many individuals. As the rate of return available to individuals began to rise sharply in the late 1970s, it became necessary for the insurance industry to develop a new product offering competitive rates of return.

The insurance industry responded with universal life insurance, which is nothing more than a combination of term insurance and an investment contract. The IRS and Congress were worried about the potential of these policies to convert taxable income into nontaxable income. (Normally, all proceeds from insurance policies are tax free upon the death of the insured). The Tax Equity and Fiscal Responsibility Act of 1982 included temporary guidelines for 1982 and 1983 for determining whether flexible premium life insurance policies (normally universal life) qualified as life insurance contracts for purposes of qualifying for the death benefit exclusion. The Tax Reform Act of 1984 has expanded upon these definitions and tightened some of the requirements. However, it would appear that universal life will become a permanent tool in the insurance industry. Accordingly, any time the closely held corporation is considering the use of life insurance as a fringe benefit, to fund a buy/sell agreement (see Chapter 6) or to fulfill a myriad of other corporate needs, the feasibility of utilizing the universal life product should be explored.

NOTE: While the Tax Reform Act of 1986 had no direct effect on the universal life product, it did have a positive effect in that it may have eliminated other viable tax-shifting vehicles. Previously, there were many products that would allow the deferral of earned income from one year to the next, for example, the IRA. With the practical demise of the IRA, which will be discussed in ¶204, this tool may be utilized more commonly to allow for a deferral of income.

> **Example:** A is age 60 and wishes to shift income until he is 65. The purchase of a universal life insurance policy will allow him to accumulate funds on the "investment portion" tax free until he is 65. At that time, he can take out the investment and earnings from the investment portion and leave his insurance portion intact.

Before a program such as the one outlined above is undertaken, the provisions of the policy as well as the tax law should be closely reviewed.

The second trend that affects the universal life product is that universal life was in its ascendancy when interest rates were high. With the reduced rates that people could earn on their investments in the last couple of years, the difference between what the insurance companies will pay on fixed investments and the amount paid on the universal life product, which usually varies with some standard (the rate of interest paid on short-term Treasury bills), has diminished, and thus the favorable financial portion of this benefit has been reduced.

[203.3]   Interest-Free or Below-Market Loans

The Tax Reform Act of 1984 has breathed new life into demand loans from the corporation to an employee (be he a shareholder or a nonrelated party) at low or no interest. The law in essence has set up a wash transaction in which it reclassifies interest-free and below-market rate loans as "arm's length" transactions, with the parties treated as if:

1. The lender made a loan to the borrower in exchange for a note requiring the payment of interest at the applicable federal rate.
2. The borrower paid interest in the amount of the foregone interest.

In essence, this treatment or wash sale requires the lender to treat the foregone interest as income and enables the borrower to take an interest deduction, assuming that he itemizes. In the case of a corporation/shareholder loan, the amount has to be received by the employee as a dividend; however, he does get the deduction as interest. In the case of an employer/employee nonrelated party, the paid compensation that is includable is offset by the interest deduction.

The following example will clarify how the interest-free or below-market loans will have impact on both the corporation and the shareholder/employee:

> **Example:** XYZ Corporation loans $100,000 to its sole shareholder at 5 percent interest on January 1, 1985, payable on demand. No loan repayments are made during 1985. The loan is considered a below-market rate since the 5 percent rate is less than 10 percent (the assumed federal rate at the time of making the loan). The foregone interest is considered transferred to the shareholder and retransferred to the corporation on December 31, 1985. This amounts to $5,000 (one year at 10 percent less interest charged 5 percent). The shareholder has received a taxable dividend of $5,000. He also has an interest expense deduction in the same amount. The corporation must realize interest income of $5,000.

WARNING: The above analysis deals solely with demand loans. If a term loan is involved, it will be treated differently. If the above example was between an employer and an employee who was not a shareholder, the treatment to the employee would be the same except that the additional $5,000 would be considered as additional compensation. The corporate treatment would be the same in that it would realize interest income of $5,000, but this interest income would be offset by an additional deduction of $5,000 as compensation. In this case, it would be a wash to both the corporation and to the employee, assuming the employee itemizes.

WARNING: Note that beginning in 1987 the Tax Reform Act of 1986 inserted a disallowance of a portion or all of the interest paid on other than mortgages on a qualified residence. Basically, a qualified residence is a primary residence and cottage. In 1987, the disallowance of the interest expense is 35 percent and increases to a complete disallowance in 1991. The question becomes: Can we preserve the deductibility of this non-interest-bearing demand loan by securing it with a mortgage on either the primary or secondary residence? Also be aware that OBRA 1987 has limited interest deductible on equity loans to the lesser of the taxpayer's basis or $100,000. This will also impact on future planning.

[204] HOW TO USE MISCELLANEOUS FRINGE BENEFITS

This section will familiarize you with a variety of specialized fringe benefits which, under the right circumstances, can provide tax windfalls to the individual taxpayer.

These benefits are sprinkled throughout the tax law in the Code and Regulations and in judicial decisions interpreting tax law. Many of these benefits are controversial and have been subjected to challenge by the Internal Revenue Service. The discussion that follows assumes the continued viability of these benefits, however, the Tax Reform Act of 1984 has had an impact on the use of some of these benefits. While ¶201 will provide you with a general framework within which you can analyze the continuing viability of any of the benefits which you are currently receiving or considering adopting, you should proceed with extreme care in light of the recent tax law changes.

Living Expenses: Normally there is nothing more personal and less likely to provide a tax deduction than the expenses incurred in maintaining one's home. Except for the portion of the home expenses which are otherwise deductible (mainly taxes and interest), the expenses of maintaining the home (including things such as insurance, heating, and utilities) usually must be paid in after-tax dollars. In certain limited situations, these expenses may be paid by the corporation and deductions obtained.

The following is an example of how to deduct living expenses:

Example: A client of our office is the major shareholder in a corporation which operates a fishing resort on one of Wisconsin's prime rivers. The family is attempting to build up the business of the resort. In order to keep the expenses of the business as low as possible, the family has, in the past, lived in one of the old lodges. As the business prospered and the family grew, these accommodations became unacceptable. It is decided that the family would purchase one acre of land from the corporation that owned the resort to build a personal residence.

If this procedure is followed, the tax result will be unfortunate. The expense of maintaining this property is not deductible. For tax purposes, the most advantageous approach is to have the corporation build and pay for the house on the land owned by the corporation. An acceptable alternative would have been for the shareholders to buy the land, build the house, and then lease it back to the corporation. The shareholder's family could live in this house. The corporation would pay all expenses with tax deductible dollars. These shareholders will not have to include these household expenses in their gross income.

This example fulfills the threefold test of deductibility of lodging. The tests are as follows:

1. Expenses must be furnished on the employer's premises. The house was built on the resort premises not separate from the resort property.

2. The lodging must be furnished for the convenience of the employer. As a practical matter, it is necessary for the family to be on these premises, especially during the peak fishing periods. They are required to be present at all times of the day and night at either the lodge, cabins, bar, or restaurant that comprises the resort. Breakfast is served from 5:00 A.M. and the bar does not close until 1:00 A.M..

3. The employee must be required to accept the lodging as a condition of his employment. Since this is a controlled corporation, there is no problem in inserting in the minute book a resolution to the effect that the chief operating officers of the company are required to live on the premises of the resort in order to qualify for employment.

The happy result is that nondeductible expenses are converted to deductible expenses with only the format changed. For these purposes, lodging expenses include items such as heat, electricity, gas, water, and sewer service. The question arises as to the deductibility of the meals which are served on the premises. In the above example, during peak fishing periods almost all meals are consumed in the lodge restaurant. Those meals, which are furnished for the convenience of the employer, are also deductible for the employer and not includable in the income of the employee.

> **Key Idea:** An area in which this fringe benefit may have been overlooked in the past is the farm corporation. Farmers are normally required to live on the farm, especially if the farm corporation is engaged in milk production or in any other type of farming in which a herd is maintained. This fringe benefit should be considered if the following facts are present:
>
> 1. The house is on the real property on which the farm is maintained.
> 2. A herd is maintained, or other good reasons could be established for requiring that employees be lodged on the premises.
> 3. The corporation must own the house or lease it from the employee.
> 4. The farm must be incorporated.

WARNING: If the house is leased to the corporation, the personal residence converts to rental property. Upon sale, the normal tax-free deferral of gain on sale of a personal residence and the $125,000 exemption from gain on the sale of residence by certain qualifying taxpayers over the age of 55 may be lost. Accordingly, if the house is to be sold within the near future, even if this fringe benefit is available, further analysis of the benefits of the fringe versus the possible loss of the favorable tax treatment upon sale should be weighed. This fringe benefit will not be available if the corporation has made an "S" election.

Checklist of Instances Where Meals Could Be Excludable from the Income of the Employee and Deductible to the Employer

☐ Meals supplied to an employee who must be available for emergencies. Employees who serve at the desk and who are needed in the event of urgent business or because special circumstances may occur could qualify.

☐ If any individual works in a restaurant, meals that they get from the restaurant are not taxable income.

☐ Meals furnished to employees who, because of their workload are restricted to a short lunch period and cannot be expected to eat elsewhere, may also qualify.

☐ If there are insufficient eating facilities in the vicinity, the employees may be able to eat tax free if the meals are made available to a vast majority of employees.

The following are illustrations of instances when personal living expenses can be converted into tax deductible items. The key to this fringe is that it must be an employer need that gives rise to the expenditure, not the desire of the employee. When this element is present or when the facts could be structured to satisfy this requirement, a review of the law should be undertaken.

Business Travel and Entertainment: Travel and entertainment expenses are not normally considered fringe benefits. The Internal Revenue Code allows deductions for travel and entertainment expenses that are business-oriented and strictly prohibits from deductibility the personal expenses of the individual employee. As a practical matter, personal travel, food, and lodging may be deducted if they meet the requirements set down in the Code and Regulations. A general discussion of the items which are deductible will show how this fringe can be utilized. In order to deduct expenses for transportation, food, and lodging while traveling, the taxpayer must meet three conditions:

1. The expenses must be incurred while away from home.

2. The expenses must be incurred in pursuit of business. There must be a direct connection between the expenses and the taxpayer's or his employer's business. The expenses must be necessary and appropriate to the development and furtherance of the trade or business.

3. The expenses must be reasonable and necessary.

Entertainment includes any activity generally considered to constitute an amusement or recreation. Examples of these are nightclubs, theaters, baseball games, restaurants, country clubs, yachts, hunting, fishing, and similar trips. Since these expenses generally satisfy the personal needs of an individual, they are ordinarily not deductible. They may qualify for the deduction where the taxpayer can show a relationship between the expense and his business.

Entertainment can be broadly divided into three major areas: the business meal, wining and dining, and entertainment facilities.

The Business Meal: During this meal, conversation occurs under circumstances that are generally considered conducive to a business discussion. This is ordinarily deductible if the proper records are maintained.

Wining and Dining: Wining and dining or a "night out on the town" is the meal with accompanying drinks, a nightclub, ball game, or similar entertainment. The deductibility becomes more difficult to substantiate because the activity itself usually precludes direct business discussions. During a nightclub act, it is difficult to substantiate that business was discussed. Therefore, this type of "wining and dining" must either directly precede or follow a substantial and bona fide business discussion. It is important to note that while business must be discussed, it is not necessary that a contract be consummated. On the other hand, monies expended to develop goodwill are usually not allowed as a deduction.

Several situations will illustrate how these general rules are implemented by the Internal Revenue Service and the courts, as follows:

Situation A: Business prospects arrive in town on Monday night. You take them to dinner and then to a nightclub. All day Tuesday you and they enter into substantial bona fide business discussions. Tuesday night you are back at the same nightclub.

Result: Your entertainment expenses are deductible.

Situation B: Prospective local customers come to the office for lengthy discussions. Immediately after the discussions, you treat them to dinner and the theater.

Result: Again, your entertainment expenses are deductible.

Situation C: Smith, a valued customer, comes from a small town to the big city for a good vacation. You decide that it should be all on you, including a few trips to local nightclubs. Why not? His company has over the years given you thousands and thousands of dollars worth of business. You are simply trying to maintain his goodwill.

Sad Result: You cannot deduct a penny—the entertainment did not precede or follow a substantial business discussion.

Key Idea: When you are planning what is generally defined as "goodwill entertainment," you should take the customer or client to a place that is conducive to business discussion. This is an exception to the general rule of nondeductibility of goodwill entertainment.

WARNING: Under law prior to 1985, the taxpayer was required to substantiate travel and entertainment deductions by sufficient evidence corroborating his own statement. Otherwise he lost the deduction. Beginning in 1985, the laws have become more stringent as to the type of corroborating evidence that could be available.

WARNING: The Tax Reform Act of 1986 has changed the law. The amount of an otherwise allowable deduction for meal or entertainment expense is reduced 20 percent. Specifically, this reduction applies to any expense for food or beverages and any item with respect to an activity generally considered to constitute entertainment, amusement or recreation, or with respect to a facility used for such activity. There are exceptions, but generally a corporation that has a significant amount of meals and entertainment expenses is going to have to reduce those expenses by 20 percent.

Example: XYZ Corporation has its president take a client to dinner and a show and spends $200. We will assume for this example that before the Tax Reform Act of 1986, the entire $200 was deductible. After the Tax Reform Act, only $160 is deductible. There are exceptions to this rule, and regulations will probably be promulgated; however, the area of entertainment expenses will obviously be the subject of discussion and of the IRS's scrutiny in the next couple of years.

WARNING: The law as to the deductibility of certain listed property has been vastly curtailed. The restrictions as to deductibility (and correspondingly the amount that must be picked up by the employee as additional income) have been increased. In particular, this applies to the company car. These types of mixed-use property, which come within the definition of listed property, must be reviewed, and a determination of the amount that is deductible by the closely held corporation and the amount that must be reported by the employee as additional income should be reviewed.

Entertainment Facility: The third type of entertainment is the luxury facility such as yachts, hunting clubs, athletic clubs, country clubs, golf clubs, and so on. The Revenue Act of 1978 has excluded all these facilities from the realm of a fringe benefit, except for the country club. The country club is deductible if the primary use of the club could be considered an ordinary and necessary business expense.

Generally, the computation is made on the actual use of the facility and not on its availability for use. If the facility is not primarily used for business, then no portion of the dues or monthly charges can be allocated as a deductible business expense. On the other hand, even if you use the country club primarily for business purposes (more than 50 percent of total use), the portion which is used individually without any business purpose must be allocated to the individual employee.

> **Example:** Jake Smith, president of Smith Manufacturing Company, belongs to a country club. All expenses are paid by Smith Manufacturing Company. His records show that of his time spent at the country club, 62 percent is business-related. The club dues are $100 per month plus the expenses incurred. His total expenses for the year in addition to the club dues were $2,000. Since Smith Manufacturing Company pays his club dues and all expenses incurred during this year, Smith will have to include in his individual income $1,210. This represents 38 percent of the expenses plus 38 percent of the $1,200 yearly dues.

Note that if Jake Smith, in the above example, could substantiate only 40 percent of the time spent at the country club as business-related, no portion of the $100 per month dues would be deductible. However, 40 percent of the $2,000 that he spent in addition to the club dues would be an appropriate expense of the corporation and not includable as income. In this instance, Smith would have to report $1,200 in dues plus 60 percent of $2,000.

Uniforms: A deduction for special work clothing had previously provided a tax benefit solely for the police, firefighters, and postal workers. This deduction has recently played an increasingly important role in corporate tax planning. Employers in increasing numbers have been requiring their employees to wear a uniform designating the corporation's logo. Many bank tellers, retail clerks, and employees in service-related occupations are now required to wear such uniforms. Generally, the cost of acquisition and maintenance is deductible only if it meets two requirements:

1. The uniforms are specifically required as a condition of employment.
2. The uniforms are not adaptable to general or continued use to the extent that they take the place of regular clothing.

For those occupations that require special work clothing such as work shoes or job-required safety equipment, the employer provides a fringe benefit when he pays for these costs. Service organizations' uniforms that bear the name of the organization or garments that are specifically made in such a manner that they are not adaptable for general use will also be acceptable for a deduction. The moral is that a uniform required by the employer may not only be smart business and good advertising but also smart tax planning.

Employee Death Benefits Up to $5,000: The Code provides that death benefits paid by an employer to the beneficiaries or to the estate of any employee by reason of the employee's death may be excluded from income as long as they do not exceed $5,000. This sum cannot represent payment for past services rendered such as bonuses, payments for unused leave, uncollected salaries, or other amounts that the deceased employee was entitled to during his lifetime.

Thus, if this death benefit is to be implemented, it must be inserted in the minutes or in the employment contract in such a manner that the employee did not have an unrestricted right to receive this sum of money prior to his death. It is suggested that a resolution be drafted to the effect that upon the death of the executive, officer, or key employee, in appreciation for the past services rendered to the corporation, $5,000 (or less) is paid to the estate of the employee. (A sample of this resolution appears in Appendix H.) This death benefit can be paid in a lump sum or over a period of time, whichever best suits the corporation.

[205] HOW TO GET MAXIMUM TAX MILEAGE OUT OF PROFIT-SHARING AND PENSION PLANS

[205.1] Four Benefits of a Qualified Deferred Pension or Profit-Sharing Plan

A great deal has been written about qualified deferred compensation plans. It is, therefore, difficult to ascertain where a discussion of these plans should start. A description of the tax benefits to be derived from the institution of such a plan is one appropriate starting place. These benefits are fourfold, as follows:

1. All money contributed to this plan is currently tax deductible to the corporation.
2. The money contributed and allocated to the employee's account is not taxable to him at the time of contribution. It is only reportable as taxable income when he receives the benefits.
3. All income earned during the accumulation period is tax free as long as no distribution is made.
4. There are a variety of methods for disbursing the funds at death, retirement, or disability of the employee. This provides flexibility to meet the tax and economic needs of the employee or his family, as the case may be.

The following is an example of the practical benefits of a qualified profit-sharing plan:

Example: FVTI Corporation is a corporation whose sole shareholder is Joe Owner. Joe, for the last several years, has been drawing a salary of $74,000, which is sufficient to meet his current expenses. Individually, he is in the 40 percent tax bracket (combined federal and state tax). The corporation which he owns has been profitable and over the past five years has earned, before taxes, between $100,000 and $150,000 per year. It has been the corporation's policy to grant a cash bonus at the end of the year to all employees who have worked during the entire year. The cash bonus has historically amounted to the lesser of 15 percent of the net payroll of the corporation or 35 percent of the excess of the corporation's income over $75,000.

Since Joe's salary of $74,000 has been sufficient to cover his ordinary living expenses he, in the past, has invested the net bonus (gross bonus less taxes) at 8 percent. At age 45 he is beginning to worry about retirement. He expects to work an additional twenty years. He has requested an analysis of the benefits that could be derived if the corporation adopts a qualified profit-sharing plan with the money it has previously disbursed as cash bonuses.

In 1988, FVTI Corporation earns $125,000, and the payroll for 1988 is $116,666.67.

	No Plan	With Cash Bonus Plan	With Profit-Sharing Plan
Profit before Taxes	$125,000	$125,000	$125,000
Contribution		17,500	17,500
Income Subject to Tax (No State Tax)	$125,000	$107,500	$107,500
Assume Federal Tax at 15% First $50,000; 25% Next $25,000; 34% Next $25,000; 39% of Excess	32,000	25,175	25,175
Income after Tax	$93,000	$82,325	$82,325
Actual Cost		$10,675	$10,675

The effect on Joe if he either receives a cash distribution or if the cash is paid into the qualified plan is as follows:

	With Cash Bonus Plan	With Deferred Profit-Sharing Plan
Salary	$74,000	$74,000
Bonus	11,100	-0-
Total Salary	$85,100	$74,000

Cash available for deposit for savings without plan is $6,660 (11,100 × .6). If, as set forth in the example, Joe is depositing this money at 8 percent, his effective after-tax rate is only 4.8 percent (.08 × .06). This will result in an accumulation over twenty years of approximately $215,000 upon retirement. At age 65, he could buy an annuity for life, 120 months certain at $8.79 per thousand (see Appendix J). This would yield a monthly income of $1,889.00. Only a small portion of this amount would be taxable to him as interest income. The tax laws allocate the remainder as a tax-free return of capital.

If, on the other hand, the qualified deferred compensation plan had been instituted, instead of being able to deposit $6,660 in each year, the full amount of $11,100 could have been invested. The full amount can be contributed because no tax is paid on any amount contributed to this plan. The earnings are at 8 percent because during the accumulation period no tax is paid. Instead of $215,000 available at age 65, there would be $507,947. This could provide, on the same assumptions as set forth above, an annuity payment of $4,465 per month. The only disadvantage of this approach is that this entire amount is taxable. To mitigate this factor, after retirement Joe should be in a lower tax bracket. He is no longer receiving any salary, and except for this passive income he probably has no outside sources of revenue. In addition, if, instead of an annuity payment, Joe elects a lump-sum distribution of his benefits, this total distribution may qualify for the favorable five-year averaging treatment on lump-sum distributions.

At the current tax rate, this would approximate a tax of $113,570. The benefits are therefore self-evident. If he accepts an annuity, his retirement benefits are more than 2.25 times greater through the use of a qualified plan than if the cash bonuses were made. On a lump-sum distribution upon retirement and payment of tax during the year which he receives a distribution, his benefits are better than 1.75 to 1 under the qualified plan.

WARNING: Prior to the enactment of the Tax Reform Act of 1986, in addition to the qualified plan contribution, Joe could have contributed $2,000 to an IRA from his salary. Also, in the proper instances, it was possible to direct an additional $2,000 of salary to his spouse and have her contribute $2,000 to an IRA. Since the enactment of the Tax Reform Act of 1986, if either spouse is an active participant, the couple has no ability to contribute to an IRA if their adjusted gross income exceeds $35,000. The prior planning devices of splitting income between spouses and each contributing to an IRA is no longer available.

What to Watch Out For: The following are several factors to be concerned with when considering the institution of a deferred compensation plan:

1. What is the benefit to be derived by the officer/shareholder in relation to the total amount contributed? In the above example, it was simplified because FVTI Corporation was already granting a cash bonus. This is not usually the case.

2. It becomes imperative to analyze what portion of the total contribution is going to benefit those persons that the corporation desires to cover. In this particular instance, Joe Owner's allocable portion was $11,100, and this was approximately 63 percent of the total contribution; it may be advantageous to follow special procedures in implementing such a plan.

3. It must also be decided whether the plan is to be used solely to maximize the benefits to the officer/shareholder or whether it is also implemented as a general fringe benefit for all the employees of the corporation. The method

and amounts of contributions will be geared to the profitability, the stability, and the needs of the business.

NOTE: In making the above analysis, the question raised is if an individual can justify both the $2,000 payment to him and his spouse whether or not it would be more beneficial for him to terminate the plan and have both spouses establish an IRA.

Example: In the above instance, if, instead of Joe Owner receiving $11,100, the contribution had been only 5 percent of the total, he would have received $3,700 in allocable benefits. The remaining $13,800 would have been allocated among the other participants. If he could justify a salary to his wife, and then if each established an IRA, the $4,000 that they would put away would definitely be a greater benefit. It would appear that in the future, unless the allocable benefits are sufficiently high, many plans will be terminated.

FURTHER NOTE: With the enactment of the Tax Reform Act of 1986 and the lowering of the effective tax rates for corporations, the benefit to be derived by small corporations will be less. Accordingly, many plans may be terminated.

Corporate Income	Tax Benefits of $10,000 Contribution	After-Tax Cost
0–$50,000	$1,500	$8,500
$50,000–$75,000	2,500	7,500
$75,000–$100,000	3,400	6,600
$100,000–$325,000	3,900	6,100
$325,000 and over	3,400	6,600

If you contrast this schedule with the prior tax rates for a corporation which imposed a tax of 46 percent on all funds over $100,000, you will see that most corporations will have a minimum of $6,600 and as much as $8,500 of after-tax costs. Prior to the Tax Reform Act of 1986, a corporation with an income of over $100,000 would have had an after-tax cost of only $5,400. This would tend to show that the benefits to the corporation of establishing these plans are going to be reduced.

In addition to the above corporate considerations, there are also individual needs to be considered. The individual needs will vary by reason of the shareholder/officer's outside income and assets and the need to accumulate funds through this particular device. A complete discussion and analysis of all the considerations that go into the implementation of a deferred compensation plan is beyond the scope of this book. If even a cursory review indicates that a corporation is producing sufficient taxable income and cash flow, the possibility of establishing a qualified deferred compensation plan should receive careful attention.

[205.2] Analysis of the Nondiscrimination Provisions of the Internal Revenue Code and Regulations and How They Affect the Implementation of a Deferred Compensation Plan

All deferred compensation plans which receive qualification under the Internal Revenue Code Section 401 are required to be nondiscriminatory. The coverage, contributions, and benefits should be for the general welfare of the employees and not solely for the benefit of the officers, supervisors, and highly paid employees (prohibited group). The concept of nondiscrimination as defined in the Code and Regulations provides for a good deal of flexibility. A plan can be adopted in a vast majority of cases to allow for requirements which funnel significant benefits to the prohibited group. These benefits make the plan appear worthwhile from the prohibited groups' perspective and nondiscriminatory from the IRS's viewpoint.

How Salary Affects the Benefits to Be Derived from All Deferred Compensation Plans

The key element in the IRS's definition of nondiscrimination is that the benefit need not be equal, for example, $100 per month for each employee. It may be proportional to the salary received by each employee. In other words, the benefit can be $100 per month for each $1,000 of salary the employee receives. Accordingly, each employee is really receiving as a retirement benefit 10 percent of his salary. The lower paid employee receiving a salary of $10,000 a year receives $1,000 a year in retirement benefits. As a practical matter, in a small corporation, the individual officers who are also shareholders wish to reap disproportionate benefits from the contributions for themselves and certain other key employees. In addition to the inherent disparity of benefits built in by reason of salary differentials, there are several methods of maximizing the amount that will be distributed to the prohibited group.

Methods for Maximizing the Dollar Amount

Integration with Social Security: Within parameters, it is possible to completely exclude all employees whose earnings do not exceed the social security limits, which during the year 1987 has risen to $43,800. Even if it is not possible to derive the benefits desired by the prohibited class and completely exclude the other employees through integration with social security, the lower paid employees will proportionately share in less of the benefits if the plan is integrated.

The following example will help illustrate this concept:

Example: XYZ Corporation has a total yearly payroll of $250,000. Two employees are in the prohibited group, the father earning $50,000 and the son earning $40,000. The remaining payroll of $160,000 is divided equally among 16 employees, each earning $10,000. A profit-sharing plan which is proportional to salary could be established. The contributions would be based on 10 percent of the wages for qualifying employees. Thus, $25,000 would be contributed. Father would receive an allocation of $5,000. Son would receive an allocation of $4,000, for a total allocation to father and son of $9,000. This amounts to 36 percent of the total contribution. The profit-sharing plan could be integrated with social security by providing that before any allocation is made to all employees, an allocation of 5.7 percent is made to employees earning in excess of $10,000.

The following is a description of how integration with social security will reallocate the contribution:

A. Before any allocation is made to the lower basis employees, 5.7 percent of the excess of $10,000 is allocated to father and son. This amount is multiplied by 5.7 percent for a total of $3,990 preliminary allocation to father and son.

B. The remaining contribution is allocated equally ($25,000 less $3,990 is divided by the total payroll of all qualifying employees—$250,000). This provides an average benefit for the individual employee of 8.04 percent on his salary.

C. The above 8.04 percent is multiplied by the father and son's total salary to provide a benefit for father and son of $7,236. This amount is added to the preliminary allocation of $3,990 for a total allocation of $11,226. By integrating with social security, the allocation to the father and son has increased to approximately 45 percent of the total contribution.

D. Note that after the enactment of the Tax Reform Act of 1986, defined contribution plans integrated are now limited to the lesser of 5.7 percent or 200 percent of the percentage applicable to compensation below the integration level. There is no problem in this case since the percentage below the integration level is 8.04 percent.

WARNING: The Tax Reform Act of 1986 has increased the minimum coverage requirements needed to qualify either a defined benefit or a defined contribution plan. Prior law required that the qualified plans be for the benefit of the employees generally rather than for the benefit of only the officers, shareholders, and highly compensated employees. To ensure that the plans did not proportionately benefit members of the prohibited group, minimum coverage requirements were imposed. To meet these requirements, plans had to either cover at least 56 percent of all sponsoring employers/employees or cover a classification of employees the secretary/treasurer found nondiscriminatory.

Under the new law, at least 70 percent of the sponsoring employers' non-highly compensated employees must be covered by the plan, or the percentage of covered non-highly compensated employees must be at least 70 percent of the percentage of highly compensated employees who are covered. Plans which do not satisfy either of the new percentage tests will still be deemed to be in compliance with the test if they satisfy an average benefit percentage test.

These rules obviously are fairly complicated, and once regulations are imposed, it will be clear to see how they will actually affect the administration of the plans. However, in establishing any new plans, the new coverage requirements of the Tax Reform Act of 1986 should be closely reviewed.

WARNING: Please note that the Tax Equity and Fiscal Responsibility Act of 1982 reduced the maximum permissible integration level to the amount of the employer's social security tax less the health insurance portion. This amount is 5.7 percent in 1984. This affects all plans beginning after December 31, 1983. Accordingly, all plans which are integrated under the old laws should be amended to reflect this change.

WARNING: Also note that the Tax Equity and Fiscal Responsibility Act of 1982 had required that minimum contributions be made to profit-sharing plans and minimum benefits be provided in pension plans for all top-heavy plans. Thus, while prior to the Tax Equity and Fiscal Responsibility Act of 1982 it was possible to have an integrated plan and provide no benefits for the non-key employees, this is no longer possible if the plan is considered "top heavy."

The Vesting Structure

The following is an example of how the vesting structure can be utilized. The benefits set forth in a pension plan provide $100 of retirement income for each $1,000 of salary. The vesting formula could restrict the benefits payable to the employee if his employment is terminated prior to a fixed period of time. Assume the following:

1. The employee's actuarial equivalent at age 55 (to provide the pension at retirement) is $10,000.
2. The pension has a graduated five-year vesting (20 percent for each full year of service).
3. The employee has been employed for three full years.

He would, therefore, be entitled to 60 percent or $6,000 of his total benefit. The Pension Reform Act of 1974 (ERISA) and subsequent acts have placed severe restrictions upon the vesting formula. After the full enactment of the Tax Reform Act of 1986, generally for all plan years beginning after December 31, 1988, other than for top-heavy plans, which will be discussed subsequently, there are two vesting schedules: five-year vesting—under this vesting schedule, an employee who completes at least five years of service has a nonforfeitable right to 100 percent of his accrued benefit derived from employer contributions—and three to seven year vesting—this vesting schedule is a "graded" schedule where the participants have a nonforfeitable right to a percentage of their accrued benefit derived from employer contributions determined under the following schedule:

Years of Service	Nonforfeitable Percentage
3	20%
4	40%
5	60%
6	80%
7	100%

Example: An employee of X Corporation, which has established a qualified deferred compensation profit-sharing plan and adopted the three to seven year vesting schedule, has been employed for five full years and quits after the fifth year of participation. His allocation in each of the five years he has been a participant was 15 percent of salary, and the total contribution has amounted to $15,000. The income earned on this account for the total period of time was $5,000, for a total account balance of $20,000. Under the three to seven year vesting schedule, he would be 60 percent vested. In this example, he would receive $12,000 from his account balance, and the remaining $8,000 would be forfeited. This remainder would either be allocated among the remaining participants or applied against the corporation's next year's profit-sharing contribution.

Benefits to be derived: It may be possible to structure the benefit formula in such a manner as to increase the ultimate benefit to the prohibited group. In a defined benefit plan, it may be possible to increase the benefits to be paid to employees who have longevity with the corporation. It is more likely that the prohibited group will be with the corporation for a longer period than the remainder of the employees. For example, the benefit for the participants upon retirement will equal 1 percent of salary for each year of service under ten years, and one and one half percent for each year after ten years.

Participation requirements: This was severely limited by the Pension Reform Act of 1974. However, it is still not necessary to cover part-time employees or employees who have been with the corporation for less than a full year. Part-time employees, for the purpose of this section, have been defined as all employees who work fewer than one thousand hours per year. Therefore, it becomes fairly significant to determine whether an employee who is considered part time by the employer may be considered full time for the purposes of the deferred compensation plan.

Top-heavy plan: In addition to the restrictions on discrimination set forth above, any plan for a plan year commencing after December 31, 1983, which would be considered a top-heavy plan will have to comply with additional requirements. These additional requirements were instituted by the Tax Equity and Fiscal Responsibility Act of 1982. A top-heavy plan is defined as one in which 60 percent or more of the benefits are provided for key employees. The definition of key employees (before the Tax Reform Act of 1986) included officers, owners of 5 percent or more of the outstanding stock and owners of 1 percent of outstanding stock who also have earnings of $150,000 or more, and the ten employees who have the largest interest in the corporation.

The Tax Reform Act of 1984 excludes from the definition of key employee any officer whose annual compensation is no more than $45,000. However, be aware that if he is an owner of more than 5 percent or is one of the top ten paid employees of the company, he may come within the purview of the definition of key employee notwithstanding the fact that his salary is less than $45,000. The term has been changed and is now referred to as "highly compensated employees" and applies to qualified plans as of January 1, 1987. Paragraph 201.1 sets forth those who would be classified as highly compensated.

The additional requirements which a top-heavy plan will need to incorporate and which have particular application to the closely held corporation are as follows:

1. The vesting schedule set forth above would not be permitted. A top-heavy plan will be limited to the choice of two vesting schedules: either 100 percent vesting after three full years of service or 20 percent per year beginning with the second year of service.

2. All top-heavy plans must provide a minimum contribution to each employee of at least 3 percent of his total compensation. Integration with social security does not relieve the employer of this obligation. Accordingly, it would appear that the minimum integration that would ensure compliance with the new law would provide contributions of 3 percent of all compensation plus an additional 5.7 (in 1984) percent of compensation above the integration level. In a top-heavy pension plan that is integrated with social security, there must be a minimum benefit for each participant. The amount of this minimum benefit amounts to 2 percent of the covered compensation for each year of service. The maximum amount of the minimum benefit is 20 percent of the covered compensation.

3. Benefits for key employees may commence no earlier than age $59\frac{1}{2}$ and must commence no later than April following the year of attaining age $70\frac{1}{2}$. This is true even if the employee continues employment.

4. There are several other provisions which normally will not be applicable to the small corporation. However, if there are combined pension and profit-sharing plans, these rules applicable to the top-heavy plans should be scrutinized very carefully.

[205.3] Creating the Plan That Best Suits Your Corporation

Once you've decided that a qualified deferred compensation plan is an appropriate vehicle to provide for retirement, the question then is: "Which type of plan should be chosen?" Basically, for an unincorporated business, such as a sole proprietorship or partnership, the only deferred compensation plan available is what is commonly known as the HR-10 plan.

HR-10 plans are available for any self-employed individual. Prior to the Tax Equity and Fiscal Responsibility Act of 1982, the limitations for contributions was the lesser of 15 percent of earned income or $15,000. After 1983, HR-10 plans have the same limits as corporate deferred compensation plans and can thus provide a defined benefit of $90,000 or a maximum annual addition of $30,000. Earned income, for this purpose, is basically income earned by the business minus business deductions. However, income earned from rents, investments, and capital gains and losses are not usually counted as earned income.

If both capital and personal services of self-employed persons are material income-producing factors, all the net profits from the business are considered "earned income." HR-10 plans still have some of their own rules regarding qualification and nondiscrimination; however, with the increased emphasis on parity, the importance of these differences is becoming less important. There are also specialized rules as to types of investments and other regulations.

Prior to the enactment of the Tax Equity and Fiscal Responsibility Act of 1982 (TEFRA), a review of the various regulations applicable to HR-10 plans would indicate that they are a great deal more restrictive than those applicable to the deferred compensation plans available to corporate employees. TEFRA has attempted to alleviate this disparity and the disparity between Subchapter S Corporations and regular corporations.

TEFRA reduced the maximum annual benefit of a defined benefit plan from $136,425 to $90,000 and also decreased the maximum annual contribution to a defined contribution plan to $30,000 from $45,475. At the same time, the maximum contribution by a self-employed person to a defined contribution Keogh plan is increased from $15,000 in 1982 to $30,000 in 1984. There was a corresponding increase in the benefits available in defined benefit plans for the self-employed individual. Accordingly, Congress in enacting TEFRA has attempted to strive for parity between qualified corporate plans and those plans available to self-employed individuals. Whether or not the parity will be achieved is still in doubt; however, in the near future, it would appear that corporate plans will still retain their advantage over plans available to the self-employed individual.

Key Idea: Before incorporating solely to gain the benefits of corporate deferred compensation plans, it would be a good idea to compare the benefits and costs of instituting an HR-10 plan to provide the contemplated benefits.

For a corporate employer, there are basically four different types of plans, each serving different needs. They are as follows:

1. Pension plans (also known as defined benefit plans)
2. Profit-sharing plans (also known as defined contribution plans
3. Money purchase plans (actually a form of a defined contribution plan)
4. 401 (k) plans (cash or deferred compensation)

There are many variations on the four types of plans, and each can be known under different names. For example, a profit-sharing plan could be presented by an employer as a thrift plan. The employer contributes a certain percentage of salary if the employee makes a like contribution.

1. *Pension plans:* The concept of a pension plan is to provide the employee with a fixed benefit. Usually the plan provides a calculable benefit to an employee upon his retirement or upon another occurrence such as death or disability. This benefit becomes a predetermined amount which may be dependent upon years of service and salary.

Example: X Corporation establishes a pension plan that provides the following:

1. One percent salary for each year of service.
2. Salary is defined as the average of the five consecutive highest years of service.

3. Payment to begin at date of retirement or age 62, whichever is later.

A, an employee of X Corporation, retires at age 65 after completing twenty-five years of service. His last five years of employment (highest consecutive five years of salary) averaged $30,000 a year. He would be entitled to a retirement benefit of $7,500.

One of the benefits of a pension plan is that it is easy to ascertain from the employee's point of view. The corporate contribution, on the other hand, is determined by the actuarial determination of the amount which must be contributed to the plan to produce sufficient funds to provide the retirement benefit. The contribution must be made whether or not there are corporate profits, and it becomes a determinable fixed cost of operation. The cost, of course, will vary from year to year depending upon the actuarial determinations.

Example: X corporation employs fifteen persons with an average age of 25. The turnover of the employees is high, and the pension plan provides that any employee with twenty years of service will receive 30 percent of his compensation upon retirement. The basic fixed yearly cost to the corporation in this instance will be very small.

Because of a long accumulation period and a high turnover rate, the cost will be low. If you compare this cost with a plan containing the same number of employees, with an average age of 50, many of whom have already fulfilled the twenty-year requirement, the years of accumulation are relatively few and the amount which will be needed to fund is greater. The implementation of a pension plan in this case would make sense if there are a number of older, highly compensated employees that the employer wishes to reward.

WARNING: Under the new laws applicable to top-heavy plans, many of the defined benefit plans that were designed for the select few may be significantly affected in small corporations by the Tax Equity and Fiscal Responsibility Act of 1982 and the Tax Reform Act of 1986. Thus, before implementing new plans or in reviewing old plans, the restrictions applicable to these top-heavy plans should be analyzed thoroughly.

2. *Profit-sharing plans:* A profit-sharing plan provides a benefit that is not predictable and depends upon the earnings of both the corporation and the funds in the profit-sharing plan. Theoretically, profit-sharing plans, if properly used, serve as an incentive to increase corporate profits because the employees participate in the higher earnings. Profit-sharing plans do not afford the stability of the pension plan which provides a predetermined benefit. The profit-sharing plan does not require a fixed payment, and the company can alter the amount that they wish to contribute to the plan each year. There is no need for a predetermined formula. The contribution can be geared to the best interests of the corporation on a year-to-year basis. If there are no profits, then no contributions need to be made. In an extremely profitable year, a greater amount may be contributed; however, there are limitations on the amount that can be contributed in any year.

Because most small corporations do not wish to make a predetermined monetary commitment, they will usually consider profit sharing the more appropriate plan. There are exceptions to this rule. The most obvious occurs in those cases where the persons who are to be benefited are older, and their accumulation period is not long enough to provide for sufficient benefits under a profit-sharing plan. The utilization of a pension plan in those instances becomes imperative.

An employee, at age 55, wishes to provide a retirement benefit of 50 percent of his current salary of $60,000. In the ten years remaining before his retirement, a profit-sharing plan contribution of a full 15 percent could provide only a small portion of the desired benefits. A pension plan properly established could provide the benefits desired.

3. *Money purchase plans:* A money purchase plan is a variation of both the pension and profit-sharing plans. The corporate contribution must be made whether or not there are profits in the corporation, making it similar to a pension plan. However, the costs of this plan are not based on an actuarial determination but solely on the covered compensation.

Example: X Corporation establishes a money purchase plan that provides that 10 percent of covered compensation will be contributed for each participant every year. Accordingly, the contribution will be made whether or not X Corporation has a profit. However, the benefit to the individual participant will be at least 10 percent of his compensation for each and every year.

In addition, there are instances where a combined pension and profit-sharing plan is appropriate. This is particularly true for service-oriented professional corporations where there is no need to retain capital for future growth.

The following is a situation where a combined pension and profit-sharing plan could be used. Doctors Incorporated is a corporation of four doctors. All are 45 years or older and have become concerned with retirement planning. The corporation had previously established a profit-sharing plan, and contributions from 10 percent to 15 percent have been made in each of the years of the corporation's existence. However, during the past five years, the net salary paid to the doctors has increased dramatically. Their present salary is substantially more than their yearly cash requirements. Each doctor is now drawing in excess of $70,000 in addition to the $10,500 being contributed to the profit-sharing plan on his behalf.

A money purchase plan could be added to the profit-sharing plan now in effect. An additional 10 percent could be contributed to this pension plan. Thus, if a combined plan is established, each of the doctors would receive a salary of $64,400, with the remaining $16,100 being contributed to both the pension and profit-sharing plans. The establishment of the money purchase plan would increase the available contribution by $5,600 per year. If this amount is compounded over a term of twenty years, the remaining working life, it will yield an additional $245,645. This, of course, will substantially increase the doctors' retirement benefits.

WARNING: In the past, in addition to a combined money purchase plan and profit-sharing plan, a combination of a defined benefit plan and profit-sharing plan could have been implemented. Under the old rules, there was what was called the 1.4 rule. Together, the defined contribution and benefit plans could reach 140 percent of the total benefits. In other words, if annual additions to a defined contribution plan represented 60 percent of its limit, then the projected annual benefit being funded could not exceed 80 percent of the defined benefit limit. TEFRA has reduced the total multiplier to 125 percent for plans which are not top heavy and 100 percent for many top-heavy plans.

WARNING: The Tax Equity and Fiscal Responsibility Act of 1982 also added new provisions relative to personal service corporations. In the past, professionals incorporated in order to obtain benefits from both the corporation and the deferred compensation plans in two particular instances. An example of the first instance involved the doctor who had an emergency room practice, employed no one other than himself, wanted to fully fund his deferred compensation plan, and was not happy with the limitations of the HR-10 plan. The second instance was the group of professionals who could not agree on an overall deferred compensation structure, so each formed his own corporation and may have collectively owned a corporation employing all other support personnel.

In either of these cases, the owners of these corporations should review the provisions of the Tax Equity and Fiscal Responsibility Act. This act attacks the corporations whose principal activity is personal service substantially performed by the owner/employee. However, even if a personal service corporation is formed for the primary purpose of reducing taxes or securing retirement benefits not otherwise available, it will be subject to the provisions of TEFRA only if it performs substantially all of its services for one other corporation, partnership, or entity. Then the IRS can reallocate tax attributes: income, deductions, credits, and exclusions to employee/owners.

This provision was inserted in the act to give the IRS a new arrow in its bow since it had consistently lost in its attacks on these personal service corporations. The owners of these corporations should immediately reevaluate their current position and ascertain whether or not they should liquidate and determine what impact this would have. New personal service corporations should be formed only at a time when complete benefits and problems can be ascertained.

4. *401 (k) plans (cash or deferred compensation):* As the cafeteria plan is the rising star in the area of general fringe benefits, the 401 (k) is the rising star in the qualified deferred

compensation area. The two keys which have given rise to its popularity are "containment of cost" (an employer benefit) and "employee choice" (an employee benefit). As employers become more and more concerned about rampant increases in noncontrollable costs, the cash or deferred plan has increased viability. In addition, it may be possible to implement a combined cafeteria and 401 (k) plan wherein all nonused benefits under the cafeteria plan are considered as an employee contribution under the 401 (k) plan.

The concept of a 401 (k) plan is nothing more than giving the employee the choice of receiving additional compensation as taxable salary or placing it into a qualified deferred compensation plan. Since the 401 (k) is really nothing more than a profit-sharing plan, it must meet the general requirements and qualifications of a profit-sharing plan. For example, the contribution cannot exceed 15 percent of the compensation, and it must meet the general nondiscrimination qualifications. In addition to the general nondiscrimination provisions applicable to all qualified deferred compensation plans, there are specific nondiscrimination provisions applicable to 401 (k) plans, as follows:

1. It cannot discriminate in favor of the highly compensated (see ¶201.1).

2. The percentage of salaries that can be deferred are limited as follows:
    (a) The actual deferral percentage for highly compensated employees must not be more than the actual deferral percentage for all other eligible employees multiplied by 1.25, or
    (b) The excess of the actual deferral percentage for the highly compensated employees over all other employees must not be more than 2 percent, and the actual deferral percentage for the highly compensated employees must not be more than the actual deferral percentage of all other employees multiplied by 2.

The following example will illustrate the concept set forth above:

Example: If the actual deferral percentage of compensation for the non-highly compensated employees is 2 percent and for the highly compensated employees is 4 percent, the plan would not qualify under test (a) since 1.25 × 2 percent is only 2.5 percent. However, under test (b), the plan would qualify since the highly compensated employees are not more than 2 times the other employees or more than 2 percent.

3. The amount contributed to the employee's account must not be forfeitable. Employer and employee contributions made to the trust pursuant to the participant's election must be 100 percent vested.

4. The benefits under this plan may not be made available earlier than the participant's retirement, death, disability, separation of service, hardship, or attainment of age $59\frac{1}{2}$.

Note that the Tax Reform Act of 1986 added a limitation to the amount that the employee may defer. Even if all other rules are met, the maximum that the employee can defer in any one year is $7,000. This limitation applies to all years after December 31, 1986.

While the requirements for contributions that can be made to the plan appear rather cumbersome, there seem to be two ways to simply comply with the law. First, you can allow for a yearly determination. In the event that the amount deferred by the highly compensated employees would disqualify the plan, then they must take this amount into compensation. Second, it must provide that, a certain amount of the amount contributed be deferred, and 2 percent over that amount can be taken at the option of the participant. For example, if 5 percent was contributed, 3 percent must be deferred, and 2 percent is at the option of the employee to be cash or deferred. If 10 percent was contributed, 8 percent must be deferred and 2 percent be at the option of the employee.

There is no doubt that in the future the cash or deferred plan will play an increasing role in the planning. The two negative factors once the percentage contribution rules are understood are that the plan cannot be integrated with social security and that all amounts paid are 100 percent vested when made.

If these two provisions can be lived with, the 401 (k) has distinct planning possibilities.

[205.4] Structuring a Nonqualified Deferred Compensation Plan for the Older Officer or Other Employee

From time to time, it becomes necessary to individually design a plan for a specific employee or a small group of employees. This is particularly true where there is an old and trusted employee who has rendered faithful service over a long period of time. For any of a number of reasons, he has either not been sufficiently compensated during time, or his retirement benefit is not sufficient to provide for a comfortable retirement.

An example of a situation similar to this was presented to me recently. A very successful real estate brokerage firm in town had been established ten years ago. Of the three key managing parties (a father and two sons), the original founder and key employee had worked continuously for less than full compensation from the inception of the corporation in order to help establish the firm. He was nearing retirement and the deferred compensation plan which had been instituted three years earlier did not supply him with sufficient retirement income. The remaining two key employees deemed that his prior services warranted additional benefits.

A Possible Solution: A partial answer to this problem was a nonqualified deferred compensation plan. This is an agreement by and between the corporation and employee which defers a part of the current compensation until retirement. In this situation, it was determined that the founder was entitled to approximately $50,000 in total yearly compensation. He would receive $24,000 a year in current salary, and the remainder would be deferred until his retirement. The employee's tax objective in this case is to ensure that he will be taxed only when the payments are received. It is anticipated that the payments will be received at a time when he is in a lower tax bracket, allowing him to retain a greater portion in after-tax income over the entire compensation period. The corporation is not allowed to deduct the payment at the time the obligation is incurred but only when the obligation is paid at retirement. This type of agreement can be funded with the deferred portion of the compensation being paid into a trust. In neither case is a current deduction allowed.

The alternative is to accrue on the books of the corporation the excess as an obligation of the corporation. As with the qualified deferred compensation plans, there is a need to include in this agreement the benefit formula, the manner in which the benefits are to be paid, the obligation to make the payments upon death or disability, and the reason why any portion of the benefits can be forfeited. (A sample of the employment contract establishing this agreement appears in Appendix I.)

If the employee is taxed when the obligation is accrued rather than when it is paid by the corporation, the tax benefit is completely defeated. This can be economically disastrous because the employee is currently taxed on money he does not have until retirement.

The Internal Revenue Service's most frequent attack utilizes the tax concept known as "constructive receipt". If the taxpayer has an unrestricted right to receive the income and chooses not to, he is subject to this attack. The classic example of constructive receipt is a coupon bond which matures on December 31, but the taxpayer chooses not to cash it in until January 1.

Constructive receipt becomes particularly relevant in two instances. The first is when nonqualified compensation plans are funded. The second is when the employee has the right to demand the income whenever he wants and chooses to have it deferred until some future date. It is usually prudent, especially when the plans are funded by a trust, to enter into this agreement prior to the rendering of services. Special care in the implementation of a nonqualified deferred compensation plan is required when the benefit is to be paid to an employee who is related to the remaining officers and directors. The exact implications and ramifications of taxation in this area are still unclear. However, this fringe benefit in the appropriate instance may provide substantial benefits and solve many problems.

[205.5] Economic Recovery Tax Act of 1981 Breathes New Life into Stock Option Plans

Under the law in effect through 1981, most compensatory stock options were not taxed to the employee at the time of grant but were taxed when the option was exercised. The value of the stock at the time of exercise less the price paid was ordinary income to the employee who had exercised the option. The employer was entitled to a corresponding expense deduction equal to the amount included in the employee's income. A major stumbling block to the employee was that he realized ordinary income and had to pay a tax at a time when he had just expended cash to exercise the option to purchase company stock. Thus, stock options had relatively little effect upon most corporate planning.

However, the Economic Recovery Tax Act of 1981 provides that incentive stock options will be taxed differently. While there is generally no tax consequences when an incentive stock option is granted or exercised, the bargain element on the exercise of the incentive stock option is a tax preference subject to the alternative minimum tax. Normally, if the requirements of the law are met, the employee will be taxed at capital gain rates when the stock that he purchased pursuant to the exercise of the option is sold. Correspondingly, there will be no expense deduction to the employer with respect to incentive stock options that qualify for the benefits. An incentive stock option is defined as an option that is granted to an individual by the corporation which employs him if all the following requirements are met:

1. The option is granted under a plan which specifies the number of shares of option stock to be issued and the employees who are eligible to receive them.
2. The option is granted within ten years of the date the plan is adopted or the date the plan is approved by the shareholders.
3. The option is by its terms exercisable only within ten years of the date it is granted.
4. The option price equals or exceeds the fair market value of the option stock at the time the incentive is granted.
5. The option by its terms is nontransferable other than at death and is exercisable during the lifetime of the employee to whom the option was granted only by such employee.
6. The employee to whom the incentive option is to be granted is not eligible for such option if immediately be-

fore the option is granted, he owns more than 10 percent of the voting power of the common stock. To determine the amount of stock owned by the employee at any one time, the stock attribution rules will be applied. This stock ownership limitation is waived if the option price is at least 110 percent of the fair market value at the time the option is granted and is not exercisable more than five years after it is granted.

7. There cannot be any other preexisting stock option exercisable by employee.

8. There must be an annual limit on the amount of stock for which an employee may be granted an incentive stock option. This limit is based on a aggregate fair market value of the option stock and cannot exceed in any calendar year an aggregate fair market value of $100,000 plus any unused carryovers. The carryover amount for any year is limited to one-half of the amount by which $100,000 exceeds the value of the stock for which incentive options were granted in the prior year. An unused limit carryover may be carried over for three years.

Not only are there restrictions on the terms and conditions of the employer's stock option plan, but there are also restrictions as to the time sequence relative to the exercise and sale once an option has been granted in order that the employee may obtain the maximum benefits. If the employee is to receive the full benefit, he must meet the following requirements:

1. The employee who has acquired the stock through the exercise of an option cannot dispose of it within two years after the option is granted and must hold the stock for at least one year.

2. The holder of the option must be an employee of the company for the entire period commencing on the date the incentive stock option is granted to three months prior to its exercise.

If the above rules are not fulfilled by the employee, the gain on the sale of the stock will be taxed to the employee not as capital gains but as ordinary income. In this case, the employer will be entitled to a deduction which, like the employee's ordinary income from the sale, will be limited to the difference between the amount realized and the option price. These new incentive option rules have interesting ramifications for the purchase of corporate stock by nonrelated parties and also for the purchase of stock of the company by related parties. The full implications are not yet known since temporary regulations have only recently been issued. However, tax planners should be aware of this new tool, especially where transition from one generation to the next or from one ownership group to another is contemplated. When money is so dear, the granting of stock options by corporations with growth potential should be carefully investigated.

WARNING: With the elimination of the favorable capital gains rates enacted by the Tax Reform Act of 1986, it would appear that the prior impetus to the establishment of stock option plans may be reduced. Exactly what the future will hold in this matter is still in doubt.

The entire field of fringe benefits is in constant flux. Current high tax rates and inflation have increased the inventiveness of the tax planners. Congress and the IRS have met those plans not with complete rejection but from the viewpoint that the fringes are deductible if they are for the general benefit of all employees and not for the selected few. This position has set up a conflict that produces interesting results.

3

How to Utilize Salary for Maximum After-Tax Payments to Corporate Officers

[300] HOW TO FIT SALARIES INTO YOUR OVERALL TAX PLANNING

[300.1] Maximizing the Salary

The two most important factors in establishing corporate salaries are beyond the planner's control. These factors concern the economic status of your client. The first factor is the individual's cash requirements necessary to maintain his standard of living. The second is the ability of the corporation to establish an earnings record that provides for the payment of an adequate salary and also allows for the expansion of the corporate business through the retention of earnings. Acknowledging these limitations, it becomes imperative to ascertain the goals in arriving at the proper game plan for paying salaries. In most instances, the game plan will rely on the concepts of dividing and shifting income, as was discussed in Chapter 1.

A simple situation reported to me while fishing in Wisconsin's Northwoods will illustrate both concepts and help to establish a framework for determining the proper tax salary. Once this salary is determined, it will be necessary to review the payment of this salary in light of the Internal Revenue Code's requirements. The Code contains terms and conditions which will disallow a salary paid as a deductible expense if it is not

147

reasonable in relationship to the services rendered by the employee.

Joe Daley, D.D.S., while casting his fishing lure, described to me the circumstances surrounding a recent monthly dental meeting. At the meeting, he sat at a table during dinner with a number of his contemporaries. The monthly meetings of the county dental association are usually concerned with procedures and practices relative to dentistry. This night, however, about 90 percent of the conversation at his table revolved around complaints regarding the inordinate portion of their total income going to pay federal and state taxes. Joe sat there quietly because he had no particular complaint with his tax burden.

Because this story was related to me in a boat, it was not possible for me to explain the planning already accomplished for Joe and the benefits he had already derived until he was in my office about two weeks later. At this time, I showed him how tax planning beneficially affected him and reduced the amount of taxes he paid.

> **Example:** Joe Daley, who was married, was netting from his practice approximately $110,000 before taxes and any deferred compensation payments. For the purpose of this example, it will be assumed that his other income equaled his deductions and exemptions thus giving him a net taxable income of $110,000. If he had been unincorporated and had earned $110,000, his only additional deduction would have been the $22,000 HR-10 payment (see Chapter 2). This indicates the maximum amount which can be contributed to the benefit of a self-employed individual. Accordingly, his federal tax burden would have been approximately $24,877.50.
>
> Because Joe's practice was still growing and because of his age (44), relatively basic and unsophisticated planning had been implemented. It is usually best to maintain maximum flexibility during the client's early working life so that the constraints placed on him do not outweigh the benefits derived by the tax planning. Tax planning is like everything else: You don't get something for nothing. Even minimal tax planning will place restraints on the current disposition of funds. The client who is most difficult to deal with is the one with substantial earning capac-

ity who each year spends more than his net after-tax income.

The planning which had been established for Joe included the incorporation of his practice. In this service corporation, both money purchase and profit-sharing plans had been instituted. He contributes a full 25 percent of his salary each year to these plans. His salary had previously been determined at $70,000. This amount was sufficient to provide him with a comfortable life-style. Individually he was subject to a federal tax of $15,732.50. The corporation was subject to a $4,875 tax on its net income of $32,500 ($110,000 less salary of $70,000 and $17,500 pension and profit-sharing contributions). His total tax burden of $20,607.50 is less than the $24,877.50 he would have paid in the unincorporated form. **NOTE:** OBRA 1987 has a significant impact on this planning. For all tax years after 1987, all taxable income of personal service corporations will be taxed at 34 percent. Unless a change in planning occurred, the total tax would have increased to $26,782.50. Alternate planning would be either to elect "S" status or pay a salary of $88,000. If the salary of $88,000 is paid, the tax, whether incorporated or unincorporated, is the same.

In addition to a substantial direct cash savings, there were indirect savings because of the other fringe benefits that had been implemented. The indirect savings are usually more than sufficient to equal and, in most cases, substantially exceed the additional cost of incorporating the business. The major additional costs usually incurred in incorporating the business are legal and accounting fees, social security tax, unemployment taxes, and workers compensation insurance expense. The goal of the salary in this particular instance, was to provide Joe with sufficient income to live and maintain his life-style. The pension and profit-sharing plans were to provide for his retirement.

It was estimated at the time the deferred compensation plans were established (nine years ago), that he wished to work approximately twenty-five more years. The assumptions made in establishing these plans were the following: (1) That $17,500 would be contributed during each of the twenty-five years, and (2) that 7 percent was an appropriate rate of return on the money invested.

The compounding effect of these contributions was to provide $1,181,354 in the retirement fund at the date of his retirement. Even with inflation, this should provide a reasonable retirement benefit in addition to the social security benefits he would receive. The corporation, upon his retirement (age 60), could purchase a single-payment life annuity with a ten-year certain in the amount of $117,237 per year based upon standard mortality tables (see Appendix J). A a practical matter, with the amount of money involved in this particular plan, a better rate of return could almost assuredly be obtained from the insurance company.

The corporation in this instance was Joe Daley's investment vehicle. The net after-tax income retained by the corporation was approximately $27,625 per year. These retained proceeds were used to repay all the debts that had previously been incurred to establish the dental practice. Once this was accomplished, the remaining yearly amount of $27,625 could be accumulated until such time as the danger of an accumulated earnings tax arose. It was anticipated that this would probably occur between the fifth and sixth year. At this time, no further earnings should be accumulated in the corporation.

For Joe Daley, this danger would occur after he had accumulated $150,000 in the corporation. (See Chapter 8 for the restrictions on accumulating earnings in both personal service corporations and other corporations.) At that time, assuming that the corporate income before salary to himself was $110,000, $88,000 would be paid as salary to him, and the remaining $22,000 would be contributed to the qualified deferred compensation plans.

An alternative to this plan would be the utilization of a nonqualified deferred compensation plan for Joe Daley. If the maximum amount is being contributed to the qualified deferred compensation plans for Joe Daley, and if he does not need the excess income, it would still be worthwhile to use the corporation as a lower basis taxpayer. However, it is usually difficult to justify accumulating earnings in excess of $150,000 for a service corporation such as this. In this situation, it may be beneficial to establish a nonqualified deferred compensation plan for Joe Daley and continue to divide the income among the corporation, Joe, and the qualified plan. In case of an IRS audit attempting to assert the accumulated earnings penalty, the corporation would be able to show the liability for payments to Joe upon retirement. This planning tool in specialized situations may be useful; however, before it is implemented, a complete review of the facts and the law prevailing at that time should be undertaken (see ¶202.4 and ¶801).

It was further anticipated that all cash accumulations would be used to fund a common stock investment fund. The reason that common and preferred stocks would be utilized in this particular instance is that the dividend income earned on common stock held by a corporation is 70 percent excludable from gross income. In other words, if this $27,625 net income could be invested in preferred stock yielding 6 percent annually, approximately $1,657.50 of dividend income would be produced. If this dividend income would be earned individually, it would be virtually 100 percent taxed to him, and the 6 percent yield would result in an after-tax yield of only 4 percent. If the corporation invested in the preferred stock, it would receive the income. The marginal tax rate on this $497.25 would be 34 percent, or $169.07. The yield to the corporation in after-tax dollars would be slightly under 5.4 percent. **NOTE:** While planning such as this after 1987 will no longer be viable for personal service corporations, this planning would still be available for all other "C" corporations.

The corporation utilized as an investment vehicle has many opportunities. There is an overriding fear expressed or implied by many tax planners that once the money is retained, it is "locked in" the corporation forever. There are three methods for unlocking the funds, assuming the corporation is not a personal service corporation.

[300.2] Taking the Accumulated Money Out of Other Than the Personal Service Corporation at the Time of Retirement: Method One

Sell the Business for Cash and Liquidate the Corporation

The first and probably the simplest method is, at the date of Joe Daley's retirement, to have Joe sell his business and liquidate the corporation (see Chapter 7). If the corporation is liquidated over two years, his overall tax burden should not exceed 31 percent. Assume that Joe's balance sheet is as follows:

	Cost	Fair Market Value
Cash Securities	$150,000	$150,000
Equipment	10,000	10,000
Goodwill	–0–	50,000
TOTAL ASSETS	$160,000	$210,000
Liabilities	–0–	–0–
Capital Stock	$10,000	$10,000
Retained Earnings	150,000	150,000
Unrealized Income	–0–	50,000
TOTAL LIABILITIES AND EQUITY	$160,000	$210,000

If Joe sells the goodwill and equipment for a $50,000 profit ($60,000 sales price less $10,000 book value), there would be a corporate tax on the sale of the assets of $7,500. He would have a total of $202,500 in this corporation. When the corporation with $202,500 is liquidated, his total after-tax capital should be approximately $145,800 ($202,500 proceeds less tax on liquidation of $56,700).

The following is an example of how timing, especially after the Tax Reform Act of 1986, could significantly reduce the total tax burden:

Example: It would be possible to liquidate this corporation in several calendar years and significantly reduce his tax burden if he retired and did not receive any other income during the second year. For example, assume he retired in 1988 when he was 62. During the three calendar years, 1988, 1989, and 1990, he could receive as a liquidation distribution from the corporation $67,500. When he was 65, he could begin receiving both his prior qualified deferred compensation plans and his social security. If this procedure were followed, the corporate tax would not be reduced. However, his total individual tax burden would be reduced from $56,700 to $45,098. As noted, just a little structuring can produce significant tax benefits.

A variation on this approach could occur if either one of Joe's children or a nonrelated party is eager to purchase the physical assets and goodwill of the corporation, but has no real desire to purchase the liquid assets.

Key Idea: During the years 1987 and 1988, it is still possible to elect the benefits of Section 337 and eliminate a portion or all of the corporate tax. (See Chapter 7 for a full discussion of the tax benefits of this election).

[300.3] Taking the Accumulated Money Out of Other Than the Personal Service Corporation at the Time of Retirement: Method Two

Converting the Business to a Personal Holding Company

The second method that has interesting possibilities is the conversion of the corporation at the time of retirement to a personal holding company. (A full discussion of the ramifications of the personal holding company appears in Chapter 8). Again, if a majority of the assets are invested in common stock, there should be no burdensome penalty taxes that would make this approach inappropriate. If you use this method, then the total amount of the assets would be available for investment since there would be no taxes upon the liquidation of the corporation because the corporate entity is retained. The sale of the business at a profit would be a taxable event and would reduce the net proceeds available for investment. Assuming the same facts where the business was sold for a $50,000 profit, $52,750 would be available after taxes are paid $60,000 sales price less tax on $50,000 gain, or $7,500. This $52,750 net after-tax proceeds would be added to the $150,000 previously retained, and there would be $202,500 available for investment. The problem with this solution is that the principal is not available for individual use.

The eventual decision of which of these two conventional methods is the most appropriate will have to occur at the time of retirement under the existing tax laws and investment possibilities at that date. An analysis such as this would certainly involve the following:

1. The dividend rates that are appropriate
2. The amount of income tax and costs to be paid by the personal holding company

3. Any further benefits that can be obtained from maintaining a personal holding company, such as medical insurance, maintenance of an office, payment of reasonable salary, and so on

4. Age at retirement

5. The profit to be realized on the sale and the total available proceeds

6. The outside income of the shareholder, including any payments he is receiving from the qualified deferred compensation plan or plans

7. The personal financial needs of the shareholder

In the above example, there are approximately $56,700 of additional assets available by maintaining the personal holding company. If Joe retires at age 72, it will have a significantly different impact than if he retires at age 59. The reason for this is that upon his death, the stock, which has a basis to him of only $10,000 but is currentl; worth $202,500, receives a basis of $202,500. Thus, $192,500 is not taxed for income tax purposes. At that time, the corporation could be liquidated at no tax cost. Accordingly, the older an individual is at retirement, the more likely it is that retaining the personal holding company will be a tax benefit.

[300.4]   New Tax-Planning Tool—Method Three

The recently passed Tax Reform Act of 1986, while eliminating many of the prior tax-planning tools, has increased the opportunities for planning in many areas which in the past had been, if not totally, partially neglected. The reasons for this are twofold, as follows:

1. The elimination of the beneficial capital gains rates after 1987.

2. The highest taxed individuals are the middle income taxpayers. Therefore, significant tax savings can be accomplished. (18 percent) by diverting taxable income to different years.

If you review the opportunities presented by the personal holding company set forth in ¶300.3 and consider the use of a personal holding company with either partial liquidation distributions or dividend, income distributions over the various years will yield sizable tax benefits. An example was set forth in ¶300.2 where the tax savings accomplished by dividing the liquidation distribution in only three years produced approximately $12,000 in tax benefits. The liquidation of the corporation can occur over time to coincide with the taxpayer's individual and tax needs.

> **Example:** Joe Daley retired at age 59 (not the scheduled 62) and needs an additional $50,000 to maintain his lifestyle until his social security and his qualified deferred compensation plans commence. Assuming an 8 percent yield on the net corporate assets, a plan incorporating both a distribution of the net dividend income and partial distribution of retained earnings in each year could be adopted, as follows:

Age of Joe Daley	Assets of Corp.	Corp. Income	Tax on Corp. Income	Net Pers. Holding Company Dividends	Distribution from Assets of Corp. (Previous Retained Earnings)	Total Distribution
57	$202,500	$16,200	$2,430	$13,370	$36,230	$50,000
58	$166,270	$13,302	$1,995	$11,307	$38,693	$50,000
59	$127,577	$10,206	$1,531	$ 8,671	$41,325	$50,000
60	$ 83,252	$ 6,660	$ 999	$ 5,661	$44,339	$50,000
61	$ 38,911	$ 3,113	$ 467	$ 2,646	$38,911	$41,557

The concept of liquidation of these corporations in the future may involve the following:

1. Deferral of qualified deferred compensation benefits until the last possible date. This is April 1 following the attainment of age 70½ under current law.

2. The conversion of otherwise taxable income into tax deferred or nontaxable income: either the purchase of municipal bonds or, in lieu thereof, the purchase of a tax-deferred annuity.

3. Timing of the commencement of social security benefits at a later than usual date.

4. The possible early retirement of an individual (see the Joe Daley example in ¶300.2).

5. The sale of the assets and conversion of the corporation into a personal holding company.

6. The liquidation of the corporation over a number of years.

[300.5] Deciding When It Is Advantageous to Divert Income to the Employee

Even before the Tax Reform Act of 1986, there were many times when it was advantageous to maximize the salary payments to an employee. This could arise when the goal was to contribute a maximum amount to the deferred compensation plans. Another situation when maximum salaries were paid occurred when a corporation had an accumulated earnings tax problem. The retention of any further funds by the corporation raised the spector of the imposition of penalty tax. After the enactment of the Tax Reform Act of 1986, the maximization of salaries will become even more important. The payment in the form of salary provides a tax deductible item to the corporation. In addition, in all likelihood, after the retention of $75,000 of income in the corporation, the individual's marginal tax bracket will be less than the corporate tax bracket. This, in conjunction with the fact that a portion of the income can be diverted to a completely tax deductible form (qualified deferred compensation payment), makes this planning tool even more significant.

The following example will illustrate the utilization of this planning:

Example: Profitable Corporation is in the business of making widgets. Over a period of years, it has accumulated excess capital which is currently not being utilized in its corporate business. The nonbusiness capital raised the problem of an unreasonable accumulation of earnings. Jack, its principal officer and shareholder, has in the past been drawing a salary of $75,000 per year. In 1988, Profitable Corporation again is going to earn, as it has in many recent years, $175,000 after tax. The net after-tax income is going to be invested directly in certificates of deposit and other marketable securities.

Jack suggests that because of his expertise in managing this corporation, he should be paid an additional $75,000 bonus. His reasoning is that if this money is retained by the corporation, it will pay 39 percent tax on the retained income, and it will increase the already present accumulated earnings. If, on the other hand, this money is paid directly to him, he will be taxed at no more than 33 percent. He volunteers that if the corporation ever needs this money in the future, he will be glad to loan the money to the corporation. If Profitable Corporation had enacted a qualified deferred compensation plan which provided that 25 percent of the salary is paid into a combination profit-sharing and money purchase plan (see Chapter 2), the benefits could be even more significant. In this case, $60,000 would be paid as a bonus, which would result in a maximum tax to Jack of $19,800, and the additional $15,000 would be paid into the combination money purchase pension plan and profit-sharing plan, assuming that he had not previously exceeded the limits. If successful, this planning would produce a benefit of $9,450. This benefit could be computed as follows:

$75,000 taxed to the corporation at 39%   ($29,250)
Less:
$60,000 taxed to Jack at 33%   ($19,800)

In this instance, the goal is to utilize the maximum salary possible to ensure the minimum overall tax burden.

While there is little fault in the logic, planning along this line is fraught with many tax-planning difficulties. The most apparent one is that of having the $60,000 bonus and $15,000 contribution to the qualified deferred compensation plans established by Profitable Corporation deemed a constructive dividend. (The full ramifications of this result and how to avoid it will be discussed shortly.) It should be noted that the major risk of this device rests with the corporation. If it was determined that $75,000 of his salary was unreasonable, there would be little or no additional tax on the amount received by the shareholder/employee. The corporation, on the other hand, would be disallowed a $75,000 deduction, resulting in $29,250 of additional taxes.

[301] HOW UNREASONABLE COMPENSATION AFFECTS TAX PLANNING

With all the planning possibilities previously indicated, the IRS has imposed its own interpretations on salary planning. It has issued a set of factors that determine what is a reasonable salary and thus a proper expense.

Section 162 of the Internal Revenue Code provides the parameters on the tax-planning possibilities. This section states that "ordinary and necessary" expenses deductible by a business include a "reasonable allowance for salaries or other compensation for services already rendered." This section grants the Internal Revenue Service the power and jurisdiction to police the various compensation agreements that have been devised.

A precise definition of "reasonable compensation" has been impossible to formulate. However, there are certain factors that consistently appear within the definition of reasonable compensation. These also provide guidelines for determining what is reasonable under various factual situations. The basic premise is that reasonableness can be determined by comparing the amount of compensation paid to the employee with the value of the services rendered. The case histories in this area are of little value except to give rise to the general principles applied. The reason for this is that most of the cases are limited by the facts presented to the court.

The following factors are considerations which the tax planner, the IRS, and finally the courts will consider in determining the concept of reasonableness in relationship to compensation paid:

[301.1] Seven-Point Checklist in Determining Reasonable Compensation

1. *Salary history:* Since an employee's services should be of relatively constant worth to the corporation, inconsistent salary

history will come within the scrutiny of the Internal Revenue Service. This lack of consistency would indicate that the employee's compensation is not based on his services rendered but results from tax considerations of the employee and the corporation. Particular scrutiny is warranted when the shareholder's salary substantially increases without a corresponding increase in his responsibility. In the same vein, there is validity to the premise that prior history is some indication as to the future worth of the employee.

> **Key Idea A:** Consistent increases in salary reflecting the general increase in the amount of business conducted or the net profits of the corporation lend credibility to the compensation paid.

The following is an example of the effect of salary history on an internal revenue service audit:

> **Example:** X Corporation, which is currently undergoing an audit, is owned by its sole shareholder, Mr. Executive. Mr. Executive's salary for the last three years and the profits of the corporation are as follows:

	1988	1989	1990
Salary	$75,000	$50,000	$100,000
Taxable Income of Corporation	$48,000	$49,000	$47,000

The salary for Mr. Executive is particularly suspect. This salary seems to have been manipulated and utilized solely as a tax-planning tool. It would appear that the goal in each year was to pay Mr. Executive a salary sufficient to reduce the corporation's taxable income to a marginal tax bracket of 15 percent.

In 1988, 1989, and 1990, the corporation would have had a marginal tax bracket of 25 percent for all taxable income in excess of $50,000. Accordingly, the salary of Mr. Executive was fixed to reduce the taxable income to just under that amount.

This salary history is inconsistent and would help substantiate the personal motivations rather than the payment of reasonable compensation. It would be even more difficult to sustain the reasonableness of this compensation if a major portion of the salary paid in 1988 and 1989 was in the form of a bonus near the end of the year.

WARNING: The Tax Reform Act of 1984 has changed the law regarding the reporting of income and expenses between related parties. In the past, an accrual basis taxpayer had to pay accrued interest or expenses (salary) in the year of accrual or within two and one-half months therafter, or else the taxpayer lost the deduction. This is no longer the case. While the taxpayer no longer loses the deduction, it can be taken only when the cash basis recipient must include it in income. Thus, the matching of services rendered to salary paid may be more difficult in the years beginning after 1983. For example, a bonus accrued for a corporate taxpayer on a calendar year basis in 1984 for services that the shareholder/employee rendered in that year but not paid until 1985 will not appear as a deduction during 1984. This will appear as a deduction to the corporate taxpayer during the calendar year 1985 and will be reported as additional compensation to the cash basis employee/shareholder during that year.

Key Idea B: Because of the change in the reporting of income and expenses between related parties by the Tax Reform Act of 1984, it may be best to change calendar-year taxpayers to fiscal-year taxpayers with corporate years ending in January, February, or March. Beware of the implications of the Tax Reform Act of 1986 and OBRA 1987 which limits the ability of personal service corporations to elect other than a calendar year. To be classified as a personal service corporation for these purposes, the corporation must have the following characteristics:

1. The principal activity must be the performance of personal services that are substantially performed by employee/owners.

2. Employee/owners are persons who own outstanding stock for at least one day during the tax year.

Key Idea C: If neither the corporation's profits nor its sales would justify an increased payment of salary to the executive, it is a good idea to tie the salary increase with the increase in the cost of living. Even if all cost of living payments are not made each year, the minutes should reflect that these increases were deferred until the corporation was able to pay them.

The inflation rate over the past decade makes this approach particularly useful, especially when there is a doubt as to the reasonableness of the salary. The only justification for increasing his salary in these instances may be the rapid rate of inflation.

2. *Dividend history of the corporation:* If in conjunction with a rapid increase in the controlling shareholder's salary there are no dividend payments, this again indicates personal or tax-dictated motives rather than a realistic appraisal of the worth of the employee's services, as follows:

Example: X, the sole shareholder of Profitable Corporation, is currently under audit. The salary history, profits, and dividends of the corporation are reflected as follows:

	1988	1989	1990
Salary of X	$ 50,000	$100,000	$ 50,000
Taxable Income of Corporation	$100,000	$ 50,000	$100,000
Dividend payments	–0–	–0–	–0–

In addition, the revenue agent has ascertained that in 1989 Mr. Executive bought a new house. The additional $50,000 was in the form of a bonus during the middle of the year, the net proceeds of which were used as a down payment for the new house. The lack of dividend history and this additional bonus during 1989 would cast some doubt as to the reasonableness of the compensation. Of course, there would have been no problem if that $50,000 had been a dividend payment.

These first two points are particularly important when trying to differentiate between intent which involves personal motivation and intent which is dictated by business factors. Intent is not normally listed as a relevant criterion. However, there is no doubt that if it can be shown that the intent of the salary payment is for personal or tax purposes without sound business reasons, the reasonableness of the salary payment is particularly susceptible to attack. For example, if the individual controlling shareholder needed additional funds to pay his children's college tuition, his bonus is particularly vulnerable to attack as a disguised dividend rather than a reasonable salary payment (see ¶402.1).

Key Idea: Pay a dividend when needs are obviously personal.

3. *Salary scale for the general employees:* A review of the general salary and compensation scale of the shareholder/employee and other employees may adversely or beneficially affect the reasonableness determination. If the shareholder's salary was increased along with the general increase in all employees, it solidifies the reasonable compensation concept. If, on the other hand, the only employee to receive a salary review is the shareholder/officer, the motives again become suspect. A comparison of the general compensation levels of all employees may have some weight for or against the compensation paid. The question becomes: "Is the salary scale in this company generally above or below normal?"

Key Idea: From time to time, include in the minutes an analysis of the general salary scale of your employees.

4. *Salary scale in the industry:* There is no doubt that the single most important factor in a reasonable compensation determination is a comparison of the compensation paid to the officer/shareholder with that paid by other companies in the industry. The regulations state the following:

> It is, in general, just to assume that reasonable and true compensation is only such amount as would ordinarily be paid for like services by like enterprises under like circumstances.

5. *Qualifications of the employee:* The particular qualifications of the individual coupled with the amount of work and the time spent at work are also factors that must be considered. Inordinately hard work, few vacations, and a heavy travel schedule are persuasive factors supporting a higher compensation rate.

6. *Contribution to the success of a particular business:* In some instances, there is no real way to measure a person's dollars-and-cents contribution to a business. This is particularly true in a highly technical business involving patents and other specialized training and information. If, in addition to being the chief administrative officer, he is also the chief innovator of the products being manufactured by this particular business, a higher than usual salary could be supported.

Key Idea: Document in the minutes the specific contribution of the employee to the profitability of the business, that is, the acquisition of a key account during the year which can be directly attributable to his efforts.

7. *Necessity of formal corporate action:* There is little doubt that corporate action timely taken and employment contracts properly drawn lend a good psychological and legal foundation for reasonable compensation. The practical problems which frequently occur are that the action is taken after the fact and that it is self-serving. However, the courts are still reluctant to place their judgment in lieu of the economic judgment of the corporate officers and directors. As long as the corporate minutes and/or employment contracts properly reflect the compensation actually paid, they cannot detract from the taxpayer's position. If, on the other hand, there are no minutes, or if the minutes only reflect the basic compensation and not the bonuses paid, the IRS's position becomes stronger.

Key Idea: It is extremely important to document in writing all corporate action and to properly draw an employment contract. It is my belief that contracts between related parties should be kept as simple as possible. The clear-cut concepts should be stated in as few pages as possible. There is nothing as self-serving as a ten-page employment contract or lease between the corporation and its sole shareholder.

Key Idea: It is a good idea to make sure that the minutes correlate with the information on the corporate income tax return. There is nothing as embarrassing and disastrous as having the minutes reflect a salary payment different from that reported on the corporate tax return and received by the individual officer.

[301.2] Planning Can Help Avoid the Problem of Unreasonable Compensation

Before discussing a plan of action which would provide for the maximum possibility to sustain an attack by the Internal Revenue Service, it is important to review the case of *Charles McCandless Tile Service v. U.S.*, 422 F.2d. 1336 (Ct. Cl. 1970). In this case, the court introduced a new concept which has created problems and clouded the future of compensation planning.

The way it was: Prior to this decision, it was generally considered that as long as the compensation is reasonable under the tests previously discussed, there is no necessity to pay dividends. The court in *McCandless* found that the two shareholders received a salary reasonable under all standard tests. The court stated: "Accordingly after examining the record in its entirety, with particular emphasis upon the elements discussed above, we consider the compensation paid by plaintiff to the McCandlesses during the pertinent period, in and of itself, to have been within the realm of reasonableness."

The approach: The court went on and found the following: "Even a payment deemed reasonable, however, is not deductible to the extent that it is in reality a distribution of corporate earnings and not compensation for services rendered." The court found it particularly relevant that there had been no dividends declared and paid to the shareholders during this particular time.

An observation: If this is the landmark in a new series of cases establishing the concept that a corporation must not only pay reasonable salaries but must also pay reasonable not just token dividends, then all compensation planning will have to go under review. If, on the other hand, this case is just another decision in the long and colorful series of cases discussing reasonable compensation, then the concept may find a quick demise. It would then appear in tax history as one of those unexplainable cases that deviates from the established norm. Because of the passage of time, it does appear that *McCandless* is a mere footnote in tax history for the reason that since its decision in 1970, neither the courts nor the IRS has attempted to impose this doctrine. However, it still appears as a cloud in the area of tax planning.

The following is an example illustrating the concept of the *McCandless* doctrine:

Example: Shareholders X and Y own all the stock in Profitable Corporation. Each has received, during the last three years, salaries starting at $75,000 and ending at $125,000 a year. X and Y can demonstrate that these are reasonable salaries for the services which they render to Profitable Corporation. It is determined that X and Y's stock in the corporation has a value of $300,000. Corporations such as Profitable Corporation have been paying a dividend of 6 percent per year. Under the *McCandless doctrine*, it could be considered that $18,000 of the salary paid in each year was dividend income which would represent a reasonable return on their investment. This, of course, would significantly deviate from the prior approach.

The initial fear in the tax-planning community was that the IRS would attempt to strictly impose the *McCandless doctrine*. This would result in the imposition of a dividend for a profitable corporation even though the compensation was otherwise reasonable. This fear was somewhat lessened by the Internal Revenue Service's recent Revenue Ruling 79-8, 1979-2, IRB 6. In part, this Revenue Ruling states the following:

The failure of a closely held corporation to pay more than an insubstantial portion of its earnings as dividends on its stock is a very significant factor to be taken into account in determining the deductibility of compensation paid by the corporation to its shareholder/employees. Conversely, where after an examination of all of the facts and circumstances (including the corporation's dividend history) compensation paid to shareholder/employees is found to be reasonable in amount and paid for services rendered, deductions for such compensation under Section 162(a) of the Code will not be denied on the sole ground that the corporation has not paid more than an insubstantial portion of its earnings as dividends on its outstanding stock.

With the *McCandless* case and this Revenue Ruling, you should still consider the payment of dividends reflecting a reasonable rate of return on the capital invested in those instances where either of the following conditions are present:

1. The salary level of the officer/shareholder gives rise to the possibility that it may be considered unreasonable.

2. A corporate taxpayer has more than sufficient income and earnings to pay not only reasonable salaries but also dividends, but chooses to retain said income.

NOTE: The Economic Recovery Tax Act of 1981 eliminated the difference in the maximum marginal tax rates between earned and unearned income (now, 50 percent is the maximum rate on all income), so a reclassification of salary as dividends has no tax consequences for the employee. However, from the corporation's perspective, a disallowance changes deductible salary expense into a nondeductible dividend distribution, thus increasing its tax liability. (See Chapter 4.)

[301.3] Five Steps to Defend against an Unreasonable Compensation Attack

In compensation planning, as in other areas of tax planning, prior thought can alleviate, if not eliminate, many problems that can arise in the future. The basic tactics which could be utilized in compensation planning are as follows:

1. *Establish a salary or form of paying a salary before the fact:* If at all possible, this salary should be based on the highest reasonable compensation at the original date of employment, giving due consideration to the benefits of income splitting, as explained in ¶100.1. Even if the corporation is unable to pay this amount, it will provide for its payment at a later date if the company prospers. The theory is that the compensation is not for the services rendered in the year of payment. This payment, if prior substantiation is present, can be attributed to prior years' salary deficiencies and will reflect a reasonable salary over the entire term.

Recently, there has been an increasing trend to maximize salary payments. This trend first became accentuated under the Economic Recovery Tax Act of 1981 (ERTA) when the corporate rates were not reduced on income over $100,000, while there was a decrease in individual rates. This trend should become even more pronounced after the enactment of the Tax Reform Act of 1986. In this case, the individual tax rates could be as much as 24 percentage points less than the corporate rates (individual rates begin at 15 percent, corporate rates can be as high as 39 percent). Successful small corporations will have a corporate tax rate of 39 percent, while the individual rates probably will be at 28 percent. When you combine this factor with the fact that increased contributions can normally be paid into a qualified deferred pension or profit-sharing plan without the payment of any tax, with the increase in salary to the employee shareholder, the necessity of maintaining the maximum reasonable salary becomes even more apparent. The goal in salary planning henceforth (or at least until the law is changed) will be the maximization of salary payments.

Schedule Showing Tax Benefits of Maximizing Salary with Qualified Deferred Compensation Plans Determined at 25 Percent of Salary

Individual Employee at a Marginal Tax Bracket	Distribution of Bonus*	Tax if Corporation Does Not Distribute Bonus but Retains the Funds	Tax to Individual if $8,000 Bonus Is Distributed	Tax Savings by Distributing Bonus
15%	($10,000)	$3,900	$1,200	$2,700
28%	($10,000)	$3,900	$2,240	$1,660
33%	($10,000)	$3,900	$2,640	$1,260

* If a bonus of $8,000 is paid to employee, then $2,000 will be contributed to qualified deferred compensation plans.

The tax savings are obvious. The following constraints should be kept in mind:

(A) That contributions to qualified deferred compensation plans can only be made to certain limits (see Chapter 2 and Internal Revenue Code Section 415).

(B) That restrictions are inherent to the law on unreasonable compensation.

2. *Show consistency in payment of both salary and bonuses:* If at all possible, compensation should be paid at regular periods of time, that is, monthly. Bonuses should relate to a fixed standard. In other words, if there is a year-end bonus of 10 percent for all employees, this year-end bonus should also be applied to the individual officer/shareholder. If the employee is entitled to bonuses for services rendered, it should be at specific periods of time, that is, Christmas, year-end, and so on. Bonuses granted at irregular times and satisfying the personal needs of the officer/shareholder are particularly suspect.

3. *Explore the possibility of a flexible salary arrangement or contingent compensation agreements:* Many times it is difficult, if not impossible, to ascertain the exact compensation of an individual on a reasonable basis. It may be worthwhile to establish a salary that is contingent upon profits or sales at a predetermined rate. While this arrangement may provide flexibility to the corporation, it will result in a great deal of scrutiny by the Internal Revenue Service. The Regulations state that in order for it to be acceptable, the agreement must result in a free bargain between the employer and the employee before the services have been rendered. An agreement such as this becomes even more suspect if there are two or three equal shareholders and each one shares in the bonus or salary payments equally.

4. *Gear salaries to payments in the general industry:* A review of the basic salaries paid to similar and like parties may give rise to a determination of the salary range which would be appropriate in the individual business.*

5. *Pay salaries that are not proportionate to the individual shareholders in the corporation:* If there are three equal shareholders, it would be best if the salary payments are not the same. Many times it is impossible to convince the individuals that this is

---

* For a comparison of salaries paid to top-level and middle management executives in various industries, see "Top Management Report" and "Middle Management Report" published by AMACOM (contact: Executive Compensation Service, American Management Association, 135 West 50th Street, New York, NY 10020) or "Executive Compensation Report" published by the Compensation Institute (contact: Compensation Institute, 3407 West 6th Street, Suite 706, Los Angeles, CA 90020).

appropriate. If it is possible to differentiate and compensate their services unequally; this will help substantiate a reasonable salary.

Any planning that can be done which would indicate that the salary compensation arrangement by and between the shareholder/officer and the employer resulted from a legitimate bargain for his services will help substantiate a reasonable salary. Any of those factors that would, to the contrary, indicate that the corporation was used solely as the shareholder's own tool for the gratification of his individual monetary desires will make the salary payments susceptible to attack.

[302] WHAT TAX STRATEGIES TO USE TO MAXIMIZE THE SALARY DEDUCTION

Checklist

☐ Try graduated increases in salary rather than big jumps. Do not tie salary to fluctuations in profits but solely to services rendered.

☐ Increase salary when there is an increase in duties and responsibilities.

Example: Profitable Corporation's sole owner, X's son, Y, has been working as a machinist in the plant. As such, he has been receiving union wages and benefits. He is promoted to assistant foreman and made assistant secretary/treasurer of the corporation. This is the time to substantially increase his salary. The increase should be reflected in the minutes and indicate that the additional compensation is the result of the increased duties and responsibilities he has undertaken. Without the promotion to foreman, to pay him in excess of union wages and benefits, even under the guise of additional compensation as assistant secretary/treasurer, may be hazardous.

☐ Documentation of services rendered and comparable services could be particularly important, especially with high compensation.

☐ If at all possible, do not pay equal shareholders equally. Reward each according to his services rather than according to his shareholdings.

Example: Profitable Corporation is owned by X and Y, each owning 50 percent of the authorized issued and outstanding stock. X has been the chief executive officer for many years, and as such his salary has increased over the years. Y is responsible for all the salesmen. In 1984, Y acquired a new customer, producing substantial revenue to the corporation. At the end of the year, it probably would be good strategy to pay Y an additional bonus based on the acquisition of this customer.

☐ If full salary is not being paid, document this fact; that is, other employees have received cost of living increases, but not officer/shareholders because the corporation is unable to pay the additional compensation.

☐ Make sure you document everything properly. Documentation in the minutes and employment contracts should reflect that information reported on the tax return for the corporation.

[302.1] Utilizing the Salary to Split Income among Family Members

The goal of this tax-planning technique is to shift income from the higher basis taxpayer to a taxpayer in a lower bracket. It has already been seen that dividing the income between the corporation and the salaried officer/shareholder produces significant tax savings. It becomes even more advantageous, especially in those years of high education or other costs, to shift a portion of the earning capacity of the corporation to the children.

Assume a situation where the officer/shareholder is in the 33 percent bracket, and the corporation is in the 39 percent bracket. Further assume that there is an additional $10,000 of income that could be distributed to the shareholder as reasonable compensation. If this income is retained, the corporation will pay a 39 percent tax. If the income is distributed as a salary, the shareholder will pay approximately the same 33 percent tax. If, on the other hand, the same $10,000 could be paid to the officer/shareholder's son as salary, the son's tax will be no more than $1,500. This will result in a tax savings of between $1,800 and $2,400.

There are various factors which must be taken into consideration before an attempt should be made to shift a portion of the income to a taxpayer in a lower bracket. The factors vary depending upon the age and relationship of the parties.

[302.2] Justifying Shifting Income to the Spouse

The most common relationship where a reasonable salary may be paid is to a spouse. In many cases, a spouse works in the business either on a part- or full-time basis and contributes substantially toward the profitability of the corporation. The payment of a salary to the wife can provide certain tax benefits, as follows:

1. For the period between 1982 through 1986, there were substantial direct income tax benefits to be derived from the payment of a salary to a spouse. Prior to 1982 and after 1986, these benefits were eliminated. During this time, there were two direct benefits that were available in two-wage-earner families. The first was the marriage deduction. This equaled 10 percent of the qualified earned income of the spouse with the lower income and reached a maximum of $3,000. Second, both spouses could make contributions to an IRA. The first benefit was completely eliminated, and the second will be useful only in rare cases.

After the Tax Reform Act of 1986, it would appear that both individuals, if they have earned income, can contribute to an IRA if neither is an active participant in a qualified plan. While direct benefits are no longer available, indirect benefits can produce positive planning situations.

WARNING: In an attempt to equalize the salaries between the married individuals, the following three additional factors should be considered:

A. By increasing one spouse's salary, you may increase the total tax liability through the payment of social security and federal and state unemployment taxes. Up to $43,800 of compensation in 1987 would be subject to a combined employer/employee social security tax of 14.3 percent. The question becomes: "Will the increased contributions to social security substantially increase the total benefit from social security upon retirement?"

B. Any attempt to equalize salaries can be construed as a tax scheme, and the equalization may have to take place over a period of years in order to avoid attack.

C. If the corporation had an integrated qualified deferred compensation plan (either profit-sharing or pension plan), the equalization of the salaries may reduce the overall benefits received by the couple.

It should be noted that the attempt to equalize salaries because of the above factors probably reached its heyday during the period 1982 through 1986. The question becomes: "With the repeal of the marital deduction and the increased restrictions on the ability to contribute to a deductible IRA (see Chapter 2), what is the future of planning that involves the shifting of income to the spouse?" Any answer at this time is probably premature. However, it would appear that in profitable corporations where it is impossible to elect an S Corporation (see Chapter 5) and where the further increase in salary can increase the specter of unreasonable compensation, the payment of a salary to the other spouse is still a viable tool.

2. Shifting income can increase the deferred compensation benefits being paid to the family unit. This is especially true if the corporation is already making the maximum contribution to one spouse.

3. It can also provide positive benefits, especially where there is a possibility that the compensation paid to one spouse may be unreasonable. The total payment may look excessive if only one person is receiving the compensation, but if both parties are working, it may be more realistic.

4. Some states tax the individual taxpayer (not the couple collectively) on the portion of the total family income that he earned.

Wisconsin law, prior to 1986, taxed the income earned to the individual at a family unit. Accordingly, if an additional $10,000 was earned by the husband (at the maximum level of taxation), he would bear a total additional state tax of as much as $1,000. If his wife earned this $10,000 and she had no other income, the taxes attributable to her income would be only $492. This could result in as much as $508 in tax savings.

Any savings in state taxes should be counterbalanced against the additional social security taxes that would be incurred by the payment of a salary to the spouse. In almost all instances when this technique is utilized, the husband officer/shareholder will not incur any additional social security tax if he receives an additional payment of salary. In all likelihood, his earnings are already in excess of the social security limits. If payments are made to his wife as salary, and this is the only salary she receives, the corporation and his wife would bear a social security tax. The disadvantage of paying the additional current social security payments should be compared with the state tax savings and the additional benefits received as social security upon retirement.

[302.3] Justifying Shifting Income to Children and Other Persons

The second group of persons who could qualify for the shifting of income are the individual's children. The utilization of the child's services in the business, and the payment of a reasonable salary, may help defray the high cost of education. At least once a year, a client will call me and ask whether or not he can pay his son's or daughter's education directly through the business. I ask him what justification there is for this payment. After a pregnant pause, there is some mumbling on the phone about some services or advice given. The final question I ask is: "If your child was not working for you, how much would you have to pay to replace him? The answer is usually evident. In certain instances, however, it is not unreasonable to pay either the child a consulting fee for time or energy spent. This is especially true if the child has special talents that can be offered to the corporation. In addition, during the summer months, there is usually adequate justification for the payment of a salary to the child.

> **Example:** Profitable Corporation is a manufacturer of widgets. X, the sole shareholder of Profitable Corporation, has three children, all boys, ages 15, 18, and 23. The cor-

poration is in the 39 percent tax bracket, and X is in the 33 percent bracket in the year 1988. The following planning techniques could be utilized:

1. The 15-year-old son could act as the janitor and provide those services to the corporation after school. The corporation could either pay him a fixed amount each month for the services rendered or pay him on an hourly basis. In either event, if $2,000 is paid during the year, there should be no tax at all. If the child provides the services, $2,000 can be saved. If the father performed the services and put the additional money in the account, only $1,340 would be available after taxes.

2. The second son has just completed high school and is going to work for the summer. There is no reason that the son cannot be employed either in the production unit or in the office staff and paid the highest amount that would be paid for those services if they were paid to an outsider. There is, of course, some risk in this, but the risk is slight. Again there are substantial savings, as in Technique 1, on any money earned by this child.

3. The third son has completed business school and is currently in law school. While he is out of town most of the year, it may still be possible for him to (a) perform some accounting services and be compensated for this or (b) do some special studies or surveys and provide written reports relative to the productivity of the business.

In any case, with some imagination, services can be rendered for which you can justify compensation.

WARNING: If significant payments to the child are justifiable, there is still an additional problem. If the child provides more than half of his own support, his parents will lose him as an exemption on their tax return.

WARNING: Beginning in 1987, a taxpayer cannot claim a personal exemption if he is eligible to be claimed as a dependent of another taxpayer.

The third class of people who qualify for this type of salary payment is the parents of the individual owners of the business. In many instances, it has become incumbent upon the children to supplement their parents' income. The making of these payments in after-tax dollars becomes fairly burdensome. On the other hand, if the parents can be paid a reasonable salary for services rendered, the government is underwriting a portion of their total support cost.

In the above instances, and in others that occur from time to time, there is the ability to pay or disburse part of the funds necessary to maintain a wife, child, parent or other related party through the means of a tax deductible salary. This significantly reduces the burden on the individual taxpayer. Before a decision is made as to the mode and method of payment, the tax risks should be analyzed. It should also be considered whether or not these payments will upset any other benefits that may be available if the individual directly supports his parents or children. As in all cases of tax planning, in the final analysis, the question is: "Are the benefits worth the risk incurred?"

[303]   WHAT THE TAX EFFECT OF THE TAX REFORM ACT OF 1986 IS ON SALARY PLANNING

The long-term effects of the Tax Reform Act of 1986 on salary planning are at this time difficult to project. However, there appears to be little if any doubt that there will be a significant impact on planning for all C Corporations in the not-too-distant-future. The impact will be felt particularly on those medium-size corporations that generate between $200,000 and $500,000 in income to the "family group" and who have developed fairly sophisticated qualified deferred compensation plans. An analysis such as the following will probably be utilized by these corporations in determining the appropriate salary. First, it is necessary to look at the graduated individual rates and corporate rates before determining the appropriate salary. The following rates include the 5 percent surcharge:

Married Individual*—Taxable Income	*Tax Rate Applicable*
0–$ 29,750	15 percent
$ 29,750–$ 71,900	28 percent
$ 71,900–$149,250	33 percent
$ 149,250 and over	28 percent

Corporate Taxable Income	*Tax Rate Applicable*
0–$ 50,000	15 percent
$ 50,000–$ 75,000	25 percent
$ 75,000–$100,000	34 percent
$100,000–$335,000	39 percent
$335,000 and over	34 percent

* Note that there are different tables for single individuals, head of household, or married filing separately. Also note that the deduction for personal exemptions are phased out for income over $149,250. Depending upon the number of exemptions claimed, this will continue the 33 percent marginal tax rate for all income over $149,250.

To illustrate the type of planning that will probably be applicable, I will use the following example:

Example: XYZ Corporation is a successful corporation which has earned income before payments of salaries and qualified deferred compensation of $150,000. Joe Executive is the sole owner of XYZ Corporation and wishes to determine the maximum salary and retention of income to minimize his total tax burden. For this example, we will assume that 25 percent of his salary (up to the applicable limits) can be paid into qualified deferred compensation plans. We will further assume that all contributions to the deferred compensation plan are made for his benefit and that no other employees will share.

What is the salary which would produce the maximum results? The optimum salary would be $80,000. This would allow $20,000 to be paid into the qualified deferred compensation plans, and $50,000 would be retained in the corporation. The total tax incurred would be approximately $26,437.50. In the future, I am sure that one of the tax services will produce a computer program that will produce this information without the necessity to go through the thought process. However, the thought process will usually combine the following:

1. Pay the salary that will generate the maximum allowable deferred compensation benefit.
2. Do not retain in the corporation more than $75,000 of taxable income. Normally maximum tax planning will indicate a corporate income of $50,000 or less.
3. Retain, if at all possible, a salary level for the individual of $71,900 or less. Note that the tax rate for married individuals between $71,900 and $149,250 produces the highest individual tax rate of 33 percent.

The above example is artifical since it was determined that all payments to the qualified deferred compensation plans would be made for the benefit of the individual. This, of course, is not usually the case, and many times the amount that will go for other than the key individual or groups of key individuals will have to enter into the factor. In this case, some "number crunching" can produce sizable benefits.

The following chart will serve as a guide to compute what will produce the maximum tax savings. Trial and error will be needed to determine both the maximum tax benefit and the practical implications of this planning.

(1) Total Disposable Income	(2) Salary	(3) Qual. Deferred Compen- sation Plan Contribution	(4) Corp. Taxable Income (a)	(5) Corp. Tax	(6) Ind. Taxable Income (b)	(7) Ind. Tax	(8) Total Tax (c)

(a) Column 1 less Columns 2 and 3
(b) Column 2 plus other income less personal exemptions and itemized deductions
(c) Total of Columns 5 and 7

Key Idea: In determining the maximum beneficial salary, it is a good idea to keep the following goals in mind:

1. Retain in the corporation less than $75,000.
2. Pay the salary which will produce the maximum qualified deferred compensation benefits.
3. If possible, keep the employees total taxable income at 28% marginal tax rate.

[303.1] Checklist of Reasonable Compensation Cases

How to Justify Reasonable Compensation

1. Special attributes:
    (a) Brought profitability to corporation—*Skyland Oldsmobile, Inc.,* ¶72,017 P-H Memo TC; *Federal Lithograph Co., Inc., v. U.S.* (Ct. Cl. Trial Judges Opinion; 1975) 36 AFTR 2d 75-6390; *aff'd* (1976) 37 AFTR 2d 76-997, 209 Ct. Cl. 789
    (b) Long hours and hard work—*Skyland Oldsmobile, Inc.,* ¶72,017 P-H Memo TC
    (c) Executive helped develop corporation—*Gordy Tire Co. v. U.S.,* 155 Ct. Cl. 759, 296 F.2d 476 (1961)
    (d) Success or failure rested with the executive—*Hower & Seamen, Inc.,* 4 BTA 261
    (e) Specialized knowledge—
        (1) *Reserve Knitting Mills, Inc.,* ¶49.093 P-H Memo TC: *John A. Dunn Co.,* 8 BTA 955
        (2) Denied where managerial duties delegated—*Langley Park Apartments,* 44 TC 474, *aff'd* 359 F.2d 427 (4 Cir. 1966)
    (f) Technical knowledge and skills—*Polak's Frutal Works, Inc.,* 21 TC 953 (NA; 1972-1 CB 3): *William C. Neils, et al.,* 82, 173 P-H Memo TC
    (g) Inventive ability—*Soabar Co.,* 7 TC 89 (A CB 1946-2 p. 5); *Appleton Electric Co.,* 67, 211 P-H Memo TC
2. Increase in responsibilities:
    Danly Machine Specialists, Inc., ¶45, 326 P-H Memo TC; *J.E. Craig Finance Co., Inc., v. U.S.,* (DC SC; 1962) 9 AFTR 2d 713, 200 F. Supp. 554
    Denied where no increase in responsibilities;

Hoffman Radio Corp. v. Comm., 177 F.2d 264 (9 Cir. 1949)
Giles Industries, Inc., v. U.S. (1974) 33 AFTR 2d 74-1142;
204 Ct. Cl. 202, 496 F.2d 556

3. Volume of business justifying increase in salaries:
Ray Watts Motors, Inc., v. U.S., (DC SC; 1956) 145 F. Supp.
269
Denied when not enough increase to justify; *Barto Co.*, 21
BTA 1197

4. Comparison of salaries paid in other businesses:
   (a) Generally—*Loesch & Green Construction Co. v.
   Comm.*, 211 F.2d 210 (6 Cir. 1954), *rev'g* ¶52,351
   P-H Memo TC
   (b) Volume of business and profits—*Pfeiffer Brewing
   Co.*, ¶52,179 P-H Memo TC
   (c) Rate—*Wright-Bernet Inc. v. Comm.*, 172 F.2d 343
   (6 Cir. 1949), *rev'g* ¶47,325 P-H Memo TC

5. Salary history compared:
   (a) Favorable—*J. R. Holsey Sales Co.*, ¶45,163 P-H
   Memo TC
   (b) Denied where no substantial change and salary
   increased—*Fritzinger Co., Inc.*, ¶43,076 P-H Memo
   TC, *aff'd* 139 F.2d 486 (3 Cir. 1943)

6. Compensation for prior services:
Marshall & Spencer Co., 7 BTA 454 (A, CB Dec. 1931, p.
45)

4

Dividends:
How to Avoid
Problems
and Take
Advantage
of Opportunities

**WHY CLOSELY HELD CORPORATIONS GENERALLY
AVOID PAYING DIVIDENDS**

In the past, dividends played an unusual role in planning for a
closely held corporation. In addition to the planning possibilities of the past, all indications are to their increased use after
the full implementation of the Tax Reform Act of 1986 in
1988.

Prior to the Tax Reform Act of 1986, most planners
avoided dividends like the plague. The reason for this aversion
is that, even in advantageous situations, dividend payments
usually result in double taxation. The following two examples
demonstrate the maximum negative effect attached to any distribution which resulted in double taxation.

> **Example:** Prior to the Tax Reform Act of 1986, Profitable
> Corporation earns $1,000, which is subject to tax at a 46
> percent marginal rate. Profitable Corporation declares a
> dividend of the net after-tax income from the $1,000 to its
> shareholders. The dividend will equal $540 (income of
> $1,000 less federal tax of $460). If this dividend is paid to
> a shareholder who is in the 50 percent marginal income
> tax bracket, he will then pay $270 in personal income tax.
> Of the $1,000 earned originally by the corporation, there

has been an effective 73 percent tax before consumption by the shareholder. Only $270 of the original $1,000 is available to the individual shareholder in after-tax income.

Example: After the full implementation of the Tax Reform Act of 1986 in 1988, using the facts in the above example, the effect upon the shareholders of Profitable Corporation on the $1,000 earnings of Profitable, assuming both the corporation and the individual are in the maximum tax brackets (corporation 39 percent and individual 33 percent), can be calculated as follows:

Earnings of Profitable Corporation	$1,000
Tax on Earnings	390
Net after Tax Corporate Income	$ 610
Tax on Dividend Income	$201.30
Net After-Tax Income to the Individual	$408.70

As can be seen, the total tax impact upon both the corporation and the individual, if both are in the maximum tax brackets, can still exceed over 60 percent. While substantial, this is considerably less than the total tax impact prior to the implementation of the Tax Reform Act of 1986, which was 73 percent.

The two examples above illustrate the most disastrous effect that can occur upon the distribution of dividend income. The extreme result is the product of both the corporation and the individual being in the maximum marginal tax brackets. The examples also show the negative side of the dividend income.

The following chart shows the effective after-tax rate to the shareholders depending upon the tax rate of the corporation and individual.

CORPORATE TAX RATE

		15%	25%	34%	39%
Individual Tax Rate	15%	72.25%	63.75%	56.10%	51.85%
	28%	61.20%	54.00%	47.52%	48.24%
	33%	56.95%	50.25%	44.22%	40.87%

The previous schedule indicates the effect of double taxation on the individual taxpayer.

Example: In our previous example of Profitable Corporation, if the individual and corporation were each at the 15 percent marginal tax brackets, the total effect upon the individual of after-tax dividend income is only 27.75 percent (100% − 72.25%).

This schedule indicates the positive planning characteristics of dividends after the Tax Reform Act of 1986. An officer/ sole shareholder is in the maximum 33 percent tax bracket during the period of time that he is between ages 60 and 65. It may be in his best interest not to take $10,000 of salary in each of those years and to accumulate this income and pay a tax at 15 percent at the corporate level. The accumulated income is distributed to him after he attains the age of 65 at the time he is in the 15 percent bracket.

Method 1: Distribute $10,000 to Executive for the five-year period between 60 and 65. Executive is in the 33 percent marginal tax bracket.

CORPORATE TAX—THE CALCULATION OF CORPORATE TAX:

Corporate Income	$10,000.00
Less Salary	10,000.00
	-0-

INDIVIDUAL TAX—CALCULATION OF INDIVIDUAL TAX:

Salary	$10,000.00
Marginal Tax Rate	.33
Tax per Year	3,300.00
	× 5
Total Tax	$16,500.00
Net Distribution to Individual During Five-Year Period	$50,000.00
Less Tax	16,500.00
Net After-Tax Income	$33,500.00

Method 2: Retain $10,000 in corporate income in each year and distribute as dividends after Executive retires.

CORPORATE TAX—CALCULATION OF CORPORATE TAX

Corporate Income before Bonus	$10,000.00
Bonus	-0-
Net Income	$10,000.00
Corporate Tax Rate	× .15
Corporate Tax	$ 1,500.00
	× 5
Total Tax during Five-Year Period	$ 7,500.00

DISTRIBUTION TO INDIVIDUAL AFTER RETIREMENT

Corporate Income	$50,000.00
Less Tax	7,500.00
Available Dividend Distribution	$42,500.00
	× .15
Tax upon Dividend Distribution to Shareholders	$ 6,375.00
Net After-Tax Distribution to Individual Shareholder	$36,125.00

Even if he is in the 28 percent bracket, the difference in tax rates will be fairly small since the combined effect of the double taxation is just under 39 percent versus the immediate tax of 33 percent that he would have to pay. The time value of money as well as the ability to have the money available during those five years probably would more than offset the difference in tax rates.

Key Idea: Whenever the corporation can accumulate income at 15 percent and one of the owners is older, the planner should consider the retention of funds for future distribution as dividends.

Key Idea: It is probably a good idea to consider the distribution of funds as dividend in lieu of salary if the salary payments will affect receipt of social security.

[401] HOW A DIVIDEND IS DEFINED FOR TAX PURPOSES

There need not be any correlation between the concept of a dividend, as interpreted by the courts for tax purposes, and the concept as understood for corporate purposes. The tax law will consider certain distributions as dividends which would not be so interpreted under corporate law and vice versa.

A dividend, as defined in tax law, is a distribution or payment made by the corporation to its shareholders out of its current or accumulated earnings and profits. Thus "dividend" is a term which has been developed by the courts in conjunction with the Internal Revenue Code and Regulations.

Significance of Understanding Earnings and Profits

Another term which is sometimes not fully understood is "earnings and profits." It would be easy to equate earnings and profits to retained earnings or surplus on a balance sheet. "Surplus," for accounting purposes, may include additional paid-in surplus and evaluation surplus created upon incorporation. Neither of these amounts appear in earnings and profits. On the other hand, even retained earnings may receive adjustments in order to be equated to earnings and profits.

The following is an example of how earnings and profits are calculated:

Example: New Corporation in 1986 has an operating profit for its first fiscal year of $10,000. This operating profit excludes $1,000 of dividends, $1,200 of municipal bond income, and property sold, which resulted in a net capital loss of $1,500. The net taxable income on the corporation's tax return will be $10,200. This income will result in a corporate tax of $1,530. The earnings and profits of the corporation at the end of the year will be $9,170, determined as follows:

Operating Income		$10,000.00
(plus) Tax Exempt Income	$1,200	
Dividend Income	1,000	(+) 2,200.00
		$12,200.00
(less) Capital Loss		(−) 1,500.00
		$10,700.00
(less) Income Tax		(−)
		1,530.00
		$ 9,170.00

This example is presented only to illustrate the fact that there is no equivalent accounting category on the balance sheet. Earnings and profits are significant because distributions for tax purposes can only be categorized as dividends to the extent that the corporation has earnings and profits subsequent to February 28, 1913. (For a full discussion of how earnings and profits are determined, refer to Section 312 of the Internal Revenue Code, IRS Pub. 542 and Rev. Proc. 75-17.)

WARNING: The Tax Reform Act of 1984 made several changes in the computation of the corporation's earnings and profits. This essentially made earnings and profits more closely conform to economic income. In general, these changes will increase earnings and profits and therefore could affect dividend distributions. Before utilizing certain techniques which would presuppose no earnings and profits, an extensive review of the new law that changes the concept of earnings and profits should be undertaken. Remember, the lack of retained earnings does not equate to the lack of earnings and profits for dividend distributions.

Example: On January 1, 1986, XYZ Corporation loans $100,000 to its sole shareholder and charges him 5 percent simple interest. Said note is a demand loan, and no loan repayments other than interest are made during 1985. This loan is considered a below-market loan since the 5 percent rate is less than the 10 percent applicable federal rate. The foregone interest is considered to be transferred to the shareholder and retransferred to the corporation on December 31, 1985. Accordingly, the shareholder has received a taxable dividend of $5,000. He has also had an offsetting interest expense of a like amount. The corporation has interest income of $5,000. This amount is calculated at the federal rate of 10 percent on $100,000 less 5 percent on $100,000, which was the interest charged.

Because the Tax Reform Act of 1984 has given credence to these loans, does it now mean that planning no longer necessitates the care set forth above? My own feeling on this, until the full impact of the Tax Reform Act is fully known, is that it would appear the safe course to treat these loans as gingerly as in the past and ensure that these loans are paying interest at a rate comparable to the federal rate and are being repaid in a commercially reasonable way. The fear, as in the past, involves not only the characterization of the interest, but that the "loan" is not a loan for tax purposes but is considered as a dividend distribution to the shareholder. The same analysis and caveat is also applicable to the following discussion on the open account.

The Tax Reform Act of 1986, beginning in 1987, will have an effect on these loans. Prior to the enactment of the Tax Reform Act of 1986, if the above analysis was "correct," the shareholder received "a wash" for tax purposes. His income was increased by the $5,000, and he had a corresponding deductible $5,000 interest expense (assuming he did itemize). After the 1986 Tax Reform Act, this constructive dividend can have adverse effects upon the individual shareholder. The reason for this is that starting with tax years beginning January 1, 1987, personal interest is no longer fully deductible.

The disallowance of deductions for personal interest is phased in over a five-year period as follows:

PERCENT OF PERSONAL
INTEREST ALLOWABLE
AS DEDUCTION

1987	65 percent
1988	40 percent
1989	20 percent
1990	10 percent
1991	0 percent

WARNING: While the Tax Reform Act of 1984 apparently opened a loophole where constructive interest would not have its prior negative adverse effects, it appears that the Tax Reform Act of 1986 has inadvertently closed this loophole by dissallowing a portion or all of the personal interest deduction. A question is raised on whether or not this otherwise partially or completely disallowed interest can be converted into deductible interest by securing these non-interest-bearing loans with a mortgage on a qualified residence. A qualified residence is the taxpayer's principal residence and second residence. Interest paid on an equity loan, which is a debt secured by a qualified residence, is deductible as long as the debt does not exceed the lesser of the taxpayer's basis or $100,000. There are additional restrictions and allowances, but normally they are not applicable.

The Open Account: In the same vein, it is not unusual for the shareholder to have an open account with the corporation. Personal advances are made periodically, and some repayments, usually in the form of bonuses, are made at the end of the year. This is a particularly dangerous situation and can pose a problem when there is an audit. Accordingly, an open account should be avoided if at all possible.

Key Idea: Make sure the open account is converted into a shareholder loan at the end of the year. As an alternative, a bonus should be paid to the officer to eliminate any remaining amount in this account. Watch out that the bonus does not result in unreasonable compensation.

Corporate Expenditures for Shareholder's Personal Benefit: If the corporation makes payments for the shareholder's personal living expenses, these are considered dividends. The method used is not important. The expenditures can either be a direct payment or reimbursement to the individual shareholders. Travel and entertainment expenses are the most common trouble area. The corporation pays what it considers "business" travel and entertainment expenses incurred by its officer/ shareholder. During an audit, it could be ascertained that a portion of these expenses were personal. As shown in Chapter 1, provisions in the bylaws may help alleviate this problem (see Appendix A). However, if there is no provision or if it is considered to be self-serving by the Internal Revenue Service, these personal expense payments will usually be considered dividends.

> **Key Idea:** A possible solution to this problem is a hedge agreement. (A sample can be found in Appendix A.) Hedge argreements state that the officer of a closely held corporation must repay any corporate payments which are subsequently disallowed as expenses to the corporation. This permits the executive to eliminate the imposition of dividend income upon the disallowance of these expenses.
>
> Some doubt has been cast upon the viability of these agreements by the Tax Court and the 8th Circuit Court. (See *Steel Constructors, Inc.*, 1978 P-H TC ¶78,489.) Closely held corporations are now faced with a difficult decision. On one hand, the agreement, if successful, will avoid double taxation to the extent of the disallowed expenses. On the other hand, the use of this agreement may in itself be regarded by the court and the IRS as evidence that the parties actually considered some corporate expenses personal.
>
> If it is decided by the corporation not to establish a hedge agreement, there should be minutes to that effect that a hedge agreement was purposely omitted. The minutes should state that there was no doubt as to either the reasonableness of the compensation or that all of the reimbursed expenses were properly deductible. (See ¶105.2).

Shareholder Loans to Corporation: The problem in this area is whether the IRS can recategorize a shareholder loan as stock in the corporation. If the shareholder loan can withstand IRS scrutiny, the interest paid on the shareholder loan will be deductible to the corporation, and the repayment of the loan will be tax free to the shareholder. On the other hand, if the IRS succeeds in reclassifying the debt as stock, any payments on the stock will be classified as nondeductible dividends, and the repayment of the debt, now classified as stock, will in all likelihood be taxed as dividend income.

As set forth in Chapter 1, the regulations that were to be promulgated under Section 385 have been withdrawn, and thus there is no definitive rules as to when debt will be recategorized as stock. Historically, there was rarely a problem with shareholders loaning money to a corporation as long as general planning was instituted. This planning usually involved evidencing said loan with a note and paying a reasonable rate of interest on the money borrowed. In addition, if the loan was sizable, a repayment schedule should have been established and religiously followed. If the new regulations had been implemented, extreme care would be necessary to ensure the loan could withstand the scrutiny of the regulations so that the repayment of these advances with interest will not be considered dividend income (see Section 104).

Because of the current clouded status of the law, all shareholder loans should be reviewed carefully with the existing law under Section 385 to be sure that the IRS could not sustain a reclassification of loans as stock in the corporation. You should also be aware that if the interest charged on shareholder loans to the corporation are too low, it may result in the loan being classified as an original issue discount note.

WARNING: As noted, personal interest is in part or fully disallowed beginning on January 1, 1987. Accordingly, the prior loans that were executed by individuals and their corporations should be reexamined to determine the effect of the Tax Reform Act of 1986.

> **Key Idea:** If a shareholder loan is made, the corporation and shareholder should consider granting to the corporation a second mortgage on either the house or cottage. The Tax Reform Act of 1986 provided an exception to the disallowance of a portion or all of personal interest for interest related to a qualified residence. A qualified residence's interest is deductible in full if it is interest on debt instrument secured by a security interest perfected under local law on the taxpayer's primary residence or secondary residence. The amount dedictible on an equity loan consists of interest on the debt which is the lesser of the taxpayer's cost of the residence plus the cost of any improvements or $100,000.

Diversion of Corporate Funds—Assigning Income to the Shareholder: This problem can occur if the shareholder attempts to obtain rents or other income earned by the corporation directly for his own use. In our more sophisticated day and age, this is no longer a real problem except in those cases of embezzlement or other appropriation of funds for the individual's use. However, in the past, shareholders had no trouble assigning income to the corporation, imposing taxation on the corporation, and also, taxing the payments made to the shareholders as dividends.

Key Idea: Recognizing assignment of income is in itself a solution to this problem. As long as the individuals are attuned to the fact that the corporate assets produce corporate income and cannot be utilized individually, this should be sufficient.

Bargain Purchases of Corporate Property: A bargain sale is normally defined as the sale of corporate property to a shareholder at a price below fair market value. The shareholder, in this instance, wishes to obtain a withdrawal of the corporate property at less than its fair market value. The spread between the fair market value and the amount paid is in effect a distribution of earnings and profits to the shareholder in the form of a dividend to the extent of the corporation's earnings and profits.

Example: Active Corporation, twenty years ago, purchased vacant real estate for investment. It paid $10,000 for this property. The current fair market value of this real estate is $100,000. A shareholder wishes to "purchase" the land from the corporation for $10,000 and sell this property for $100,000 to X, a nonrelated third party. He anticipates that the $90,000 gain upon the sale to X will be treated as a capital gain. Since he "bought" the real estate from the corporation, he expects that this will not be a taxable event to him. The tax result is not what is anticipated. The shareholder will realize the full $90,000 as dividend income upon the transfer from Active Corporation to himself. There is, of course, no further taxation to him upon the sale to X. However, if he does not dispose of the property by selling it to X, he will be taxed on a gain which produced no liquid assets.

Key Idea: Before any sale of corporate assets is anticipated, obtain documentation giving the reasons for the sale as well as documentation establishing the fair market value of the property. It is not unusual for a corporation to sell some of its assets to obtain working captial. Minutes documenting this fact and also documenting the value of these assets through appraisals or independent determinations can shortcut any problems that may be encountered.

Excessive Compensation: As discussed in Chapter 3, if the compensation paid to the individual officer/shareholder is unreasonable, the difference between the reasonable salary and the amount paid will be considered dividend income.

Key Idea: The best ways to short cut any problems that may be encountered is to (1) determine a reasonable salary and (2) initiate a periodic payment of this salary. When a salary is increased, a statement of the reasons for the increase should appear in the minutes, for example, cost of living, increased responsibilities, quality of work performed, and so on.

With these concepts firmly established, the following example will illustrate how constructive dividends could play havoc to effective planning:

Example: Profitable Corporation is run by X, the son of the original founder of the corporation. X, many years ago, had purchased all the stock from his father and mother. At a later date, it was ascertained that the parents' income was not sufficient to maintain their life-style. X had a moral obligation to support his parents since he had purchased the business on favorable terms. He also felt that it was better if the government helped subsidize his parents' retirement. Accordingly, he pays a salary to Mom and Dad. The services rendered by Mom and Dad are negligible.

X would like to have the salary payments considered as compensation and thus deductible to the corporation. However, upon audit, it could easily be determined that the salary payments were constructive dividends to X, not deductible by the corporation, and reportable as additional income on X's return. If the salary payments were $10,000 and the corporation was in the 39 percent marginal tax bracket, then the total cost to X and Profitable Corporation would be $6,100 ($10,000 less tax of $3,900). On the other hand, if the salary payments are a constructive dividend, then the amount paid to Mom and Dad would not be deductible. It would cost the corporation a total of $10,000 in after-tax income. In addition, if X is in the 33 percent bracket, it would cost him $3,300 in additional tax. The final straw is that X would be considered as having made a gift of $10,000. The only good news in this example is that the $10,000 is within the yearly gift tax exemption (maximum of $10,000 to each individual). Thus, it will not be necessary for X to utilize any part of his unified credit or to pay any gift tax.

[402] HOW TO USE DIVIDENDS IN CREATIVE TAX PLANNING

Notwithstanding the possibility of double taxation, dividends do play an important, although sometimes not fully understood, role in tax planning. The opportunities available have been greatly enhanced by the enactment of the Tax Reform Act of 1986.

There are three types of dividends which can be distributed by the corporation: cash, property, and stock dividends. Stock dividends may or may not be a taxable event, as will be shown in ¶402.3.

Basic cash or property dividend planning usually attempts either to rectify a problem that has previously existed or to prevent a future problem from occurring. An example of rectifying a preexisting problem is where the corporation owns appreciated investment property. It is anticipated that this property will be sold in the near future. If the corporation sells the property and then distributes the net proceeds as a dividend, this typifies classic double taxation. It may be more beneficial in these instances to distribute the property as a dividend and then, at a later date, sell the property. (See ¶403.1 for a complete explanation of the benefits of this procedure.)

Dividends can be used to prevent future problems when the corporation has excessive accumulated earnings. Dividends can also lessen the possibility that salaries will be deemed unreasonable. Dividend payments in both instances provide some hedge against the imposition of an accumulated earnings tax or the Internal Revenue Service's imposition of a constructive dividend through the finding of unreasonable compensation.

The stock dividend may give rise to planning for future needs and can provide positive benefits. This planning tool may also involve the recapitalization of the corporation in conjunction with the issuance of stock dividends.

[402.1] Structuring Property Dividends to Result in Significant Tax Savings

The payment of a dividend in cash out of the earnings and profits, either current or accumulated, yields definitely determinable tax results. Dividends which may be declared and payable in the form of property complicate planning for both the corporation and the shareholders. The shareholder will have to report this distribution as dividend income at the fair market value of the property received. In addition, the difference between the fair market value and cost basis of the property distributed may also result in taxable income to the corporation.

The major considerations in making property distributions are threefold as follows:

1. The taxable effect of the distribution on the corporation
2. The taxability of the distribution to the shareholders
3. The tax basis of the property, in the hands of the shareholders

Prior to the 1984 Tax Reform Act and even after its enactment, there was the possibility in some situations to distribute appreciated property to the shareholders as a dividend and to effectively eliminate taxation on the appreciated value at the corporate level. An example of how this tax-planning technique was utilized and its benefits will illustrate the change in the law effected by the Tax Reform Act of 1986.

Example Showing the Positive Tax Planning That Could Be Effected by the Distribution of Appreciated Property as a Dividend Prior to the Enactment of the Tax Reform Act of 1986

(A) The following is an example of the wrong way of handling a property distribution before the Tax Reform Act of 1986:

Example: Active Corporation owns vacant real estate which it purchased many years ago for $5,000. It was anticipated that this property would be used for future expansion of the business, and in the interim it was used as a parking lot. The property is no longer needed, even for parking, and its current worth is $50,000. Active Corporation has decided that it would like to liquidate this real estate and distribute the net proceeds to the shareholders. If it can realize $50,000 from the sale of the land, this will result in a capital gain of $45,000. At long-term capital gains rates of 28 percent, a tax of $12,600 will result. The net dividend would be $37,400. If it is then distributed to the shareholders, all of whom are in the 50 percent bracket, they will incur a tax of $18,700 on dividend income. This leaves the shareholders with $18,700 as after-tax income.

(B) The following is an example of the proper way of handling a property distribution before the Tax Reform Act of 1986:

Example: There was a better way in certain instances of accomplishing the above transaction. The procedure if the dividend distribution would have qualified was to distribute the real property as a dividend distribution to the shareholders. If the dividend distribution qualified, there was no taxation at the corporate level. The shareholders, when they sold the property, therefore, would not realize any capital gains since their basis for the real property was $50,000. Their sole tax burden would have been $25,000, which would have resulted in a tax savings of $6,300.

(C) What is the effect of the Tax Reform Act on dividend planning for appreciated property? Basically, a distributing corporation recognizes income on the distribution to its shareholders of appreciated property no matter how the property would have been taxed previously. In other words, in the above example, the corporation would realize income at the corporate level under all circumstances.

WARNING: Any dividend distribution of appreciated property by a distributing corporation will result in income to the corporation. A possible exception would appear to be a nonliquidating distribution made by qualified corporations prior to January 1, 1989. A qualified corporation is defined as a corporation that at all times on and after August 1, 1986, has its stock owned by ten or fewer qualified persons and has a value of not more than $10 million. A qualified person means an individual, an estate, or certain trusts. It should be noted that the total benefits available to a qualifed corporation are phased out for corporations with a value of between $5 million and $10 million. Accordingly, if dividend distributions of appreciated property are contemplated by a qualified corporation before January 1, 1989, a complete analysis should be made to determine the following:

1. Whether or not the corporation is a qualified corporation
2. Whether or not the shareholders are qualified shareholders
3. Whether the distribution will be taxable at the corporate level or can escape all or a part of the corporate tax

(D) How is the individual shareholder taxed upon the receipt of a property dividend? Passing reference has been made to the tax effects of a property dividend upon its distribution to the individual shareholders. If the shareholder is an individual, trust, estate, or other noncorporate shareholder instead of a corporation, it will be taxed as an ordinary dividend to the amount of the fair market value of the property as long as the corporation has earnings and profits since February 28, 1913. If, on the other hand, the earnings and profits are insufficient to cover the full value of the property, the taxable dividend is limited to the earnings and profits. The remainder of the distribution reduces the tax basis of the stock of the shareholder. If the distribution also exceeds the tax basis, the remainder will be taxed as capital gains.

Example of How an Individual Shareholder Is Taxed upon Receipt of a Property Dividend

Example: Ordinary Corporation has been doing business for many years. It has earnings and profits since February 28, 1913, of $11,000. The corporation distributes ten acres of vacant investment property to its sole shareholder, X. The property has a basis on the books of the corporation of $15,000 and a fair market value of $15,000. X started the corporation many years ago, and his basis in the corporation is $1,000. X's taxation will be as follows:

1. $11,000 will be realized as ordinary dividend income (limited to the earnings and profits of Ordinary Corporation).
2. $1,000 will be a nontaxable return of property (the tax basis of the shareholder).
3. $3,000 will result in capital gains (15,000 − 11,000 − 1,000).

After this transaction, X will have zero basis in the stock of the corporation. The tax basis of the ten acres received by the shareholder will be $15,000.

There are three separate instances where it may be necessary and beneficial to distribute dividends in the form of cash on a regular basis, as follows:

1. The corporation has an accumulated earnings problem.
2. The specter of unreasonable compensation to the shareholders may be mitigated if not alleviated by the payment of dividends.
3. The shareholder is in a low tax bracket.

The first instance of eliminating or alleviating the accumulated earnings tax through the payment of dividends is examined in detail in Chapter 8. It is sufficient here to say that timely cash dividends reduce the earnings and profit accumulation from which this tax can be extracted. Unreasonable compensation, the second reason for dividends, has been covered in Chapter 3. The third situation and its possibilities will now be explored.

If the stock of a corporation is held by the founding father, who is no longer working for the corporation and is in a lower tax bracket, dividend payments may be appropriate. The payments of dividends may also be appropriate if the stock of the corporation is owned by another corporation. In both of these illustrations, the problem of double taxation is mitigated by the fact that both recipients are in low tax brackets.

Impact of Double Taxation Can Be Effectively Reduced If Two Conditions Are Met

1. If the corporation is in a marginal tax bracket of 25 percent or lower.
2. If the marginal tax bracket of the individual is not more than 28 percent (the net taxable income for a married taxpayer, filing a joint return in 1988, does not exceed $71,900). The impact of double taxation in this case would yield 54 percent in after-tax income to the stockholder on each dollar earned by the corporation. Thus, the tax bite, while still substantial, is not confiscatory.

Key Idea: If the corporation is in the 25 percent marginal tax bracket or less, the advantages of paying dividends to a shareholder who is receiving social security should be investigated. Dividends, since they are not earned income, do not affect the receipt of social security payments. The after-tax benefits of making dividend payments which do not have an impact on the social security payments deductible to the corporation, but at the same time, could reduce the social security benefits.

Example: XYZ Corporation has a total taxable income of $50,000 or less and therefore is in the 15 percent marginal tax bracket. Joe is over 65 (but under 70). If he were over 70 years of age, he could receive earned income and not have it affect his social security benefits. He is receiving $30,000 a year in salary and therefore does not qualify for

$12,000 of social security benefits. If his $30,000 was paid as dividends, the corporation would lose $4,500 in tax benefit (additional income $30,000 times tax rate 15 percent). Joe would receive $12,000 of social security, and at least one-half of this would be tax free.

WARNING: The Social Security Act of 1983 may have the impact of making a portion of the social security benefits which are normally tax free taxable. Up to one-half of the social security benefits may be subject to tax if the special gross income base exceeds $25,000 for single filers or $32,000 for joint filers. The special gross income base consists of:

1. A retiree's adjusted gross income (generally gross income subject to tax less deductions—the typical retiree doesn't take anyway)
2. Interest not subject to tax
3. One-half of the social security benefits

If the total of these items exceeds the $25,000 or $32,000, depending upon which is applicable, then there is an income tax on the lesser of one-half the social security benefits or one-half the excess of the special gross income base over the threshold amount. Thus, planning in this area must consider both the adverse impact of the possible reduction in social security benefits of compensation and the possibility of up to one-half of the social security benefits that may be taxed.

Note: If the shareholder is a corporation, normally 70 percent of the dividend income would be excluded from taxation. The payment of a dividend may help supply the other corporation with capital at a very low tax rate. If the dividend-paying corporation is a subsidiary, 100 percent of the dividends paid are excluded from taxation.

[402.2] Using Stock Dividends as a Planning Tool

There are many tax and nontax reasons for the issuance of a stock dividend. Among the nontax reasons are improving the capital position of the corporation, conserving cash, and dividing equity in order to allow a junior executive to purchase a portion of the business at a lower price. Until the Tax Reform Act of 1986, it appeared that except for the most sophisticated plans, which are usually inapplicable and inappropriate for the closely held business, the sole area of planning left for the use of stock dividends was in the area of estate planning. The object of this planning is to facilitate the transfer from one generation to the other with the minimum gift and estate costs. The stock dividend in estate planning is often used in conjunction with the Reorganization Section of the Internal Revenue Code, Section 368 (a)(1) E. (For a further discussion of the estate planning possibilities of using a stock dividend, see ¶403.3(d).) While the full effects of the Tax Reform Act of 1986 are not yet known, it would appear that there will be increased use of the stock dividend to help split income among family members. (A discussion of this will appear at E below.) However, OBRA 1987 has reduced the beneficial effects of stock dividends in certain recapitalizations, and care should be exercised; the current law should be reviewed before accomplishing any recapitalization.

(A) Different Types of Stock Dividends

A stock dividend has been defined as the distribution by a corporation to its shareholders of shares of its own stock or rights to subscribe to additional stock in the corporation. It should be noted that a distribution by the corporation to its shareholders of stock of another corporation is not considered a stock dividend but a property distribution. Basically there are six different types of stock dividends which may be declared and paid, as follows:

1. Common stock distributed on the outstanding common stock of the corporation. The common stock being distributed is of the same class as that which is currently outstanding.

2. Common stock paid and distributed on common stock. However, to differentiate this from 1, the common stock to be distributed is of a different category or class, such as nonvoting common or voting common stock.

3. Common stock distributed on the currently outstanding common stock.

4. Preferred stock distributed on the currently outstanding common stock.

5. Preferred stock distributed on preferred stock in the same class as the outstanding stock on which it is paid.

6. Preferred stock distributed on a different class of outstanding preferred stock.

(B) Basic Rules and Provisions Governing Taxation of the Distribution of Stock Dividends

Two sections of the Internal Revenue Code assume an important role in determining the feasibility of utilizing the stock dividend in tax planning. These are Sections 305 and 306. Section 305 sets forth the general rule that a distribution of stock or stock rights as dividends issued by a corporation with respect to its own stock is nontaxable. It also sets forth the exceptions to this rule. Thus, a stock dividend is tax free unless:

1. There is a provision of any kind allowing any one or all of its shareholders to make an election to receive payment in cash or stock.
2. The distribution results in the receipt of property, including cash, by some shareholders and an increase in the proportionate interest of other shareholders.
3. The distribution results in the receipt of preferred stock by some common shareholders and common stock by other common shareholders.
4. The stock distributed is convertible and the plan of distribution is such that the proportionate share of ownership of some shareholders will be increased while the other shareholders receive property in compensation for dilution of their proportionate share of ownership.

The following situations illustrate these rules as they apply to various types of stock dividends:

Situation 1: Profitable Corporation is in a highly capital-intensive industry. While its earnings are more than sufficient to justify the payment of cash dividends, its cash position is poor, and the directors decide to issue stock dividends in lieu of the cash dividend it had been paying. It has only one class of stock, and this is voting common stock. The directors authorize and the corporation pays a 10 percent stock dividend.

Result: This is the most common example of nontaxable common stock dividend issued on common stock.

Situation 2: Profitable Corporation, instead of issuing only common stock as a stock dividend on the outstanding stock, gives the shareholders of record an option of either receiving the 10 percent common stock dividend or $2 per share in cash.

Result: All stock and cash dividends are taxable pursuant to Section 305(b)(1), providing that if a distribution is, at the election of any of the shareholders, payable in either the corporation's stock or in cash, it is treated as a taxable distribution.

Situation 3: Profitable Corporation has two classes of stock. These classes are identical, except that one class receives cash dividends and the other class receives stock dividends in a like amount.

Result: All dividends are taxable because the proportionate interest of the shareholders receiving a stock dividend will be increased each and every time they receive a dividend.

Situation 4: Profitable Corporation issues to all its common shareholders, preferred stock in the amount of $100 per share.

Result: As long as all shareholders receive the same proportionate share of the issued stock, there will be no taxation. However, the sale or disposition of this stock will be taxable pursuant to Section 306. The impact of having stock classified as Section 306 stock will be discussed immediately following these situations.

Situation 5: The directors of Profitable Corporation decide to increase the proportion of earnings retained in the business by restricting future cash dividends paid on their common stock. Accordingly, they grant the option to their common shareholders of either retaining their common shares and not receiving any future dividend income or converting them into preferred stock which has a stated dividend rate.

Result: While this is not, in reality, a stock dividend but a reorganization under Section 368(a)(1)E, it has some of the characteristics of a stock dividend. (This particular technique is discussed in Chapter 6.) The taxability and the status of the preferred stock (whether it shall be categorized as Section 306 stock) must be determined on a case-by-case basis.

The distribution of tax-free dividends set forth in Situations 1, 4, and 5 has as its goal either or both of the following:

1. Estate planning. The dividend procedure may be utilized to lock in the value of the stock owned by the older generation. By converting stock with unlimited ability to appreciate, such as common stock, to stock with a fixed value, such as preferred, all future appreciation will be attributable solely to the owners of the common stock. OBRA 1987 has had a negative impact on this planning.

2. Profitable corporation may wish to acknowledge the fact that the income of the corporation would justify the payment of dividends. However, the funds are not available to pay cash dividends because of the internal needs of the business.

The remaining situations set forth above which produce taxable income are rarely used in small corporations where dividends are usually avoided whenever possible.

(C) Taxation of Section 306 Preferred Stock

Section 306 stock is any preferred stock received as a non-taxable stock dividend at a time when the corporation has earnings and profits. The classic method of distributing the preferred stock can be seen in Situation 4. Situation 5 may or may not involve preferred stock which will be issued with the Section 306 taint. Section 306 does not make the receipt of the preferred stock taxable. However, the disadvantages of 306 appear when the stock is disposed of by sale or redemption. In general, the proceeds of the sale or redemption are treated as ordinary income and not as capital gains.

There are several exceptions to Section 306 which will allow for capital gains instead of ordinary income treatment upon disposition. The major applicable exceptions are as follows:

1. If a shareholder dies owning Section 306 stock, this Section 306 taint dies with him. His successors in interest would take the stock free and clear of the Section 306 liability.

2. The stockholder sells his *entire* interest in the corporation to a nonrelated party.

3. The corporation redeems all preferred (Section 306 stock) and other stock of the shareholder.

4. The corporation redeems its Section 306 stock in a bona fide, complete, or partial liquidation of the corporation.

5. A transaction occurs in which neither gain nor loss is recognized.

6. The stock is disposed of in a transaction which did not have as one of its principal purposes the avoidance of federal income tax.

(D) Use of Stock Dividends in Estate Planning

Current income tax planning gives rise to little utilization of the stock dividend. Estate planning does allow for effective use of the stock dividend.

The following is an example using the stock dividend in an estate plan:

Example: Profitable Corporation, whose sole shareholder is X, has been in operation for many years. X is 59 years old and is considering retirement in the near future. X's son, Y, has been working for the corporation for a number of years. X now considers it time to transfer effective operational control from himself to Y. He also wants to gift as much of the stock as possible to Y and still retain income sufficient to maintain his life-style. One of the suggested solutions to this problem would be for Profitable Corporation to issue preferred stock. Assume that Profitable Corporation's capital structure was as follows:

Common Stock

Paid-in capital	$100,000
Retained Earnings	500,000

If Profitable Corporation issues $500,000 of preferred stock bearing dividends at the rate of 7 percent per annum, the corporation could issue a preferred dividend to X. X could either sell or gift to his son the common stock in Profitable Corporation. All future appreciation in value of the corporation would be attributable to the common stock. Since the common stock would be transferred to his son, X will receive no future appreciation in his estate, and the value of his ownership in the corporation is fixed at the amount of the preferred stock he has received. This preferred stock should produce $35,000 of dividends to him each year. This should be sufficient to maintain his life-style. Without a doubt, the preferred stock issued under this plan has the Section 306 taint attached to it. However, at a future date, this taint may be removed either by death or upon the complete redemption of this stock under Section 302(b)(3).

OBRA 1987 has attempted to eliminate this technique as an effective estate planning tool. In any transfer where a person transfers a disproportionately large share of the subject subject to appreciation while retaining a disproportionately large share of the income producing stock, the taxpayer will be treated as having retained a taxable interest in his estate for estate tax purposes.

WARNING: While in the past the Internal Revenue Service had ruled on whether or not a recapitalization was taxable or nontaxable as a reorganization and whether or not stock issued would or would not be considered Section 306 stock, in 1983 it indicated that it would no longer rule in this area. It should be noted that even though the IRS did rule as to the income tax effects of these reorganizations, it never did rule on whether or not a gift had resulted from the recapitalization. Accordingly, in the future, these recapitalizations are going to require a good deal of care. The only effective way of proceeding may be to obtain attorneys' opinions as to the income tax effects of the reorganization.

For example, if Profitable Corporation in the above example is worth $600,000, this value must be allocated between the common and the preferred stock. Because the $500,000 of preferred stock bears a dividend of only 7 percent, the preferred stock will not be worth its face value and will have a valuation of significantly less than $500,000. It would be unusual under current market conditions for this preferred stock to be worth anywhere near its face value, and it would not be at all unusual for it to be discounted. Thus, assuming that the preferred stock under current market conditions was valued at $400,000, the common stock would be worth $200,000, and any sale for less than that amount would have gift tax implications. The terms and conditions of the preferred stock, such as voting rights, dividend rates, period of redemption, and the general economic environment all have relevance as to the valuation of the preferred stock.

This is a satisfactory solution only in those situations where the appreciation in the value of the stock is occurring at a rapid rate. If the corporation's future is in doubt and the earnings and profits vary from year to year, there may be other more appropriate methods of shifting the control. **Warning:** Before any recapitalization is attempted, the tax implications of OBRA 1987 should be reviewed.

(E) Effect of the Tax Reform Act of 1986 on the Utilization of Stock Dividends in Effective Income Tax Planning

It would appear that with the enactment of the Tax Reform Act of 1986, the positive utilization of stock dividends in income tax planning may increase. The major problem with issuing preferred stock that had the Section 306 taint (see C earlier) is the fact that the sale or transfer of the stock would normally give rise to ordinary income instead of capital gains. With the enactment of the Tax Reform Act of 1986, which removed the beneficial tax treatment of capital gains, (after 1987) Section 306, unless the law changes again, will have minimum negative effect on future planning.

While the full impact of the law is obviously currently unknown, planning such as the following may have increased validity: It should also be noted that Congress is contemplating limiting this technique. Care and a current review of the law in this area is a necessity.

> **Example:** Son, who is married, owns all of the stock of XYZ Corporation. XYZ Corporation is in the 15 percent tax bracket. He wishes to contribute $10,000 a year to the support of his parents. Son is in the 33 percent marginal tax bracket.
>
> *Method 1:* His tax advisor informs Son that he can increase his salary by $10,000 without risk that the increase will be considered as unreasonable compensation. If Son proceeds in this manner, the tax effect is as follows:
>
> | | |
> |---|---:|
> | Additional Income to Son | $10,000 |
> | Tax 33 percent | 3,330 |
> | After-Tax Proceeds | $6,700 |
>
> Gift to parents of $6,700 will not create any additional taxable income

Method 2: XYZ Corporation accomplishes a reorganization and issues to Son in addition to all of the common stock he owns in XYZ Corporation $100,000 of 10 percent preferred stock. Son then transfers to his parents $100,000 of this stock (note that with a gift splitting and the utilization of the $10,000 yearly exemption, probably no more than $20,000 of the gift would result in a reduction of the unified credit if the gift is made in two years). The $10,000 of income can come from XYZ Corporation. If we further assume that the parents have no taxable income except for social security and that dividends are paid in 1988, the tax ramifications would be:

Income to XYZ Corporation	$10,000	
LESS:		
Corporate Income Tax	1,500	
Available for Dividends	$ 8,500	
Taxation of Dividends at the Parents' Level		$ 8,500
Standard Deduction	$ 5,000	
Plus Two Additional Exemptions for Over Age 65	$ 1,200	
Two Exemptions	$ 3,900	$10,100
		–0–

Method 3: Issuance of noncumulative preferred stock with a dividend rate at 8½ percent. XYZ Corporation can issue $80,000 of noncumulative preferred stock with an 8½ percent dividend rate. Each year, $6,800 of dividends could be paid, and a portion of the preferred stock could be redeemed. Since there is no longer any benefit from capital gains, this would produce the same tax result as set forth in method 2.

An additional benefit from the planning set forth in Methods 2 and 3 other than the tax savings of approximately $1,800 is that if the parents own the stock and at death their will leaves the stock to Son, he will receive a step-up in basis of the stock without any capital gains or ordinary income tax. In all likelihood, the owner of a closely held corporation's basis in the stock is small. In the above example, if the basis of the preferred stock value $100,000 was $10,000, this step-up in basis can be worth as much as $29,700 in the future. (Gain on sale of stock $100,000 less $10,000 basis equals $90,000 of gain. If Son's marginal tax bracket is 33 percent, this will produce $29,700 in tax savings.) Note that this step-up in basis will not occur if the preferred stock is reacquired by the son within one year of the date of the original gift.

Obviously planning such as the above has particular relevance not only with the parents but also with children over the age of 14. Utilizing the same scenario as set forth above, the gift of the preferred stock could be made to the minor children, and the preferred stock can either bear dividends or be redeemed. It should be noted that to get any benefit under the Tax Reform Act of 1986 requires the preferred stock to be gifted to children over age 14. Children under the age of 14 would be paying tax at the marginal tax rate of the parents. Also, the major benefit in utilization of the parents involves the fact that both personal exemptions and the standard deduction could be utilized. In the case of children, either over or under the age of 14, neither of these benefits could be derived. However, some tax savings should be accomplished in any event. An exact determination can be made only on a case-by-case basis.

Obviously, the above planning is for the more adventuresome and not for those timid of heart. It is difficult at this time to contemplate how the IRS would react to planning such as this because this type of planning would circumvent Congress's intent.

In conclusion, dividends can fulfill a whole range of goals for you. They can range from preventive measures to ensuring that the shareholders and officers of a corporation avoid the disaster of constructive dividends and instead use affirmative tax-planning opportunities, such as preferred stock dividends on common stock, to accomplish estate tax-planning goals. Your major goal in dividend planning should be an awareness of both the pitfalls and the planning opportunities that can be fulfilled by dividend payments. The preventive cash dividend, used to alleviate the possibility of the imposition of an accumulated earnings tax, is just as important as the dividend payment to a lower basis retired taxpayer to ensure the maintenance of his life-style. Finally, in the proper situation, you should not overlook the positive benefits of a property dividend to reduce the overall tax burden, even though the full planning opportunities are still unknown.

5

How to Utilize the Subchapter S Corporation to Obtain a Cash Flow without Double Taxation

[500] HOW THE S CORPORATION CAN BE AN EFFECTIVE TAX PLANNING TOOL

The entity designated as an S Corporation and sometimes also referred to as a Subchapter S Corporation or Small Business Corporation has been an integral part of the tax laws since enactment in 1958. Until the passage of the Tax Reform Act of 1986, the business community was only peripherally aware of the utilization of this entity in tax planning. In 1958, Congress enacted Section 1371 through 1378 of the Internal Revenue Code with the stated objective to "permit businesses to select the form of business organization desired, without the necessity of taking into account major differences in tax consequences." In other words, the S Corporation is a hybrid means of doing business. It is treated as a combination of partnership, sole proprietorship, and corporate forms. These sections permit certain corporations to elect not to be taxed at the corporate level. As a result, corporate income or loss is divided among the shareholders pro rata, considering both the percentage of ownership and the portion of the year the stock was owned by the shareholder. The allocable share is taxed to the shareholder individually whether or not it is distributed as dividends.

Misunderstanding the application of the Subchapter S provisions has discouraged its use in appropriate instances. The most common misconception is that by electing as an S

Corporation, you have destroyed the state law characteristics of the corporation, and therefore the nontax advantages of incorporating are lost. (See ¶101.1.) The truth is, the nontax advantages of incorporating, such as limited liability, are not disturbed by the election.

Congress's stated intent was to eliminate taxation as a factor in incorporating by enacting the Subchapter S provisions. In doing so, it had provided you with another tool which, if properly utilized, can produce significant benefits. However, care should be taken in dealing with the S Corporation. It was always difficult to deal with, and the Subchapter S Revision Act of 1982 and the Tax Reform Act of 1986 have had significant effects on some of the historical tax advantages of the S Corporation. For example, prior to enactment of the Subchapter S Revision Act of 1982, the S Corporation was entitled to virtually all fringe benefits of regular corporations (now referred to as C Corporations). However, for a 2 percent or more shareholder, the 1982 act has adversely affected the deductibility of such previously deductible items as medical insurance and group term life insurance. The Tax Reform Act of 1986 has added a new area of problems. These problems expand upon the events which not only will result in taxation to the shareholders but also result in taxable income to the corporation.

Until the passage of the Subchapter S Revision Act of 1982, the laws regulating Subchapter S Corporations had remained virtually unchanged for over twenty years. The terminology, concepts, and planning strategies in this area became thoroughly ingrained in the thinking of most tax planners. Thus, at this time I have chosen to build on this prior knowledge by explaining how thinking and planning must now be adjusted to take into account the new laws rather than addressing the old-law concepts. If you are familiar with the old Subchapter S regulations, you will find it easier to learn how you must now adjust your thinking and planning to take into account the new regulations. If you are new to the area of Subchapter S Corporations, the explanation of the old law will give you the conceptual framework you will need to understand the implications of the opportunities and pitfalls opened up by the new laws.

Because of the relative newness of the 1982 and 1986 acts, many of the regulations in this area have not yet been implemented or interpreted by the courts. Therefore, the full implications of the new law on tax planning are not yet totally clear, so the suggestions made in this chapter will be on the conservative side.

[501]   HOW THE S CORPORATION SHOULD BE USED

[501.1]   Inherent Dangers of Electing to Be Taxed as a Subchapter S Corporation

The Subchapter S Corporation provides substantial benefits for you during the three stages of corporate existence: inception, operation, and liquidation.

One of the major advantages of the S Corporation is that, unlike the regular corporation, it is not subject to double taxation on its earnings—once at the corporate level and again at the shareholder level. One major exception to this general rule is that the Tax Reform Act of 1986 has imposed at the time of sale a tax at the corporate level on the preelection built in gains. (The gain subject to tax, as well as the tax rate, is fully discussed in ¶505.2.)

WARNING: The rules and regulations governing the election, qualification, and continued existence of an S Corporation are complex. It is not unheard of for a corporation which has validly elected and qualified as an S Corporation to have its election inadvertently terminated. This can have disastrous consequences. The corporation may suddenly find itself subject to corporate taxes.

The Subchapter S Revision Act of 1982 attempted to alleviate the problem of inadvertent terminations by easing some of the requirements for continued qualification as an S Corporation and by making reelection easier for the inadvertently terminated S Corporation. For example, prior to the Subchapter S Revision Act of 1982, if more than 20 percent of the total income of a Subchapter S Corporation was from passive sources in any one year, the election was terminated. After the act, in order for a termination to be triggered by excess passive income, the corporation must have earnings and profits during three consecutive years and must have more than 25 percent of its total income from passive sources. Obviously, this change makes planning and avoidance of inadvertent termination considerably easier.

In addition, in the past it was virtually impossible to reelect Subchapter S status once the election was terminated for at least five years. Reelection under the Subchapter S Revision Act is significantly easier. (For a more in-depth discussion of the impact of the Subchapter S Revision Act on planning in this area, see ¶504.1.)

Example Showing Why Care Must Be Taken so That the Proper Election Has Been Made

Example: X, who owns all the stock of XYZ corporation, elects Subchapter S status for XYZ. During a three-year period, XYZ Corporation earns $50,000 each and every year. X believes that XYZ is a validly elected S Corporation. The corporation distributes $150,000 in dividends. X is in the 33 percent bracket. He pays $49,500 of tax on the $150,000 dividend income. Unfortunately, the IRS determines that the corporation has not validly elected Subchapter S status. Accordingly, it taxes the $50,000 of earned income to the corporation in each year and assesses $22,500 as tax plus interest and penalties.

Alternative Planning is Self-evident. If X had known that the corporation was not an S Corporation, he would have attempted to pay himself a reasonable salary or would have paid no salary to himself and accumulated the earnings and profits in the corporation. In either instance, the total tax on the shareholder and corporation would have been significantly reduced.

This example illustrates the care which must be exercised in dealing with the S Corporation. As noted in Chapter 4, this double taxation limits the usefulness of dividends as a planning tool for the C Corporation. However, since there is no taxation at the corporate level for an S Corporation, dividends play an important role in the S Corporation both in tax planning and in the funding of benefits.

[501.2] Strategies for Gaining Maximum Tax Savings through the Subchapter S Corporation

With necessity for care in the election and operation of the S Corporation firmly established, it is now incumbent to consider its proper utilization. Under the proper circumstances, its benefits may be incalculable. Unlike other areas of tax planning which allow for correction of prior mistakes, planning opportunities involving the Subchapter S Corporation, if not utilized at the proper time, may be lost forever.

Operating Losses Can Be Used for the Shareholder's Benefit

Operating losses of the Subchapter S Corporation flow through to the individual shareholders. The taxation of an S Corporation provides that both income and losses are allocated to the individual shareholders of the corporation. Accordingly, if either at the inception of the corporation or during its operation, it is anticipated that the corporation will operate at a loss, the election as an S Corporation is particularly valuable. These losses directly reduce the shareholder's taxes on other income. The only problem which may occur is that the losses are limited to the shareholder's individual basis in the stock and loans to the corporation. After 1982, the excess may be carried forward indefinitely for use in future years.

The following shows how losses are utilized:

Example: XYZ Corporation, a validly electing Subchapter S Corporation, has an operating loss of $50,000 in the year 1979. X owns 50 percent of the issued and outstanding common stock of the corporation. He is, therefore, allocated $25,000 of the loss to be applied against his other income. If he is in the 33 percent tax bracket, this will produce a $16,500 tax savings.

Key Idea: If the closely held corporation anticipates operating losses in the future, and if the individual shareholder has income from other sources, a Subchapter S election should be contemplated to offset his other income with the loss from the Subchapter S Corporation.

For all years ending in 1982 and before, in the event that the shareholder's loss exceeded the adjusted basis of the stock he owned plus his adjusted basis in the corporation's debt, the loss was lost forever. Since 1983, loss pass-throughs in excess of the current deductible amount can be carried forward indefinitely. This presents the tax planner with various interesting planning tools.

Key Idea: A shareholder of a Subchapter S Corporation that has a pass-through loss in excess of his basis in the corporate stock and debt can get a deduction in any year he wants by simply contributing additional funds to the corporation.

Example: The year was a bad one for S Corporation, a qualifying Subchapter S Corporation and its sole shareholder, Y. S Corporation has a loss of $20,000, and Y can use only $10,000 of that loss as his basis in the stock, and debt is $10,000. His other income in 1984 is negligible. However, in 1985, while S Corporation does not make any money, Y's other income is substantial. By conveying to the corporation $10,000 of cash, he can reduce his taxable income by $10,000.

Key Idea: Under the same factual circumstances as in the example above, instead of contributing the $10,000 as additional equity, Y loans the money to the corporation in 1985. Accordingly, the $10,000 loss that was carried over from 1984 can be taken as a loss in 1985. This will reduce his other income by $10,000. Now let's assume that in 1986, the corporation has zero taxable income and distributes to him the $10,000 in payment of debt. Y has received a corporate distribution in excess of his basis. This $10,000 should be taxable to him as capital gain.

WARNING: The Tax Reform Act of 1986 has imposed limitations on passive activity losses. Thus, before it can be considered that this loss will be "passed through" and applied to the other earned and portfolio income of the taxpayer, it is necessary to determine whether or not this loss is a passive loss under the terms of the act. If it is a passive loss, the amount of the loss that can be applied to the other income is limited during the years 1987 through 1990 to prescribed percentages. During those years, the portion of the disallowed loss can be carried forward, and after that time, the entire loss can be carried forward.

The thrust of the law is to allow only passive losses to be utilized against passive activity gains. Needless to say, the planning that would produce an S Corporation loss with the intent to currently utilize 100 percent of this loss against other income will be disrupted if this loss cannot be utilized in the current year, but all or a part must be carried forward. Accordingly, any S Corporation that is going to produce losses with the concept of utilizing this against other income should be closely monitored.

> **Example:** XYZ Corporation, a C Corporation, anticipates losses in the next three years. Joe, the sole shareholder, will be in the 33 percent marginal tax bracket. If XYZ Corporation elects S status and has a $10,000 loss in each of the three years, Joe's anticipated tax savings will be $9,900 ($30,000 times 33 percent). If the loss cannot be utilized because of the passive activity restrictions and is carried forward to a year when Joe is in the 15 percent tax bracket, his benefit will be reduced to $4,500.

Shareholders in a Lower Tax Bracket Can Use Subchapter S to Save Taxes

The officer/shareholder may no longer be able to receive income from the corporation through the payment of compensation. The services he is rendering no longer justify the payment of a substantial salary. In this case, the election as a Subchapter S Corporation may be appropriate. An example will illustrate the particular benefits.

Example of Benefits to Be Gained by the Lower Tax Bracket Shareholder

Example: Passive is the sole shareholder of Subchapter S Corporation. Passive's outside income is minimal, save and except for his salary from Subchapter S Corporation. He is retiring to Florida. It is anticipated that his son, Active, will manage the business. Passive wishes to retain an income from the corporation to support himself during retirement. If Subchapter S Corporation elects to be taxed as a small business corporation, the dividend income will not be taxed first to the corporation and then to the shareholder. It can be taxed directly to the shareholders. This eliminates double taxation. Assume that Subchapter S Corporation earns $50,000 after a reasonable salary payment to Passive's son, Active. As a regular corporation which has not elected Subchapter S status, only $42,500 would be available for dividend payments ($50,000 income less $7,500 income tax). As a Subchapter S Corporation, all $50,000 can be utilized.

Key Idea: If a shareholder in a corporation retires, and if he does not have sufficient outside income to support himself, a Subchapter S election should be contemplated to avoid double taxation on the dividend distribution to the retired shareholder or the possibility that any salary paid to him would be considered unreasonable compensation.

Social Security Benefits Are Not Disturbed by Subchapter S Dividends

In a case similar to that in the one above, Passive, the sole shareholder, may be able to justify a reasonable salary payment during his retirement years. This is particularly true when Passive is commuting between his major residence and his retirement home. However, these salary payments may be counterproductive. Any salary payments he receives may reduce his current social security payments. In 1987, every dollar earned as salary in excess of $8,160 a year by a taxpayer 65 or older will reduce his benefits by 50¢ until it completely eliminates any social security benefits he is entitled to. If, on the other hand, he receives dividend income through Subchapter S distributions, this may have no effect on his social security payments. Notwithstanding this fact, the receipt of social security benefits, which are normally completely nontaxable, may be taxable up to one-half of the social security amount received. After 1983, in the event that the taxpayer receives $25,000 for single taxpayers or $32,000 for married of special gross income, there is an income tax on the lesser of one-half of the social security benefits or one-half of the excess of the special gross income base over either the $25,000 or $32,000 figures, whichever is applicable.

Key Idea: Unlike salary, Subchapter S distributions do not reduce the social security benefits owed to a retired shareholder.

NOTE: It is important to note that the only time that salary reduces the amount of the social security benefits that can be received is the period commencing when the taxpayer first qualifies at age 62 through age 70. After reaching that age, the individual can collect full social security no matter how much he earns. Accordingly, the use of the Subchapter S election for this particular purpose may be of rather short duration.

Accumulated Earnings Tax Can Be Avoided by Electing Subchapter S Status

If a corporation is running the risk of the imposition of an accumulated earnings tax on its earnings and profits (see Chapter 8), it is possible to avoid the imposition of the tax by having the corporation elect the Subchapter S status. Future earnings and profits will not be subject to this tax.

Key Idea: A corporation which may be subject to an unreasonable accumulated earnings tax should consider the election as a Subchapter S Corporation. A Subchapter S Corporation is not subject to an accumulated earnings tax.

Certain S Corporations may still reap benefits for fringes paid for the benefit of their shareholder/employees.

The Subchapter S Revision Act of 1982 has had a substantial impact on the use of fringe benefits for Subchapter S corporations and employees who own more than 2 percent of the stock. Prior to 1983, various fringe benefits applied to all employees of Subchapter S Corporations to the same extent as employees of regular corporations whether or not they were also shareholders of the corporation.

Among others, these included the following:

1. The $5,000 death benefit exclusion provided in Section 101(d) of the Internal Revenue Code
2. The accident and health provisions of the Internal Revenue Code Sections 105 and 106
3. Group term life insurance
4. Exclusion from income for meals and lodging provided for the convenience of the employer

The Subchapter S Revision Act now completely changes the treatment of these fringe benefits to any person owning more than 2 percent of the stock of the Subchapter S Corporation. These individuals will generally be treated in the same manner as a partner in a partnership. The amount paid for these employees will be included as income.

Example: Y, the sole shareholder of Subchapter S Corporation in 1984, received $50,000 in salary, and the corporation paid $1,500 in health insurance for him and all other employees of the corporation. Prior to 1983, the $1,500 would have been a deductible expense for the corporation and would not have been included in the income of Y. Commencing in 1983, he will report the $50,000 as income plus the $1,500 of health insurance payments as additional income.

There appears to be little benefit or positive planning that can be utilized in this particular change. It will now be necessary for all new corporations electing Subchapter S status to reevaluate the amount of the fringe benefits which are currently deductible and the cost to the individual shareholders if the Subchapter S election is made. Some small relief is provided for currently electing Subchapter S corporations.

Key Idea: If a corporation was a qualified Subchapter S Corporation as of September 28, 1982, the new fringe benefit rules will apply only for years beginning after 1987. There are some restrictions to the utilization of this transitional rule. However, if a corporation is a Subchapter S Corporation and if it had fringe benefits in effect prior to September 28, 1982, before changing, amending, or in any way affecting these plans or the Sub S status, you should review the law.

NOTE: The Tax Reform Act of 1986 has imposed nondiscrimination rules for statutory employee benefit plans including health insurance, group term life, benefits under group legal service plans, educational assistance programs, and dependent care or assistant care programs. These provisions are currently projected to take effect on 12/31/88. All corporations, be they S or C Corporations, are of necessity going to have to review their entire fringe benefit program in light of the new provisions imposed by the Tax Reform Act of 1986.

It Is Possible to Shift Income to Lower Base Taxpayers

As in the following illustration, the S Corporation can be used to shift the income to the shareholder's children. The following is an example of how to divide income among shareholder's children:

Example: X is the sole shareholder of two corporations, Capital-Intensive Corporation and Service Corporation. Capital-Intensive Corporation is a manufacturing corporation that generates substantial income ($100,000 before taxes but after salary payment to X). All the net income must be retained for business expansion. Service Corporation, on the other hand, is a distributor of widgets (manufactured by Capital-Intensive Corporation) and generates approximately $50,000 a year after salary payments but before income tax. There is no need for business purposes to retain this income for expansion. X is married and has four children. If Service Corporation had been a Subchapter S Corporation with X being allocated the income, the tax which would have been incurred (assuming 33 percent marginal tax bracket), would have been $16,500. A good planning technique would be for X to gift to each of the children who are 14 or older 10 percent of the outstanding stock of Service Corporation. After the gift, X would own 60 percent of the outstanding stock of the corporation. The tax on the $30,000 of allocable income to him would be $9,900. Each of his four children (who for the purpose of this example we will assume have no other income) would report $5,000 of income on their individual return, and each would pay less than $750 in tax. The total family group tax liability would be reduced from $16,500 to $12,900.

The above example illustrates not only the use of the S Corporation to shift income among the family group but also the use of multiple corporations. There are restrictions to the use of these savings. The optimum planning device is to have all the income as dividend income because it reduces the family's overall tax burden. In the above example, we assumed X had been paid a resonable salary. The IRS imposes the restriction that the corporation pay a reasonable salary to the individual officers. This position has been reinforced and expanded by the Subchapter S Revision Act of 1982. Now, adjustments may be made for the value of capital contributed as well as services rendered. Income can be reallocated even if the party rendering the services or contributing capital is not a shareholder.

WARNING: The Tax Reform Act of 1986 has had substantial detrimental effects upon this planning. The major impact on this planning is felt in the following two separate and distinct areas:

1. The corporate tax being higher than the individual tax
2. The "kiddy" tax

The first problem has already been addressed. The second imposes a marginal tax rate on the family unit rather than on the individuals. The Tax Reform Act of 1986 taxes net unearned income for a child under the age of 14 at the parents' marginal tax rate. In the above example, if the children had been under the age of 14 rather than over the age of 14, there would have been no tax benefit from the allocation of income to the children.

When There Is a Tax at the Corporate Level
for S Corporations

The Tax Reform Act of 1986 has had a significant impact upon the taxation of the S Corporation upon sale of appreciated property. This act has significantly changed the law as far as the ability of a prior C Corporation to elect S status, to sell appreciated property, and avoid tax at the corporate level. In order to understand the full impact of the new law, it is necessary to analyze the act's provisions, the prior provisions, and the ability of certain small corporations to currently avoid the full impact of the change in the law at least until January 1, 1989.

The new act imposes a corporate level tax on pre-S election appreciation (known in the act as built-in gain) if the assets are disposed of within ten years after the corporation has become an S Corporation. The gains on the disposition of assets are presumed to be built in except to the extent the taxpayer can establish that the appreciation occurred after the S election (such as where the asset was acquired by the entity in taxable acquisition after the S election). The tax rate imposed upon the gain is the maximum corporate tax rate for the year in which the sale occurs applied to the lesser of (a) the recognized built-in gains or (b) the amount that would be the taxable income of the corporation if the entity was not an S Corporation. This obviously has a significant impact upon those corporations which wish to elect S status to avoid the corporate level gain. The change in Section 1374 is part of Congress's overall intent to repeal the effects of the General Utilities Doctrine which also has had a significant impact upon liquidations under Section 331, Section 333, and Section 337, all of which are discussed in Chapter 7.

The new law came into effect for corporations on January 1, 1987. However, a qualified corporation is allowed to avoid the full impact of this act if it elects Sub S status prior to January 1, 1989. A qualified corporation includes any corporation if, on August 1, 1986, and at all times thereafter, more than 50 percent (by value) of its stock is held by ten or fewer qualified persons and the applicable value of the corporation does not exceed $10,000,000. Full relief is allowed only for corporations with a value not in excess of $5 million.

Since the act's relative newness, it is impossible yet to determine exactly how the new act will be interpreted. There seems to be no doubt that the concept of gains includes both long-term capital gains, short-term capital gains, and ordinary income. The question becomes: How will this transitional rule of the new law be interpreted? The current interpretation seems to be that long-term capital gains will be excluded from tax treatment; however, the penalty tax would apply to the ordinary income and short-term gains.

Even with the partial relief of the transitional rule, you should still be aware that the Internal Revenue Code imposes restrictions upon the utilization of this election to avoid double taxation upon the sale of long-term capital gain property. If the net capital gains in any one year are less than $25,000, there will be no additional tax consequences. If they exceed $25,000, Section 1378(b) and other relevant sections should be reviewed to determine whether or not the restrictions set forth in these sections can be complied with and still retain the contemplated benefits. The utilization of an installment sale allocating a certain amount of capital gain to each and every year should also be explored when contemplating the sale of appreciated property in conjunction with a Subchapter S election.

Key Idea: If a qualified C Corporation has "built-in long-term capital gains," it should consider electing S status prior to January 1, 1989.

Key Idea: The qualified C Corporation may be required to make an S election for the years beginning before 1989. Care should be exercised since the terminology of the Tax Reform Act of 1986 is unclear. It appears that the election must be made during 1988 and be effective for the corporate year beginning in 1988. Accordingly, an election made during December 1988, while it is effective for the plan year beginning January 1, 1989, may not protect the new S corporation from taxation on preelection gains. Regulations may be enacted to indicate whether or not such an election would be effective.

S Corporations Must Adopt Permitted Taxable Year

Prior to the Tax Reform Act of 1986, many S Corporations were "grandfathered" and had fiscal years other than a permitted taxable year. The 1986 Tax Reform Act has altered this procedure, and now all S Corporations must have a permitted year for the taxable years beginning after 1986. A permitted year is either a "calendar" year or any other accounting year for which the corporation shows a business purpose that is satisfactory to the IRS. Accordingly, the Tax Reform Act of 1986 has provided the same tax treatment for partnerships, personal service corporations, and sole proprietorships. Only C Corporations that are "not personal service corporations" appear to have the flexibility of choosing a year without regard to IRS regulations.

OBRA 1987 provides that a partnership, S corporation, or personal service corporation that is otherwise required to change to a calendar year can elect to retain the tax year it used for the last tax year beginning in 1986. OBRA 1987 permits these entities to retain fiscal years, as long as there is a deferral of deduction for payments to owner/employees, if disproportionately high payments occur toward the end of the fiscal year. If a Sub S corporation has substantial nontax reasons for a fiscal year, the provisions of OBRA 1987 should be reviewed.

Net Operating Losses Can Be Carried Forward Indefinitely

The Subchapter S Revision Act of 1982 turned a prior disadvantage into a positive attribute of the Subchapter S Corporation. For all tax years beginning before 1983, a net operating loss could not be carried forward. During this time, a loss in excess of the shareholder's basis could not be utilized in the year in which the loss occurred. This is the same under current law. However, under prior law, this loss could not be carried forward and thus was lost forever. There were two methods of avoiding this prior to the Subchapter S Revision Act of 1982. At a time when the shareholder's basis in the corporation was minimal, it was beneficial for him to terminate the Subchapter S election. As an alternative, the shareholder who anticipated a loss in excess of his basis could contribute additional capital or could have loaned money to the corporation. This would have allowed for the full utilization in the year.

As noted above, the new law does continue the prior rules that limit the deduction that a Subchapter S shareholder can claim to the amount of his adjusted basis in the stock that he owns plus the adjusted basis in any debt the corporation owes him. However, the positive impact of the Subchapter S Revision Act is that the loss in excess of the basis is not lost. It can be carried forward indefinitely and allowed in any subsequent year in which the shareholder has adequate basis in his stock and debt.

The change in the law allows a shareholder with a pass-through loss to time a deduction. All he has to do in a subsequent year is convey property to the corporation. This increases his basis and allows for a deduction in that year. In the alternative, of course, this loss can be used against a future gain in the corporation. The full range of planning techniques offered by this change in the law are just now beginning to show themselves to the tax practitioner.

Election as a Subchapter S Corporation Can Allow for a Change of Accounting Methods and Techniques

Incorporating can permit the corporation to change accounting methods which would not otherwise be allowed without the prior consent of the Internal Revenue Service.

At times, a taxpayer wishes to make a change in accounting procedure that normally would require Internal Revenue Service approval. However, if he incorporates the business, the new entity will be able to adopt its own accounting procedures even if they deviate from the procedures previously adopted by the sole proprietorship or partnership.

The following is an example of the accounting procedures that could be changed in this instance:

1. If the business had previously elected to report its inventory on a LIFO basis and if now wishes to change to FIFO.
2. The business has been reporting on a cash basis and wishes to adopt accrual, or vice versa.

The above is not an inclusive list of the financial advantages of the Subchapter S Corporation but solely those major techniques which can be used. A Subchapter S Corporation can provide the flexible tool needed alone or in conjunction with another corporation, partnership, or trust which can result in significant tax savings.

[501.3]   Considering the Disadvantages Prior to Electing to Be a Subchapter S Corporation

In addition to the care which must be exercised in operating a Subchapter S corporation, there are several disadvantages that must be considered prior to electing Subchapter S status, as follows:

1. *Incorporating may incur additional unemployment taxes and increase the liability under the Federal Insurance Contributions Act:* If the partnership or sole proprietorship is initially incorporated as a Subchapter S Corporation, the individual partners or sole proprietor becomes subject, as employees of the corporation, to the Unemployment Compensation Act. In addition, the total contribution for FICA is increased. The exact after-tax cost can be calculated only on an individual basis. This additional cost is limited to those individuals who were partners or to the sole proprietor. The cost for all other employees remains the same. The changes in both the Social Security Laws as well as the laws relating to Unemployment Compensation have reduced this problem.

2. *State taxation may be complicated by a Subchapter S election:* Many states do not recognize the status of the Subchapter S Corporation. Accordingly, the accounting will be complicated by this election. In these cases, for state purposes, the corporation will be considered an ordinary corporation and, therefore, taxed as such. On the other hand, for federal purposes, the income is allocated to the individual shareholders with no taxation at the corporate level. The duality of the tax concepts imposed complicates the accounting and bookkeeping which must be maintained for the corporation.

3. *For all taxable years prior to 1983, tax-sheltered income was converted into taxable income:* Prior to the Subchapter S Revision Act of 1982, except for capital gains, income received by a Subchapter S Corporation lost any beneficial tax characteristics it originally had. On the other hand, if a Subchapter S Corporation had tax-sheltered income such as municipal bond interest, it was not taxed to the shareholders upon receipt by the corporation, but it was taxed upon distribution as a dividend.

Example: Muni Corporation, an electing Subchapter S Corporation, had taxable income of $75,000, plus $25,000 of municipal interest in 1982. If the corporation distributed, during the year, $100,000, the entire amount would have been taxable as a dividend. In contrast, if Muni had been a partnership, the partners would only have been taxed on $75,000.

The distribution of tax-exempt income to the shareholders was a taxable event. This result for tax purposes was disastrous. In planning, we attempt to convert taxable income to tax-free income not tax-free income to taxable income. Thus, prior to electing Subchapter S status, it was necessary to review the corporate income to determine if any tax-sheltered income was being received and what effect this would have upon the election. Also, the purchase of tax-exempt securities by a Subchapter S Corporation should have been avoided.

Good News: The Subchapter S Revision Act of 1982 removed this particular negative characteristic for corporations electing Subchapter S status. For all taxable years beginning after 1982, tax-exempt interest passes through to shareholders retaining its character. This interest merely increases the shareholder's basis for his Sub S Corporation's stock. As a result, a subsequent distribution of tax-exempt interest will not be taxable; it will simply reduce the shareholder's basis in the stock.

4. *The benefits of using the lower tax rates of a corporation are lost by electing Subchapter S status:* As described in ¶100.1, the lower tax rates of the corporation can be utilized to effectively minimize the overall tax burden of the business and individual. However, by electing Subchapter S status for the corporation, the income is taxed to the shareholder, and this benefit will not be available.

5. *The election by a C Corporation of an S status can cause an increased tax burden upon the sale of appreciated assets:* If a corporation elects S status after January 1, 1989, for qualified corporations and after January 1, 1987, for all other corporations, and if the corporation subsequently sells the property at a gain within ten years of election, not only the shareholder but also the corporation can be subject to a tax on the built-in gains. If this is the case, the tax at the corporate level would be the maximum corporate tax. This, in essence, alleviates the benefit of the surtax exemption which would have been available if the

C election had not been terminated. The maximum tax rate at the corporate level is 34 percent.

Before an S election is made when the sale of appreciated property is anticipated, a determination of the amount of the gain should be made and a review of the law undertaken. The planner should also be aware that even if the corporation is a qualified corporation, if the gain on the sale would result in a long-term capital gain the S corporation may still result in taxable income. Prior to the implementation of the Tax Reform Act of 1986, the Internal Revenue Code imposed a tax upon net long-term capital gains in any one year of $25,000 or more. On $25,000 or less, there was no additional tax consequences. If they exceed that amount, Section 1378(b) and other relevant sections should be reviewed to determine whether or not the corporation will incur any additional tax.

> **Example:** ABC Corp. (owned 50% by A, 30% by B, and 20% by C) made an S election after 1986 to be effective as of 1/1/90. ABC Corp. owned property which, on 1/1/90, had a fair market value of $1,200, with a basis in the hands of the corporation of $100. In addition, ABC Corp. had a net operating loss carryforward of $100 as the result of prior years' operations. In 1992, while still an S corp, ABC Corp. sold the property for $1,500. Assuming that ABC Corp. could establish that $300 of the appreciation constituted post-S election appreciation, the results would be:

1. Gain on sale

$1,500	Amount realized
(100)	Adjusted basis
$1,400	Gain
(300)	Post-S election appreciation
$1,100	Built-in gain

2. Tax to ABC Corp.

$1,100	Built-in gain
(100)	Net operating loss carryforward
$1,000	Taxable built-in gain
34%	Maximum corporate rate
$ 340	Tax

3. Tax to shareholders

	A-50%	B-30%	C-20%
(a) Tax on built-in gain:			
Taxable built-in gain	$500	$300	$200
Corporate-level tax	(170)	(102)	(68)
Net gain taxable to shareholders	$330	$198	$132
Maximum tax rate	28%	28%	28%
Tax to shareholders on built-in gain	$ 92.40	$ 55.44	$ 36.96
(b) Tax on post-S election appreciation:			
Capital gain	$150	$ 90	$ 60
Maximum tax rate	28%	28%	28%
Tax to shareholders on post-S appreciation	$ 42	$ 25.20	$ 16.80
Total tax to shareholders	$134.40	$ 80.64	$ 53.76

TOTAL TAX PAID $608.80

Please note the marginal combined tax rate of over 55% on this built-in gain. Those who are considering conversion as an S corporation whose corporation owns property which can be subject to substantial built-in gains (real, personal, or intangible property that has appreciated) should consider getting an appraisal of this property at the time of conversion. This, at least, will provide a basis for determining pre- and post-election gains.

[502] HOW TO DECIDE WHICH CORPORATIONS ARE ELIGIBLE TO ELECT SUBCHAPTER S STATUS

The designation "Small Business Corporation" is a misnomer because neither the Internal Revenue Code nor the Regulations place any requirement as to the size of a business. The requirements for Subchapter S are as follows:

1. *The corporation must be a domestic corporation:* For the purpose of this election, the corporation must be created or organized in the United States or under the laws of the United States.

2. *The corporation must not be a member of an affiliated group:* An affiliated group for Subchapter S purposes is a group of corporations in which one of the corporations owns 80 percent or more of all classes of stock of another corporation. As will be noted later, no shareholder of a Subchapter S Corporation may be another corporation. Accordingly, the only possibility that a Subchapter S Corporation is a member of an affiliated group is to have a Subchapter S Corporation own more than 80 percent of the stock of another corporation.

> **Example:** X Corporation is contemplating the election to a Subchapter S corporation status. It has a wholly owned subsidiary, Y Corporation. Therefore, X does not qualify as an eligible corporation to elect Subchapter S status because it is a member of an affiliated group. The officers and directors of X have two choices if they believe that Subchapter S status is the appropriate tax-planning technique. The first choice is to merge Y into X. The second is to sell 21 percent of the common stock of Y to another party. If this sale is accomplished, X will no longer be a part of the affiliated group since it owns less than 80 percent of the stock of Y.

3. *The Subchapter S Corporation may not have in excess of thirty-five shareholders:* Prior to the Subchapter S Revision Act of 1982, a Subchapter S Corporation was limited to twenty-five shareholders. The Subchapter S Revision Act of 1982 now provides that a Subchapter S Corporation can have thirty-five shareholders at its inception or may increase the number of shareholders to thirty-five at any time. To comply with this requirement, the ownership of stock by a husband and wife will be counted as only one shareholder. This determination is made without regard to the manner in which the stock is owned by the married couple. In all other cases of joint ownership (joint tenancy, tenancy in its entirety, or ownership as tenants in common), each joint owner is counted in the number of shareholders.

4. *Not everyone is eligible to own stock in a Subchapter S Corporation:* Prior to the Economic Recovery Tax Act of 1981, the only eligible shareholders of a Subchapter S Corporation were individuals (other than nonresident aliens), their estates (either bankrupt or decedents), voting trusts, grantor trusts, and testamentary trusts (but only for a period of sixty days after such transfer). Specifically excluded from those eligible parties are corporations and inter vivos irrevocable trusts.

The Economic Recovery Tax Act of 1981 liberalized the rules regarding the eligibility of trusts as Subchapter S shareholders. As indicated above, prior to the act, only grantor trusts (revocable trusts used many times as will substitutes), voting trusts, and certain testamentary trusts (only for a sixty-day period), could qualify as Subchapter S shareholders.

The Economic Recovery Tax Act of 1981 provided two additional types of trusts which will be eligible, as follows:

☐ A trust which is treated as wholly owned by a person other than the grantor
☐ A qualified Subchapter S trust

Therefore, the following trusts can now own stock in a Subchapter S Corporation without affecting the election.

(a) A voting trust, although its full utilization is still somewhat suspect. (See page 238 for a discussion of the problems entailed in utilizing a voting trust.)

(b) A grantor trust which, as indicated above, is nothing more than a revocable trust and in many cases is used as a substitute for a will.

(c) A testamentary trust; however, only for a period of sixty days.

(d) A trust wherein a person other than the grantor is treated as the owner. An example of this type of trust would be the marital deduction trust created by a marital deduction will, which grants the beneficiary the unlimited right to withdraw principal. This trust would provide the surviving spouse with the life income and the unrestricted right to obtain the principal of the trust at any time.

(e) The qualified Subchapter S trust: The prerequisites to qualify as such are that:

    i. The trust holds stock in one or more Subchapter S Corporations

    ii. The trust is a simple trust in that all income must be distributed currently

    iii. The beneficiary must be a U.S. citizen or resident

    iv. The trust can have only one income beneficiary at a time. The income interest must terminate at the earlier of the termination of the trust or death of the income beneficiary. For example, the trust will terminate at the earlier of the death of the beneficiary or at the time the beneficiary becomes age 25.

    v. Upon the termination of the trust during the life of the beneficiary, all the corpus and income must be distributed to said beneficiary. However, if the income beneficiary dies prior to obtaining said age, the corpus can be distributed to another party.

Key Idea: A shareholder in a Subchapter S Corporation who has either been supporting his parents or who wishes to provide for the education of his children but does not want them to participate in any corporate decisions could establish a qualified Subchapter S trust which would hold stock in the corporation. The income could be paid to the child or parent without giving them any control in the future of the business. Note the new restrictions contained in the Tax Reform Act of 1986 relative to shifting income to minor children under the age of 14.

(f) It should be noted that stock transferred to a custodian for a minor under the Uniform Gifts to Minors Act is not held in trust even though a form of fiduciary relationship is created.

5. *There must be only one class of stock:* Section 1361(b)(1)(D) defines a Subchapter S Corporation as a corporation which has no more than one class of stock. There are several minor exceptions to this rule which permit two classes of stock. One of

the commonly used exceptions is to have two classes of voting stock. Each class has the same rights except for electing members to the board of directors. This technique is utilized to maintain control within a family group.

The following is an example of how two classes of common stock can be used:

Example: Mr. Hatfield and Mr. McCoy have for years owned 50 percent of the stock of Kentucky Corporation. Under their leadership, this corporation has been successful and has run smoothly for many years. The two founding fathers are getting older, and each has several children who are ready to take their place in control of the corporation. Hatfield and McCoy wish to preserve their families' interest in the corporation and also wish to commence a gifting program to help eliminate estate taxation.

What to Watch Out For: If either Hatfield or McCoy gifts even one share of the stock to any of his children, this could create potential problems. If a child of McCoy's voted with the Hatfields, the Hatfields could completely divest the McCoys from any effective control of the corporation. Fifty-one percent of the stock could vote an entire new board of directors. These directors could then appoint new officers.

How to Solve this Problem: This problem is completely eliminated if Hatfield receives 100 shares of Class A common stock and McCoy receives 100 shares of Class B common stock. Class A and Class B will be exactly the same, except for the fact that each will elect two directors of a four-person board. As long as either Hatfield or McCoy owns 51 percent of the class of stock of his family, he can retain control and still begin a gifting program. This technique, of course, is not limited to Subchapter S Corporations. However, a device using this technique does not upset planning if a Subchapter S Corporation is the appropriate tool.

The Subchapter S Revision Act of 1982 expanded upon the prior concepts and has stated that "a corporation shall not be treated as having more than one class of stock solely because there are differences in voting rights among the shares of common stock." It would appear that now it will be possible to have a nonvoting common stock and different classes of voting common stock as long as all other rights are equal (such as rights to receive dividend income or rights upon liquidation). If this is the case, the ability to use a Subchapter S Corporation to shift control between generations and as an estate-planning tool will be greatly expanded. However, until regulations are promulgated, it is not possible to determine the full scope of these planning opportunities.

In tax law, very few things are what they seem. The IRS has attempted to terminate Subchapter S elections in two situations which would appear to pose no problems. In both types of cases, the IRS had tried to establish that there are two classes of stock which would preclude the Subchapter S election (Section 1374[a][4]). Under the first theory, the IRS attempts to create a second class of stock by reclassifying the debt of the corporation.

> **Example:** Two Corporation, an electing Subchapter S Corporation, has three separate shareholders, A, B, and C. Each owns one-third of the authorized and issued common stock of the corporation. In addition, A has loaned to Two Corporation the sum of $50,000, which bears interest at the rate of "the greater of 9 percent per annum or 25 percent of the net taxable income."

This type of situation produced a great deal of litigation over the past two decades. In the above example, the IRS would attempt to establish that the "debt" owed to A is a second class of stock. The debt has some attributes of stock because its interest is dependent upon either a fixed rate or a percentage of profits. However, even if A had just loaned money to the corporation and it bore interest at a fixed rate, the IRS still may attack this debt as a second class of stock.

In an attempt to clarify when debt will be considered stock, Congress has attempted in the Subchapter S Revision Act of 1982 to establish a safe harbor wherein debt will be classified as debt and not as a second class of stock. The safe harbor provides that a straight debt instrument will not be treated as a second class of stock for purposes of the one class of stock requirement. A "straight-debt instrument" has been defined to include a written unconditional promise to pay, on demand or at a specified date, a sum certain as long as it incorporates the following additional characteristics:

1. The interest rate and payment dates are not contingent on the corporate profits, the discretion of the corporation, or similar factors
2. The instrument is not convertible into stock
3. The creditor is a person, estate, or trust eligible to hold Subchapter S Corporation stock

It should be noted that even though the interest rate is dependent upon the prime rate or some other similar factor, this will not disqualify the safe harbor treatment.

The question was then posed: "What if the debt instrument was considered stock under the stock equity rules?" In the Congressional Committee Reports, Congress attempted to deal with this and indicated that a safe harbor debt instrument may nevertheless be treated as stock under general tax principles. In that event, the secretary of the Treasury may prescribe rules or regulations relating to the treatment of these instruments for purposes of applying Subchapter S and other provisions of the Code. It is intended that these rules will treat the instrument in such a way as to prevent tax avoidance, on the one hand, and also to prevent unfair, harsh results to the taxpayer, on the other. It is anticipated that these safe harbor instruments will be treated as debt under Subchapter S so that no corporate income or loss will be allocated to the instruments. Again, the regulations should give further insight as to what will and will not be allowed.

The second area of controversy has involved agreements among the individual shareholders to provide for voting control. These agreements have included such devices as voting trusts or irrevocable proxies. While the IRS had very little success with the courts in trying to substantiate a second class of stock where these voting agreements were present, the fear of a retroactive termination had previously precluded their full utilization. The Tax Reform Act of 1976, which added grantor trusts and voting trusts as eligible shareholders, should put to rest any fears about using this planning device. In additon, the Subchapter S Revision Act of 1982, which has provided Subchapter S Corporations with the ability to have stock with different voting rights, seems to have put to rest any further worry about the use of voting trusts in Subchapter S Corporations.

[503] HOW TO TIME A SUBCHAPTER S ELECTION FOR THE MAXIMUM TAX BENEFIT

In the areas of election and termination, the changes by the Tax Reform Act of 1976, the Revenue Act of 1978, the Economic Recovery Tax Act of 1981, and the Subchapter S Revision Act of 1982 have substantially liberalized the ability to timely elect Subchapter S status. These laws have also effected changes in the Subchapter S election and termination. The changes have limited the possibility of involuntarily terminating the election once validly made. Nonetheless, you should use caution whenever tax planning involves the use of the Subchapter S Corporation.

[503.1] Making the Election

A corporation may make the election at any time during the entire taxable year preceding the year in which the election is to be made effective, or on or before the fifteenth day of the third month of the election year. If the corporation makes an untimely election (after the fifteenth day of the third month), it will be treated as if the election was made for the next year.

The following example will help illustrate these concepts:

Example: XYZ Corporation is a calendar-year corporation. It wishes to make an election effective January 1, 1985. If it makes this election any time in 1984 or up to March 15, 1985, the election will be effective for 1985. On the other hand, if it makes an election for 1985 on April 1, 1985, this election will only be effective starting January 1, 1986.

In addition, even if the election is timely made, it will not be effective until the following year if the corporation was not eligible to make the election, for example (if we have a corporate shareholder in the electing corporation), at any time during the period commencing on the first day of the year to the date of election.

If the corporation meets all the qualifications for Subchapter S status, it must first file a form which contains the written consent of each shareholder to the election with the district director of the Internal Revenue Service. (The form which is accepted by the IRS is reproduced in Appendix K.)

Normally, the party who should make the election is self-evident. This was particularly true prior to the expansion of the law to include qualified Subchapter S trusts. The question now becomes: How and when should qualified Subchapter S trusts make an effective election? There appears to be two separate elections that must be made, as follows:

1. In order to qualify, the trust must elect and qualify as a Subchapter S trust.
2. The corporation itself must elect as a Subchapter S Corporation.

If a trust is a stockholder prior to filing the Subchapter S election, the trust cannot consent to the election at its inception because it is not an eligible stockholder. For the income beneficiary to elect qualified Subchapter S treatment, thereby making the trust eligible to hold stock, the trust must already be a Subchapter S stockholder. Therefore, the income beneficiary cannot elect to qualify the trust until the Subchapter S election is made. It would appear that the Economic Recovery Tax Act of 1981, as amended by the Tax Reform Act of 1984, provided a solution to this dilemma by allowing the beneficiary's election to be made retroactively up to two months and fifteen days. This conforms to the time the corporation has to make a Subchapter S election.

One procedure that could be followed seems logical and appears to comply with the Internal Revenue Service procedure outlined in its Temporary Regulations. First the Subchapter S election is filed. The trustee, as the legal title holder of the stock, could consent to the election, although at that time, the trust is ineligible to elect. The beneficiary of the trust, after said election, could request that the trust be treated as a qualified Subchapter S trust retroactively to the initial date of qualification as a Subchapter S Corporation. The duality of election and procedures to implement this will in due course be clarified by the IRS in the final regulations. Until such time, all planning must proceed with extreme care.

It is interesting to note that the qualified Subchapter S trust election can only be revoked with the IRS's consent. This trust, of course, can hold stock in more than one corporation, and, there would seem to be nothing that would prevent the income beneficiary from joining with the other shareholders and voluntarily revoking the Subchapter S election.

On the other hand, it would appear impossible for the trust to try to convert itself into a nonqualifying trust and therefore kill the election without the IRS's approval. (See ¶504.1 for a review of the various methods of terminating a Subchapter S election.)

[504] HOW THE SUBCHAPTER S CORPORATION IS TERMINATED

[504.1] Methods of Termination

Voluntary Termination

A valid Subchapter S election is effective for the year of the election and all subsequent years until it is terminated or voluntarily revoked. For all taxable years beginning after 1982, voluntary revocation will be effective if it is filed with the district director of the Internal Revenue Service by a shareholder or a group of shareholders owning more than 50 percent of the corporation's stock by the fifteenth day of the third month of the year in which the revocation is to be effective. In the event the revocation is filed later than that date, then, as in the case of the original election, it will be effective in the subsequent year. (See Appendix L.)

Under the law prior to the Subchapter S Revision Act of 1982, revocation was effective for the entire taxable year in which it was made or became effective on the first day of the next taxable year. The corporation did not have any alternative. Under the Subchapter S Revision Act of 1982, the effective date of revocation can be specified even if the date causes the corporation's taxable year to be split. If the corporation's taxable year is to be split, then the corporation will have a short Subchapter S year (from the first day of the taxable year to the day before the revocation is effective); therefore, for the remainder of the year, it will be taxed as a regular corporation. You should be aware that any time the corporation is taxed as a regular C Corporation, the taxable income must be annualized. For example, S Corporation, a qualifying electing Subchapter S Corporation reporting on a calendar year basis, files an election on January 1, 1988, that as of September 30, 1988, the Subchapter S election will cease. If the corporation reports $100,000 of income for the full year, then $75,000 (three-quarters or nine months of the year's income) is allocated to the Subchapter S Corporation, and $25,000 (one-quarter or three months of the year's income) is allocated to the C Corporation. Subchapter S is taxed on the C Corporation income as follows:

1. The annualized income is determined as follows:
$$\frac{365}{92} \times \$25,000 = \$99,185$$

2. The tax on the $99,185 of income is $21,972.90.

3. The portion of the tax to be paid on the last three months is determined as follows:
$$\frac{92}{365} \times 21,972.90 = \$5538.37$$

WARNING: Before a Subchapter S election is terminated in the middle of the year, the impact of the corporate income tax on the remainder of the year should be studied. Annualization of income reduces the benefit of the lower corporate tax rates on the annualized C income in excess of $50,000.

Involuntary Termination

Previously, in all cases of involuntary termination, the election was retroactively terminated to the first day of the fiscal year. For all taxable years beginning before 1983, there were four methods of triggering involuntary termination, as follows:

1. A new shareholder who affirmatively failed to consent to the Subchapter S election within sixty days of his becoming a shareholder.

2. The Subchapter S Corporation failed to meet any of the initial qualification requirements; for example, a corporation became a shareholder of the Subchapter S Corporation.

3. More than 20 percent of the corporation's gross receipts for the taxable year were from passive income.

4. More than 80 percent of the corporation's gross receipts for the current taxable year were from foreign sources.

The Subchapter S Revision Act of 1982 changed all the rules regarding involuntary revocation. The following discussion outlines the changes and shows how they will affect future planning:

First, a new shareholder will not have the right to affirmatively refuse to consent to a Subchapter S election and have it retroactively terminated to the beginning of the year. Prior to the act, this was an effective tax planning tool. At the end of the year or near the end of the year, if it was determined that Subchapter S election adversely affected planning and that a regular corporation would be substantially more beneficial to overall planning, any shareholder could gift a portion of his shares to a related party, for example, his wife or children. They would then affirmatively refuse to have the Subchapter S election, and the election would be ineffective from the first day of the year. The change in the law, of course, will adversely affect this particular planning technique.

On the other hand, Subchapter S Corporations will no longer have to worry about the possibility of a malcontent who has acquired some stock in the corporation and who would attempt to ruin the majority stockholder's planning through an affirmative refusal to consent to the Subchapter S election. The change in the voluntary revocation rules, which now allows for a revocation only if signed by more than 50 percent, will allow the majority to operate the corporation without regard to the minority interest. This will have both good and bad effects in the future on electing as a Subchapter S Corporation.

The second method of having the Subchapter S election involuntarily revoked (the corporation failed to meet any of the

initial requirements) has also been changed. Prior to the Subchapter S Revision Act of 1982, the revocation was effective to
the first day of the year. Now, the day before the terminating
event occurs will be treated as the last day of a short Subchapter
S taxable year. The day the terminating event occurs will be
treated as the first day of a regular corporation taxable year. At
the end of the year, the corporation will allocate its income
between the Subchapter S portion of the year and the C corporation. In the alternative, with the consent of the shareholders,
the income or loss can be allocated as actually earned. If this
election is made, there will be additional accounting costs; however, it should provide a tax-planning tool if the accounting
records indicate a loss during the first part of the year and a
gain during the later part of the year. (The notification which
should be sent to the IRS is set forth in Appendix N.)

Third, while the effect of a Subchapter S Corporation
earning passive income has been completely overhauled, in the
event that the Subchapter S election is terminated by reason of
its earning excess passive income, this election will be involuntarily revoked to the beginning of the year. A further discussion will follow.

The final method of involuntary revocation, that being the
Subchapter S Corporation's income from foreign sources exceeding 80 percent of total income, is no longer applicable.
Under prior law, if more than 80 percent of the electing corporation's gross receipts for the taxable year was from foreign
sources, the election terminated as of the beginning of the year.
This is no longer the case for the simple reason that beginning
for taxable years in and after 1983, an electing corporation can
have 100 percent foreign income and still not affect its Subchapter S status.

Involuntary Termination through Excess of Passive Income Limitation

Prior to the Subchapter S Revision Act of 1982, a relatively
common problem leading to involuntary termination was to
have investment income exceed 20 percent of gross receipts.
Investment income has been defined to include royalties, rents,
dividends, interest, annuities, and gains from the sale of stock
and securities.

The following is an example of what could have happened if the officers and directors did not attend to the problem when investment income exceeded 20 percent of the gross receipts:

Example: X Corporation is in the construction business. In the past, it has constructed residential and multifamily dwellings for sale to others. During periods of low demand, in order to keep its entire workforce intact, it has built multifamily homes and has retained these buildings in the corporation as rental units. The entire rental income did not normally exceed $180,000 a year (fifty units at $300 per month). The corporation's gross sales usually exceed $2,000,000 in any one year. However, during the current year, through a combination of high interest rates and a strike by their employees, the total gross receipts, including rental income, are only $750,000.

The officers may be so preoccupied with the lack of sales and the strike that they would not be aware that the rent now exceeds 20 percent of the gross income. Accordingly, the Subchapter S election had been terminated as of the first day of the current fiscal year.

Effective for tax years beginning after 1982, the law repeals the passive income rule for corporations that do not have any earnings and profits at the close of the taxable year and eases the rules considerably for those that do. Thus, under the rules as changed, the Subchapter S election will only terminate under this passive income limitation if the corporation has earnings and profits as an ordinary corporation at the end of each of three consecutive taxable years, and more than 25 percent of its gross receipts for each of those years is from passive income. Thus, a Subchapter S Corporation that was never a regular corporation can have as much as 100 percent passive investment income.

In addition, Subchapter S Corporations that do have earnings and profits left over from their days as a C Corporation are much better off. The new rule does not provide automatic revocation of a Subchapter S election if you violate the passive income limitation in any one year. You can avoid revocation by earning less than 25 percent passive income by the third year.

There should be plenty of advance warning before revocation becomes effective.

WARNING: While the Subchapter S election has not been terminated because of the excess passive income, the corporation itself may be forced to pay an income tax. If the Subchapter S Corporation ends up with excess net passive income for the year, it must pay a tax at the maximum corporate tax then applicable.

At this point in our discussion, certain terms must be defined. "Net passive income" is defined as normal passive investment income less any allowable deductions. To determine how much of the passive income is "excess net passive income," you must multiply the corporation's *net* passive income by a fraction, the numerator of which is the corporation's passive income for the year that exceeds 25 percent of the gross receipts, and the denominator of which is the corporation's passive investment income for the year.

For example, assume that during a taxable year, a Subchapter S Corporation has $200,000 of gross receipts, passive investment income of $75,000, and expenses attributable to passive income of $10,000. As a result, its net passive income is $65,000 ($75,000 investment income minus $10,000 of expenses) and the amount by which its passive investment income for the taxable year exceeds 25 percent of the gross receipts is $25,000 ($75,000 passive income minus $50,000 [$200,000 gross receipts times 25 percent]). The income subject to the tax is determined as follows:

$$\$65,000 \times \frac{25,000}{75,000} = \$21,666.67$$

This amount is multipled by the maximum current corporate tax rate to yield the appropriate tax.

The rules above are fairly complicated; however, there is one limitation. The excess net passive income cannot exceed the corporation's taxable income for the year computed without a deduction for a net operating loss. Therefore, if we have a Subchapter S Corporation which incurs an operating loss for the year, it may be able to wipe out any of its tax on the net taxable income.

Reinstatement of Subchapter S Election Once Terminated

Once the election has been revoked, it cannot normally be reelected for five years. Prior to the Subchapter S Revision Act of 1982, once an election was terminated for any reason, it was impossible to reelect for that five-year period. Effective for the tax years beginning after 1982, the new law authorizes the IRS to waive the effective and inadvertent termination for any period, provided that:

1. The corporation corrects the event that created the termination in time.

2. The corporation and all of its shareholders agreed to be treated as if the election had been in effect for that period.

The Committee Reports indicate that the IRS might find it appropriate to issue a waiver and treat the election as never terminated in the case where a Subchapter S election was terminated by the corporation inadvertently violating the one class of stock requirement. As discussed, under prior law, once the revocation occurred, there was no possibility of correcting the situation. Under the new law, even if the IRS found that the election was not inadvertently terminated and it would not waive the revocation for the current year, the IRS could waive a portion or all of the five-year waiting period.

It should be noted that a voluntary revocation is not an inadvertent termination and, therefore, none of the new rules relative to reelecting because of an inadvertent termination apply. The IRS is, therefore, given broad discretion as to correcting an inadvertent involuntary revocation or waiving a portion or all of the waiting period before the corporation could again elect as a Subchapter S Corporation. It is anticipated that the regulations will set forth the guidelines as to when the IRS will act.

[505] HOW THE SUBCHAPTER S INCOME IS TAXED

[505.1] Taxation of Subchapter S Income at the Shareholder Level

Under Subchapter S, taxation is virtually eliminated in all instances at the corporate level except for the taxation of built-in gains, discussed in ¶505.2, and excess passive income, discussed in ¶504.1. All corporate income is taxed directly to the individual shareholders. The shareholders must include as part of their own income their pro rata share of the income of the corporation plus specially treated items of income and deductions.

Before the Subchapter S Revision Act of 1982, many people incorrectly attempted to analogize Subchapter S Corporation taxation to that of a partnership. This was a misleading generalization. After the Subchapter S Revision Act of 1982, this analogy is more appropriate. Now the computation of taxation to the individual shareholders is virtually the same for Subchapter S Corporations as for partnerships. The corporate income is divided pro rata among the shareholders, and the special treatment of items of income, loss, and deduction are also passed directly to the shareholders of the corporation in proportion to their shareholdings.

> **Example:** Subchapter S Corporation has three shareholders, A, B, and C. Each owns one-third of the stock. During the year, Subchapter S Corporation has income of $15,000, long-term capital gains of $24,000 (not included in its income and not considered "preelection gain"), and $12,000 of charitable deductions (also not included in its income). Accordingly, each of the shareholders will report on his individual tax return income as follows:

Ordinary Income	$5,000
Long-Term Capital Gains	8,000
Charitable Deductions	4,000

The problems of computing taxable income and deductions for Subchapter S Corporations during the next couple of years will not so much involve the complexity of the law as relearning what has already been learned. The following types of items will be passed through to the shareholders and will retain their own characteristics:

1. Capital gains and losses. This is slightly different under the new law. Under the old law, capital gains were passed

through; however, capital losses were not allowed as a deduction but were only allowed to be carried forward against capital gains of the corporation. Now capital gains and losses will retain their own characteristics and will be passed through to the shareholders. Note that if these gains resulted from preelection built-in gains, the corporation and the individuals can be subject to taxation.

2. Section 1231 gains and losses.

3. Charitable deductions. Previously Subchapter S Corporations were limited, as were regular corporations, as to the amount that they could give. Now there are no limitations since the amount a Subchapter S Corporation gives will pass through to the individual shareholders as a deduction.

4. Tax-exempt interest. As noted in ¶501.3, prior to 1983, tax-exempt interest could create earnings and profits for the Subchapter S Corporation which could create taxable income from nontaxable interest. This is no longer the case since tax-exempt interest passes through to the shareholders.

5. Excludable interest and dividends.

6. Credits and various other items, including foreign taxes, depletion, foreign income, and loss.

The method of handling net operating losses has also gone through a complete revision. While prior to the Subchapter S Revision Act of 1982, a loss could only be taken to the amount of the basis in the stock and debt that a shareholder had, a loss in excess of that basis was lost forever. Now, under the new rules, a Subchapter S loss in excess of its basis can be carried over indefinitely. It can be taken as a loss or against income in the year in which:

1. The shareholder contributes additional property to the corporation

2. The corporation earns a profit

Another significant change was that previously the shareholder on the last day of the year recorded the income that he received. In other words, it was common in a corporation that was producing a great deal of income to transfer stock to children on the last day of the year. The children would report the income on their shares for the entire year.

> **Example:** Subchapter S Corporation earned $100,000. A was the sole shareholder until December 31, at which time he conveyed 10 percent of the stock to each of his five children. Since his five children were shareholders on the last day of the year, each would report $10,000 of income, and A would report $50,000 of income. The rule for losses stated that the loss would be pro rated over the number of days that the stock was owned by the shareholder. Now, the law has been changed so that income loss or specially treated items of income and deductions will be pro rated to the time that an individual owns the stock. In this instance, each child would report 1/365 × 10 percent × $100,000, or $273.97 of income. A will report the remainder of the income ($98,630.15). Note that the Tax Reform Act of 1986 taxes children under the age of 14 at their parents' marginal tax rate.

Another area of taxation of the Subchapter S income that has been completely changed is the concept of basis. Previously, a Subchapter S Corporation could have earnings and profits while it was a Subchapter S Corporation. It could also have undistributed taxable income and many other complicating items. Because of the change in the law that now makes the taxation of Subchapter S virtually the same as partnership taxation, partnership rules play a greater role in determining the basis of the stock and debt of a Subchapter S shareholder. However, the basic rules remain unchanged as follows:

1. The amount that you pay for the stock and debt is the amount of basis in the Subchapter S stock and debt.
2. The basis in the stock will be increased by the amount of profits and reduced by the amount of loss.
3. Any transfers of cash will reduce the stock basis first, and if there is no longer any basis in the stock, the basis of the debt will be reduced.
4. Any distribution by the corporation in excess of its previously taxed income will be applicable to the earnings and

profits during the period of time prior to the Subchapter S election, if the corporation had earnings and profits. If there were no profits, then any distributions will be taxed as a reduction of basis and thereafter as capital gains.

The complications arise on the heirarchy of stock and debt and the transferring of appreciated property from the corporation to the shareholder. A complete discussion is beyond the scope of this book because of its complicated nature and because, if the problem is known in advance, it rarely presents a problem in overall planning.

[505.2] Taxation of Built-In Gains

The Tax Reform Act of 1986 has added a new complication into the taxation of S Corporations. Prior to the Tax Reform Act of 1986, there were only two instances when an S Corporation could be taxed at the corporate level. The first was discussed in ¶501.2 and involved the sale by the S Corporation of an asset that yielded net long-term capital gains in excess of $25,000. The second instance when the S corporation could be subject to a tax at the corporate level arose when the corporation had net passive income. The taxation in this instance was discussed in ¶504. The first will cease to be a problem for all but qualified small corporations after January 1, 1989. The second continues to be a problem.

A tax on the net unrealized gain is a new problem which must be dealt with, and appropriate planning must be enacted in order to avoid the full impact in the future. An S Corporation is subject to a corporate level tax on built-in gains tax in any taxable year beginning after 1986 but only if the corporation made its election to be an S Corporation after 1986 (certain qualified corporations may not be subject if they made the election before 1989). If the Subchapter S election was made before 1987 (for qualified corporations before 1989) the prior rules will continue to apply. The tax is imposed on the net unrealized built-in gain, which means the excess of the fair market value of the corporation's assets as of the beginning of its first taxable year as an S Corporation over the aggregate adjusted basis of the assets at any time. The recognized built-in gain is defined as any gain recognized during the recognition period by an S Corporation on the disposition of any assets except to the extent that the S Corporation demonstrates that (1) the asset was not held by the S Corporation as of the beginning of its first taxable year as an S Corporation or (2) the gain recognized on the disposition is more than the excess of its fair market value of the asset at the beginning of the corporation's first taxable year as an S Corporation over its adjusted basis.

It appears that Congress intends to tax sales or dispositions of any assets at the corporation level, and it will be presumed to be a built-in gain except to the extent that the corporation can show that the appreciation accrued after the election. The most obvious case would be where the asset was not acquired until after the election. The act uses the concept of a recognition period, which means the ten-year period beginning with the first day of the first taxable year the corporation is an S Corporation. So the applicability of the gain is only in that ten-year period. The amount of the tax imposed is determined at the lesser of the recognized built-in gains or the taxable income the corporation would have had if it were determined as a C Corporation. In some instances, because of things such as dividends-received deduction or net operating loss carryforward, it may be beneficial to take a built-in gain in the year when there is a net operating loss.

Obviously, this concept is completely new, and the interpretation of many of its provisions still need further definition. The full ramifications will not be known for some time, and so planning should be done with a great deal of care.

[506] WHAT THE EFFECT OF THE TAX REFORM ACT OF 1986 IS ON THE SUBCHAPTER S ELECTION

There is no doubt that the Tax Reform Act of 1986 will speed the conversion of many C Corporations to S Corporations and will prompt many newly formed corporations to elect initially S status. The reasons for this are twofold, as follows:

1. The lowering of the individual tax bracket. The prior ability to shelter in small corporations significant amounts of income at substantially lower corporate rates will in 1988 totally disappear. At that time, the effective corporate rate

can be as much as 6 percent higher than the maximum individual rate (39 percent for corporations and 33 percent for individuals). With this disparity, positive planning as a C Corporation can only occur if the corporate taxable income can be maintained at $50,000 or less and the individual's marginal tax rate is 33 percent. The ability of small businesses to plan within such small parameters may necessitate the election of more S Corporations. This is particularly true of personal service corporations which do not have the benefits of the graduated tax rates. Before a business is elected as an S corporation, the law on built-in gains as it applies to cash basis taxpayers and their receivables should be reviewed.

2. The potentiality of a corporate level tax on built-in gains as previously discussed, will prompt C Corporations if they are qualified corporations to elect S status prior to January 1, 1989, to ensure that there will be no corporate level tax upon sale of assets.

As a general concept, it appears that Congress may have overreacted, and while electing an S status appears to be favorable at this time, it may work to the disadvantage of the general economy. In the past, the ability to shelter income at the corporate level has encouraged individual small businesses to retain money in the corporation for future expansion. The Tax Reform Act of 1986 will have a completely different effect upon the economy. The full impact is not fully known or contemplated. In this instance, the pendulum may have gone too far, and we may in the future see an increase in the individual rates or a lowering of the corporate rates. At that time, the benefits of the S election, discussed in this chapter, may no longer be applicable. In addition, the concept of taxation of built-in gains is extremely complicated, and the imposition of this tax may prove to be more difficult than originally contemplated. However, in the short term, there is no doubt that the S Corporation has reemerged as a valuable tool for the tax planner.

6

How to Purchase the Interest of Older, Disgruntled, or Deceased Shareholders at Minimum Tax Cost

[600] HOW TO MINIMIZE THE TAX COST FOR A RETIRING SHAREHOLDER

Previously, we dealt with methods for maximizing after-tax distributions for the benefit of all the office/shareholders of a corporation. Now, our goal is to maximize the after-tax distribution to a single or small group of retiring or deceased shareholders. In most instances, it will be their last chance to obtain funds from the corporation in exchange for their stockholdings. In this chapter, we will analyze how this transfer of stock may come while the shareholder is alive or after his death. In either case, it will be extremely important for you to arrive at the proper method and procedure for distributing to the shareholder or his estate, cash and/or property in the most beneficial manner.

Prior to the Tax Reform Act of 1986, from the shareholder's point of view, the goal was to have this distribution classified as either a return of capital or to have it result in a transaction taxed at capital gains rates. Without careful planning, these distributions may be considered as dividend income. In closely held family corporations, the question of attribution among the various family members complicates an already complex problem. The recently passed Tax Reform Act has made the solutions even more costly from a tax standpoint and will in the future require even greater care in developing the proper tax strategy to minimize after-tax proceeds.

257

During the life of a corporation, there may be times of stress or divergence of interest among the controlling shareholders. There are several reasons for such problems that occur among shareholders. At times they are precipitated by the death or disability of one of the parties. However, it is more likely that the interests of the shareholders no longer coincide. This may occur because one of the parties is much older than the remaining ones and may now be facing retirement. A change in family circumstances may also give rise to problems. A major inheritance by one of the parties may make him less dedicated to the pursuit of the business. Any of these or other psychological, physical, or emotional changes in the individual shareholders has an impact upon the general business. When these situations occur, it may be necessary to effect a change in ownership or find another accommodation between the parties.

The three methods used to resolve these problems are as follows:

Method 1: Purchase the individual shareholder's interest. There are three possible groups of purchasers—a third party or parties, the remaining shareholders, or the corporation.

Method 2: Dispose of the entire corporate business. It then becomes incumbent upon all shareholders to find a willing buyer for either the stock of the corporation or the corporate assets.

Method 3: Arrive at a financial accommodation among the various shareholders. This is usually difficult, if not impossible, for three reasons: First, it may not be possible to evaluate the active shareholder's worth: second, it may be disastrous for tax purposes to divert sufficient income to the inactive shareholder; third, there may not be sufficient income to accomplish all the goals. The active shareholders will want to extract their entire cash flow from the corporation through salary. The inactive shareholder, on the other hand, may be in a position where any salary he receives will be deemed payment in the form of unreasonable compensation. Therefore, any compensation payment would necessarily be classified as dividend income. As a long-term solution, this is usually the least viable of the alternatives.

Once a shareholder decides to accomplish a sale or transfer of the disgruntled or deceased shareholder's interest, either alone or in conjunction with the other shareholders as a total sale of the business, you have several areas of concern. The selling shareholder's goal is to have his entire transfer of shares classified either as a return of capital or as a capital gain. Without careful planning, however, the selling shareholder may be shocked to discover that a portion or all of the receipt of the purchase price is considered dividend income. This problem occurs most frequently when all of the stock in the corporation is owned by one family. Congress, in conjunction with the Internal Revenue Service, has developed the theory of attribution (also known as constructive ownership of stock).

Within this theory, an individual, partnership, estate, trust, or corporation for certain purposes, is considered to own not only its own shares but also those of other persons or entities. The attribution rules have different applications depending upon the method of extracting funds. Thus, a complete analysis should be made not only of the redemption or liquidation rules but also of those rules concerning attribution when there are related parties involved.

The following two examples will help illustrate this principle:

Example 1: A, the sole owner of Profitable Corporation, retires and transfers the active management of the corporate business to his son, B. He reads all there is to know about unreasonable compensation and realizes that little, if any, income can be paid to him by the corporation to maintain his life-style. He currently owns 100 shares of stock with a basis of $100,000 and a fair market value of $1,000,000. His lawyer explains to him that a sale of his stock to Profitable Corporation will be designated a redemption. He intends to sell 5 shares per year to the corporation and to report the net income as capital gains. In each year, he anticipates a $50,000 sale, of which $45,000 will be capital gains and $5,000 will be return of capital.

Sad Result: A is the owner of 100 percent of the authorized and issued common stock before and after the redemption. The entire receipt of money ($50,000) or the earnings and profits of the corporation, whichever is less, will be taxed as dividend income.

Example 2: A is initiated into the concept of constructive ownership after the sad results of **Example 1** are explained to him. He understands that the prior redemption would be completely ineffective as a tax savings device. Instead, he intends to give his son 20 shares of stock in the corporation and pays the applicable gift tax. Then, pursuant to a prearranged plan, the corporation will, each year, redeem 5 shares of his remaining 80 shares of stock. He now argues that while under **Example 1** he owned 100 percent before and after the redemption, under the current plan, his ownership in the corporation is being reduced by approximately 5 percent each year. His son's interest in the corporation is being increased by a similar amount.

Sad Result: Pursuant to the attribution rules set forth in Code Section 318, the father would be considered the owner of his son's stock. Thus, before the redemption took place, he owned, in addition to his 80 shares, the 20 shares that his son owned, or 100 percent of the stock. After the first redemption, he owns 75 shares individually plus the 20 shares that his son owns, or 100 percent of the outstanding shares. Therefore, the entire $50,000 gain is classified as dividend income.

The above two examples illustrate the problems of constructive ownership. The remainder of this chapter will illustrate plans and techniques which will either skirt the rules of constructive ownership or utilize the exceptions that are specifically included in the Code and Regulations. In addition, this chapter will also help you devise plans and methods for saving the seller taxes by classifying the distributions as either a tax-free return of capital or as a capital gain. Any receipt classified as dividend income will usually serve no useful purpose. In utilizing these plans, it will be necessary to ensure that if a redemption occurs and property other than cash is distributed, the corporation will not be taxed at the time of the property distribution. In addition, while the remaining shareholders' tax position will rarely be the key impediment to proper tax planning, their position should be reviewed and analyzed.

WARNING: It is conceivable that the IRS will attempt to tax the remaining shareholders upon redemption with a constructive dividend if the proper redemption format is not utilized.

IRS Position: There are two major areas where this problem can occur. The first is when the shareholder has an unqualified obligation to purchase the decedent's stock in the corporation and instead the corporation rather than the shareholder exercises this right. (See ¶601.7.) The second is the case of the minnow swallowing the whale. The corporation redeems the 90 percent shareholder. The 10 percent shareholder's interest in the corporation increases to 100 percent. An argument can be made that corporate funds have been used for individual benefit. (See ¶601.7.) The Internal Revenue Service accepts the position that a redemption which increases and even gives the remaining shareholder control of the corporation does not result in dividend income to the remaining shareholder. (See Rev. Rul. 58-614, 1958 2 C.B. 920; *Holsey v. Commissioner,* 258 F.2d 865 [3d. Cir. 1958]). Nevertheless, caution should still predominate where the shareholder who is being redeemed owns more than 50 percent of the stock.

The Tax Reform Act of 1986 may have some long-range effects upon the problems and solutions posed in this chapter. Commencing in 1988, the tax rates for capital gains and ordinary income will be the same. If this is the case, there will be little if any difference in tax treatment if the redemption is considered as a capital transaction or as dividend income. In example 1 above, prior to the Tax Reform Act of 1986, assuming A was in the 50 percent marginal tax bracket, the redemption, which in effect is a dividend distribution under pre- and post-Tax Reform Act of 1986, would be taxed as dividend income and result in a $25,000 tax. If the gain had been taxed as a long-term capital gain, the tax would have been only $9,000 (sales price $50,000 less $5,000 or basis times tax at 20 percent). After the Tax Reform Act of 1986 in 1988, (there are still some benefits to long-term capital gains remaining in 1987), again assuming A is in the maximum marginal tax rate, 28 percent in that year, the tax difference is significantly less and can be determined as follows:

1. If the distribution is considered a long-term capital gain, the tax is calculated as follows:

Sale Proceeds $50,000
Less Basis   5,000
Taxable Gain $45,000
                 × .28
               $12,600

2. If the transaction was considered dividend income, then the tax would be calculated as follows:

Dividend Income $50,000
                   × .28
                 $14,000

Prior to the Tax Reform Act of 1986, the difference in taxation was $16,000. After the Tax Reform Act, the difference is only $1,400. The law as to what is a capital transaction versus dividend income has not been significantly changed by the Tax Reform Act of 1986; however, the impact has. The question for tax planners is whether or not capital transactions will continue to be taxed as ordinary income or whether the law will be changed. Obviously, planning in this situation is dependent upon the future course of the law, and as tax planners we must react with a good deal of flexibility. Until the future course of the law is charted, it will be necessary to continue to analyze the old law and project the new law's consequences.

NOTE: The capital gains rates and the individual rates will be the same commencing in 1988. There is still significant benefit from net long-term capital gains during 1987. The maximum tax rate on these gains is 28 percent while the highest marginal tax rate in that year is $38\frac{1}{2}$ percent.

Key Idea: If the Tax Reform Act of 1986 is fully implemented in 1988, the benefits of capital gains treatment will be greatly reduced, and there will probably be a greater use of distributions that do not qualify as redemptions but solely as dividend income.

[601] THE STRATEGIES AND PROBLEMS IN REDEEMING THE STOCK OF A SHAREHOLDER

[601.1] Defining a Redemption

The Internal Revenue Code defines a redemption as follows:

> Stock shall be treated as redeemed by a corporation if the corporation acquires its stock from a shareholder in exchange for property, whether or not the stock so acquired is canceled, retired, or held as Treasury stock.

This chapter gives you highlights of those common areas where a redemption may be utilized to solve the problem of the deceased, disabled, or disgruntled shareholder. The term "property" as used in this chapter includes money, securities, and any other holdings, with the exception of stock in the distributing corporation.

Normally, a shareholder who holds shares for more than one year (more than six months during the period June 22, 1984, through December 31, 1987) will receive favorable long-term capital gains treatment when he sells the stock to any party other than the issuing corporation. It should be noted that the effective tax rate during the year 1987 is 28 percent or the marginal tax rate of the taxpayer whichever is less. After 1987, the effective tax rate for capital gains is the same as ordinary income.

It is often more advantageous to have the corporation redeem a portion or all of the stock the shareholder owns. If these shares are a capital asset and if the redemption is classified as a sale or exchange, the distribution will be taxed as a capital transaction. Any redemption that does not qualify as a "sale or exchange" will constitute a dividend distribution with respect to these shares of stock. To the extent that these distributions are less than the earnings and profits of the corporation, the distribution will result in dividend income. Any distribution in excess of the earnings and profits will reduce the shareholder's basis as a return of capital. The excess over his basis will be classified as capital gain. (See Chapter 4.) A redemption of capital stock will generally be considered a distribution rather than a "sale or exchange" unless it satisfies certain requirements set forth in the Internal Revenue Code.

Three significant factors which affect the ultimate determination of how the distribution is classified are as follows:

1. The shareholder's percentage of ownership before and after the redemption
2. Analysis of the other shareholders to determine whether the constructive ownership rules apply
3. Analysis of whether or not the redemption also qualifies as a partial liquidation

The Code sets forth the following four categories where the redemption will be considered as a "sale or exchange":

1. The transaction results in a complete redemption of all the stock and interest of the shareholder in the corporation (see ¶601.2).
2. With respect to the individual shareholder, the redemption is substantially disproportionate (see ¶601.5).
3. Even if conditions one and two cannot be satisfied, if the redemption is not essentially equivalent to a dividend, the distribution will be considered a sale or exchange (see ¶601.5).
4. A redemption which also qualifies as a partial liquidation may have an advantageous impact as to the tax costs to the distributing corporation if it qualifies and if the distribution occurs before January 1, 1989 (see ¶703.5).

[601.2] Complete Redemption in a Closely Held Family Corporation Can Provide for Capital Gains to the Shareholder

The complete redemption of a shareholder's stock is useful to you in three situations. However, before each of these situations is analyzed through the use of examples, it is necessary for you to know what the basic requirements are for a complete termination of a shareholder's interest through a corporate redemption. The basic concept of a termination of a shareholder's interest is relatively easy to grasp. In a corporation with two nonrelated shareholders, A and B, each owning 50 percent, a complete termination is accomplished when the corporation redeems 100 percent of A's stock in the corporation. The problem becomes more complicated if A and B are related and the attribution rules become applicable.

If A and B, instead of being nonrelated parties, are husband and wife, A, before and after the redemption, is considered the owner of 100 percent of the stock. Therefore, the entire distribution could be classified as dividend income.

The Code provides an exception to these constructive ownership rules if the following three requirements are met:

1. Immediately after the redemption, the shareholder must not have any interest in the corporation, other than as a creditor. He cannot be an officer, director, or employee of the corporation.

2. He must not acquire any interest in the corporation (save and except as a creditor) within ten years after the redemption. In addition, he must file an agreement with the commissioner of the Internal Revenue Service in which the taxpayer agrees that if he acquires an interest within ten years, he will notify the commissioner. (An example of the agreement which is required is included in Appendix N.) This agreement must be filed with the taxpayer's return for the taxable year in which the redemption took place. The requirements for notification are contained in the agreement.

3. The taxpayer must not, within ten years before the redemption, have acquired the stock from a person whose stock (at the time of redemption) had been attributable to the taxpayer under constructive ownership rules. This particular requirement applies only if avoidance of income tax is one of the principal purposes for the above acquisitions or transfers.

Example 1: W Corporation has 200 shares outstanding. Husband, the sole shareholder, transfers 100 shares to his wife, and two years later the corporation redeems her shares. These shares, having been acquired within ten years of redemption from a person who owns, at the time of redemption, stock attributed to the taxpayer under the constructive ownership rules, disqualifies the stock for capital gains treatment.

Example 2: X Corporation has 200 shares outstanding. Husband, the sole shareholder, transfers 100 shares to his wife. The corporation, two years later, redeems the husband's shares. This again would not satisfy the third requirement set forth above.

Example 3: This is an example of a technique showing how a complete termination of a shareholder's interest can be used to accomplish your client's current income tax and future estate tax-planning goals. Mom and Dad have for twenty years operated M and D's Hardware & Supply, Inc. From a very humble beginning, they have developed not only a substantial retail business but also have become the distributors for selected farm machinery throughout the Midwest. Mom has, since its inception as a corporation more than twenty years ago, owned 50 percent of the stock. Mom and Dad are now nearing retirement age. The two oldest sons have worked in the business for the last five years. It is contemplated that the two sons should take over the active management of the business.

If Mom and Dad's initial capital investment in the corporation was $10,000 and if it is currently worth $400,000, there are several planning techniques that could be currently utilized to shift the ownership of the business. One possibility is a complete redemption of Mom's stock combined with an installment sale of Dad's stock to his sons to obtain the maximum tax results.

In this situation, Mom and Dad may not have sufficient outside assets and income to maintain their life-style after retirement. This need for additional income coupled with the need to provide a method for the payment of stock normally indicates a redemption of Mom's stock. In most instances, Number 1 and 2 sons have no significant independent assets. If the corporation is to redeem Mom's stock in consideration of a promissory note bearing interest at 9 percent per annum, payable in equal monthly installments over a term of ten years, the monthly payment will be $2,534, or approximately $30,408 a year. The vast portion of these installments will, in the beginning years, be interest. This, of course, directly reduces the taxable income of the corporation. However, the remaining principal must be paid in after-tax income.

Assume that over the ten-year period, $20,000 of each $30,408 payment is applied against the principal indebtedness of $200,000.

If the corporation is in the 15 percent tax bracket, $33,937 in before-tax income must be available for the redemption— principal and interest. A portion of this income will be available from the reduction in salary expenses when Mom and Dad retire. However, the remaining amount may have to be obtained from other funds of the corporation. If the corporation is at a higher tax bracket, for example 39 percent, the before-tax income required is $43,195. The question then becomes: Why don't Number 1 son and Number 2 son pay for the stock individually?

The reason is that their individual tax rates may even be higher than the corporate rate. If each had a net taxable income prior to redemption of $72,000, he would be subject to a federal tax at the 33 percent rate. If it was determined that each of them, because of the increased responsibilities, would receive sufficient additional salary to purchase the stock of his mother individually, he would have to receive an additional $20,129 a year, calculated as follows:

Additional Salary	$20,129
Deductible Interest (average)	5,204
	$14,925
Applicable Tax on the Nondeductible Portion of the Salary at a Marginal Tax Rate of 33 Percent	$4,925
Average After Tax Payments Available for Principal Payments	$10,000

The total cost to the corporation in additional salary is $40,258. This total cost can be compared to the cost if the corporation had redeemed the stock. At the 39 percent marginal tax bracket, the cost to the corporation would be approximately $2,937 more a year. On the other hand, if the corporation was in the 15 percent marginal tax bracket, the total cost would be about $6,241 less. An additional problem could arise if the sons purchased stock. In that case, a part or all of the increased salary may be designated as unreasonable compensation. It may subject the two sons to a higher marginal bracket. In the previous example, the marginal tax bracket increases from 28 percent to 33 percent for all increase in income. Future increases in salary will be extremely difficult if they are already receiving high salaries.

WARNING: The Tax Reform Act of 1986 disallows the current deduction of a portion or all of the interest which normally was incurred by the shareholders to purchase the stock. Beginning in 1987, only investment interest up to the amount of the investment interest income may be deducted. The excess will not be disallowed but carried forward to subsequent years when there is sufficient investment income. While the full impact of the law will not be felt until 1991 (phase in during the interim), if the interest is not deductible currently this would have a definite impact on planning, as described above. It would appear that there will be an increased use of stock redemption agreements instead of cross-purchase agreements. In the above example, if the sons did not have investment interest income from other sources, the after-tax costs to each would be $22,692, or a total cost to the corporation of $45,385 beginning in 1989.

Many times it will be necessary for you to structure not only a redemption but also a sale. In the previous instance of Mom and Dad, it may be sufficient to have Mom's stock redeemed to provide the needed cash flow. For estate planning, Dad could then commence a gifting program to Number 1 son and Number 2 son. After Mom's ten-year note has been paid, Dad may sell the remainder of his stock to his two sons to maintain retirement income. If a greater cash flow is initially needed, it may be necessary to completely redeem Mom's stock and also to sell a portion of Dad's stock to Number 1 son and Number 2 son. A decision in this instance can be made only after a complete analysis of the income tax ramifications for the individual parties. It must also be ascertained whether or not the corporation can support the payments that are anticipated.

You must remember that all payments to support any redemption or sale originate from corporate income.

The planning technique you finally utilize should maximize the after-tax income to both the corporation and the individual parties. (A further discussion of a sale coupled with a redemption is found in ¶601.7.)

There are certain considerations that should be reviewed and certain steps that can be taken when a closely held corporation is contemplating the transfer from one generation to the next.

> **Key Idea:** Planning after the Tax Reform Act of 1986 will dictate the increased use of the covenant not-to-compete. Commencing in 1988, the tax rate on capital gains and ordinary income is the same. The selling shareholder no longer faces any significant disadvantages from having a portion of his payments classified as a covenant rather than as a sale of stock. On the other hand, principal payments are not deductible by the corporation while payments under a covenant not-to-compete are deductible.

Impact on Terminating Shareholder

1. Is he going to be receiving social security? If so, how much?
2. Is it anticipated that the terminating shareholder will continue to render any services to the corporation?
3. What are the terminating shareholder's cash needs from the corporation?
4. What is his marginal tax rate?
5. Are there other children, and are they going to be affected?
6. What are the estate-planning ramifications?

Impact on Purchasing Shareholder

1. What is the tax rate of the purchasing shareholder?
2. Can the corporation pay the purchasing shareholder additional compensation to fund the buy-out and not have said compensation deemed unreasonable?

3. What are the future income needs of the purchasing shareholder?

4. Does he have investment income so that he can deduct the interest paid?

Steps to Take Prior to Date of Retirement

☐ A portion of the stock should be gifted to the other spouse.

☐ Consider incorporating with preferred as well as common stock.

☐ Consider reorganization of the corporation from just common stock to common and preferred stock.

☐ Consider incorporation with debt as well as common stock.

Planning Alternatives at Time of Retirement

☐ Redemption of all the stock of either Mom and/or Dad

☐ Purchase of all or part of the stock of one of the shareholders and redemption of the stock of the other

☐ Recapitalization of the corporation into preferred and common stock

Goals of the Corporation

☐ Maintain sufficient income for the current shareholders

☐ Limit the growth of the estate of the older generation

☐ Make sure the corporation has sufficient income to sustain the transfer of ownership as well as fund the growth of the business and maintain reasonable salaries

The chart on the next page capsulizes stock redemptions that qualify for capital gains treatment and shows when to use the applicable Code section.

Buying Out Shareholders' Stock Redemptions That Qualify for Capital Gains Treatment[1]

Section and Description	Whether Constructive Ownership Rules Are Applicable	When Section Should Be Used and Its Basic Requirements
Section 303—redemption of a portion of the stock at the shareholder's death	No	1. At least 20% of authorized and issued stock of company is included in determining value of decedent's estate. For purposes of the 20% rule, the surviving spouse's interest in jointly held and community property is treated as included in the decedent's estate. 2. Fair market value of stock owned by the estate amounts to more than 35% adjusted gross estate. 3. The decedent's estate has substantial death taxes, funeral, and administrative costs.
Section 302(b)(3)—complete termination of shareholder's interest	No	1. Used to completely redeem all the stock owned directly or indirectly by the individual shareholder. 2. After the redemption, he must not be a shareholder, employee officer, or director of the corporation.

[1] Virtually all stock redemptions utilizing appreciated property will result in income to the distributing corporations, save and except for some redemptions which also qualify as partial liquidations and redemptions which qualify under Section 303. Even these limited exceptions when they are applicable should cease to have any further effect on January 1, 1989.

continued

Section and Description	Whether Constructive Ownership Rules Are Applicable	When Section Should Be Used and Its Basic Requirements
		3. Must not have received or transferred stock within ten years of redemption.
Section 302(b)(2)—substantially disproportionate redemption	Yes	1. To substantially reduce the shareholder's stock in a corporation— usually utilized in a corporation which is not closely held by one family. 2. Shareholder must, after the redemption, own less than 50% of the outstanding stock of the corporation. 3. The percentage of stock owned by shareholder after the redemption must be less than 80% of the stock which he owned prior to the redemption.
Section 302(b)(1)—distributions not equivalent to dividends	Probably	1. Not to be utilized in planning. 2. May qualify a distribution for capital gains treatment when all else fails.

[601.3] Complete Redemption of Stock Can Be Utilized among Unrelated Shareholders for Both Life and Death Planning

In the preceding section, we dealt exclusively with using a complete redemption to facilitate estate and income tax planning among family members. However, many small corporations are not owned by one family. There may be two or more families owning equal or unequal interests in the corporations. Life and death time problems can be avoided by proper planning. The most common planning device you can use between unrelated shareholders is a shareholder agreement. There are many varieties of these agreements, either funded by insurance or unfunded.

All shareholder agreements have the following two goals in common:

1. To provide for a smooth transition of the business upon the death or disability of one of the shareholders.
2. To ensure that the deceased shareholder's estate or the disabled shareholder receives a fair return on his investment upon transfer of his stock.

The provisions of each agreement are dependent upon the specific goals which the agreement serves to satisfy. Many agreements are of limited scope in that they deal only with one problem. An example of this type of agreement would be one which provides the remaining shareholders with a right of first refusal prior to the transfer to a third party.

In my practice, I consider shareholder agreements to be divided into two separate categories. The first is the type of agreement which I designate the "equal-party agreement." These agreements are entered into between the corporation and/or the shareholders in such a manner that they are "fair" to all parties. The interests are equal in the sense that each shareholder is contributing an equal amount of time and/or money to the business.

The second type of agreement is designated the "keep-them-interested" agreement. Many small corporations, in order to retain the dedication of their key employees, "sell" their employees a stock interest in the corporation. Most times, this amounts to a small percentage of the issued stock. The purpose of the procedure is to give a proprietary interest to the individual employee. This agreement is rarely used when the intent is to have the employee obtain a substantial interest in the corporation.

In theory, this technique has merit. However, without

proper planning, it can cause serious problems. The problem usually occurs when the employment of a disgruntled share-holder is terminated by the corporation. If upon termination, he goes into competition with his prior employer, he can make himself a general pest in all future planning because of the rights he has as a shareholder. For example, he could have access to all financial statements of the corporation. An agreement, classified as a "call," solves this problem. This agreement provides that the corporation may redeem the employee's stock upon his death, disability, or termination of employment with the corporation. In all of these instances, the price is based upon the real worth of the shares. (See Appendix O.) If the stock was sold to the employee at book value or a multiple thereof, the "call" price would be determined in the same manner.

> **Example:** New Corporation was founded by Eager Beaver five years ago. It is a rapidly expanding corporation which is dependent upon numerous factors, among which are the loyalty and hard work of its employees. Eager Beaver, to encourage the employees to work harder, grants that each employee who has completed a year of service may buy one share of stock for each $10,000 of compensation he receives. The purchase price of the stock is determined to be one and one-half times the current book value. If Don, an employee of New Corporation, has a salary of $30,000, and if the book value of each share of stock is $1,000, he can purchase 3 shares of stock at $1,500 a share ($4,500 total).
>
> In the first year, he exercised this option. During subsequent years, however, because of personal financial commitments, he did not exercise his option to purchase any further stock of the business. He is offered a better job and leaves the employ of New Corporation. At this time, the book value per share of New Corporation has risen to $1,500 per share. Upon Don's termination of service, New Corporation will have the right, although not the obligation, to purchase his 3 shares of stock at $2,250 a share (one and one-half times current book value), or a total price of $6,750. Don has realized an increase of $2,250 in the value of his stock.

If you use this "keep-them-interested" agreement, the employee/shareholder can see his worth increase as the business expands. On the other hand, this agreement protects the corporation from the now trusted employee whose services may be terminated at a later date. There are many formats for this agreement. (One such agreement is included in Appendix P.) There is, of course, no reason why this agreement cannot contain a mandatory buy/sell provision rather than an option to purchase. The difference between this agreement and the common "equal-parties" agreement is that, in the "keep-them-interested" agreements, there should be a provision, whereupon any "termination of service" causes the operative terms to take effect.

In an "equal-parties" agreement, this provision is harsher and less appropriate. If there are three equal shareholders, and this provision is contained in the shareholders' agreement, any two can force the third to sell. Sometimes this is appropriate. In most instances, however, it could have a counterproductive effect.

> **Key Idea:** In either the equal-parties or the keep-them-interested agreements, it is often important to contain a provision restricting the terminating employee from competing with the corporation after his stock is bought out. The last thing the corporation wants is for a prior employee to be repurchased with corporate funds and to have the terminated employee use said funds in competition. Care in drafting these restrictive covenants should be exercised since they are not favored in the law. Courts have a tendency to enforce only those that are "reasonable" to both the corporation and the selling shareholder.

[601.4] Comparison of the Cross-Purchase and the Stock Redemption Shareholders' Agreement

Provisions of All Agreements: With either the "equal-parties" or "keep-them-interested" type of agreements, there are two general types of contracts that you can use: the stock redemption and the cross-purchase agreements. In the stock redemption, the corporation purchases the stock of the deceased or selling shareholder. In the cross-purchase agreement, the remaining shareholder or shareholders purchase the stock. There are certain terms and conditions which should be considered in all agreements, as follows:

1. The event which will cause the agreement to take effect, such as death, termination of service, and disability.
2. The method of determining the purchase price (see Appendix Q). The most common methods are as follows:
   (a) Book value or some multiple.
   (b) Formula using earnings (that is, eight times the average of five years' earnings).
   (c) Formula using earnings and book value.
   (d) Book value plus appreciation of various real and personal property.
   (e) Fixed price determined by the shareholders. This is a "fair" price fixed by the shareholders at the time of the execution of the agreement and amended thereafter on a regular basis.
   (f) Fixed price determined by the shareholders at date of execution plus the increase in the book value of the corporation after the date of execution.
3. The method of paying the purchase price:
   (a) Cash
   (b) Installment payments
4. The method of funding the agreement:
   (a) Life insurance
   (b) Corporate assets
   (c) Individual assets
5. The type of obligation imposed upon the parties when the specific event occurs:
   (a) Mandatory buy/sell by all parties
   (b) Option, on behalf of the corporation, to buy the terminating shareholder's stock
   (c) Option, on behalf of the shareholders, to have their stock bought by the corporation
6. The restrictions which are placed upon the sale of the stock during lifetime:

    (a) The corporation has the right of first refusal before the sale by the shareholder.

    (b) The corporation has the right to purchase the stock at a predetermined price before the sale by the shareholder.

7. Whether or not to insert a covenant not-to-compete in the contract.

These are the major terms and conditions which these shareholder agreements can contain. They are not the only terms and conditions contained in the agreements, nor are they the only options available. Each of these agreements must be tailored to the individual needs of the shareholders and the corporation. However, the above list sets forth those considerations which are the heart and soul of a successful buy/sell agreement.

Which Agreement Should You Choose? Prior to drafting a buy/sell agreement, a review of the advantages and disadvantages of the stock redemption versus the cross-purchase should be undertaken.

The difference between a cross-purchase buy/sell and a stock redemption agreement is the party who either has the option or the obligation to purchase the stock of a deceased or terminating shareholder. It has been my experience that as long as there is only an option and not an obligation to purchase, this option should rest with the corporation. On the other hand, if there is a mandatory obligation to purchase upon death (even though there is only an option to purchase during lifetime), either of the two agreements can be utilized.

The cross-purchase agreement which places an obligation on the other shareholder will rarely be used unless there is sufficient life insurance to fund a vast portion of the purchase price. Thus, an important factor in a vast majority of cases is how much life insurance is needed to fund the agreements and what the corresponding premium cost is. These premiums must be paid in after-tax funds. If $100,000 of life insurance can be purchased for $1,000 of premiums, the additional funds can be distributed as additional compensation without too many problems. On the other hand, if the same $100,000 requires a $5,000 premium payment and if the officer is already in the 33 percent marginal tax bracket, this will require an increase in salary of $7,462, or about $620 per month. Unreasonable compensation could pose a problem.

Advantages and Disadvantages of the Cross-Purchase Agreement versus the Stock Redemption Agreement

	Advantage of Stock Redemption Agreement	Advantage of Cross-Purchase Agreement
Multiple shareholders	X	
Assurance all premiums paid	X	
Need for increase in basis of stock when purchased from shareholder or his estate		X
Corporation tax bracket less than shareholder's tax bracket	X	
Corporation tax bracket greater than or equal to shareholder's tax bracket		X
Problem of unreasonable compensation	X	
Unreasonable accumulation of earnings problem and agreement funded with insurance.		X
Various ages and differences in health of individual shareholders		X
Need for business to fund portion of purchase price	X	

The basic advantages of the stock redemption agreement are as follows:

1. Ease of administration.
2. Assurance that the life insurance policies funding the agreement are being paid.

3. Corporation's tax bracket is usually less than the individual shareholder's tax bracket.

The basic advantages of a cross-purchase agreement are as follows:

1. Upon death, the shareholder receives an increase in tax basis.
2. The payment of premiums in and of itself is "fair" in that the person who is most likely to purchase the stock pays his fair share rather than having the premium payments divided equally. This is especially true in the case of unequal ages or unequal cost of premiums for other medical reasons.

The above analysis indicates that it is extremely important to analyze each factual situation to determine which of the various agreements will be the most appropriate.

[601.5] Determining When a Partial Redemption of a Shareholder's Stock Will Qualify for Capital Gains Treatment

In the previous sections of this chapter, we discussed requirements for capital gains treatment in a complete redemption of a shareholder's stock. There are times when a complete redemption is not the appropriate vehicle. Section 302 of the Code sets forth two additional types of redemption distributions that will be considered a sale or exchange and not result in dividend income, as follows:

1. When the redemption is substantially disproportionate
2. When even if the distribution does not qualify as a complete or disproportionate redemption, it is not essentially equivalent to a dividend

In addition to these Section 302 provisions, there are two other sections in the Code where a partial redemption will not be classified as a dividend, as follows:

1. A redemption pursuant to the terms of Section 303 where the proceeds are utilized for the payment of death taxes, funeral, and administration expenses (see ¶603)

2. A redemption pursuant to a partial liquidation of the corporation (see ¶703.5)

Disproportionate Redemptions: In order to have a distribution considered substantially disproportionate, a major change in the shareholder's "stock circumstances" must take place. An analysis of the shareholder's ownership before and after the redemption must be made. In order for the redemption to be considered disproportionate after the redemption, the following three requirements must be met:

1. The shareholder must own, both directly and constructively, less than 50 percent of the combined voting power of all classes of stock.
2. The shareholder's percentage of voting stock still outstanding must be less than 80 percent of his previously owned percentage.
3. The shareholder's percentage of both voting and nonvoting common stock must be less than 80 percent of the percentage he previously owned. In making this computation, if there is more than one class of common stock outstanding, the determinations shall be made with reference to fair market value.

Example: Redeeming Corporation has 400 shares of common stock currently issued and outstanding. These shares of stock are owned equally by A, B, C, and D. None of the four are in any way related under the rules of constructive ownership. Redeeming Corporation redeems a portion of the share of stock owned by each person.

The schedule on page 281 will analyze the effects of this distribution on each shareholder:

Only shareholder A owns less than 80 percent of the shares that he previously owned. Accordingly, the redemption may be considered a dividend to B and C but not to A. These rules are fairly complex, and though a full discussion is beyond the scope of this book, an introduction to its general provisions allows the tax planner to recognize the factual situation when this section becomes applicable.

Shareholder	A	B	C	D
Shares owned before redemption	100	100	100	100
Shares redeemed	55	25	20	0
Number of shares owned after redemption	45	75	80	100
Ownership percentage before redemption	25%	25%	25%	25%
Ownership percentage after redemption	15%	25%	26⅔%	33⅓%
Individual ownership percentage after redemption/ownership percentage before redemption	60%	100%	107%	133%

This redemption vehicle should be used only when there is a desire to substantially reduce one of the minority shareholders' interest in the corporation. One particular instance in which a disproportionate redemption may be appropriate is when there are three equal shareholders, each owning 33 shares of common stock. One of the shareholders, X, needs funds for personal reasons, and the corporation has some additional cash. Accordingly, it decides to redeem 15 of the shares of stock that X owns. This redemption will qualify as a disproportionate redemption in that after the redemption, X's percentage ownership is less than 80 percent of what it was before, and he never was a 50 percent shareholder. On the other hand, the voting control of the corporation is not substantially changed since it still requires two of the three to constitute a majority. It should be noted that X's share of the future appreciation in the business will be reduced because his interest in the corporation has been reduced. In a closely held corporation controlled by family members, the substantially disproportionate redemption rarely comes into play because of the constructive ownership rules. These rules consider the individual as not only owning stock in his own name but also stock owned by his spouse, children, grandchildren, and certain other related partnerships, trusts, and estates. Thus, in a situation where there are equal shareholders or where there is a majority shareholder, usually the complete redemption is the only vehicle that can be utilized.

Redemptions not Equivalent to a Dividend: If a redemption will not qualify as either a complete or substantially disproportionate redemption, the redemption may still receive capital gains treatment if it is not essentially equivalent to a dividend. This amorphous doctrine would appear to be basically an escape clause. How wide the route is has been subject to divergent opinions among the various courts and also between the Internal Revenue Service and tax planners. In the case of *United States v. Maclin P. Davis,* 397 U.S. 301 (1970), the Supreme Court has given some guidance. The Court held that a redemption, which has the effect of distributing property to the shareholder without changing his relative economic interest in the corporation, is essentially equivalent to a dividend. In order to qualify for exchange treatment, the Court held that there must be a meaningful reduction of a shareholder's proportionate interest in the corporation. In addition, the Court held that the constructive ownership rules are to be applied in determining whether or not relative economic interest of the corporation has changed. Even after this ruling, there are no clear-cut guidelines which a tax planner can follow. In other words, this is not a section which should be utilized in planning, but only in situations when it is necessary to justify what otherwise may have been a tax mistake.

[601.6] Advantages in Using Appreciated Property in the Distributions of Stock

The Tax Reform Act of 1986 has vastly changed the law as to the recognition of gain by a corporation upon the distribution of appreciated property in a nonliquidating distribution (normally a dividend). The corporation that distributes the appreciated property after the Tax Reform Act of 1986 recognizes gain on nonliquidating distributions of appreciated property to a shareholder with respect to the stock if the distribution is considered a dividend by the shareholders. Under the pre-Tax Reform Act law, there were several exceptions to this recognition of gain. These exceptions were (1) qualified dividends distributed with respect to qualified stock (see ¶403.1B) and (2) partial liquidation distributions (see ¶703.5).

If one of the exceptions to recognition of gain applied, gain is recognized only on the distribution of certain types of property, that is, those properties that gave rise to recapture under Sections 1245 and 1250. It appears that with the Tax Reform Act of 1986, Congress intended that the repeal of these exceptions to nonrecognition of gain on dividend distributions of appreciated property is meant to apply to qualified corporations (see ¶702 for a description of a qualified corporation) on distributions before January 1, 1989, only to the extent that the gain would have produced ordinary income or short-term capital gains. Accordingly, there still may be a limited door as far as what can be accomplished for qualified corporations making distributions prior to December 31, 1988. In addition, even after the full implementation of the Tax Reform Act of 1986, certain distributions of appreciated property will not result in taxation at the corporate level, as follows:

1. A distribution which qualifies as a split-off does not result in taxation to the corporation. A split-off is a distribution by a parent/corporation of the stock of its subsidiary to its shareholders in exchange for part or all of its stock. (An analysis of the utilization of a split-off is in ¶604.) Also, an analysis of the possible tax problems to the corporation should be considered. (These are discussed in ¶702.1.)

2. A transaction which also qualifies as a reorganization does not cause taxation to the corporation. (These reorganizations are more fully described in ¶602.)

3. For all transactions prior to September 1, 1982, a complete redemption of a shareholder who owns 10 percent or more of the authorized and issued common stock of the corporation normally will not result in taxation to the corporation.

4. A debt obligation of the distributing corporation is not considered appreciated property.

   Example: ABC Corporation, a qualified closely held corporation, owns land that it purchased many years ago with a basis of $1,000 that is now worth $100,000. This land was originally purchased to provide for corporate expansion; however, the corporation has never utilized it. The corporation would like to distribute this property as a dividend. This dividend would result in taxation of $100,000 to its shareholders. On January 1, 1989, and thereafter, this distribution would produce tax at both the corporate and individual levels and could have disastrous effects. Assume ABC Corporation is in the 34 percent tax bracket and the individual shareholders are in the 28 percent tax bracket:

Tax to corporation on distribution of the property	$34,000
Tax on distribution to the individual shareholders of the property	$28,000

If, on the other hand, the property can be distributed by the corporation prior to January 1, 1989, there is no taxation at the corporate level. The sole tax would be at the individual level, which would result in a tax of $28,000.

WARNING: Except as set forth above, virtually all distributions of appreciated property in redemption of stock will result in taxation at the corporate level.

[601.7] Coupling a Redemption with a Sale to Solve Many Tax and Economic Problems

Up to this point, we have considered situations where a shareholder's stock will be completely redeemed, partially redeemed, or sold to another party or parties. At times, it may be advantageous to have the purchasing shareholders buy a portion of his stock and to have the corporation redeem the remainder. With this particular technique, the purchaser obtains 100 percent control of the corporation through the utilization of a portion of the assets of the corporation. This will reduce the actual purchase price by reducing the value of the assets transferred.

There are several factual situations where the redemption of stock may help facilitate the sale or transfer of the business. This may occur when the sole shareholder or one or more of the controlling shareholders wishes to dispose of his interest in the corporation and any of the following situations exist:

1. The prospective purchaser is a junior executive who does not have sufficient cash or credit to purchase the stock.

Example: A, the sole shareholder of XYZ Corporation, is nearing retirement age. He has no children interested in continuing the family business. In addition, because of the technical nature of the business, it is difficult to find an outside purchaser to pay him the fair market value of the corporation. Junior Executive does not have the financial capabilities to individually purchase the entire issued and outstanding stock owned by A.

Solution: A possible solution to this problem is to have A sell to Junior Executive, on a long-term sales contract, 50 percent of the stock owned by him. After this contract is entered into, XYZ Corporation will redeem, also on a long-term sales contract, the balance of A's outstanding stock. The corporation helps finance the purchase by Junior Executive. A will get the tax benefits of an installment sale.

2. The book value of the corporation is too high and there are assets owned by the business which may not directly contribute to the production of income.

Example: Value Furniture Store, Inc., is owned entirely by X. X's son wishes to purchase the business, and X is willing to sell it to him. The value of the business is determined as follows:

Net value of going concern (assets less liabilities)	$420,000
Net value of buildings (assets less liabilities)	180,000
Total Purchase Price:	$600,000

The son does not have any independent assets. Thus, the purchase of all of the stock owned by his father would be impossible without the use of a redemption. He purchases 70 percent of the stock from his father and issues to him an installment note for this stock. The corporation, after the sale, redeems the remaining 30 percent of X's stock by transferring to him the appreciated real property. With this redemption, the son becomes the sole owner of the corporation.

Key Idea: Since the Installment Sales Revision Act of 1980, the above tool has had increased applicability. Prior to that date, when the redemption exceeded 30 percent of the total purchase price, the Internal Revenue Service attempted to disallow installment sales reporting. The Installment Sales Revision Act of 1980 no longer requires that a maximum of 30 percent of the sales price be received in the year of the sale. However, there still is the problem that the redemption could be considered a dividend distribution, and thus care should still be exercised in structuring a transaction such as the above, especially among related parties. It should also be noted that after the Tax Reform Act of 1986, the distribution of the appreciated property in redemption of the stock, if it occurs after January 1, 1987, may result in income to Value Furniture Store, Inc.

3. The corporation has excess liquid assets which are not needed by the purchaser.

Example: In the event that the corporation set forth in item 2 above, had the $180,000 in cash or liquid assets instead of in real estate, it may be easy to redeem the stock of the shareholder for cash instead of appreciated property.

The above examples dealt with only one shareholder. This, of course, is artificial because many factual situations involve two or more shareholders. There is nothing in these examples that preclude their use with more than one shareholder. If the shareholders are related, it is necessary to consider the attribution rules to ensure that no further problems are incurred.

Tax Traps to Be Avoided: The first tax trap that occurs is when the redemption precedes the sale of the stock. If the redemption occurs first, it will be essentially equivalent to a dividend, and the Internal Revenue Service may attempt to tax the entire distribution as dividend income.

The second trap previously involved the ability to qualify under the installment sale provisions. If the redemption involved cash or property, and the sale of the stock would otherwise qualify for an installment sale, the Internal Revenue Service had attempted to combine the two transactions, thus disqualifying the installment sale. If the facts in the second example were changed, and the real property amounted to more than 30 percent of the total of the purchase and redemption price, the Internal Revenue Service had previously attempted to tax the entire transaction as a sale and exchange in the year of sale. This, of course, had extremely detrimental effects on the entire tax plan.

The Tax Court and the 6th Circuit took this position in the case of *Zenz v. Quinlivan,* 213 F.2d 914 (6 Cir. 1954), the leading case in the area of sale and redemption. Both courts held that the 30 percent limitation set forth in Section 453 must be computed by aggregating the redemption price and the stock sale payment received in the year of stock sale, divided by the sum of the redemption price and sales price. With the enactment of the Installment Sales Revision Act of 1980, this trap should no longer prove to be a problem. This act has removed the 30 percent limitation in the year of sale, and even if the IRS prevails, the taxation should remain the same. Prior to the enactment of this act, the IRS had established a procedure wherein it would rule on the tax status of all portions of these transactions. With the change occasioned by the enactment of the Installment Sales Revision Act of 1980, and the virtual elimination of the second trap, the question becomes whether or not a ruling should be obtained in these transactions. This will depend upon the factual situation, whether the parties are related or unrelated, and also the future course of the law.

Tax Status of the Shareholder/Purchaser—Beware of a Constructive Dividend: Normally there are no problems and no tax effects upon the purchaser of the stock or upon the remaining shareholders in the corporation. The question becomes: "Are there any tax traps to be avoided by the shareholder/purchaser?" The answer is yes, when there is a cross-purchase agreement between the two shareholders. The following example will illustrate this problem.

A and B, nonrelated individuals, own all the outstanding stock of Corporation X. An agreement between them provides unconditionally that within ninety days after the death of either A or B, the survivor will purchase the decedent's stock from his estate. Upon the death of B, A causes Corporation X to assume the contract and redeem the stock from B's estate. The assignment of the contract to X, followed by the redemption by X of the stock owned by B's estate, will result in constructive distribution to A. Immediately on the death of B, A had a primary and unconditional obligation to perform the contract.

There is obviously a better way. A review of the stock purchase agreement which appears in Appendix Q will illustrate the preferred method.

Here's how to properly structure a stock purchase agreement:

> **Example:** A and B own all the issued and outstanding stock of X Corporation. The agreement included in Appendix Q between A and B provides that, upon death of either, X Corporation will redeem all of the stock owned by the decedent at his death. In the event that X Corporation does not redeem the shares from the estate, the agreement provides that the surviving shareholder will purchase the unredeemed shares from the decedent's estate. A, in accordance with the agreement, causes X Corporation to redeem all the shares owned by the estate of B. In this case, A is only conditionally liable under the agreement between A and B. Since A is not primarily obligated to purchase the stock from the estate of B, he receives no constructive distribution when the corporation redeems the stock.

As long as you take care and as long as you follow the format set forth in the Revenue Ruling 69-608, 1962-2 C.B. 42, you should have no particular problems with these transactions.

Another area of concern for you is what I designate as an example of the "minnow swallowing the whale." If A owns 10 percent of the outstanding stock of the corporation and B owns 90 percent and if the corporation redeems B's stock, the question of a constructive dividend is raised. The answer is not clear-cut, and the only advice is "be careful."

This section illustrates those transactions where a redemption alone or coupled with a sale to a third party may be utilized to the benefit of all. It is not meant to be an all-inclusive list of the appropriate uses of these techniques. However, an awareness of the various avenues of approach may allow for solutions where none are readily apparent.

[602] HOW THE SELLING SHAREHOLDER CAN BENEFIT FROM THE PURCHASE OF STOCK BY REMAINING SHAREHOLDERS OR THIRD PARTIES

A purchaser can buy the stock of a selling shareholder with either property or cash. The transfer of property gives rise to several tax-planning opportunities. The purchaser has the opportunity to transfer property either through a taxable or a tax-free exchange. The general rule is that any transfer of property will be taxable unless specifically excluded under the provisions of the Internal Revenue Code. In other words, if X owns stock in Closely Held Corporation and wishes to transfer this stock to Y in exchange for Y's stock in GM and AT&T, this will be a taxable transaction. Both X and Y will have to report a sale or exchange and either a loss or gain, depending upon the basis of the property transferred and the value of the property received. On the other hand, if the acquiring person or corporation can structure a reorganization which will qualify under Section 368, the entire transfer may be nontaxable.

Examples of the most common types of tax-free transfers are as follows:

☐ Closely Held Corporation will be merged into another corporation. X, owner of Closely Held Corporation, will receive only stock in the merged corporation.

☐ Closely Held Corporation will become a wholly owned subsidiary of the other corporation. In this instance, if X received only stock, it should be a completely nontaxable transaction to him.

A full discussion of all the variations and ramifications of nontaxable stock and security exchanges are beyond the scope of this book for the reason that in closely held corporations the availability of such transactions usually does not satisfy the needs of the parties. However, from time to time, it will be possible for you to acquire another business through the use of a tax-free exchange, or, in the alternative, have your own corporation acquired by another in a tax-free exchange.

Usually a cash transaction will involve only one or a small group of purchasers. However, at times, this stock may be sold to the general public through an underwriter. The corporation will be considered as "going public." In this instance, the shareholder will dispose of a portion or all of his stock through a public offering. Commonly, the underwriter will purchase a portion, but usually not all of the shareholder's stock, and dispose of this stock after complying with approved federal and state Securities Laws. In this instance, it is possible to convert the unmarketable stock into cash without losing effective control of the corporation. This becomes particularly important when the controlling shareholder is getting older and the stock of the corporation comprises an inordinate portion of his total assets. Upon death, there must be enough liquid assets to pay state inheritance and federal estate taxes.

The following is an example of a problem which may force a corporation to go public:

> **Example:** A owns all the stock of Old Line Corporation. Old Line Corporation has been a family corporation for many years and has prospered under A's tutelage over the last thirty-five years. A is 62 years old and owns the following assets:

> | | |
> |---|---|
> | House | $150,000 |
> | Cash and Negotiable Securities | 200,000 |
> | All the Stock in Old Line Corporation | 2,500,000 |

> Upon A's death, assuming his wife predeceases him, his federal estate tax will exceed $1 million. There will not be sufficient liquid funds for his estate to pay this amount. In this case, it may be beneficial for him to sell a portion of his business to the public—for example, 50 percent. This will produce ($1.250 million less brokerage fees and taxes) sufficient liquidity to provide for the payment of his death taxes and expenses.

[603] HOW TO UTILIZE REDEMPTIONS TO PAY DEATH TAXES

An individual with assets such as those in the example in ¶602 faces an extreme liquidity problem. The estate needs sufficient liquid assets to pay death taxes and administration expenses. The personal representative of the estate of the deceased is faced with a liquidity crisis. One alternative is for him to arrange for a disposition of the shares in the closely held corporation. Since the buyer of these shares will often be a larger competitor, Old Line Corporation will tend to become consolidated in larger businesses. Congress, to help prevent this trend toward consolidation, enacted Section 303 of the Internal Revenue Code.

Section 303 has had a checkered history and has been revised directly and indirectly several times since its enactment. Its interrelationship with Section 1014 became particularly significant during the period from 1977 to 1980 when the question arose of whether the basis of stock at the date of death would carry over or whether the estate would receive a step up in basis. If the rules of carryover basis had continued in effect, the difference between the basis of the decedent's stock and the current market value would have been taxed as capital gains upon redemption. However, with the demise of the rules under carryover basis and the enactment of the Economic Recovery Tax Act of 1981, Section 303 has become particularly important.

Section 303 redemptions should be considered if 20 percent or more of the stock in two or more corporations is included in determining the value of the decedent's estate, and when the stock in these corporations is combined it amounts to more than 35 percent of the decedent's adjusted gross estate. In the Old Line Corporation example, if it was not for Section 303, the redemption of any portion of the stock held by A's estate would be considered dividend income. The estate interest in the stock of the corporation would have been 100 percent prior to the redemption and 100 percent after the redemption. However, with Section 303, the corporation may redeem a portion of the stock and have the redemption treated as a sale or exchange rather than a dividend. Because the estate gets a stepped up basis at date of death equivalent to the fair market value of the stock at that date or the alternative valuation date, there should be no capital gains by the estate upon this redemption. Accordingly, the difference between the fair market value at either the date of death or alternative valuation date and the redemption date will, in most instances, be insignificant.

In addition to liberalizing the rules for qualification under Section 303, this section, used in conjunction with the installment provisions of Section 6166, provides numerous planning opportunities for the estate with a liquidity problem.

Currently, the amount and timing of the redemption are subject to the following restrictions:

1. Generally, the amount of the redemption from the corporation cannot exceed the sum of the following:
    (a) Death taxes and interest thereon imposed because of the decedent's death
    (b) Funeral expenses allowed as a deduction
    (c) Administration expenses allowed as a deduction
2. The amounts distributed as a result of the redemption must be distributed to the decedent's estate within a certain time period, which is no later than:
    (a) Three years and ninety days after the due date of the federal estate tax return
    (b) Sixty days after the Tax Court decision in a contest of estate tax liability has become final
    (c) Within the time provided by the provisions allowing for installment payments of the estate tax due

The requirements for the utilization of Section 303 are as follows:

1. There must be a distribution and redemption of part or all of the decedent's stock of the corporation.
2. The stock redeemed must be included in the gross estate of the decedent, and the fair market value of the total stock must amount to more than 35 percent of the adjusted gross estate. Adjusted gross estate for this purpose is basically the gross estate less administration taxes, losses, and debts which are generally charged against the estate.

Under Section 303, two or more corporations can be combined if the decedent's estate owns 20 percent of the value of the outstanding stock in each corporation.

[603.1] Using Section 6166 in Conjunction with Section 303

Normally, estate taxes are due nine months after the death of the decedent. The need for substantial cash to pay the tax has created a liquidity crisis for many estates. The estate at this period of time must have cash available to pay not only the estate taxes, state inheritance taxes, and administrative costs but also to provide available cash for the needs of the beneficiaries. This need for cash has prompted many estates to sell the stock to the closely held corporation. For the past decade, Congress has been particularly worried about the consolidation of big businesses and the merger of small corporations.

The example on the next page highlights this problem. In this example, and in many more like it, it became apparent that the only real salvation for the estate was the sale of the corporation. In virtually all instances, the corporation purchasing stock was a bigger corporation, and thus, business was becoming more and more consolidated into big corporations. Congress viewed the consolidations as a direct result of the liquidity crisis at the death of the shareholder. Not only was this true in the business community but also in the farming community.

Since the farm is a capital-intensive, low cash-flow asset, it did not matter if the farm was owned by a corporation, a sole proprietorship, or a partnership. The death of the owner produced a liquidity crunch. Congress has attempted to remedy this problem in the Economic Recovery Tax Act of 1981 in the following two ways:

1. *Unlimited marital deduction and increased unified credit.* The law provides a unified credit of $192,800 which has an exemption equivalent of $600,000 in 1987. With proper planning, this credit coupled with the unlimited marital deduction will allow for the passing of $1.2 million by a married couple to the next generation tax free.

2. *Consolidation and attempt at coordinating the provisions under Sections 303, 6166, and 6166A.* This act in essence repeals the old provisions of 6166A and expands and liberalizes

the coverage under Section 6166. The Economic Recovery Act of 1981 now provides that Section 6166 will allow for a fifteen-year installment payment of the estate tax attributable to the decedent's estate if the closely held business or the value of the farm exceeds 35 percent of the adjusted gross estate. If the estate chooses this installment payout, only the interest need be paid annually for the first five years. The tax owed with interest may be paid in annual installments over the next ten years. The interest will be charged at the rate of 4 percent of the tax due, if the tax liability is less than $345,800. However, if the tax liability exceeds $345,800 (less the appropriate unified credit), the interest on any excess will be at the normal IRS interest rate. The interest is determined at 3 percent over the short-term federal rate. The deferral of the payment of the tax under this provision is limited to the tax attributable to the closely held business or family farm.

Example: X dies and it is determined that the total estate tax due is $750,000. The estate tax attributable to the closely held corporate stock is $500,000. The $500,000 can be deferred, and $250,000 must be paid within nine months. Since X dies in 1987 when the estate's unified credit was $192,800, $153,000 ($345,800 − $192,800) will bear interest at 4 percent, and the remaining $347,000 will bear interest at 3 percent over the short-term federal rate.

There were certain other changes enacted by ERTA which have an impact upon post-mortem estate planning, as follows:

1. Deferral of the tax is continued provided not more than 50 percent of the assets of the business are disposed of and not more than 50 percent of the value of the business is withdrawn.

2. The rule for aggregation of two or more closely held businesses has been changed. As long as the estate owns at least 20 percent of the outstanding stock, this stock may qualify for aggregation.

3. The unpaid balance of the tax will not be accelerated upon the death of the decedent's heir or subsequent transferor

provided the interest of the business passes to a family member or heir or a subsequent transferee.

4. In the event of default in the making of any payment, there is no longer an automatic acceleration of principal and interest due if the delinquent payment is made within six months of the due date.

The following chart provides a bird's-eye view of the choices open to you when a retiring or deceased shareholder must obtain funds from the corporation to pay estate taxes and administration costs:

Comparison of Requirements and Advantages of Sections 303, 6166

	Section 303	Section 6166
1. Percentage of the total gross estate which the business interest represents	Must be more than 35% of the adjusted gross estate	Must be more than 35% of the adjusted gross estate
2. Maximum amount of tax eligible for deferral, or in reference to Section 303 the maximum redemption	Death taxes (attributable to business) funeral and administration expenses	Total tax multiplied by the total value of the business divided by the adjusted gross estate
3. Interest rate on unpaid principal balance	Not applicable	4% on the lesser of total deferred taxes or deferred taxes on the first $1 million of fair market value; variable rate on the balance, based on 3% over the federal rate
4. Percentage required if two or more businesses are combined	20% of each corporation must be owned	20% of each corporation must be owned
5. Maximum number of shareholders	None	15

[603.2] Using Before-Death Planning to Ensure Qualification under Section 303 and Section 6166

Your planning prior to the date of death should involve the structuring of the decedent's estate in such a way that it will qualify for the Section 303 redemption or an installment payment under Section 6166.

Planning Tips

1. Husband and wife own stock in a closely held corporation as joint tenants. If nothing is done, it will be impossible to redeem the stock upon the death of either husband or wife and qualify under Section 303. While the stock is part of the adjusted gross estate, the taxes cannot be paid from the proceeds of the redemption because the surviving joint tenant and not the estate will own the stock. This unfavorable result can be avoided by converting joint tenancy property into tenancy in common prior to death.

2. The same problem would occur if the will left the shares to the wife and made the estate liable for the entire payment of the taxes and administration costs. Instead of bequeathing the shares of stock to the opposite spouse, a specified amount can be paid to him or her.

3. Creative gifting of nonbusiness property may also produce the desired results.

The use of the $10,000 annual exclusion and gift splitting may also reduce the adjusted gross estate to an amount where the business interest would qualify. In addition, the unlimited marital deduction for lifetime gifts offers another possibility for reducing one's nonbusiness estate. For example, an owner of substantial liquid assets who also owns stock in a closely held business may with proper planning divide the marketable and nonmarketable assets between his wife and himself.

The following example will illustrate some possibilities in this regard:

Example: An elderly married couple own the following property:

House in Joint Tenancy: $ 400,000
Marketable Securities: 1,000,000
Closely Held Corporation: 2,000,000

Proper planning may dictate that one spouse own only stock in the closely held corporation and the other spouse own the house and marketable securities. This would provide for the maximum deferral of estate taxes upon the death of the husband. In this instance, he may wish to limit his marital deduction to one-half of the gross estate. If he dies first, his estate would pay a tax on the excess of $600,000. He could, of course, reduce his estate to zero by granting a maximum marital deduction to his wife. However, it may be more advantageous to provide that upon his death, $1 million will be given to his wife, and therefore $1 million would remain in his estate.

In this case, there would be a deferral of $153,000 at 4 percent for fifteen years. His wife, upon her death, assuming that the stock represents at least 35 percent of her adjusted gross estate, would also have this right of deferral of payment of a portion of the tax due or could have the corporation redeem a portion of the stock pursuant to Section 303.

The full impact of creative planning such as this is difficult to determine prior to the death of the first spouse. Thus, appropriate planning would indicate that flexibility should be maintained, and the surviving spouse should be given the right to disclaim all or a portion of his or her interest.

> **Key Idea:** With the enactment of the Economic Recovery Act of 1981, and its liberalization of Sections 303 and 6166, post-mortem planning becomes extremely important; thus, wills should be drafted to provide for the effective use of a full or partial disclaimer.

[603.3] Using Postmortem Planning to Allow for a Section 303 Redemption through a Recapitalization of the Corporation

There are certain actions that can be taken after death to qualify for a Section 303 redemption. Any type of stock interest can be redeemed using this unique post-death planning tool for bailing out cash from a corporation. This interest can either be voting, nonvoting, or preferred stock. In addition, the timing of a recapitalization can occur not only before the death but also in the post-mortem period.

The following is an example of how a recapitalization can occur and how it can benefit the individual shareholders (assuming there is cooperation among all parties):

> **Example:** X and Y each own 50 percent of the common stock of ABC Corporation. After X's death, the corporation has sufficient liquid assets to make a Section 303 redemption. In addition, the stock that X's estate owns satisfies the requirements for a Section 303 redemption. If a portion of this common stock is redeemed, his family's percentage of voting control in the corporation will be adversely affected. Accordingly, ABC Corporation can issue, through a nontaxable pro rata stock dividend preferred stock of the corporation. The amount of this stock could approximate the taxes, administrative costs, and so on. The corporation could then redeem the preferred stock from X's estate, without changing the voting control of the corporation. While it is not likely that Congress intended to upset this type of planning when it passed OBRA 1987, a review of the law's provisions should be undertaken before implementing a program such as set forth above.

[604]   HOW TO USE SPIN-OFFS, SPLIT-UPS, AND SPLIT-OFFS TO DIVIDE THE BUSINESS

[604.1]   Dividing the Business into Separate Corporations Allows for the Solution of Business and Personal Problems at No Tax Cost

WARNING: From time to time, dissension within the corporation may threaten the future profitability of the business. Nothing can ruin a profitable business more quickly than the inability of the principal parties to agree on the proper course of action.

One viable solution, in the appropriate instance, is to divide the business with each of the shareholders retaining one operation. This, of course, is not always feasible, but when the opportunity presents itself, you should explore it.

The following is an example showing the technique for dividing the business into separate corporations:

Example: X Corporation is owned equally by A and B. X is in the retail clothing business and operates two stores in different cities. A and B find it impossible to continue the operation of the business together. One solution to this problem would be to develop a technique where A would become the sole owner of one store and B would become the sole owner of the other.

Another possibility for using the technique of dividing up a corporation into separate operations presents itself when there are two or more businesses. One has historically been profitable and the other either has not been profitable or is in a high risk area. Your goal in this particular instance is to divide the entity so that the profitable business is insulated from the losses which may be incurred in the nonprofitable or high risk area.

The following is an example showing the technique for dividing the business when there are two or more businesses:

Example X is in the business of fire protection equipment sales and service. Historically he has sold fire extinguishers and other equipment to be utilized by commercial and manufacturing businesses. As a sideline of this business, he began to establish fire control systems in restaurants and in computer rooms of major companies in his service area. These systems contained many products which were relatively new in the field of fire protection and thus had no history as to their reliability. The potential magnitude of a loss through a products liability suit in this portion of the business was enormous.

In order to protect his long established and profitable business, he decided to create a subsidiary to run its installation of fire prevention systems. The old business, which was profitable and had little risk, was retained as the parent corporation.

[604.2] Techniques for Dividing a Corporation

There are three basic techniques which you can use in order to divide a corporation. They are designated spin-off, split-up, and split-off, as follows:

1. *How to effect a division of the business through a spin-off.* Old Corporation is conducting two separate and distinct businesses. One is the manufacture and distribution of pool tables and accessories from its plant and warehouse. The other is the operation of various retail stores selling the pool tables and accessories to the general public throughout the Midwest. The method of effecting a spin-off would be to have Old Corporation form New Corporation and transfer to it the retail stores. After creating this new subsidiary, Old Corporation would distribute to its shareholders a pro rata dividend of all of New Corporation's stock. The shareholders who previously had owned shares only in Old Corporation would now own both Old Corporation and New Corporation stock. Their ownership in each would be equivalent.

2. *How to divide the business through a split-off.* A split-off is accomplished in exactly the same way as a spin-off, except for the final step where shareholders X and Y surrender a portion of the stock that they own in Old Corporation for the shares in New Corporation.

3. *How to divide a corporation through a split-up.* The split-up uses a different format. In the split-up, Old Corporation would create two wholly owned subsidiaries, New Corporation 1 to own and operate the retail outlets and New Corporation 2 to own the manufacturing and warehouse facilities. Then Old Corporation would be liquidated, and X and Y would exchange their shares of stock in Old Corporation for new shares of stock.

[604.3] Effect of Non-Pro Rata Distribution in Eliminating Dissension

The above examples have illustrated the concept of a pro rata distribution for the division of the business. A pro rata distribution, while it will facilitate the sale of a portion of the business, usually serves no purpose in resolving internal dissension. The non-pro rata distribution, on the other hand, can serve to separate the business between two waging factions. Using the example under item 1, one faction would receive the shares of the manufacturing and distributing corporation while the other faction would receive the retail outlets.

[604.4] Tax Consequences of the Distribution of Stock When the Business Is Divided

There are basically two methods you can use to classify, for tax purposes, the distribution of the stock in a separation of a business. You could consider the distribution tax free if it satisfies the requirements set forth in Section 355 and related sections of the Internal Revenue Code. You could also consider it a property distribution in the form of a dividend to the various shareholders if it fails to satisfy the requirements set forth in these sections. (The taxation of property dividends has been discussed in ¶403.1.) It should be evident that the usual goal is to satisfy the requirements of a tax-free exchange and not have the distribution classified as a dividend. In a pro rata distribution of the stock of the corporation, there is a greater possibility that this distribution will be considered a dividend. The pro rata distribution is a common subterfuge for obtaining a distribution of the earnings of the corporation without dividend taxation. (See ¶604.5.) The non-pro rata distribution is used for many nontax-oriented goals, one of which is the resolution of internal dissension. Because of the obvious business purpose, the Internal Revenue Service has indicated that it will apply less stringent tests to a non-pro rata division, especially one in which a shareholder terminates his entire interest in the distributing company. (See Revenue Ruling 64-102, 1964-1 C.B. 136.)

[604.5] Using a Pro Rata Division of Business to Accomplish Tax-Oriented Goals

In many cases, the shareholders of a corporation, such as Old Corporation (¶604.2), may have a buyer for one of its businesses. In the above instance of a manufacturing and distributing company in one corporation supplying a retail business in the other corporation, the possibility of selling is less likely than if Old Corporation conducted two unrelated businesses. In the latter case, Old Corporation may not need to utilize the cash realized in its other business. The shareholders of the selling corporation may want the sale proceeds distributed directly to them and not retained by the corporation.

In this instance, a division of the business with a pro rata distribution to the shareholders can convert what would otherwise be dividend income into capital gains, as shown in the following example:

Example: Old Corporation conducted two businesses. It owned retail clothing stores in various cities and also owned and operated appliance stores under completely separate management in the same cities. To divide the business and allow for the distribution of the sales proceeds to the shareholders, Old Corporation could create a wholly owned subsidiary and transfer to this subsidiary, pursuant to a tax-free Section 351 incorporation, all the assets of the appliance stores. This stock could then be distributed through a tax-free dividend to the shareholders. The shareholders, after receiving the stock of the corporation owning the appliance stores, could either sell the shares of stock to a third party or liquidate the corporation and obtain capital gains treatment.

Because tax-free divisions of businesses provide a planning technique for distributing earnings of a corporation at capital gains rate, the IRS has attempted to limit its availability and use through a myriad of complicated restrictions. The complexity of these restrictions coupled with the fact that the intent almost always is tax-oriented makes it highly desirable to obtain an advance ruling from the Internal Revenue Service before attempting a distribution.

[604.6] Accomplishing the Division of a Business Tax Free

There are four basic requirements which must be satisfied to have a division of a business classified as a tax-free distribution under Section 355. In addition, there is an overriding requirement that the separation must be for business purposes and not for personal reasons.

These requirements can be summarized as follows:

1. *Property subject to distribution:* In general, only stock or securities of a controlled corporation may be distributed in a tax-free spin-off. A controlled corporation, for the purpose of Section 355, is defined as a corporation that has 80 percent of its total combined voting power of all classes of stock entitled to vote and at least 80 percent of the total number of shares of all other classes of corporate stock owned by another corporation. Money or other property (collectively considered as "boot") distributed in addition to the stock or securities of a qualifying controlled corporation will be taxed separately. It should be noted that

the distribution of boot will not necessarily make a non-taxable distribution taxable in its entirety.

2. *Conduct of business after distribution:* After the division of the old and new corporation and the distribution of the new corporation stock, the parent and the subsidiary must be engaged in the active conduct of a trade or business.

3. *Active conduct of business five years before distribution:* It is not enough that the spun-off controlled corporation be actively engaged in the business immediately after the distribution. It must also have conducted business actively for five years prior to the distribution. If this were not a requirement, it would be a simple matter for the shareholders to avoid classifying the distribution as a dividend. The technique would be to have the old corporation purchase a new business with the free assets of the old corporation. The old corporation would then immediately distribute the shares of the new business to the shareholders of the old corporation. The purchased corporation could then either be sold or liquidated.

4. *Types of businesses that qualify for separation:* The question that has plagued tax planners and the Internal Revenue Service is whether or not a tax-free separation can occur in a single business. The IRS, through its Regulations, states that a tax-free separation can occur only if there are two or more existing businesses. The courts have been more liberal in the application of the law than the regulations. For example, a tax-free division has been approved by the courts pursuant to Section 355 where a construction company divided its business, with each 50 percent shareholder taking one-half of the unfinished contracts and half the equipment.

IRS Position: In recent years, the IRS has begun to modify its position. It would seem that, while a vertical division would now be permitted, a horizontal division would apparently still not qualify unless the spun-off activity would also qualify as a separate business.

A common problem in this area involves the distribution of the stock of a corporation owning real property to the shareholders in a supposedly tax-free separation. The question is whether a corporation owning real estate can place this real estate in a subsidiary and distribute the stock tax free. Is the ownership and operation of the real estate a separate business which would qualify for a tax-free division? It would appear that the sole occupant of a factory building is not in the real estate business. A bank that uses one and one-half floors of a two-story building (renting out the remainder) is also not in the real estate business. But what about a bank that occupies only the ground level of a major real estate building? This distribution will probably qualify as a tax-free division. Favorable rulings have been issued for divisions in which the buildings were less than 40 percent owner occupied.

5. *The business purpose rule:* The separation must not be a device for distributing any corporate earnings to the shareholders tax free or at capital gains rates. In other words, there must be a business purpose for this separation. Some of the business purposes that will qualify resolving internal dissension, functionally operating different businesses, and valid personal reasons, such as the desire to leave different segments of the business to different legatees. As noted in ¶604.5, if it is anticipated that the subsidiary will be sold or liquidated after the separation, this could be considered a prearranged transaction. This could have serious ramifications on the taxability of the division. The regulations, in this instance, state that a prearranged sale is evidence that a spin-off is a device to take earnings out tax free or at capital gains rates.

NOTE: The distribution of stock in a tax-free reorganization is an exception to the general rule enacted by the Tax Reform Act of 1986 that the distribution of appreciated property by a corporation results in tax at the corporate level. It is my belief that there will be an increased use of spin-offs in the future since decentralization will provide additional flexibility to tax planners. Multiple entities, not centralized businesses, will provide maximum benefits in the future.

OBRA 1987 has placed new restrictions on tax-free spin-offs. While in the normal instance these should have no negative effects, the current law should be reviewed prior to undertaking any division of the corporation.

7

How to Maximize the Distribution of Assets Upon Termination of the Corporation

[700] THE THREE MOST COMMON METHODS OF LIQUIDATING THE CORPORATION

Up to this point the name of the game has been how to get the most value out of the corporation at the least tax cost. We have discussed all the steps you should take to help you achieve specific financial objectives for your client prior to incorporation and during the life of the corporation. But for one reason or another, it is impossible to continue the corporation. You will now be shown how to effectively deal with assets to preserve the corporation's tax benefits.

When the final liquidation of a corporation is contemplated, there are many planning opportunities open to you, but there are also many pitfalls. The timing of the sale of corporate assets, how the cash and/or other property is distributed to the shareholders, and the type of property distributed have significant impact on both the corporation and the shareholders. Usually, substantial tax can be saved or deferred through proper planning. Unfortunately, you are often presented with a fait accompli. If a sale of the assets to a third party is contemplated, the "deal" may already be worked out. Then you would be instructed not to act as a planner but only as a scrivener. By that time, the restructuring of the transaction is usually extremely difficult. Also, any change may upset the entire sale.

307

Therefore, prior conditioning of the client to planning is particularly important, especially after the enactment of the Tax Reform Act of 1986. If proper planning is not implemented, the after-tax proceeds can be greatly reduced.

Prior to the enactment of the Tax Reform Act, there were three techniques utilized in liquidating a corporation as follows:

1. Section 333: The liquidation of a corporation, which may result in no tax to either the shareholder or the corporation. The planning opportunity presented by this section is the distribution to the individual shareholders of appreciated property upon the liquidation of the corporation with little or no taxation. While the application is rather limited, if you use it properly, it can be a tremendous tax-saving device. (See ¶703.1 for a discussion on how to use Section 333.)

   This option is no longer available to all but qualified corporations after December 31, 1986, and for qualified corporations after December 31, 1988. To completely understand the impact of the Tax Reform Act of 1986, a discussion of both the pre- and post-Tax Reform Act ramifications will follow.

2. Section 337: Use this to avoid any tax to the corporation upon liquidation. You should use this particular technique when there is a bulk sale of the major assets of the corporation. The goal of this planning technique is to avoid double taxation—taxation at the corporate level and again at the individual level upon distribution of the assets to the shareholders. If Section 337 is elected, you can avoid most, if not all, taxation upon the sale of the assets at the corporate level. This particular section has received renewed attention after the enactment of the Installment Sale Revision Act of 1980, which allowed for the increased use of its provisions through the liberalization of the law. Again, the Tax Reform Act of 1986 has had a significant impact upon the utilization of this section. This section will become unavailable for all but qualified corporations on January 1, 1987, and for qualified corporations on January 1, 1989. (See ¶703.2 for a discussion on how to use Section 337.)

3. Section 331: Use this section to minimize the tax impact on the individual. You should use this section when the liquidation of the corporation is going to occur over a long period of time or when, in addition to cash, other assets are going to be distributed to the individual shareholders. The goal here is to ensure that (1) none of the distributions to the shareholders during the period of liquidation are treated as dividend income and (2) all such distributions are considered as liquidating distributions. This will ensure that the corporate distributions will receive capital gains treatment. Again, the Tax Reform Act of 1986 has had a significant impact upon the use of this liquidation section. The major adverse effect has come in two separate areas:

   (a) The creation of taxation upon distribution of appreciated property at the corporate level
   (b) The removal of the favorable capital gains rates

   However, there is no doubt that the use of a liquidation over a number of years for tax-oriented reasons will become even more prevalent under the Tax Reform Act of 1986 than it was in the past. (See ¶703.3 for a discussion on how to use Section 331.)

[701] HOW TO CHOOSE THE BEST LIQUIDATION METHOD FOR YOUR SITUATION

In liquidating a corporation, your goals are easy to define. However, accomplishing all or a major portion of these goals is sometimes more elusive. The following are the goals you should keep in mind:

Goal one is not to have the distribution from the corporation to the individual shareholders create any taxation to the corporation or shareholder.

Goal two is to have this distribution or distributions classified not as dividend income but either as a tax-free return of capital or as a sale or exchange of a capital gain.

Goal three is to reduce taxation at the corporate level upon distribution of appreciated property.

The Code provides you with certain planning tools which, if used properly, can produce the maximum after-tax return to the shareholders in a wide variety of cases. Although each case is unique, the following are the variables you *must* consider in choosing the most advantageous liquidation method:

1. What are the earnings and profits of the corporation?
2. What is the period of time over which the assets can either be (a) sold and the cash distributed to the individual shareholders or (b) distributed to the individual shareholder?
3. What are the types of assets owned by the corporation?
4. Is the corporation's fair market value of its assets greatly in excess of the book value?
5. Is there any need to retain the corporate shell to pay off contingent liabilities?
6. What is the financial reason for the liquidation?
7. Are there other problems?

Prior to January 1, 1987, you used Section 333 if the corporation had the following attributes:

1. The corporation had no earnings and profits.
2. The assets of the corporation are greatly appreciated.
3. The liquidation does not result in recapture of depreciation or distribution of appreciated LIFO inventory.

Section 333 provided rules for a complete tax-free liquidation (to both shareholders and corporations) where the corporation had no earnings and profits and where the liquidation distribution included neither cash nor securities. In the proper instance, a corporation could be liquidated and the in-kind assets returned to the shareholders without any taxation. The Tax Reform Act of 1986 repealed this section as of December 31, 1986. The reasons for this repeal are not clear, and subsequent to its enactment, the IRS ruled that this section would be available for continued usage by qualified corporations until January 1, 1989.

A "qualified" corporation should use Section 337 if there is a bulk sale of the assets (which would have yielded capital gain), and if the sale occurs prior to January 1, 1989. This liquidation is commonly referred to as the one-year liquidation. In this instance, the liquidation must be accomplished within a one-year period. Prior to the enactment of the Installment Sales Revision Act of 1980, it was extremely costly in taxes to sell the bulk assets for anything but cash. With the change in the law, there are no longer any adverse effects from an installment sale, and the shareholder will report the income as received, rather than at the time of liquidation and distribution of assets. This particular liquidation alternative is most viable when the bulk sale is anticipated and when the earnings and profits of the corporation are high. This planning technique is still available until January 1, 1989, for qualified corporations (see ¶703.2).

The ability to effectively utilize Section 337 is complicated by the presence of installment obligations created prior to the election under Section 337 and property subject to depreciation and investment credit recapture. If none of these complicating factors exist, the corporation can convert the major portion of the property to cash at no corporate tax and distribute all the assets to the shareholders at capital gains rates.

AVOID THESE PITFALLS: If a binding contract for sale is entered into *prior* to the date of the election, the whole transaction may be taxable, or, if the transaction is not accomplished within a year, the entire tax benefits of this transaction could be defeated.

You should use Section 331 when it is necessary to accomplish the liquidation over a long period of time. The goal here is not to eliminate taxation to the corporation but only to ensure that the distributions will occur not in one year but over a number of years and will be treated as liquidation distributions—not as dividend distributions. Under this method, it is important that proper documentation be established in the corporate minutes to set the time frame for the liquidation. Dribble liquidations over a long period of time will become more prevalent after the Tax Reform Act of 1986. Since there is no longer any favorable treatment to long-term capital gains even if the distribution is considered as a dividend distribution rather than a liquidating distribution, it should have little if any tax impact upon the shareholders.

You should use Section 302(e) for a partial liquidation when one of the various businesses of the corporation is being liquidated. This is a useful method for extracting funds from the corporation upon the termination of one segment of the business.

WARNING: The distribution in a partial liquidation could be considered a dividend distribution rather than a partial liquidation under Section 302(e).

The chart on pages 314-317 lays out the techniques for each liquidation method and shows how you can use each method to accomplish a specific result.

[702] HOW TAX AND FINANCIAL CONSIDERATIONS AFFECT YOUR CHOICE OF METHOD

Before trying to decide which liquidation method you should follow, it is best to analyze the financial and tax considerations that can prompt a liquidation of the corporation. In liquidating the corporation, it is necessary to consider two tax questions. The first is: "Will the liquidation of the corporation result in any corporate tax?" The second is: "How will the proceeds received by the shareholders be taxed?" The goals of complete liquidation are to realize no taxable income at the corporate level and to have the distribution treated as a sale or exchange or tax free at the individual level. If the liquidation is not planned properly, the distribution could be taxed at the corporate level and considered a dividend to the individual shareholder. There are several tools available to you which will produce favorable tax results to all parties and avoid double taxation.

Four of the more common financial reasons for liquidation are as follows:

1. A sale of the business
2. A division of the assets of the business among the shareholders

3. An effort to continue the business without one or more of the shareholders

4. A continuation of the business in another form

If the business is going to be sold in bulk, the entire transaction is dependent upon the tax ramifications. Basically, the sellers will attempt to have no taxation at the corporate level and have the entire receipt of cash and property taxed as capital gains. On the other hand, the purchaser's goal will be to have a stepped-up basis for the assets which he is purchasing. If the corporation is going to be liquidated over a period of time, the tax ramifications are again the primary motivation. In this instance, your goal will not be to avoid taxation at the corporate level (this is usually impossible) but to have all distributions taxed at capital gains rates.

In your analysis, you may find that financial circumstances may dictate a division of the business. The continued overhead of operating the business may be too great, and each of the individual shareholders may wish to receive a portion of the assets. An example of this occurred when a real estate investment corporation, after many years of successful operation, ascertained that the overhead was becoming too great to justify the profits being generated. Accordingly, the corporation was liquidated, and each of the shareholders received a portion of the assets of the corporation. In this case, each shareholder's portion of the overhead was significantly less than the total cost of operation.

Another motivation is that certain shareholders may decide that it is more advantageous to eliminate one or more of the current shareholders. If the assets of the corporation allow for this type of division, this may be very productive.

A planning area which was extremely complicated in the past has become even more difficult since the enactment of the Tax Reform Act of 1986. This act repealed what was known in tax law as the "General Utilities Doctrine." This doctrine, named after a 1935 Supreme Court case, was interpreted to mean that a corporation did not realize gain on distributions of appreciated property. The doctrine was codified in the 1954 code in IRS Code Section 11 for nonliquidating distributions, in IRS Code Section 336 for liquidating distributions, and in IRS Code Section 337 for sales under a twelve-month plan of

TECHNIQUES FOR LIQUIDATING THE CORPORATION

	Method One: Section 333[1] Complete Liquidation	Method Two: Section 337(1) Complete Liquidation	Method Three: Section 331 Complete Liquidation	Partial Liquidation[1]
Benefits of Transaction	The liquidation of a corporation may result in no tax to either the shareholder or the corporation.	Used to avoid any tax to the corporation upon liquidation.	Used to minimize the tax impact on the individual.	Used to extract money or property from the corporation at capital gains rates for the shareholder on contraction of business.
Code Section	333	337	331	302(e)
Paragraph Reference to the Main Text	¶703.1	¶703.2	¶703.3	¶703.5
When to Consider	1. Appreciated property. 2. Little or no earnings and profits. 3. Little or no cash or securities.	1. Appreciated assets which, if sold, will yield long-term capital gains. 2. Necessity for sale of the	1. Neither Section 333 nor 337 liquidations are available. 2. A long	1. Two or more businesses have been operated by corporation for five or more years. 2. One business is either going to be sold or the

[1] These liquidation sections are available to qualified corporations until January 1, 1989. To all other corporations, these techniques ceased to be available on December 31, 1986.

314

	business discontinued. 3. Individual shareholder could use the proceeds of the sale.	winding-down period. 3. Little appreciated property held by the corporation. 4. Consider continuing the business in unincorporated form.	appreciated assets under the installment sale provisions.
Why Use	To reacquire assets at shareholder level with little or no tax consequences to corporation or shareholder.	To avoid double taxation.	Spread the capital gains to the individual shareholders over a number of years. When a corporation has more than one business, one of which will either be sold or is no longer expanding and will be phased out.

continued

TECHNIQUES FOR LIQUIDATING THE CORPORATION

	Method One: Section 333[1] Complete Liquidation	Method Two: Section 337(1) Complete Liquidation	Method Three: Section 331 Complete Liquidation	Partial Liquidation[1]
Tax Consequences to the Corporation	Basically no taxation except if distribute recapturable items, installment obligations, or LIFO inventory.	Most of the assets which are sold during the year are tax free. Inventory items must normally be reported as ordinary income.	All sales, exchanges, and operations during the period of liquidation are taxable.	None, unless property is distributed, then investment credit or depreciation recapture property could cause taxation, or installment obligations being distributed could also cause taxation to the corporation. In addition, for all partial liquidations, beginning in 1983 gain may be realized by the corporation if appreciated property is distributed as part of the liquidation.
Tax Consequences to the Noncorporate Shareholder	Possible dividend income to the greater of the amount of earnings and profits or cash and	1. Distributions to shareholders will qualify for capital gains.	The initial receipt of funds will reduce the basis of the stock in the	Part return of capital and part capital gain/loss.

[1] These liquidation sections are available to qualified corporations until January 1, 1989. To all other corporations, these techniques ceased to be available on December 31, 1986.

316

securities distributed.	2. If the corporation distributes to shareholders installment obligations received in exchange for assets pursuant to Sec. 337, the shareholders will report income as received, not upon distribution.	hands of the shareholder; thereafter, all profit will be reported as capital gains.		
Restrictions on the Use	1. Collapsible corporations. 2. Sale of property contemplated by shareholders immediately after liquidation. 3. Certain corporate shareholders excluded.	1. Collapsible corporations generally not available. 2. Liquidation must occur within one twelve-month period.	1. The corporation must properly adopt a liquidation posture. 2. Not available to collapsible corporations except in limited situations.	1. Each business must have been in existence for at least five years. 2. Cannot be equivalent to a dividend. 3. Gain to the corporation could result if appreciated property is distributed.

complete liquidation. While later amendments to the code narrowed the scope of nonrecognition by providing recapture rules (see ¶703.2[B]), the code did provide a substantial tax preference for liquidating distributions. Obviously Congress believed that the General Utilities Doctrine tended to undermine the corporate income tax by allowing a corporation to dispose of its assets without realizing gain even though the acquirer gets step-up basis for the assets.

> **Example:** XYZ Corporation owned only one asset—land with a basis of $1,000 and a fair market value of $11,000. If Section 331 were utilized and if the corporation were liquidated prior to the implementation of the Tax Reform Act of 1986, the individual shareholders would have paid tax on the distribution to them of the land with a fair market value of $11,000. Assuming they had no basis for the stock, they would have paid a capital gains on $11,000. However, the corporation would have realized no income at the corporate level.

> **Example after the Full Implementation of the Tax Reform Act in 1989:** In the above example, if the corporation is liquidated under Section 331 after the full implementation of the Tax Reform Act, a gain of $10,000 would have occurred at the corporate level and resulted in a tax of $1,500 (assuming no other income). The net distribution available to the shareholders would then have been reduced to $9,500.

The Tax Reform Act of 1986 contained an exception to the general rule that all distributions of appreciated property would result in corporate taxation for distributions by certain closely held corporations that are completely liquidated before January 1, 1989. In these cases, a liquidating corporation does not recognize gain or loss on the liquidating distribution that would be otherwise recognized under the 1986 act on distributions for sale in complete liquidation if the liquidating corporation is:

1. A qualified corporation
2. Is completely liquidated before January 1, 1989

A qualified corporation is defined as follows:

1. On August 1, 1986, and at all times thereafter, more than 50 percent of the stock in the corporation is held by ten or fewer qualified persons, which include individuals, estates, and certain trusts.
2. The corporation has an applicable value of $10 million. It should be noted that if the value is more than $5 million, the full relief of this section is not applicable.

WARNING: If there is a controlled group of corporations, the value of the entire group must be considered, and in many cases action must be taken as to all the corporations involved—not just one. The rules as to when relief will be available are complex and, accordingly, any qualified corporation with qualified individuals which wants to avail itself of these relief sections should proceed with extreme care.

Key Idea: Many qualified closely held corporations will find tax advantages to liquidate prior to January 1, 1989. A complete analysis of whether or not they are a qualified corporation and what will be the tax effects should be undertaken before a liquidation is attempted.

There are many reasons that a corporation may no longer be a viable form for operating a business. In most instances, it is usually easier to obtain the sought-after benefits as a Subchapter S Corporation by having the income taxed individually. However, this is not always possible because the income earned may be passive, and the corporation may not qualify for a Subchapter S election, or double taxation on built-in gains may make the election tax-wise inappropriate. The Subchapter S Revision Act of 1982 has provided corporations that earn passive income the opportunity to elect Subchapter S status. An example of a corporation that still may not be able to use fully the positive benefits of the Subchapter S election is a corporation that has invested solely in apartment buildings and has accumulated earnings and profits. It is now considered in the best interest of all parties to conduct business in an unincorporated form. Thus, liquidation of the business may be necessary. (For a complete analysis of the impact of a corporation earning passive income on both the Subchapter S status and taxation, see ¶504.1.)

The approach that I will use in this chapter is to analyze both the law prior to the enactment of the Tax Reform Act of 1986 and the changes effected by this act. The reason that it is particularly important to understand both the prior law as well as the changes that are effective is that closely held corporations have a "window of applicability to the prior law" until January 1, 1989, and may wish to avail themselves of some of the planning opportunities. In addition, without understanding the prior law, it is difficult to understand the changes in thinking that will be necessitated by the Tax Reform Act of 1986.

[702.1(A)] Liquidation of the Corporation May Result in Corporate Income Tax—Law in Effect Prior to the Tax Reform Act of 1986

This problem usually involves the type of property which will be distributed upon liquidation. Cash distributed by the corporation to the shareholders will not result in taxation to the corporation. However, in complete liquidations, it is not always feasible to distribute only cash. Generally, when a corporation distributes property in complete liquidation, it realizes no gain or loss regardless of how much the assets have appreciated in value since their date of acquisition. However, as with all tax rules, there are certain exceptions.

The most commonly encountered exceptions are as follows:

1. *Distribution of installment obligations:* If the distribution contains installment obligations, the corporation must recognize as income the difference between the basis and the fair market value of the obligation at the date of liquidation (*Commissioner v. Culbertson* 337 U.S. 733 [1949]).

> **Example:** X Corporation, a retail appliance store, has in the past sold its goods two different ways: cash and in installments. All financing was at least 10 percent at the date of sale, the remainder payable over thirty-six months with interest at commercial rates. X Corporation has reported all credit sales pursuant to the installment method.

When it liquidates and distributes to its shareholders the installment notes which it owns, the corporation, at the date of liquidation, will recognize the entire realized profit.

There Is a Major Exception to This Rule: A corporation sells its assets on an installment sale basis during the twelve-month liquidation period pursuant to the terms of Section 337 and then distributes these obligations to a shareholder as a liquidation distribution. Unlike the example above, in this instance, the distribution of the installment obligation because of the election under Section 337 has no tax impact to the corporation.

2. *Depreciation recapture:* In the event that the corporation distributes personal property or real property subject to depreciation recapture, a taxable event occurs at the time of corporate liquidation (IRC Sections 1245 and 1250).

Example: X Corporation owns depreciable personal property with a basis after depreciation of $1,000 and a current market value of $2,000. Prior to liquidation, $3,000 of depreciation is expensed. Upon distribution by the corporation, in complete liquidation of its stock, the corporation will realize $1,000 in taxable income (fair market value of $2,000 less basis of $1,000, but not greater than the total depreciation).

3. *Investment credit recapture:* A distribution of tangible personal property in complete or partial liquidation results in a disposition (equivalent to a sale) of investment credit property. A complete or partial recapture will occur if the required holding period has not elapsed prior to the distribution (Regs. 1.47-2(a)(1); 1.47-3(a)(1); 1.47-3(f)). This should become less of a problem since the Tax Reform Act of 1986 has repealed the investment credit retroactively to January 1, 1986. Thus, there should be less problems with investment credit recapture in the future.

4. *There are other miscellaneous areas that may pose some problems in liquidation:* In one case, the IRS, utilizing the tax concepts set forth in the Court Holding Case, attempted to assign the sale of certain assets to the corporation rather than to the shareholders. In another, the IRS established that the corpora-

tion was not utilizing a method of accounting which properly reflected its income. Upon liquidation, the corporation was required to realize income.

5. *Distribution of LIFO inventory:* If a corporation has adopted the LIFO method of reporting its inventory, and if it adopts a plan in partial or complete liquidation after 1981, the corporation will realize a gain to the extent of LIFO recapture. LIFO recapture is defined as the difference between the value of the LIFO inventory and the same inventory valued under the FIFO method. LIFO inventory has been increasingly used in the last five to ten years because of increased inflationary pressure. LIFO (last in first out) has a tendency to match current costs against current sales. The inventory in essence becomes frozen at historical cost. In other words, if we were to value a LIFO inventory at today's cost, the inventory would be substantially greater. While a complete discussion of LIFO inventory is beyond the scope of this book, it should be noted here that any corporation liquidating under any section that has adopted the LIFO method of reporting its inventory could realize taxable income.

[702.1(B)] Law That Will Be in Effect after the Full Implementation of the Tax Reform Act of 1986

As indicated in ¶702, the law as set forth in ¶702.1(A) has changed for all but qualified corporations on January 1, 1987, and will change for all corporations as of January 1, 1989. The 1986 Tax Reform Act provides that a gain or loss is recognized by a liquidating corporation on the distribution of property in complete liquidation as if the property had been sold to the distributee at its fair market value. The identity of the distributee, of course, can have some importance in determining the type of gain that is recognized. For example, all gain on the sale of depreciable property by a corporation to a related shareholder is treated as ordinary income. Therefore, if we treat a pro rata portion of each asset as sold to each shareholder, the corporation will recognize some ordinary income instead of Section 1231 gain or capital gains on distributions of appreci-

ated property to its shareholders if one of its shareholders is a
related person even if the depreciable property is not distributed to that shareholder. It can be clearly seen that after the
full implementation of the Tax Reform Act of 1986 the tax
implications will be dramatic.

Example: XYZ Corporation has the following balance
sheet:

	Basis	*Fair Market Value*
Cash	$1,000	$ 1,000
Land	1,000	10,000
	$2,000	$11,000

Assume XYZ Corporation is in the maximum marginal tax bracket:

1986	*1987*	*1988 and thereafter*
46%	40%	34%[1]

and A, the owner of all the issued and outstanding common stock of XYZ Corporation, is also in the maximum
marginal tax bracket:

Ordinary Income	50%	38.5%	28%[1]
Capital Gain	20%	28%	28%[1]

In this example, I will assume that the corporation is completely liquidated in one year and that the liquidation would
qualify under Section 331. I will also consider that the basis for
the stock in A's hands is $1,000. I will contrast the taxation for
the years 1986, 1987, 1988, and 1989 under the assumption
that XYZ Corporation is both a qualified corporation and that
XYZ does not qualify for the transitional rules.

---

[1] For neither the corporation nor the individual, have I considered the implications of the 5 percent surcharge.

ASSUME XYZ IS A QUALIFIED CORPORATION

	1986	1987	1988	1989
Corporate Tax	-0-	-0-	-0-	$3,060
Net before Tax Proceeds to XYZ	$11,000	$11,000	$11,000	7,940
Tax on Distribution to A	2,000	2,800	2,800	1,943
Net after Tax Distribution to A	9,000	8,200	8,200	5,997

ASSUME XYZ IS NOT A QUALIFIED CORPORATION

	1986	1987	1988	1989
Corporate Tax	-0-	$3,060	$3,060	$3,060
Net before Tax Proceeds to XYZ	$11,000	7,940	7,940	7,940
Tax on Distribution to A	2,000	1,943	1,943	1,943
Net after Tax Distribution to A	9,000	5,997	5,997	5,997

As can be seen in the above example, the variations in tax treatment are fairly great, and, therefore, various tax results can occur depending upon the facts. It should be noted that approximately 44 percent of the total tax liability can be saved by XYZ if it is a qualified corporation and liquidates in the year 1988 rather than 1989. It would appear that liquidations of corporations with appreciated property over the next couple of years will be more prevalent.

[702.2] Receipt of Property in a Liquidation May Be Tax Free, Taxable as Ordinary Income, or Taxable as Capital Gains to the Shareholders

The general rule is that a distribution to the shareholders in a complete or partial liquidation of a corporation is taxed to them when the proceeds are received. If the stock qualifies as a capital asset in the hands of the shareholder, the distribution will be treated as a capital gain or loss. The major beneficial exception to this rule was set forth in Section 333 of the Internal Revenue Code. Under this section, the receipt of property was taxed differently. (The benefits of electing Section 333 and the taxability of the receipt of proceeds are discussed in ¶703.1.)

The distribution upon complete liquidation may contain not only cash but also assets owned by the corporation. In computing gain or loss, the value of the distribution is determined by subtracting from the fair market value of the property received any liabilities that the shareholder assumes upon the liquidation distribution.

Example: X corporation is liquidating and distributes to its sole shareholder, A, in complete liquidation of his stock, assets subject to liabilities as follows:

1. Real estate with a fair market value of $20,000 subject to a first mortgage in the amount of $10,000
2. Cash in the amount of $10,000
3. Accounts payable in the amount of $5,000

If A's basis in the stock, prior to liquidation was $5,000, upon receipt of the assets shown above, he would realize a capital gain of $10,000 (fair market value of the cash and property ($30,000) less the total of the mortgage and the accounts payable assumed ($15,000) less the basis of $5,000).

When the complete liquidation is payable in installments, the question becomes: "How do you report the receipt of each of the installments?" As a rule, the value of each installment is applied against the shareholder's basis, and no gain is recognized until the value of the assets received exceeds the basis of the stock in the shareholder's hands.

Example: XYZ Corporation adopts a plan of liquidation on June 1, 1981. It distributes to A, its sole shareholder, $50,000 during 1981 and makes a final distribution of $50,000 in 1982. A has a basis in the stock of the corporation of $10,000. He will realize a $40,000 gain in 1981 and a $50,000 gain in 1982.

The assumption has been that the liquidation results in a gain. If the liquidation results in a loss, this loss is generally not deductible until the year of the final distribution. However, the retention of some assets by the corporation will not postpone claiming the loss if the amount of the assets can reasonably be determined. Such amount can be taken into account when determining the loss.

NOTE: The basic taxation to an individual shareholder was not greatly altered by the Tax Reform Act of 1986.

[703] STRATEGIES FOR LIQUIDATING THE CORPORATION

The techniques for liquidating a corporation were discussed in ¶700. Here you will see what arrangements can be made to enable the corporation to divert income for officers, shareholders, and directors at the termination of the corporation.

[703.1] Using Section 333 so That There Is No Taxation to Either the Stockholder or the Corporation

An unusual relief provision in the Code is included in Section 333 and is known as the "one-month liquidation." This was originally enacted in 1938 to allow personal holding companies an opportunity to liquidate in order to escape the personal holding tax which was enacted in that year.

However, these provisions and their use were far broader than the original purpose for which they were enacted. The provisions generally allowed shareholders to defer all or part of their gain on liquidation until they disposed of the property in a taxable transaction. The scope of this relief provision was rather narrow and was generally applicable only to corporations that had both of the following characteristics:

1. The corporation had little or no accumulated earnings and profits.
2. The major part of the corporate assets or assets used in the trade or business that will qualify for capital gains if and when sold. If these assets (upon sale) would result in both capital gains and recapture (depreciation and LIFO), the benefits could be lost because this otherwise tax-free trans-

action can be converted into a transaction that will result in dividend income.

The following is an example of how it is possible to avoid tax liability to the shareholder or corporation using Section 333:

	Book Value	Fair Market Value
ASSETS		
Cash	$ 1,000	$ 1,000
Equipment	20,000	20,000
Inventory	50,000	50,000
Real Estate	50,000	150,000
TOTAL ASSETS	$121,000	$221,000
LIABILITIES AND EQUITY		
Mortgage against the Real Estate	$ 81,000	$ 81,000
Untaxed Appreciation	-0-	100,000
Capital Stock	30,000	30,000
Earnings and Profits	10,000	10,000
TOTAL LIABILITIES AND EQUITY	$121,000	$221,000

Example: Old Corporation's earnings and profits were the same as its retained earnings ($10,000). The corporation had a buyer for its inventory and equipment but currently did not have a buyer for the building. Since the basis and fair market value of the equipment and inventory are the same, no gain would be realized from the sale. The cash realized from the sale ($71,000) should be used to reduce the remaining indebtedness against the real estate. The real estate subject to the remaining unpaid liability should be distributed to the shareholders. The sole asset available for distribution would be the real estate subject to a $10,000 ($81,000 − $71,000) first mortgage.

If the shareholder's basis in the stock is $30,000 and no election is made under Section 333, the shareholders would realize, upon the liquidation, a $110,000 gain (fair market value of building $150,000 less liabilities of

$10,000 less basis of $30,000). On the other hand, if a Section 333 is timely filed, the only income that will be realized upon distribution to the individual shareholders is $10,000 of dividend income. Note that if the real estate is subject to depreciation, additional Section 1250 income would be generated and a greater portion of the distribution would be ordinary income.

Section 333 permits the shareholders to reacquire the real estate individually with minimum tax liability. At a subsequent time, they can either lease the property and receive rent or dispose of the property on an installment sale. Real estate utilized in a Section 333 liquidation may be of a specialized nature. These single-purpose specialized buildings usually require owner refinancing in order to sell. If the building had been retained in the corporation, and the corporation had either leased or sold the building pursuant to an installment sale, the corporation could face the imposition of a personal holding tax (see ¶803).

The Tax Reform Act of 1986 repealed these provisions for all but qualified corporations commencing January 1, 1987, and for qualified closely held corporations commencing January 1, 1989. For small closely held corporations, this window of applicability is of particular importance, especially during the years 1987 and 1988. Prior to the implementation of the Tax Reform Act of 1986, there was a definite benefit to have all payments in liquidation deemed a sale or exchange qualified for capital gains purposes rather than ordinary income. The maximum taxation upon a long-term capital transaction would be only 40 percent of ordinary income. This differential has been greatly reduced in 1987 and will be completely eliminated in 1988. Thus, Section 333 may have a tremendous amount of applicability in a sales context as well as in a pure liquidation, especially when the corporation has a net operating loss or other favorable tax characteristics.

After the full implementation of the Tax Reform Act of 1986, it seems to be a general rule that, under this act, the taxpayers will suffer greater problems for mistakes that occurred in the past than they did prior to its enactment. In other words, the new tax act is not at all forgiving. Proper planning will have to be implemented at each step of the corporate process if tax disasters are to be avoided.

[703.2(A)] Requirements for Section 337 Liquidation

The directors of the corporation must adopt a plan of complete liquidation. (See Appendix T.) The date of its adoption is particularly crucial because it triggers the commencement of the twelve-month period. There is a problem if any assets are inadvertently sold prior to the adoption of the plan. In this case, the corporation will recognize income upon the sale of those assets. On the other hand, if the liquidation distribution is not completed within the twelve-month period, the entire income realized by the corporation will be taxable income.

[703.2(B)] Exceptions to the Nonrecognition of Gain upon Liquidation by the Corporation

Section 337 applies only to a gain or loss recognized by a corporation in liquidation of its business and not from a gain or loss resulting from sales in the ordinary course of business. The general rule that all other sales or distributions after the sale of the major property are tax free is subject to the following major exceptions:

1. The sale of stock in trade or other property which is normally included in inventory at year-end, or property held primarily for sale in the ordinary course of the business will result in taxable income. However, if there is a bulk sale of the inventory items to a nonrelated party, this will not be considered a sale in the ordinary course of business and will be excluded from any taxability.

2. A distribution of an installment obligation received as a result of a sale or exchange of property will be taxable upon distribution if the sale occurred prior to the date of adoption of the plan for complete liquidation.

3. A liquidation under Section 337 will spark the recapture provisions under Sections 1245 and 1250. The investment credit recapture provisions are also applicable on either the sale or distribution of property in liquidation.

4. If a corporation distributes LIFO inventory, it realizes a gain in the amount of the excess of the FIFO inventory amount over the value of the inventory determined under the LIFO method.

In addition to these specific statutory exceptions, there are several court-imposed instances where the corporation will recognize a gain. These court-imposed exceptions usually involve the assignment of the income doctrine or the tax-benefit rule. Before a liquidation under Section 337 is attempted, the exceptions to the nontaxability rules should be analyzed to ensure that the "tax-free sale" will not produce significant taxation to the corporation.

The Installment Sales Revision Act of 1980 has substantially liberalized the method of reporting gain by a shareholder on the distribution of obligations qualifying for special treatment under Section 337.

The following example will illustrate the taxation before and after the Installment Sales Revision Act of 1980:

Example: Using the factual situation and example of X Corporation on page 331, we will assume that the sale of the "property" will result in capital gains which will not give rise to either depreciation or investment credit recapture, nor does it involve LIFO inventory. The purchaser is willing to pay for the property as follows:

Purchase Price	$110,000
Down Payment	20,000
Balance Due	$ 90,000

The balance due of $90,000 will be payable pursuant to a promissory note containing the following terms:

(a) 120 equal monthly installments of $1,291.24

(b) Interest on the unpaid principal balance at the rate of 12 percent

WARNING: The Tax Reform Act of 1984 changed the rules relative to the interest which should be charged on installment sales pursuant to Section 483. In order not to give rise to imputed interest, a safe harbor rule has been engrafted in the act. As long as interest is 110 percent of the applicable federal rate, there will not be any imputed interest. If it is not 110 percent of the applicable federal rate, the imputed interest rate will be at 120 percent of the applicable federal rate. The federal rates have been divided into three separate categories: short-term debt instruments (term of three years or less), medium-term debt instruments (over three years but not more than nine years), and long-term debt instruments (term of over nine years). An example of the interest rates allowable (110 percent AFR) as determined in December 1986 is as follows:

Short-Term	*Medium-Term*	*Long-Term (annual)*
6.81	7.89	8.5

Before the enactment of the Installment Sales Revision Act of 1980, this sale would have been tax free to the corporation pursuant to Section 337. However, upon distribution of the installment note, the shareholder would have had to report the entire gain in the year of distribution.

Example: In our example of X Corporation, A would have received cash of $21,000 plus an installment note of $90,000 for a total value received of $111,000. This would have resulted in a capital gain of $96,750 (total proceeds received $111,000 less basis in stock of $14,250). Under the Installment Sales Revision Act of 1980, only the cash and other property received will have to be reported in the year of distribution. Thus in this particular example, only $18,304 of gain will be reported by the shareholder upon distribution. This gain is calculated as the cash received multiplied by the fraction, the numerator of which is the gain and the denominator of which is the total proceeds ($21,000 × $96.750/$111,000). The remainder of the gain will be reported as the principal is received under the terms of the promissory note. This relieves the shareholder from the current taxation on the distribution of the installment note.

Key Idea: Prior to the enactment of the Installment Sales Revision Act of 1980, it was inappropriate for tax purposes to sell pursuant to the terms of an installment sale. The Installment Sales Revision Act of 1980 has provided relief, and thus sales can be accomplished in this manner.

WARNING: Effective for installment sales made after June 6, 1984, the entire amount of depreciation recapture must be included in taxable income in the year of sale. This rule applies even if no cash is received in the year of sale. If the down payment is inadequate, a transaction can generate more tax liability than cash in the year of sale. In those situations with the potential of substantial depreciation recapture, installment sales will now be a less attractive income-averaging technique.

WARNING: The Tax Reform Act of 1986 has repealed the benefits of Section 337 for qualified closely held corporations commencing on January 1, 1989, and for all other corporations commencing January 1, 1987. It is particularly important to determine whether or not you are a closely held corporation and what the tax ramifications would be in either event.

[703.3] Utilizing Section 331 to Minimize the Tax Impact on the Individual

The complete liquidation of a corporation can mark not only the termination of the corporation but also the termination of the business which had previously been operated by the corporation. However, the complete liquidation of the corporation may also be motivated by reasons other than the termination of the business. This liquidation may be nothing more than a step in the transfer of the business from a corporate form to the partnership or sole proprietorship form. There are many reasons that a business may wish to shed the corporate form. If the continuation of the business is contemplated, the corporation, rather than converting all of its assets to cash, could distribute all of its assets in kind, subject to any liabilities which may be outstanding, to the shareholders. This distribution will result in a complete liquidation of the business just as if the corporate assets had been sold, converted to cash, and the cash distributed to the shareholders in exchange for their stock.

When a corporation distributes all of its assts, be they cash or other assets, to its shareholders in a complete liquidation, the tax law treats the transaction as a sale and exchange of these assets for and in consideration of the stock. The shareholders report any gain or loss that may result by ascertaining the value of the assets received versus the basis of their stock in the corporation. If Section 331 is utilized, the entire gain will be taxable to the shareholders in the year of the transaction.

Distributions in a complete liquidation are treated as a sale or exchange, which will normally result in capital transactions. If the distribution is not considered a distribution in complete or partial liquidation of the corporation, these distributions will be taxable as ordinary income if the corporation has earnings and profits. Under Section 331, when a liquidation is planned over a number of years, it is important to ensure that the distribution in each and every year is considered as a liquidation distribution qualifying for sale and exchange, resulting in capital gains treatment.

Since Sections 333 and 337 were utilized for special problems, there are many situations when neither of them is applicable. Hence, Section 331 is probably the most commonly used liquidation section. Even this section can produce substantial tax savings. When a corporation has to liquidate over a number of years, the overall tax burden to the shareholders can be reduced. It may be neither practical nor desirable from a tax standpoint to retain cash in the corporation until such time as the sale of all of the assets is accomplished and complete liquidation is feasible. The goal of this situation is not to have the distributions which may occur over a number of years designated as dividend income, but to have them classified as an installment distribution in complete liquidation of the corporation. The advantage of liquidating over a number of years is that it usually reduces the overall taxation.

Example: Contracting Corporation has been in the business of constructing various properties for sale to municipalities and private individuals. At the time liquidation is contemplated, the corporation has several projects in various stages of completion. In addition, it owns parcels of real estate which will be disposed of within a year. It is impossible to determine how long it will take the other property, including the equipment to be sold. The equipment can be disposed of only after the last project is completed. The founding father has retired and is interested in receiving cash over the next several years. He is the sole shareholder and has left his chief assistants to accomplish the liquidation. It is anticipated that upon complete liquidation of all properties, there will be $300,000 in cash to be distributed after payment of all expenses.

Assume the sole shareholder's basis is $0. If the corporation accumulates the cash during the five years and then distributes it, it will be necessary to realize $300,000 of capital gains in one year. Assuming that the sole shareholder has no other income, this would result in a tax of approximately $84,000. If, on the other hand, a partial liquidation distribution of $60,000 is made in each year, the capital gains which will be recognized in each year will be only $60,000. Again assuming no other taxable income, the tax each year would be about $12,932. This would result in a total tax savings over the five-year period of approximately $19,337.

There is no definite time schedule that must be followed in a complete liquidation. The Internal Revenue Service has announced that it will ordinarily not issue advance rulings or determination letters on the tax effects of a complete liquidation when the liquidation distributions are to be made over a period of time greater than three years. However, the courts have been more lenient and have permitted liquidations that have extended over a period of time up to twenty-three years. It is a prerequisite that every reasonable effort must be made to dispose of the properties and liquidate within the shortest possible time. If taxes are the sole reason for maintaining the corporate entity, the liquidation will not be able to extend over the desired period. In the cases where tax motivation has been the primary reason, the courts have imposed a constructive liquidation dividend prior to the date of distribution.

The requirements for a complete liquidation under Section 331 are relatively simple to satisfy. In order for Section 331 to apply, a status of liquidation must exist at the time the first distribution is made. However, neither the Code nor the Regulations defines exactly what the term "complete liquidation" means. Whether the corporation, at the time this distribution is made, is in the status of liquidation involves a factual determination. Neither the retention of the corporate charter to protect the corporate name nor the retention of sufficient assets to satisfy any contingent liabilities will disqualify the liquidation.

However, where the retention of any assets is contemplated or any business is transacted after the adoption of the liquidation resolutions, a complete analysis should be made to ensure that Section 331 is being complied with. A failure to comply could result in a dividend distribution. Proper documentation setting forth the resolutions in the minutes, while it may not be required by law, is useful in establishing the format which gives rise to favorable tax results.

Spread the Liquidation Distribution under Section 331 over as Many Years as Possible to Obtain Tax Reduction

The ability to spread the distribution over as many years as possible is particularly important. Basically, in utilizing Section 331, the distribution can be spread over three taxable years in as little as fourteen months. For example, one distribution can be made in December of 1984, one in January of 1985, and one in January of 1986. An example of a complete liquidation that took place over a long period of time is illustrated in *William C. McGuire v. Comr.*, 222 F.2nd 472 (7th Cir. 1955), when the corporation was liquidated in successive installments over a period of ten years because of pending litigation. However, if the IRS could have established that the only reason in delaying the complete liquidation is to defer taxes, it can impose a constructive liquidation distribution of the total net assets to the shareholders in an earlier taxable year. See *Williams v. U.S.*, 219 F.2d 523 (5th Cir. 1955), and *Everett Pozzi*, 49 T.C. 119 (1967).

Procedure to Follow: To play it safe, it is usually a good idea to have a formal plan of liquidation (although it is not required) and to have a systematic sale of the assets. Business reasons, even if tax tempered, should dictate the procedure.

NOTE: With the elimination of Sections 333 and 337 even for closely held corporations on January 1, 1989, planning utilizing Section 331 either alone or in conjunction with a personal holding company is going to become even more prevalent. The total tax effects of both a sale at the corporate level, with the resulting taxation, and the taxation upon liquidation is going to become so onerous that many corporations will either liquidate over a long period of time or convert to personal holding companies. Note that the prior negative effects of the receipt of

funds as dividend income have been largely overcome by the
Tax Reform Act of 1986.

[703.4] Utilizing the Partial Liquidation to Extract Money or Property from the Corporation

A partial liquidation is very much akin to the redemption of
corporate stock. In reality, a partial liquidation is nothing more
than a distribution of assets to the shareholders in exchange for
a portion of their stock. This distribution will virtually always
be made pro rata. Thus, if the redemption does not qualify as a
partial liquidation, it will result in dividend income to the
individual shareholders. A partial redemption, on the other
hand, may involve a reduction of the stock ownership by one
shareholder or a group of shareholders. In this instance,
the redemption will not qualify as a liquidation but will have
to qualify as a disproportionate redemption or a redemption
not equivalent to a dividend in order to receive capital gains
treatment. (The requirements for a partial redemption are
shown in ¶601.5.) This section will deal only with those distributions which would qualify as a partial liquidation.

The distinction between redemptions and partial liquidations has become even more important since the enactment of
the Tax Equity and Fiscal Responsibility Act of 1982 (TEFRA).
The 1982 law has placed the partial liquidation rules and regulations under Section 302, which had traditionally dealt with
redemptions. This law repeals some of the prior law's rules
defining partial liquidations. While capital gains treatment is
generally preserved for distributions or property to noncorporate shareholders, distributions to corporate shareholders
are generally treated as dividends with carryover basis for any
property distributed. The question that is asked is whether or
not appreciated property can be distributed tax free by the
corporation. Under prior law, there was no doubt at all. Under
the new rules, the answer to the question of whether or not the
corporation will report any gain on distribution of appreciated
property is a great deal more complicated.

If the corporation is a "qualified corporation" and the partial liquidation occurs before January 1, 1989, the following
important questions must be asked:

1. Are the shareholders receiving the distribution, corporate or noncorporate?
2. Is the distribution made pursuant to a partial liquidation?
3. Is the distribution made to a shareholder who holds qualified stock?

A full discussion of the ramifications of the answers to these questions will follow shortly. If the corporation is not a qualified corporation or if the liquidation occurs after January 1, 1989, the distribution of appreciated property will result in gain at the corporate level.

The partial liquidation plays a unique role in tax planning. While most planning involves the minimization of taxes during the profitable expansion years, the partial liquidation has applicability when the business is not expanding and has begun a period of contraction. In these instances, a partial liquidation becomes useful to minimize the overall tax burden. An example of its application is as follows:

> **Example:** Real Estate Corporation has been in existence for many years. From its inception, it has conducted a small mortgage loan business and has also been in the business of purchasing and selling vacant real estate for its own account. There are approximately fifteen shareholders in this corporation, of which two are the principal officers. One of the principals has had a severe heart attack, and it is evident that the business can no longer expand. As a practical matter, this corporation has commenced liquidation of its real estate interests. At this time, the mortgage business accounts for approximately one-third of the total gross sales, and real estate sales represent the remainder.
>
> Because of a change in the law, the mortgage business has become very unstable, and the corporation becomes involved in a lawsuit that will probably take many years. It is decided that the real property of the corporation will be distributed to the shareholders. Each shareholder will receive approximately sixty-six lots. The individual shareholders treat this exchange as a partial liquidation of the business. The corporation maintains the mortgage business

and operates it for several years until after the settlement of the lawsuit. At that time, the mortgage business is
liquidated and the cash is distributed to the individual
shareholders. Since the redemption qualified as a partial
liquidation, the distribution becomes a sale or exchange
rather than a dividend. In addition, if the shareholders
are receiving lots that have appreciated in value and if the
corporation is a qualified corporation making a distribution prior to January 1, 1989, it is possible that no gain
may be realized at the corporate level.

Why It Is Advantageous for a Partial Redemption to Qualify as a Partial Liquidation

It should now be obvious to you that the partial liquidation
is similar in many respects to a distribution in partial redemption of stock. Both involve a distribution of corporate property
in exchange for stock owned by the shareholders. A single
distribution may qualify under both sections. The partial liquidation has definite advantages over the redemption for the
following reasons:

1. If the corporation has previously issued Section 306 stock,
   a partial liquidation will result in capital gains treatment,
   while a redemption will be treated as dividend income.
2. If property having a mortgage in excess of basis is to be
   distributed, a partial liquidation will not result in any taxation to the corporation.
3. Partial liquidations may be made pro rata without any regard to the constructive ownership rules. Redemptions, to
   qualify for the sale of exchange treatment, must take attribution into consideration and must qualify as either a substantially disproportionate redemption or a redemption
   not equivalent to a dividend.
4. Redeeming the stock of any shareholder with appreciated
   property will result in income to the distributing corporation in the event of a redemption. However, in certain
   limited instances, if appreciated property is distributed to
   a noncorporate shareholder in a partial liquidation, the
   distribution *may* be tax free to the corporation. Prior to the

enactment of the Tax Reform Act of 1986, the distribution of appreciated property by a qualified closely held corporation in partial liquidation may have avoided taxation at the corporate level. Even before the Tax Reform Act of 1986, the distribution of appreciated property by the corporation will result in taxable income upon partial liquidation if the property distributed was installment obligations, property subject to depreciation recapture, or appreciated LIFO inventory. After the full effects of the Tax Reform Act of 1986 are implemented (for closely held qualified corporations January 1, 1989, and for all other corporations January 1, 1987), it will not be possible to distribute appreciated property at the corporate level and escape taxation. The distinction between redemption and partial liquidation will then become less important.

What the Requirements Are for a Partial Liquidation

Section 346(a)(2) of the Internal Revenue Code was amended by the Tax Equity and Fiscal Responsibility Act of 1982. It is now reincorporated within Section 302 which deals with distributions in redemption of stock. While there was a substantial change in the law, the definition of partial liquidations was continued. Basically, a distribution shall be treated as a partial liquidation if:

1. The distribution is not essentially equivalent to a dividend
2. The distribution is pursuant to a plan and occurs within the taxable year in which the plan is adopted or in the succeeding taxable year.

A distribution is not essentially equivalent to a dividend if it is attributable to the distribution of a qualified trade or business. Therefore, the question revolves around what a qualified trade or business is. A business will qualify if:

1. The trade or business was actively conducted throughout the five-year period preceding the date of distribution
2. Said trade or business was not acquired by the distributing corporation within that period of time in a taxable distribution

Section 302(e) states that whether or not a redemption meets the requirements of a partial liquidation shall be determined without regard to whether or not the redemption is pro rata with respect to all shareholders of the corporation. Thus, a pro rata distribution may still qualify for a partial liquidation.

It should be noted that while the Tax Equity and Fiscal Responsibility Act of 1982 affected what qualifies for a partial liquidation, the major changes in this area involved how the corporation is taxed upon the distribution. (This will be discussed in the next section.)

How Partial Liquidations Are Taxed to the Corporation and Shareholder

Taxation to the Corporation: The general rule to the enactment of the Tax Reform Act of 1986 was that a partial liquidation will not result in any taxation to the corporation except if the property distributed is either an installment obligation (other than an obligations of the corporation distributing the property), property subject to recapture (investment credit or depreciation), or appreciated LIFO inventory.

With the enactment of the Tax Equity and Fiscal Responsibility Act of 1982, the ability to distribute appreciated property to its shareholders without taxation to the corporation was reduced to those cases where the following prerequisites were met:

1. The distribution must qualify for a partial liquidation and not solely as a redemption of stock. It should be noted that all redemptions of stock with appreciated property except for redemptions pursuant to Section 303 (redemption to pay death taxes and other administrative costs) will be taxable.

2. The distribution must be to a noncorporate shareholder of qualified stock. In order to have the stock owned by the shareholder qualify, it must meet the following prerequisites:

   (a) The noncorporate shareholder must have been a shareholder for at least the five-year period ending on the date of distribution or the entire period during which the distributing corporation was in

existence if the corporation is less than five years old.
(b) The shareholder must have held at least 10 percent of the outstanding stock of the distributing corporation.

The following example will show how this exception can be utilized:

Example: ABC Corporation was authorized to issue only one class of stock, and during the five-year period ending January 1, 1985, 1,000 shares of stock were issued and outstanding. On January 1, 1979, X, an individual, bought 100 shares of ABC's stock and held those until the date of distribution, January 1, 1985. On March 1, 1982, X acquired an additional 200 shares of ABC's stock. On January 1, 1985, pursuant to a plan of partial liquidation, ABC makes a distribution of appreciated property to X in redemption of 100 shares of his stock. The distribution does qualify as a distribution in partial liquidation. ABC recognizes no gain as a result of the distribution since all of the redeemed stock is qualified.

After the Tax Reform Act of 1986, it is no longer clear whether or not there is any ability to distribute appreciated property that qualifies for a partial liquidation without incurring a tax at the corporate level. It initially appeared that qualified closely held corporations would be able to continue the same treatment as under prior law, at least until January 1, 1989. However, there is some question as to whether or not this intent was incorporated into the act. Thus, if appreciated property is to be distributed in a partial liquidation, care should be exercised.

WARNING: After the Tax Reform Act of 1986, there is no doubt that appreciated property distributed in a partial liquidation will result in taxation to the corporation for all other than qualified closely held corporations after January 1, 1987. There is a question of whether or not this will result in taxation to a qualified closely held corporation for the period January 1, 1987, to and through December 31, 1988. There is no doubt that after that time, a liquidation will result in taxation at the corporate as well as individual level.

> **Key Idea:** Instead of partially liquidating the corporation, a qualified division of the corporation under Section 355 should be considered with at least one of the corporations electing as an S Corporation.

In the above example, if X had acquired all his shares on January 1, 1982, even though the distribution may have qualified as a partial liquidation, the corporation would still have had to report the gain upon distribution. The distribution of appreciated property, therefore, can have ramifications on the corporation and shareholder.

The chart on page 343 will give the general rules as to how this is treated.

Congress was worried about the inventive shareholder attempting to turn a partial liquidation into a complete liquidation. The following example will illustrate the particular fears in this matter:

> **Example:** XYZ Corporation conducted two businesses. In Appleton, Wisconsin, they manufactured pallets. In Neenah/Menasha, they acted as a paper converter. The Appleton plant was leased. The Neenah/Menasha plant and assets were all owned by XYZ Corporation. If it had not been for the restrictions included in the Tax Equity and Fiscal Responsibility Act of 1982, it would have made good sense to have XYZ form a subsidiary corporation and convey the paper converting business to the subsidiary. The stock of the subsidiary could then have been distributed to the shareholders of XYZ as a tax-free spin-off. The subsidiary corporation could then have been liquidated.

In essence, this is really nothing more than a partial liquidation. If this partial liquidation could have been accomplished at the corporate level, the converting plant would have been conveyed directly to the shareholders of XYZ in partial liquidation. Unless the partial liquidation included the distribution to noncorporate shareholders of qualified stock, the difference in

	Taxation to Shareholder	Taxation to Qualified Closely Held Corporation
Dividend Income (see Chapter 4)	Normally ordinary income to the amount of earnings and profits of the corporation	Corporation will normally recognize gain on distributions of appreciated property unless the dividend is a qualified dividend made on qualified stock.[1]
Qualifying Redemption of Stock Not Qualifying for Liquidation (Note: This discussion excludes the treatment available under certain redemptions qualifying for special treatment under Section 303.) (See Chapter 6.)	Capital transaction	Recognizes gain on difference between fair market value and basis on all appreciated property distributed
Partial Liquidation—Distribution to a noncorporate shareholder who does not own qualified stock	Sale or exchange	Recognizes gain on difference between fair market value and basis on all appreciated property distributed
Partial Liquidation—Distribution to a noncorporate shareholder who owns qualified stock	Sale or exchange	Does not recognize gain, except on distribution of appreciated LIFO inventory, installment obligations; and/or recapture property.[2]

[1] Appears to be the law until January 1, 1989. Thereafter, all distributions of appreciated property will result in taxation to the corporation.

[2] This appears to be Congress's intent, although the interpretation of the Tax Reform Act of 1986 may be that all distributions will result in taxation. However, even if this interpretation is correct, this will only apply to closely held qualified corporations until January 1, 1989. Thereafter, all distributions in partial liquidation of appreciated property will result in taxable income at the corporate level.

value between the basis of the real estate and its fair market value would have been taxed at the corporate level. Therefore, if the above procedure was allowed, the use of a tax-free incorporation to establish the subsidiary, followed by a Section 355 tax-free spin-off and finally by a complete liquidation, could have escaped taxation at the corporate level. The IRS has been given powers to issue regulations that would prohibit this result. Thus, the ability to convert a partial liquidation into a complete liquidation through the use of Section 351 tax-free incorporation and Section 355 spin-off is going to be subject to IRS regulations to prohibit the same.

Taxation to the Individual Shareholder Upon Distribution: If the distribution qualifies as a partial liquidation, it is necessary to ascertain what portion of the stock basis must be allocated to the exchange. The gain or loss is not necessarily determined by subtracting the adjusted basis of the shares actually surrendered from the fair market value of the distribution. Regardless of the actual number of shares surrendered, the Internal Revenue Service considers that the total number of shares surrendered to be the total number of shares owned multiplied by the fraction, the numerator of which is the fair market value of the property received in the distribution and the denominator of which is the total fair market value of the property owned by the corporation.

> **Example:** Contracting Corporation has assets of $200,000. It conducts two businesses, and one is liquidating for $80,000. The corporation intends to distribute these proceeds pursuant to a qualifying partial liquidation. Contracting Corporation has 1,000 shares of authorized and issued common stock. All the stock is owned by one shareholder, whose basis is $5 a share. The shareholder surrenders 500 shares of stock. The Internal Revenue Service will disregard the fact that 500 shares were surrendered. Since the property distributed represented only 40 percent of the total assets ($80,000 distribution divided by $200,000), it will consider only 400 shares redeemed (40 percent of the 1,000). The capital gains will be $78,000 (proceeds received $80,000 less stock basis $2,000).

[704] HOW TO REINCORPORATE THE BUSINESS TO OBTAIN A HIGHER BASIS

Prior to the enactment of the Tax Reform Act of 1986, there was a tax gambit known as "liquidation and reincorporation." The goal of this gambit was to distribute accumulated earnings of the corporation at capital gains rates while continuing the corporate entity. This planning tool was useful when the old corporation had liquid assets exceeding its business needs. In this type of liquidation, the excess liquidity could be distributed to the shareholders while the active business assets would be reincorporated.

The benefits of this particular transaction were dependent upon the following two factors:

1. The favorable long-term capital gains rates at the individual level

2. The ability to distribute appreciated assets to the individual shareholders in complete liquidation tax free at the corporate level

Since the enactment of the Tax Reform Act of 1986, there seems to be little if any benefit left in this planning gambit. The tax stakes were always high, and the ability of the IRS to attack was always great since there was little business justification for such a procedure. Now, under the Tax Reform Act of 1986, even during the period of time when a qualified closely held corporation can avoid taxation, the elimination of the any favorable capital gains rates after 1987 seems to be the death knell of this technique.

Chapters 6 and 7, while being treated independently in this book, have interrelated concepts. The basic goal in both chapters is to shift the ownership of the business or businesses. This shift of ownership may be occasioned by the death or disability of a shareholder or the transfer of some of the shares of stock of the corporation. It could also be occasioned by the contraction of the business. The Internal Revenue Code presents numerous planning techniques to allow for a favorable tax transfer. However, the unwary can encounter numerous risks. Care for future planning through the utilization of stock purchase agreements and corporation redemption agreements of the shareholders is essential. It is also necessary for the individuals faced by particular problems to discuss the alternatives in conjunction with the tax effects that each present.

[705] STEP-BY-STEP GUIDE TO A SUCCESSFUL SECTION 331 LIQUIDATION

Key Idea: You should spread the liquidation distribution under Section 331 over more than one year. This will reduce the capital gains tax impact upon the individual shareholders.

Checklist of Steps You Should Take to Accomplish a Section 331 Transaction

1. Adoption by the shareholders and directors of a resolution recommending the corporation to liquidate completely under Section 331, including a resolution as to the proper steps to accomplish said liquidation. Depending upon the reason for the liquidation, this may be nothing more than obtaining an appraisal for the assets and a resolution authorizing the distribution of said assets pro rata to the shareholders. In the alternative, it may require the sale of some of the assets and the appraisal and distribution of the remainder of the assets.

2. File Form 966 with the Internal Revenue Service within 30 days of the adoption.

3. Take whatever steps are necessary to sell those assets that are to be sold, and distribute the remaining assets.

4. File the appropriate dissolution documents that are required by state law. Each state requires slightly different procedures; however, the general format is to require a final article of dissolution or certificate of dissolution.

5. File the corporation's final income tax returns, and file the necessary 1096 and 1099L forms with the Internal Revenue Service.

6. File with the commissioner of the Internal Revenue Service a request for a prompt assessment of all taxes which are due from the corporation.

7. Take any and all steps to wind up and close out the corporation's affairs, including the cancellation of all stock certificates and miscellaneous other acts.

8. Consider the benefits of liquidating the corporation over a number of years.

Helpful Hints and Problems to Avoid

1. Be sure that all documentation establishing the mode of liquidation has been accomplished prior to the first distribution. Also beware of taking on new business after a liquidation distribution has been accomplished.

2. Beware of qualified closely held corporations distributing property before January 1, 1989, such as unrealized accounts receivables or installment obligations. This would create taxable income to the corporation as well as capital gains tax to the individual shareholders.

3. Beware of qualified closely held corporations distributing LIFO inventory property before January 1, 1989. This would create taxable income to the corporation as well as capital gains to the individual shareholders.

4. Be sure that liquidation is accomplished in the quickest possible time.

5. If the corporation has elected to report on the cash basis, liquidation under Section 331 or any of the other methods may cause additional taxation if there are sizable accounts receivables and no accounts payables.

6. Beware of distributing any appreciated property to shareholders. This could cause taxation at the corporate level.

7. Beware of the many tax problems created by the Tax Reform Act of 1986.

[706] HOW TO ACCOMPLISH A SUCCESSFUL SECTION 333 LIQUIDATION

Key Idea: You should consider liquidating a qualified closely held corporation which owns appreciated assets and has little or no earnings and profits and cash or securities prior to January 1, 1989.

Checklist of Steps to Take to Accomplish a Section 333 Liquidation

1. Adoption by the shareholders and directors of a resolution recommending the corporation to distribute all of its assets under Section 333 within one month.

2. The reduction of all liabilities of the corporation through the use of cash and securities.

3. File Form 964 by at least 80 percent of the shareholders of each class of stock of the corporation.

4. File Form 966 with the Internal Revenue Service within thirty days after the adoption of the liquidation.

5. Distribute assets within one month.

6. File the appropriate dissolution documents that are required by state law. Each state requires slightly different procedures; however, the general format is to require final articles of dissolution or certificate of dissolution.

7. File the final corporate income tax returns.

8. File Form 1096 and 1099-L with the Internal Revenue Service.

9. It may be beneficial to file with the commissioner of the Internal Revenue Service a request for the prompt assessment of all taxes which are due from the corporation.

10. Take any and all steps to wind up and close out the corporation's affairs, including the cancellation of all stock certificates and miscellaneous other acts.

Helpful Hints and Problems to Avoid

1. If a sale of the property is contemplated by the shareholders immediately after liquidation, problems may arise. Hence, a significant time lag should occur, or a different liquidation approach should be utilized.

2. In certain instances, corporate shareholders may not qualify for the benefits under Section 333. Also, it may be more beneficial for them not to have it qualify. If the shareholder is a corporation, alternatives may need to be considered.

3. Care should be used by qualified closely held corporations in distributing property subject to recapture (depreciation

or investment credit), installment obligations, or LIFO inventory before January 31, 1989. If this type of property is being distributed, this would have severe adverse effects on the corporation.

4. Beware of the many tax problems created by the Tax Reform Act of 1986.

5. Beware that unless the law changes as of January 1, 1989, this provision will not be available for even qualified closely held corporations. For all other corporations, this section has ceased to be available as of January 1, 1987.

[707] WHAT YOU MUST DO FOR A SUCCESSFUL SECTION 337 LIQUIDATION

Key Idea: If all assets are to be sold rather than distributed in kind to the shareholder, you should consider the sale by the qualified closely held corporation and election under Section 337. This sale could reduce the overall tax impact on the corporation and shareholders.

Checklist of Steps You Should Take to Accomplish a Section 337 Transaction

1. Ascertain the goals of the liquidation.

2. Ascertain which, if any, assets are to be sold and distributed and which assets are to be distributed in kind. Compare Section 337 with the alternative Section 331.

3. Determine an action by the board of directors and shareholders of the corporation approving the liquidation of the corporation and the sale of the assets in conformity with Section 337.

4. File Form 996 with the district director within thirty days after the adoption of the resolution.

5. Determine the sale of those assets to be sold by the corporation and a distribution of the remainder of the assets within the twelve-month period.

6. Satisfy all corporate debts.

7. File, along with information which must be supplied pursuant to Regulations 1.337-5, final income tax returns.

8. Submit and file formal dissolution documentation with the appropriate state agency.

9. Request a prompt assessment with the commissioner.

10. File information returns Forms 1096 and 1099L.

11. Complete the liquidation, including cancellation of stock certificates, and so on.

Helpful Hints and Problems to Avoid

1. Qualified closely held corporations should be careful when they distribute property subject to depreciation or investment credit recapture or LIFO inventory.

2. Qualified closely held corporations should be careful when distributing installment obligations not incident to the sale of assets during the year of liquidation or from inventory.

3. Beware of retaining corporate shell beyond the twelve-month period of time, except in very limited situations.

4. Be aware that Section 337 can ordinarily not be utilized to liquidate a collapsible corporation, except under very restrictive instances.

5. Review the positive aspects of liquidation under Section 337 in coordination with the changes made by the Installment Sales Revision Act of 1980.

6. If the corporation has elected to report on the cash basis, liquidation under Section 337 or any other method may cause additional taxation if there are sizable accounts receivables and no accounts payables.

7. Beware of the many tax problems created by the Tax Reform Act of 1986.

8. Beware, unless the law changes as of January 1, 1989, this provision will not be available for even qualified closely held corporations. For all other corporations, this section has ceased to be available as of January 1, 1987.

8

How to Avoid the Pitfalls of Operating and Terminating a Corporation

[800] FOUR KEY TAX TRAPS

In the preceding seven chapters we have dealt with the various methods of taking money out of the corporation at minimum tax cost. This chapter investigates four major problem areas that could unknowingly produce unplanned complications for you. The problems of collapsible or multiple corporations may be present from inception and continue throughout corporate existence. Problems such as the accumulated earnings tax or the personal holding company can occur at any time during the operation of the corporation with little, if any, warning. All four of these tax traps may have their risks mitigated or completely avoided by proper planning.

[801] HOW TO AVOID THE ACCUMULATED EARNINGS TAX TRAP

The accumulated earnings tax was inserted into the law as a method to ensure that corporations, which have a dividend-paying capacity and no reasonable need to accumulate the assets in the business, would distribute these assets in the form of dividends. In essence, Congress through Section 531 of the Internal Revenue Code placed a tool in the hands of the IRS to

353

allow it to exact a "penalty" on corporations which retain earnings in order to avoid taxation to the shareholders on the distribution of these earnings as dividends. Chapter 4 analyzed the negative effects of unplanned dividends resulting in double taxation.

As a rule, in closely held nonpublicly traded corporations, it was found that dividends should be avoided. In addition to the general reluctance of corporate directors to pay dividends, corporations have often withheld dividends in the early years of the corporate existence when the majority shareholders are in high tax brackets. Dividends are paid in the later years when the majority shareholders have retired and are in lower tax brackets (see ¶403.2).

To prohibit excess accumulation, Congress enacted Section 531. This allows the corporation to retain sufficient funds for the legitimate needs of a growing business and to pay a penalty solely upon the accumulated earnings in excess of reasonable current needs or reasonably anticipated needs.

When a corporation finds that it may be subject to an accumulated earnings tax, there are certain steps that can be taken to minimize the problem. Some of these acts require only the documentation of actions already taken by the corporation, others necessitate the restructuring of the corporation.

The following is a list of the six positive steps to be taken to minimize the problem of an accumulated earnings tax:

1. Documentation of the purposes for which the earnings and profits of the corporation are being retained. This should include minutes stating the actions taken by the officers, the success they have met, and any and all outside documentation, such as offers, letters, and so on.

2. Payment of dividends. Any corporation subject to the accumulated earnings tax should consider paying dividends.

3. Maximization of salaries. This will result in the reduction of the earnings and profits. If the additional salary produces a cash drain to the corporation to the extent that the corporation cannot meet its current operating needs, then, in all likelihood, the corporation did not have an accumulated earnings problem in the first place.

4. Liquidation. Consider the possible liquidation of the corporation, if all else fails.

5. The purchase of business assets. If the corporation had been leasing its building, it may be more advantageous to purchase it.
6. Election as a Subchapter S Corporation.

Example of Positive Steps to Be Taken to Limit the Imposition of the Accumulated Earnings Tax

Example: Profitable Corporation has been in existence for 15 years and currently has the following balance sheet:

Cash and Equivalents	$250,000
Equipment and Inventory	200,000
Accounts Receivables	100,000
Unrelated Investments	200,000
TOTAL	$750,000
Accounts Payable	$ 75,000
Capital Stock	100,000
Retained Earnings	575,000
TOTAL	$750,000

Obviously, on the face of the above example, Profitable Corporation has an accumulated earnings problem. The steps that may be taken to mitigate this problem are as follows:

1. Profitable Corporation may be engaged in a business where technological changes necessitate a substantial reinvestment in new equipment. This fact could be well documented in the corporate records. These corporate records, of course, should also include outside documentation.
2. Profitable Corporation should probably consider the payment of dividends.
3. If salaries in the past have not been at the highest reasonable compensation, they at least should be raised to this figure.
4. Serious consideration should be given to the liquidation of the business. In this case, this may not be appropriate because of the great amount of gain that would have to be realized by the shareholders upon the liquidation. The

possibility exists that the corporation may also have to realize taxable income upon liquidation by reason of owning appreciated property.

5. Nothing vindicates the retention of earnings to a greater extent than the spending of said earnings for the expansion of the business. Substantial expenditures for either real or personal property justifies the retention of the earnings. As a corollary to this principle, if the business is expanding in sales, the retention of earnings and profits to maintain a rapidly increasing inventory and accounts receivable could also be justified.

6. In the final analysis, a review of the reason for the retention should always be made. If in the past, money had been retained to sustain the maximum tax benefits through the dividing of income (see ¶100.1), a reevaluation of the goals should be instituted. It may indicate that the tax advantages of retaining the corporate system of taxation may be more than counterbalanced by the possible imposition of an accumulated earnings tax. Usually the easiest way to avoid this particular problem, if the corporation is eligible, is to elect as a Subchapter S Corporation. Subchapter S Corporations are not subject to the accumulated earnings tax.

Before attempting to elect as a Subchapter S Corporation, a complete review of the prerequisites should be undertaken to ensure that the corporation qualifies. In the above example (because of the value of the unrelated investments, cash and equivalents, and the accumulated earnings and profits), while a Subchapter S election probably could be utilized, the corporate taxation caused by such election may effectively prohibit its proper utilization.

[801.1] Requirements for the Imposition of an Accumulated Earnings Penalty

The penalty tax imposed by Section 531 applies to any corporation formed or operated for the purpose of enabling its shareholders to avoid income tax by permitting its earnings and profits to be accumulated instead of being distributed. For the purposes of this Code section, tax avoidance has not been defined. While the statute itself does not define reasonable needs of the business, it does define the term "reasonably anticipated needs," which includes, in addition to business needs, several personal needs of the shareholders, as follows:

1. Amounts needed (or reasonably anticipated to be needed) in the year of death and later years to redeem the stock and to pay death taxes to the extent they are eligible for capital gains treatment under Section 303

2. The amount needed (or reasonably anticipated to be needed) to redeem from private foundations, stock held on May 26, 1969 (or received pursuant to a will or irrevocable trust treated as binding on May 26, 1969)

The regulations adopt a positive attitude toward establishing a set of criteria consistent with that of a prudent businessman. If the prudent businessman would consider a certain accumulation of earnings and profits for present business purposes and for reasonably anticipated future business needs, then the accumulation is not unreasonable. Therefore, a plan to expand into a new facet of the existing business would definitely qualify.

> **Example:** Film Processing Corporation is a business that plans to expand. Film Processing Corporation has, in the past, processed only black and white film. Eastman Kodak, pursuant to a consent agreement filed with the court, has agreed to end its color processing monopoly. If Film Processing Corporation goes out and purchases new equipment and leases temporary headquarters until a more permanent location could be established to begin color film processing, it could allocate a portion of its retained earnings for future expansion. This planned expenditure would be considered a reasonably anticipated need.

However, a mere statement that technological changes caused the need for a possible expansion is not sufficient. Another reason for the accumulation is that a prudent businessman could prepare for contingencies. The regulations indicate that for the accumulation to be appropriate, the contingency must be realistic. Exactly what is "**realistic**" depends upon the particular situation. The corporation which faced the possibility of losing its largest customer could reasonably retain earnings to conduct an advertising campaign to attract new business. However, a contingency which has no reasonable chance of occurring could not justify the accumulation.

Checklist of Commonly Considered Reasonable and Unreasonable Needs of the Business

Reasonable needs are as follows:

☐ Provide for business expansion.

☐ Provide for replacement of physical assets or purchase of new assets.

☐ Provide for assets to acquire another business, in the proper circumstances.

☐ Provide for the payment of indebtedness.

☐ Provide for necessary working capital. During a period of rapid inflation, it is very important to retain capital for the current and the anticipated increase in inventories and receivables. This particular provision has substantial validity during certain business cycles.

☐ Provide for investments and loans to suppliers or customers, if necessary.

Unreasonable needs are as follows:

☐ Loans to shareholders or expenditure of corporate funds for personal benefit

☐ Loans which have no reasonable relation to the corporate business

☐ Loans to a related corporation

☐ Investments and unrelated activities

☐ Retention of earnings to provide against risks which are unrealistic

[801.2]   Taxing Unreasonable Accumulations

The accumulated earnings tax is a tax in addition to all other taxes and is imposed as follows:

1. 27½ percent of the accumulated taxable income not in excess of $100,000

2. 38½ percent of the accumulated taxable income in excess of $100,000

Accumulated taxable income is exempted from taxation to the greater of:

1. The reasonable needs of the business

2. The aggregate sum of $250,000 ($150,000 for certain personal service corporations).

The Economic Recovery Tax Act of 1981 increased the minimum accumulated earnings credit from $150,000 to $250,000 for all corporations except certain personal service corporations, which are only eligible for the old $150,000 credit. For this purpose, service corporations include those corporations whose principal function is the performance of services in the fields of health, law, engineering, architecture, accounting, actuarial science, performing arts, or consulting. It is extremely important to watch for an unreasonable accumulation when the earnings exceed the appropriate minimum credit and one or more of the following indicia for unreasonable accumulations are present:

1. Large shareholder loans

2. Investments in unrelated business activities, for example, savings accounts, corporate stocks, or Treasury bonds

3. Lack of a dividend-paying policy

The following example will illustrate how the accumulated earnings tax can be applied to a specific factual situation:

Example: Unreasonable Corporation is a corporation doing business as a manufacturer's representative. (It would appear that while this is a *service corporation* as commonly defined unless the regulations promulgated under Section 535 are given a broader interpretation, the $250,000 accumulated earnings limitation would be applicable.) The corporation rents an office and owns furniture and equipment. Virtually all of its business is written through its twenty-five registered representatives, who are independent contractors. The balance sheet is as follows:

Cash	$ 10,000
Government Securities	200,000
Furniture and Equipment	50,000
Shareholders Loans	150,000
TOTAL	$410,000
Accounts Payable	$ 10,000
Corporate Stock	20,000
Accumulated Earnings	380,000
TOTAL	$410,000

This corporation is definitely susceptible to the imposition of an accumulated earnings tax. Two indicia make this corporation particularly vulnerable, as follows:

1. The shareholders' loans in the amount of $150,000
2. The unrelated investment in government securities of $200,000

If the accumulation in the corporation is less than $250,000, no threat of the tax would exist. However, because the accumulation in this example is in excess of that amount, the minimum credit does not apply, and the income in excess of $250,000 would be subject to the tax.

Before the tax is imposed, seven adjustments are subtracted from the total accumulation. Some of the more common adjustments to be subtracted are the reasonable accumulation (or the $250,000 credit, whichever is greater), a consent dividend, taxes, charitable deductions, capital losses, and capital gains. The Tax Reform Act of 1984 has had a significant impact on how adjustment for capital gains and losses are treated. Under the prior law, the accumulated taxable income against which the accumulated earnings tax is applied was reduced by a deduction of the net capital loss for the year, or by a deduction of the net capital gain (computed without loss carrybacks or carryovers) minus the tax attributable to such capital gains.

To prevent corporations from scheduling capital gains in some years and capital losses in others to minimize the tax, these rules have been significantly changed. Under this act, in determining the net capital gains deduction, net capital gain is first reduced by the tax attributable to it. The law then provides that the net capital gains must be reduced by net capital losses from prior years. As far as the net capital loss deduction is concerned, this must be reduced by the prior capital gains deductions from the accumulated taxable income. Under this "recapture" rule, the net capital loss is reduced by the previous net capital gain deduction which has not already been recaptured. However, this reduction cannot be more than the amount of the earnings and profits as of the close of the preceding taxable year. The rules regarding these adjustments are extremely complicated and should be reviewed, especially in light of the changes made by the Tax Reform Act of 1984.

In the above example, a reasonable accumulation would include the current operating capital plus assets needed in the operation of the business. Assume that this reasonable accumulation was finally ascertained at $70,000 ($10,000 of cash, $10,000 of accounts payable, and $50,000 of furniture and fixtures). Assume further that the entire accumulation was the result of one year's earnings and that there were no adjustments to taxable income other than the amount needed to be retained as a reasonable accumulation. Therefore, the $70,000 is less than the $250,000 minimum deduction; accordingly, the appropriate reduction from the accumulated earnings is $250,000, and this is subtracted from the $380,000. The unreasonable accumulation would appear to be $130,000 and would be subject to a tax determined as follows:

$100,000 times 27½ percent $27,500
$ 30,000 times 38½ percent   11,550
         TOTAL $39,050

The above example of Unreasonable Corporation has been simplified, since all $380,000 is shown as income in one year. The accumulated earnings tax is a tax on current earnings and not a tax on the total accumulated earnings. However, the reason it is called an accumulated earnings tax is that this tax does not apply until such time as there is an excess of earnings and profits. Assuming in the previous example that the corporation paid the accumulated earnings tax and again accumulated an additional $100,000 of earnings and profits in the next year, in that year, there would again be an additional $27,500 in tax. This, of course, assumes that there was no justification for accumulating the earnings during the subsequent year.

[801.3] Avoiding the Accumulated Earnings Tax

Checklist of Planning Opportunities to Avoid the Accumulated Earnings Tax

Indications that the corporation may be subject to an accumulated earnings tax:	☐ Accumulated earnings and profits are in excess of $250,000 ($150,000 for certain personal service corporations); and ☐ Loans have been made to the various shareholders; or ☐ The corporation has unrelated investments such as stocks and bonds; or ☐ Surplus of corporation's funds are in liquid assets; or ☐ The corporation during the year does not have substantial amounts of indebtedness.
What to do?	☐ Maximize salaries; and/or ☐ Pay dividends; and/or ☐ Purchase additional business assets; and/or

	☐ Elect under Subchapter S; and/or
	☐ Consider corporate liquidation.
When to do it?	☐ As soon as the problem appears, you should document in minutes and through outside verification any and all actions and reasons for the accumulation of earnings.
Helpful hint:	☐ If a problem appears, it would be a good idea to review the working capital needs of the business pursuant to the formulas originally set forth in *Bardahl International Corp.*, 25 CTM 935 (1966), and *Bardahl Manufacturing Corp.*, 24 TCM 1030 (1965) (see Appendix *U*).

[801.4] Dealing with the Accumulated Earnings Tax if There Is No Other Way

Checklist of Alternative Steps to Take if a Corporation *Is* Faced with a Possible Accumulated Earnings Penalty

☐ Dividends are not your best tax-planning tool. However, if the only way to avoid the penalty is to pay dividends, this may be your best alternative. Prior to the payment of the dividends, it may be worthwhile to gift a portion of the stock to a lower base taxpayer. This technique, if used either immediately prior to the payment of dividends or pursuant to a long-range program of gifting, may allow for minimization of the double taxation upon the payment of dividends.

Example: Unreasonable Corporation has the balance sheet and characteristics of that described in ¶801.2. The officers of the corporation have made an analysis and have ascertained that there is no reason to retain the earnings. They have further ascertained that the imposition of a tax on unreasonable earnings with the resulting $39,050 expense is imminent. Currently, Unreasonable Corporation has two shareholders, X and Y, and each owns 50 percent of the stock. If it were possible to spread the dividends over two years ($65,000 in each year) and if X and Y were each in the 33 percent bracket, at least $21,750 of taxation would be incurred in each year. If X has three dependent children over the age of 14, he can minimize this taxation on his $65,000 share of dividend income by conveying 10 percent of the stock to each of these children prior to the payment of the dividends and retaining 20 percent of the corporate stock. If X does convey to each of his children 10 percent of the stock and if these children do not have any earnings other than his income, tax savings will result, calculated as follows:

WITHOUT INCOME SPLITTING

	1988	1989	Total
X's Dividend Income	$32,500	$32,500	$65,000
Tax	$10,725	$10,725	$21,450
Net After-Tax Income	$21,775	$21,775	$43,550

WITH INCOME SPLITTING
(10 PERCENT OF STOCK GIFTED TO EACH OF THREE CHILDREN, 20 PERCENT RETAINED)

	Child 1	Child 2	Child 3	X	Total
Dividend Income (each year)	$6,500	$6,500	$6,500	$13,000	$32,500
Tax	$ 900	$ 900	$ 900	$ 4,290	$ 6,990

TOTAL TAX EFFECT ON X WITH INCOME SPLITTING

Tax on children's portions ($900 × 3 × 2 yrs.)	$ 5,400
Tax on X's remaining 20 percent (2 yrs.)	8,580
TOTAL	$13,980
Tax if X had retained entire 50 percent of stock	$21,450
Tax savings with income splitting	$ 7,470

Tax savings may be derived from splitting the income into two years. If the corporation is a fiscal year corporation (for example with a year-end of January 31), it is possible within one corporate year to pay out the total dividends and have the dividends reported by the shareholders in two calendar years. If, on the other hand, the corporation is a calendar year tax-payer, the dividend income splitting may be more difficult. In addition to the splitting into two years, we have allocated a significant amount of the dividends each year, $19,500, to lower base taxpayers.

> **Key Idea:** Note that under the Tax Reform Act of 1986 the maximum benefit is the difference between the minimum marginal tax rate—15 percent—and the maximum marginal tax rate with the surcharge of 33 percent or 18 percent. The benefits of the savings of the tax should be counterbalanced with the fact that a gift has been made to a lower basis tax-payer, and the ability to reacquire the property at a later date may not be possible.

☐ The corporation can maximize the payments to the various officer/shareholders in the form of reasonable compensation.

☐ The corporation can take no action at all and risk the imposition of the tax. An analysis should be made of whether or not the payment of the tax is a greater or lesser burden than the payment of dividend income.

If it is decided that it would be in the best interest of the corporation to risk the imposition of an accumulated earnings tax, certain additional factors should be considered, as follows:

1. The age of the shareholders. If the shareholders are old and there is a real possibility of one or more of their deaths in the not so distant future, it should be considered whether or not it would be possible to withdraw the money tax free under Section 303 (see ¶603).

2. An analysis should also be undertaken as to whether or not it would be possible to accomplish a redemption of stock so that a portion of these accumulated earnings could be returned as either a tax-free return of capital or, in lieu thereof, at capital gains rates.

The following example shows when no action is taken:

Example: X, the sole shareholder of Unreasonable Corporation, is in the 33 percent marginal tax bracket. The unreasonable accumulated earnings for 1988 is $100,000. If this $100,000 is distributed as a dividend distribution, X will realize $67,000 in after-tax income. If this money is accumulated in the corporation, the corporation will bear a penalty of $27,500. X may deem it in his best interest to suffer this penalty even though he still does not have the money in his possession. This would be particularly applicable if it is anticipated that in the near future his marginal tax bracket will be less. If he anticipates he will be in the 15 percent marginal tax bracket (taxable income of $29,750 or under, for a married taxpayer filing a joint return for taxable years beginning after 1987), his after-tax income would be computed as follows:

Dividend distribution ($100,000 less $27,500)	$72,500
LESS Individual Income Tax	10,875
Net After-Tax Income:	$61,625

☐ In an appropriate situation, an attempt should be made to ensure that the accumulated earnings do not exceed $250,000 (or $150,000 for certain personal service corporations).

☐ A review should be made as to whether or not a liquidation of the corporation may not be the most advantageous method of approach.

□ It may be appropriate to elect under Subchapter S and have the income taxed directly to the individual shareholders (see ¶500).

□ The corporation should take action to substantiate its accumulation. A review of the current business needs and the anticipated needs of the business should be undertaken. Proper documentation should be inserted in the minute book.

Example: Manufacturer's Rep. Corporation is a corporation that serves as a sales agent for the midwestern distribution of widgets. In the past, it had acted solely as an agent and only solicited orders for the widget manufacturers. A complete analysis of the business was undertaken by the operating officers to ascertain the ramifications of extending into the distributorship field. As part of this survey, an analysis was made as to what the total capital needs of an extension of the business would be. Included in the capital needs survey was the need for an acquisition of a warehouse and the additional capital necessary to sustain both inventory and receivables. This survey and analysis were documented by the business with a definitive determination that until such time as the corporation had a $350,000 capital base, it was impossible to compete with an established distributor.

While not conclusive, this type of documentation, contemporaneously prepared adds validity to the accumulation of earnings. If, in addition to this survey, actual steps to effect the extension of the business had been undertaken, justification would exist. Two examples are as follows:

1. The corporation had made several offers to purchase real estate.

2. The corporation had entered into negotiations to purchase a distributorship in a nearby locality, which would have given them instant access to the markets.

If Manufacturer's Rep. purchased a distributorship, it would lend credence to the actual need and intent for the accumulation in the business. If, on the other hand, no further action had been taken, this would cast doubt as to the original intent and need for this accumulation. In most cases, where the imposition of an accumulated earnings tax is considered, the agent will be applying 20/20 hindsight. Of necessity, the audit will occur several years after the initial accumulation. Therefore, the agent will be reviewing events after the year in question to show the "real" intent for the accumulation.

[801.5] Effect of the Tax Reform Act of 1986 on the Accumulated Earnings Tax

Because of the benefits of dividing income between the individual employee/shareholders and the corporation was substantial (the potential of approximately 33½ percent on $50,000,) the desire in the past to retain money in a corporation was enhanced. However, with the enactment of the Tax Reform Act of 1986, which basically provides reduced income-splitting benefits for corporate income under $75,000 and negative benefits for retention of funds in the corporation for money over that amount, the desire both for tax and nontax purposes to retain money in the corporation will be reduced. It would appear that in the future, corporations will have greater impetus to distribute funds in the form of salary and/or dividends, and there will be less desire or benefit to retain funds in the corporation. This would seem to indicate that while the accumulated earnings tax is not a thing of the past, it may become less of a problem in the future.

QUERY: With the need for the United States to retool in order to meet foreign competition, will the law be amended in the future? The best possibility to meet future competition is the retention of funds in a corporation. The accumulated earnings tax was imposed not to prevent the retention of funds, but to discourage the abuse. The future course of the law at this time is at best murky and will have to be watched and analyzed to determine its future course.

[802] WHEN TO USE PERSONAL HOLDING COMPANIES

The personal holding company creates various planning opportunities, which we will discuss more fully later in this section. However, the major impetus of this section will be to explore certain alternatives which will eliminate or minimize the threat of the imposition of a personal holding tax on the corporation.

These alternatives can be summarized as follows:

1. Personal holding companies are sometimes the result of poor planning when a previously active business is sold.

   Key Idea: Before selling a business, consider liquidation of the corporation.

2. The liquidation of the corporation, even after the sale of the business, should be considered.

   Key Idea: Prior to liquidation, the transfer of the stock to lower base taxpayers, for example, children over the age of 14, or possibly parents, may reduce the overall tax effects.

3. Payment of dividends may eliminate any of the personal holding tax consequences and can provide positive planning opportunities for the family unit which owns the stock in the corporation.

4. Maximize the salary and other expenses to minimize the income subject to a personal holding tax.

5. Consider investing in preferred and common stock to reduce the overall tax impact of the personal holding company.

The personal holding company is a tax concept developed by the Code, which may appear at three times during the corporate existence, as follows:

1. At incorporation, as a device to be utilized to effectuate estate-planning goals (see ¶802.3)

2. During the operation of the corporation, as a trap for the unwary, which could disastrously increase the overall tax burden (see ¶802.2)

3. As an alternative to the liquidation of the corporation upon the sale of the business (see ¶802.3)

[802.1]   Requirements for a Corporation to Be Considered a Personal Holding Company

For the purposes of Code Section 542, a personal holding company is defined as a corporation which meets two separate and distinct requirements. They involve an analysis of the adjusted gross income and the stock ownership of the corporation. Both requirements must be met for the corporation to be subject to the personal holding company tax, as follows:

1. *Adjusted ordinary gross income requirement:* At least 60 percent of the adjusted ordinary gross income for the taxable year must be personal holding company income. For the purposes of this requirement, personal holding company income includes most forms of passive income, such as dividends, interest, royalties, and annuities. There are certain types of personal holding company income that present special problems. They are personal service contract income, produced film rents, copyright royalties, mineral, oil and gas royalties, and rents. Since most of these are not commonly encountered in the operation of a small corporation, they will not be dealt with in this book. However, rents are a common form of income in a small corporation and should be considered.

   Rents will be included in passive personal holding company income unless both of the following requirements are met:

   (a) The adjusted income from rents constitutes more than 50 percent of the adjusted ordinary gross income for the corporation. Adjusted gross income from rents is defined as the gross rents received less property taxes, interest, depreciation, and rent paid out.

   (b) Other personal holding company income is less than or equal to 10 percent of the ordinary gross income, or other personal holding company income exceeds 10 percent of the ordinary gross income, and the excess over 10 percent was paid out or consented to as dividends.

   Therefore, with proper planning, a corporation which owns solely rental property should not be subject to a personal holding company tax.

2. *Stock ownership requirement:* At any time during the last half of the taxable year, more than 50 percent in value of the outstanding stock is owned directly or indirectly by not more than five individuals. As a practical matter, if the stock is owned by less than ten individuals, the stock ownership test must be satisfied.

For this reason, most closely held corporations will meet the stock ownership test but avoid personal holding company status by failing to meet the adjusted gross income requirement. For the purpose of stock ownership, Section 544 establishes its own rules of constructive ownership. These deviate somewhat from the rules previously discussed in ¶600. Therefore, whenever there are related shareholders or shareholders who own interests in related entities—for example, corporations, partnerships, and so on—a complete analysis of this Section should be undertaken.

There are certain types of corporations that are excluded from personal holding company status. A partial list of the more frequently encountered are banks, savings and loans, life insurance companies, other lending or financial institutions (if they meet certain requirements), and small businesses under the Small Business Investment Act of 1958.

[802.2] Taxing Personal Holding Company

In addition to all other taxes imposed by the Code, a personal holding company is subject to a tax of 50 percent of the undistributed personal holding income for all years prior to 1987, 38.5 percent in 1987, and 28 percent thereafter. This rate is tied to the maximum individual tax rate for the applicable year. Basically, undistributed personal holding company income is computed by the same method as taxable income with the following adjustments:

1. *Taxes:* There is a deduction allowed for federal income taxes.
2. *Charitable deductions:* A deduction for a charitable contribution is increased to the 50 percent limitation allowed to individuals instead of the normal 5 percent corporate limitation.

3. *Long-term capital gain deduction:* Any excess long-term capital gain over the net short-term capital loss (less the taxes attributable to the excess) shall be allowed as an additional deduction.

4. *Dividends received:* The 80 percent dividend exclusion allowed to corporations is not allowed in figuring the personal holding company's undistributed personal holding company income.

5. *Various miscellaneous deductions involving foreign corporations and nonresident aliens which are not normally encountered.*

6. *Dividends paid deduction:* Dividends paid during the year plus consent dividends paid during a subsequent taxable year in addition to dividends paid within two and one-half months after the taxable year (as long as this does not amount to more than 20 percent of the total dividends paid) will be allowed as a deduction in determining personal holding company income.

In addition to the preceding adjustments to taxable income, the corporation is also entitled to a deduction for the dividends paid under Section 561. This section is fairly complicated, with several elections available. A critical review of this section will indicate that the statute's aim is not to impose a tax on the undistributed personal holding company income but to force payment of dividends. The payment of deficiency dividend reduces undistributed personal holding company income. This can relieve any subsequently discovered personal holding company tax liability.

The general taxation of a personal holding company can best be demonstrated by the following example:

Example: XYZ Corporation is a personal holding company subject to the tax in 1986. XYZ Corporation has the income statement shown on the top of page 373 for the first year of operation.

After deduction of the 80 percent dividend exclusion for 1988, XYZ Corporation has a loss of $2,000. This is determined by subtracting from book income of $30,000 the dividend exclusion of $32,000 (.8 × $40,000 dividend income). Notwithstanding this fact, the undistributed personal holding company income before the payment of div-

	1984
Gross Sales	$200,000
Cost of Goods Sold	190,000
Gross Income from Sales	$ 10,000
Less Operating Expenses:	30,000
Operating Income	($ 20,000)
Plus Rental Income	5,000
Interest Income	5,000
Dividend Income	40,000
Book Income	$ 30,000

idends is $30,000. Note that the total personal holding company income is $50,000 but, that it is partially offset by the loss from regular business operations. If XYZ had paid a dividend of $30,000 during the year, no personal holding company penalty tax would be imposed. Also, if it had paid $25,000 of dividends during the year and within two and one-half months after the year it had paid an additional $5,000, again there would have been no personal holding penalty tax.

The above example illustrates the fact that it is possible to have a personal holding company subject to a tax even when there is no taxable income at the corporate level.

[802.3] Using the Personal Holding Company to the Shareholder's Benefit in Estate Planning and upon the Sale of the Business

In certain instances, it may be beneficial for an individual to create a personal holding company for possible estate tax savings and ancillary income tax savings. This is particularly true if we have a stock that is rapidly increasing in value and at the same time have an individual who has a substantial outside salary.

The current income tax savings that may be obtained are as follows:

1. The deferral of tax on appreciation
2. The estate tax benefits that could be derived are:

(a) The utilization of the fifteen-year deferral under Section 6166 (see ¶603.1). However, in order to obtain the benefits of this section, the corporation must be engaged in a "trade or business," normally not the case in personal holding companies. The Tax Reform Act of 1984 permits an executor to elect to treat stock in certain personal holding companies as stock in an active business for certain purposes under the estate tax installment payment provision. Under this act, any stock in a corporation carrying on an active business, which could be considered in determining qualification for estate tax installment payments were it owned directly, generally can be so considered even if owned by a personal holding company. However, because of the complexities associated with looking through multiple corporations, the act provides that a corporation will be looked through only if at least 20 percent of the total value of the corporation is included in the decedent's gross estate, either directly or indirectly. (The complete planning ramifications are beyond the scope of this book.)

(b) The ability to gift away the property with ease.

The following is an example of some of the benefits to be derived from a personal holding company.

Example: Mr. Rich is an executive for a major corporation and is receiving a salary of $100,000 a year. Approximately twenty years ago, his parents left him with a substantial inheritance, which has increased in value. The inheritance, which originally had a basis of $100,000, currently has a value of $1.5 million. In addition to this inheritance, he owns real property—a home and a summer home worth about $300,000. He has cash and other securities worth another $100,000. His will creates a non-marital trust with credit exemption equivalent of $600,000 and gives the remainder to his wife outright. His wife has no assets at all in her own name. The dividend income from the $1.5 million worth of stock is approximately $90,000 a year.

Several years ago, Rich established a corporation to buy a resort, Resort Corporation, which has a current fair market value of $75,000. One of his children is currently the chief operating officer of this resort. Because of the heavy debt created by the purchase and the extraordinary operating expenses, this resort has a net operating loss. If he transfers to this corporation the shares of stock received from his inheritance for preferred stock in Resort Corporation (in which he is the sole shareholder), no taxation will result. This transfer will be tax free under Section 351. By transferring this dividend-paying stock to Resort Corporation, a personal holding company will be formed from a previously active corporation with a net operating loss. For the best results, the new stock should be preferred and will be issued in the amount of $1.425 million. All future appreciation will be attributable to the common stock of Resort Corporation. He could then transfer all the common stock, which has a current fair market value of $75,000, to his children and wife. Rich could then commence a gifting program and gift to each of his children $10,000 a year in preferred stock. If his wife consents, this gift can be increased by the amount of her annual exemption for a total of $20,000 to each child per year.

For gift tax purposes, this preferred stock will probably be valued at less than the $10,000 par value because it is preferred with a low dividend rate. The creation of the personal holding company would have the following beneficial results. First, it transfers future appreciation in the portfolio of inherited stock to the holders of the new common stock of Resort Corporation (his wife and children), thus reducing Rich's taxable estate. Second, as the preferred stock is gifted to Rich's children, the dividends payable on it will be reallocated to lower bracket taxpayers. Resort Corporation will be entitled to an 80 percent dividend exclusion on the $90,000 annual income from the $1.5 million portfolio transferred to the corporation. **NOTE:** OBRA 1987 has had a negative effect on planning such as outlined above. The law should be reviewed before the implementation of any such plan.

After this exclusion, the taxable income would be only $18,000, which would be more than offset by the loss from the resort. In addition, it is entirely conceivable and appropriate that Rich would receive a salary and fringe benefits for managing the corporation. He, of course, runs the risk of having any salary classified as unreasonable compensation, but if he devotes substantial time and energy to the investment and the maintenance of the personal holding company and to the operation of the resort, this has a good chance of being sustained.

It should be noted that there will be no personal holding company tax because if there is any undistributed personal holding company income, it will be more than offset by the dividends paid deduction that must be incurred because of the payment of dividends on the preferred stock.

The general format illustrated above, or any of its variations, is a sophisticated plan that can produce significant tax-planning benefits given the proper factual situations. Basically, the prerequisites for using this tool are as follows:

1. An individual taxpayer in a high marginal bracket.
2. This individual taxpayer has a significant estate producing unearned income and containing assets.
3. An active corporation which produces a net operating loss.

If these factors are present, the tax-planning opportunities are great. However, even when all the factors are present, the utilization of this vehicle must be constantly monitored. The reason is that minor errors can produce a significant tax effect through the imposition of a personal holding tax.

Another use of the personal holding company has already been shown in ¶300.1 regarding Joe Daley, D.D.S. The personal holding company not only can be used when a professional practice is sold but also when a manufacturing or other business is sold. Rather than liquidating the corporation and paying the subsequent capital gains tax, the after-tax benefits may be greater if the corporate shell is retained and the net proceeds are invested in common and preferred stocks.

Example: Here's an example of another personal holding company strategy. Mr. Able, who has other income of $150,000, also owns all the stock of Contract Corporation. A list of the corporation's assets is as follows:

	Cost	Fair Market Value
Cash	$100,000	$100,000
Furniture and Equipment	200,000	300,000
Vacant Land and Building	100,000	100,000
TOTAL	$400,000	$500,000

Able is trying to sell Contract Corporation but has been unable to find a buyer for cash. He finds he can liquidate by selling parts of the business over a five-year period. In investigating the various methods of liquidation, the most practical method for him would be to liquidate the corporation currently and, assuming that this liquidation occurs after December 31, 1988, there will be a gain on the sale by the corporation, which would yield a tax of $34,000. The net after corporate tax liquidation then would be $466,000. The capital gains would be determined as $466,000 (proceeds less $100,000 basis), which yields $130,480 in tax. However, his current cash needs are small, and the capital gains tax is too high to justify liquidation. Thus, he considers the possible retention of the corporation. If this corporation could be retained and not be considered a personal holding company until after the five years, this would produce the optimum results.

One problem that must be avoided or at least dealt with concerning the above example is the possibility that during the years of liquidation, the company would inadvertently become a personal holding company. In certain cases, this could be avoided by the nature of the business itself, especially if the corporation is operating two separate businesses. The net after-tax assets still owned by the corporation would then be approximately $466,000 ($500,000 fair market value − $400,000 basis) × .34 = $34,000 in tax. If these assets could be invested at a 5 percent dividend rate, they would yield $23,300 in dividends. These dividends (after the 70 percent exclusion) would yield a taxable income of approximately $6,990. This taxable income should be significantly reduced by costs and by a salary to Able for managing the assets. The undistributed personal holding company income would have to be distributed to the individual shareholder.

This technique allows the individual, in the proper circumstances, to defer approximately $130,480 in tax. The corporation could be liquidated immediately after his death with no tax on the appreciation. This technique is useful when an older shareholder does not need the actual assets.

The personal holding provisions were introduced to ensure that family investment companies (which had become known as "incorporated pocketbooks") would distribute their earnings to the shareholders. In limited situations, these personal holding companies provide a tax-savings device. It is a device which needs constant review and fine tuning. Left to itself, it could cause significant tax problems. Accordingly, before this technique is utilized, you should review it at length, and a plan should be firmly established by all the parties.

Unlike the accumulated earnings tax that the Tax Reform Act is making obsolete, the personal holding company is going to become increasingly useful in the future. This is especially true in the sale of small closely held corporations after January 1, 1989, where "S" corporation status could not be utilized to eliminate double taxation. The recision of Section 337 for all but qualified corporations as of January 1, 1987, and for all corporations as of January 1, 1989, increases the tax upon sale and liquidation to a point that either stock of a closely held corporation must be sold or, in lieu thereof, if the assets are sold, that the retention of the corporation as a personal holding company may be the only viable alternative to reduce the overall tax impact upon the corporation. (Although a full discussion of this topic is beyond the scope of this book, for a comprehensive discussion, see *Buying and Selling Closely Held Corporations*, by Lawrence C. Silton (Prentice-Hall, Inc., 1987.)

[803]   WHAT A COLLAPSIBLE CORPORATION IS AND HOW IT CAN TRAP THE UNWARY

[803.1]   Understanding How the Law of Collapsible Corporations Applied Prior to the Tax Reform Act of 1986

The collapsible corporation itself did not produce any tax benefits. However, a complete understanding of the collapsible corporation gave rise to an appreciation of the tax-planning opportunities which were available prior to full implementation of the Tax Reform Act of 1986.

This technique can be illustrated as follows:

1. An individual owns appreciated investment property (that is, vacant real estate) which if subdivided and developed would yield all ordinary income. He should consider the sale of this property to a corporation for development. (An example of this technique is more fully discussed in ¶102.2.)

2. Utilizing the above concept along with the gifting of the shares of stock to a lower basis taxpayer with the eventual liquidation of the corporation can also provide significant tax benefits.

3. The overall tax burden may be significantly reduced if the real estate is developed in the corporation. The net after-tax income realized by the corporation is distributed to the shareholders in a liquidation distributions and reported at capital gains rates.

Example: Assume that X, an individual, has net taxable income of $60,000. He is involved in a real estate development which will, according to projections, allocate to him additional taxable income of $50,000 in each of the years 1984, 1985, and 1986. A comparison of the utilization of the corporation versus the individual reporting the income is as follows:

Taxable income without development income		$ 60,000
Taxable income with development income		110,000
Tax without development income	$15,168	
Tax with development income	$36,924	
Increase in tax by reason of development income	$21,756	

The total tax impact of development income will be $65,268 ($21,756 × 3). The after-tax income from the development project is $150,000 less $65,268, for a net of $84,732. If the corporate form is used, the development income is retained in the corporation which could be liquidated after the three-year period with the following effect: Each year's $50,000 income will result in a tax of $8,250, or a total net after-tax income per year of $41,750. The three-year total is $125,250. Upon the liquidation of the corporation, this would result in a capital gains tax of approximately $25,050 attributable to the liquidation distribution. This produces a net after-tax income from the development project of $100,200 for a tax savings of $15,468. This procedure, especially if there is a predetermined plan, could, of course, be attacked by the Internal Revenue Service.

The problem of a collapsible corporation in pre-1986 Tax Reform Act law had a great deal in common with both the accumulated earnings tax and the personal holding company. The common denominator in all three is that Congress is trying to prevent an abuse of favorable provisions contained in the Internal Revenue Code. Congress approached the problem posed by a collapsible corporation differently than in either of the other two cases. Congress did not impose a penalty tax upon a collapsible corporation but reclassified the taxation of the income at the shareholder/taxpayer level.

Probably the best way to obtain an appreciation of the problem is to illustrate the abuse which Section 341, dealing with collapsible corporations, was enacted to correct. Two of the more popular areas in which this abuse occurred were in the film and real estate industries. In the case of *Pat O'Brien*, 25 TC 376 (1955), a taxpayer and others invested in a corporation to produce a movie. The taxpayer invested a total of $12,500. The corporation was formed, and it secured credit for $350,000 to finance the production of the film. After the production was completed and the movie was released for distribution, the corporation was liquidated, with the movie rights being assigned to the shareholders. The value of each shareholder's stock at the time of liquidation was $150,000. The taxpayer realized a capital gain of $137,500 (fair market value $150,000 less $12,500 basis) when the corporation was liquidated. After liquidation, when he individually received a cash flow from his investment, the taxpayer treated receipts up to $150,000 as tax free.

The net effect was that the taxpayer paid capital gains rates on what would have otherwise been ordinary income to the corporation or himself if either had produced and distributed the film. Assuming that capital gains rates are taxed at 40 percent of ordinary income tax rates and that the shareholder was in the 50 percent marginal tax bracket, his total burden, without taking into account minimum tax or other taxes, would have been approximately $27,500. If the $137,500 had been taxed to the shareholder individually as ordinary income, the tax would have been $68,750. There was a tax savings in excess of $40,000. This technique has no basis in economic reality. Transactions such as this are not tax-planning tools but gimmicks. Congress's and the Internal Revenue Service's approach to prohibit the utilization of this gimmick was the enactment of Section 341.

It should be noted that the difference between the planning tool illustrated on page 379 and the gimmick illustrated in the Pat O'Brien case is that in the O'Brien case, no income was realized by the corporation. The corporate income tax was completely eliminated. At times, it does not pay to be greedy. The question that still may not be completely resolved is: "If the corporation had realized a portion or all of the income in the O'Brien case, would the tax court have ruled for O'Brien?"

[803.2] The Future of the Collapsible Corporation after the Tax Reform Act of 1986

In reviewing the previous section, it becomes obvious that the technique that was abused was the conversion of ordinary income into capital gains. The pre-1986 Tax Reform Act taxed capital gains at 40 percent of ordinary income, but no more than 20 percent. The post-1986 Tax Reform Act changes the tax universe in two ways which will have a substantial impact in this area:

1. Beginning in 1988, capital gains will be taxed at the same rates as ordinary income.
2. Beginning in 1989, the liquidation of a qualified corporation (beginning in 1987 for all other corporations) with

appreciated property will produce income at the corporate level.

Thus, even if the collapsible corporation rules did not apply in the case of O'Brien, as set forth above, the corporation would have realized a taxable gain at the corporate level on the difference between the fair market value of the movies and their basis. This, in conjunction with the fact that there are no favorable benefits to classify the receipt of income as capital gains, would seemingly provide the deathknell to this planning device. However, it should be noted that the collapsible corporation was not deleted from the Code, and while capital gains will be taxed as the same rate as ordinary income in 1988, the Code maintained a distinction between ordinary income and capital gains with the idea that different rates may be applied in the future. This, in addition to the fact that qualified corporations (see Chapter 7) still receive favorable treatment on the liquidation until January 1, 1989, necessitates an awareness of the planning tools and problems posed by the collapsible corporation. It appears that the final chapter in the law of collapsible corporations has not yet been written.

[803.3] Taxing the Shareholders of a Collapsible Corporation

If a corporation is ascertained to be collapsible (see ¶803.4), the gain realized on the following transactions (which except for the provisions of Section 341 would result in long-term capital gains) shall be taxed as ordinary income:

1. The sale or exchange of stock of the corporation
2. A distribution in partial or complete liquidation of the corporation (see ¶700)
3. A nonliquidating distribution that, by reason of a lack of earnings and profits, would have been considered a distribution in excess of basis and would have been treated as a capital transaction (see ¶403.1)

It is interesting to note that the conversion of capital gains to ordinary income is not limited to a corporation that collapses but also relates to corporations and shareholders that dispose of their stock in other ways. If it were not for those restrictions, it would have been relatively easy to circumvent the intent of Section 341.

[803.4] Events That May Cause a Corporation to be Considered Collapsible

Section 341 defines a collapsible corporation as a corporation formed or availed of principally for the manufacture, construction, or production of property which is Section 341 property or for the holding of stock in a corporation so formed or availed of, with a view to:

1. The sale or exchange of stock by its shareholders (whether in liquidation or otherwise)
2. A distribution to its shareholders before the corporation realizes taxable income from the sale of 341 assets
3. The realization by such shareholders of the gain which would normally be attributable to Section 341 assets when they were sold

An analysis of the example in ¶803.1 will further the understanding of this definition. The intent of this section is clear and is "to prohibit the conversion of what would normally be ordinary income into capital gain." Basically, Section 341 assets are defined as property held for less than three years, that is:

1. Stock in trade in the corporation
2. Property held primarily for sale to customers in the ordinary course of business
3. Section 1231(b) assets, that is, real and depreciable property used in the trade or business
4. Unrealized receivables or fees pertaining to the aforementioned property

There is also a rebuttable presumption created in favor of collapsibility if both the following conditions are present:

1. The value of Section 341 assets held by the corporation constituted 50 percent or more of its total assets
2. The value of those Section 341 assets is 120 percent of the adjusted basis of those assets

The following example will illustrate the requirements of conditions 1 and 2 set forth before:

Example: Collapsible Corporation had the following balance sheet:

	Book Value	Fair Market Value
ASSETS		
Cash	$ 1,000	$ 1,000
Equipment	100,000	100,000
Land (Developed for resale 341 asset)	20,000	200,000
TOTAL ASSETS:	$121,000	$301,000
LIABILITIES AND EQUITY		
Liabilities	$100,000	$100,000
Untaxed Appreciation	–0–	180,000
Stock	10,000	10,000
Retained Earnings (Earnings and Profits)	11,000	11,000
TOTAL LIABILITIES AND EQUITY:	$121,000	$301,000

In this example, note that land (developed for resale, which is a 341 asset) constitutes 66 percent of the total fair market value of all the assets and therefore satisfies the first condition. In addition, its fair market value has increased ten times, and therefore the second condition is also satisfied. Thus, if this corporation was liquidated, the IRS has established a rebuttable presumption that the corporation was a collapsible corporation, and the gain realized on liquidation which would appear to be $291,000 (fair market value less basis in stock) would be taxed at ordinary income rates instead of as capital gains.

[803.5]   Four Methods of Escaping the Restrictions in the Collapsible Provisions

Method A: If a shareholder does not own, directly or indirectly, more than 5 percent in value of the collapsible corporation's outstanding stock, then his sale or exchange will be capital gains and not ordinary income. "Directly" or "indirectly" includes not only the stock owned by the individual shareholder himself but also the shares of stock which, through constructive ownership, could be attributable to him.

Method B: The second method of escape is to have the corporation hold the property for at least three years. The following example will illustrate how this exception is applied:

> **Example:** A group of people form a corporation to build a real estate project. Assume this had initially been the type of project that if sold upon completion would have generated ordinary income. If the corporation was liquidated as soon as the project had been completed, this would have been a classic example of a collapsible corporation. If the collapsible corporation rules did not apply, the ordinary income from the sale of the project would have been converted into capital gains. However, if this project is completed and if it is held by the corporation for three years, the subsequent sale by the shareholder will not produce ordinary income but will produce capital gains.

The question then becomes: "If this project is held for the requisite time, could the corporation then be liquidated and have the gain taxed as capital gains?" The answer is that it depends on which liquidation section is used.

Section 337, the one-year liquidation (see ¶703.2), is not available except in very limited situations not applicable to this example. Section 331 would seem to be available without restrictions (see ¶703.3). It would also appear that Section 333, which provides a one-month liquidation (see ¶703.1), would also be available.

Method C: There is also a third possible exception, known as the "70 percent provision." This provision deals with the type of assets held by the corporation and the gains attributable to these assets. To summarize this exception: If at least 30 percent of the gain from the sale of property is not attributable to Section 341 property, the corporation will not be considered a collapsible corporation.

The Tax Reform Act of 1984 allows the IRS to determine the extent that all inventory, stock in trade, or property held primarily for sale to customers in the ordinary course of business, that is, of like kind, will be treated as a single asset for the purposes of this rule.

Method D: Another possibility, which is not a specific exception to the collapsible corporation provisions, is the use of a Subchapter S Corporation. A corporation which is a collapsible corporation could make a timely Subchapter S election. It could then sell the Section 341 property and distribute the proceeds at the cost of a single tax at the shareholder level.

WARNING: The Tax Reform Act of 1984 has established a new standard for determining when an otherwise collapsible corporation can be liquidated. Prior to the 1984 act, the law provided that a corporation would not be classified as a collapsible corporation if a substantial portion of the income to be derived from ordinary income property of the type described in ¶803.3 is realized by the corporation prior to liquidation. In the case of *Commissioner v. Kelley,* 293F.2d 904 (5th Cir. 1961) affirming 32 TC 135 (1959), non acq. 1962-1CB5 withdrawn and acq. substituted, Rev. Rul. 72-48, 1972-1CB 102, the court held that the corporation will be treated as having realized a substantial part of the taxable income to be derived from such property, thereby avoiding collapsible status, if the corporation realizes as little as one-third of the taxable income from the property. The Tax Reform Act of 1984 explicitly states that a corporation, otherwise collapsible, will be collapsible unless at least two-thirds of the taxable income to be derived from the property is realized by the corporation. Thus, the new law provides a clearer standard than that found in the prior statute. However, the new standard is more restrictive than the one established by case law.

WARNING: The Tax Reform Act of 1986 added new provisions relative to taxation at the corporate level upon sale of assets with "built-in" gains. Thus, before electing S Corporation status, a complete review of the law should be undertaken. You should also review your long-term planning goals.

In addition to the general relief provisions, there are several special provisions enacted in the Code to take care of situations which have no general applicability to corporate planning.

[803.6]   Impact of the Collapsible Corporation Rules

This, as well as many other "loophole plugging sections" in the Internal Revenue Code, becomes long and very difficult to comprehend and apply without understanding the problem the section is designed to prevent. The basic thrust of Section 341 was to prevent the conversion of ordinary income into capital gains upon the liquidation of a corporation. With this knowledge, a corporation with ordinary income property that has substantially appreciated should completely review the collapsible corporation provisions prior to liquidation.

> **Example:** A real estate development corporation was formed to develop a particular tract of land. This tract was not sold as originally contemplated. After a period of time, it was considered in the best interests of all the parties to dissolve and liquidate this corporation. Upon liquidation, the distribution may be taxed as ordinary income.

Our major purpose for discussion of collapsible corporations is to ensure that the problem can be recognized before liquidation and not afterward. As noted previously, the future of the tax planning technique, as well as the problems posed by the collapsible corporations, is very much in doubt after the enactment of the Tax Reform Act of 1986.

[804]   THE CHANGING CONCEPTS OF MULTIPLE CORPORATIONS

Section 1551 and the related sections are yet another example of Congress's response to what it considered a tax-planning abuse. It was common practice, prior to 1969, to create multiple corporations. If a business was reviewing the benefits of incorporation, it may have been more advantageous to create multiple corporations instead of one for tax purposes.

The following is an example of some of the benefits of multiple corporations:

Example: Joe Dealer operates a new and used car dealership. For accounting purposes, he has separated his business into four divisions: new car sales, used car sales, automobile repair and maintenance, and insurance and financing. After all allocable costs have been applied, including a reasonable salary for himself, it was ascertained that each of the four divisions of his business produces approximately $50,000 a year in net before tax income. If he incorporated his entire business as one corporation, his total tax liability on the $200,000 of income would be $61,250. On the other hand, if there were no restrictions against the utilization of multiple corporations and if each division operated as a separate corporation, the total tax would be $30,000 (corporate tax on $50,000 of income is $7,500 times four for the total tax burden).

The creation of the four corporations would have yielded a tax savings of $31,250. In addition, if this technique were allowed, each of the individual corporations would be entitled to a separate accumulated earnings tax credit. It may also have been easier to implement pension plans, profit sharing, and other fringe benefits in one corporation to the exclusion of the employees in the others.

Congress's response to what it considered artificial separations of businesses solely for tax-planning purposes was to develop the concept of "controlled corporations." This concept combined the income from all the related businesses rather than allowing each of the corporations to take advantage of the lower tax rates for corporate income under $75,000. In addition, it limited controlled corporations to only one accumulated earnings credit.

The two instances where several corporations could be considered in a controlled relationship are designated parent/subsidiary or brother/sister corporations. In all controlled relationships, the corporate income is combined, and one accumulated earnings tax credit is allowed. This may be allocated among the various corporations if the appropriate election is filed with the Internal Revenue Service. A parent/subsidiary relationship will be established as a controlled relationship if the controlling corporation (parent) owns 80 percent of the combined voting power of all classes of outstanding stock of the controlled corporation (subsidiary). As under prior law, preferred stock is not counted as stock in determining whether the requirements explained above are met unless the preferred stock is convertible into any other class of stock. Certain employer's securities, not counted as stock under the prior law, are not exempted under the 1984 act.

Up to now, this chapter has dealt with avoiding tax traps. In this particular instance, it is relatively simple to avoid the controlled relationship by having a "nonrelated party" own 21 percent of the stock of the controlled corporation. The necessity for the party to be a nonrelated entity is that Section 1551 applies the constructive ownership rules set forth in Section 1563 of the Internal Revenue Code. The constructive ownership rules in Section 1563 are comprehensive and include options, partnerships, estates, trusts, spouses, minor children, and, in certain instances, adult children and grandchildren.

While some of the rules and regulations regarding parent/subsidiary controlled group relationships appear difficult, it is usually relatively simple to recognize the multiple corporation problem when it appears in the form of a parent/subsidiary corporation. On the other hand, the brother/sister controlled group definition has caused a great deal of litigation, and its current status is still cloudy.

We will start our examination of brother/sister controlled groups with an analysis of the regulations. These regulations have been the subject of controversy for years and just recently have been declared invalid by the Supreme Court in the case of *U.S. v. Vogel,* 49 AFTR 2d, 82-429. The reason an analysis of the regulations is so important is that they indicate what the Internal Revenue Service believes should be appropriate rather than what is currently the law. While the future is somewhat in doubt, at least for the near term it is possible to plan with a good deal of certainty with the clarification brought about by the Supreme Court in *Vogel.* According to the Internal Revenue Service in its regulations, a brother/sister relationship exists if both the following are present:

1. At least 80 percent of the combined voting stock is owned by five or fewer individuals.
2. If more than 50 percent of the stock ownership is identical with respect to each corporation. Identical ownership is

defined as the lowest percentage of stock owned by a shareholder in a group of corporations.

These rules can best be illustrated by the following example included in the regulations:

Example: The outstanding stock of corporations P, Q, R, S, and T, which have only one class of stock outstanding, is owned by the following unrelated individuals:

Individuals	Corporations					Identical Relationship
	P	Q	R	S	T	
A	60%	60%	60%	60%	100%	60%
B	40%	—	—	—	—	—
C	—	40%	—	—	—	—
D	—	—	40%	—	—	—
E	—	—	—	40%	—	—
	100%	100%	100%	100%	100%	60%

Corporations P, Q, R, S and T are members of a brother/sister controlled group.

The above rules are further complicated because of the following:

1. The concept of stock has multiple meanings. There is one definition and application for voting stock, and there is another definition that relates to the total value of all shares of stock.
2. Certain types of stock must be excluded from the computation of what is common ownership.

A full discussion of these complications is beyond the scope of this book. In a simple situation where there is only one class of stock of the corporations involved, ascertaining whether or not there is a controlled relationship among brother/sister corporations should not be that difficult to accomplish. The regulations, in interpreting the law, had created a harsh result.

In the previous example, B, C, D, and E own 40 percent of their respective corporations, yet none of these corporations are entitled to additional surtax exemptions. This would definitely prohibit a person from establishing a series of corporations with different individuals utilizing multiple surtax exemptions. In other words, A, the common denominator in all the corporations, would have to restrict his ownership to 50 percent if he wishes to obtain multiple surtax exemptions. This was an overreaction by the Internal Revenue Service in interpreting the Code. In *Vogel*, these regulations were declared invalid. Now each of the above corporations would be entitled to a separate surtax exemption because there was more than 20 percent owned by an unrelated party. Thus, under *Vogel*, as long as any brother/sister corporation has more than 20 percent owned by an unrelated party, each corporation is entitled to a separate surtax exemption. In the above, as long as A, B, C, D, and E are not related, each corporation will receive a separate surtax exemption. The concept of identical ownership has been stricken from the regulations.

Key Idea: In certain cases, having an outsider own at least 21 percent of brother/sister corporations would give rise to separate surtax exemptions.

WARNING: Be careful of additional stock being attributed to the majority shareholder in the case of a stock purchase agreement. The rules and regulations under the attribution section should be reviewed in these cases.

The question then becomes: "Is there any difference in treatment between brother/sister corporations, as discussed previously, and parent/subsidiary corporations?" Even before the positive result in *Vogel*, it was possible to obtain positive tax-planning benefits through the proper structuring of a parent/subsidiary corporation.

Example: Joe Smith is the owner of two corporations: Hard Manufacturing and Sales Corporation located in Appleton, Wisconsin, and Soft Manufacturing and Sales Corporation located in Elkhart, Indiana. Both corporations are in the farm machinery business, and while they manufacture completely distinct and separate products, they have in the past used the same salespeople and manufacturing representatives to sell their products. Joe has been looking to the future and has decided that his personal and business needs include the following:

1. A coordinated sales staff
2. The active participation of various unrelated parties in the ownership of the two manufacturing corporations
3. Development of an overall management team for the sales and manufacturing corporations
4. A long-range goal of possibly selling the entire business to management

Joe's chosen heir is John Jones, who he believes has the capabilities to manage the entire operation of the business in the future. In each of the two manufacturing corporations, he has responsible personnel who would like to participate in the growth of the business. The consolidated group of corporations generates over $400,000 in net taxable income. Joe could sell 21 percent of both Hard and Soft Manufacturing Corporations to different parties and would obtain two surtax exemptions. However, if the following steps could be taken, he may have an even better plan:

1. A new sales corporation could be formed (Sales and Administration Corporation).
2. Joe could convey all the stock he owns in Hard and Soft Manufacturing Corporations to the sales organization under Section 351 and would receive all the stock of said sales corporation.
3. Prior to the transfer by Joe to the new sales corporation, he would sell 21 percent of Hard Manufacturing and 21 percent of Soft Manufacturing to unrelated independent parties. Thus, the sales corporation would own 79 percent of Hard Manufacturing and 79 percent of Soft Manufacturing.

4. Joe will sell at least 21 percent of the sales corporation to his chosen heir, John. A chart showing ownership of the various corporations appears below.

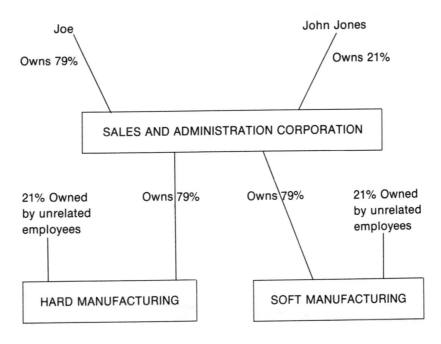

If the above steps were taken, it would appear that we could obtain three separate surtax exemptions.

APPENDIX

The tools that are included in this appendix have been designed to aid you in diverting income for utilization by a corporation's officers, shareholders, and directors for the minimum tax cost during the three stages of the corporate life—setting up, operating, and terminating. With the careful use of these forms and tables, you will be able to do the following:

☐ Avoid errors and omissions in the planning process
☐ Enhance the client's understanding and evaluation of the available tax-saving opportunities

The following forms and tables have been cross-referenced directly to the main text:

☐ Appendix A: Sample Minutes Providing for Reimbursement of Disallowed Expenses
☐ Appendix B: Sample Minutes Establishing a Section 1244 Stock Plan
☐ Appendix C: Sample Minutes Establishing a Discriminatory Medical Reimbursement Plan
☐ Appendix D: Sample Minutes Establishing Payment for Medical and Health Insurance
☐ Appendix E: Sample Minutes Establishing a Nondiscriminatory Medical Reimbursement Plan
☐ Appendix F: Regulation 1.79-3 of the Internal Revenue Code
☐ Appendix G: Sample Minutes of Corporation Establishing a Group Prepaid Legal Expense Plan
☐ Appendix H: Sample Minutes Establishing a Death Benefit Plan

- ☐ Appendix I: Sample Employment Contract Establishing Nonqualified Deferred Compensation at Retirement
- ☐ Appendix J: Sample Annuity Tables—Payments to Be Obtained by a Purchase of a Lump-Sum Annuity Upon Retirement
- ☐ Appendix K: IRS Form 2553 Election by a Small Business Corporation
- ☐ Appendix L: Sample Form of Voluntary Revocation of Election under Subchapter S
  L-1: Covering Letter
  L-2: Notification of Revocation of Election under Subchapter S Made by Corporation
  L-3: Consent Signed by All Shareholders or by Shareholders Holding a Majority of the Stock
- ☐ Appendix M: Sample Notification of Termination of Election—Nonresident Alien Shareholder
- ☐ Appendix N: Agreement Filed Pursuant to Section 302(c)(2)(A)(iii) of the Internal Revenue Code of 1954
- ☐ Appendix O: Valuation of Closely Held Corporation
- ☐ Appendix P: Stock Option Agreement
- ☐ Appendix Q: Agreement between Stockholders and Company to Purchase Stock
- ☐ Appendix R: Stock Transfer Agreement
- ☐ Appendix S: IRS Form 964 Election of Shareholder under Section 333 Liquidation
- ☐ Appendix T: Minutes of Meeting of Shareholders and Directors Adopting a Plan of Liquidation under Section 337
- ☐ Appendix U: Bardahl Formula Worksheet
- ☐ Appendix V: Flexible Benefits—A Guide to the Practitioner and a Program Booklet

APPENDIX A

Sample Minutes Providing
for Reimbursement of Disallowed Expenses

The minutes of corporate action shown below provide that all expenses which are subsequently disallowed as expenses by an Internal Revenue Service agent must be repaid by the officer to the corporation. This will eliminate double taxation due to dividend income. A full discussion of the utilization and impact of these minutes is found in Chapter 1, ¶105.3.

ACTION BY UNANIMOUS WRITTEN CONSENT
OF THE BOARD OF DIRECTORS
OF PROFITABLE CORPORATION

We, the undersigned, comprising all the directors of Profitable Corporation, hereby take the following action, without a meeting:

WHEREAS, it is in the best interest of the corporation to enact a plan whereby the officers, directors, and shareholders of the corporation reimburse the corporation for any and all expenses which are subsequently disallowed as nondeductible, in whole or in part, by the corporation:

IT IS THEREFORE RESOLVED AS FOLLOWS:
REIMBURSEMENT OF DISALLOWED EXPENSES

In the event any payment (either as compensation, interest, rent, expense reimbursement or otherwise) to any officer, director, or shareholder which is claimed as a deduction by this corporation for federal income tax purposes shall subsequently be determined not to be deductible in whole or in part by this corporation, such officer, director, or shareholder, as the case may be, shall reimburse the corporation for the amount of such payment so disallowed provided that this provision shall not apply to any expense where the board, in its sole discretion, determines such disallowance (including any concession of such issue by the corporation in connection with the settlement of other issues in a disputed case) is manifestly unfair and contrary to the facts. For the purposes of this provision, any such payment shall be determined not to be deductible when and only when either (a) the same may have been determined by a court of competent jurisdiction and either the corporation shall not have appealed from such determination or the time for perfecting an appeal shall have expired or (b) such disallowed deduction shall constitute or be contained in a settlement with the Internal Revenue Service which settlement may have been authorized by the board of directors.

This action taken at Appleton, Wisconsin, on the first day of January, 19__.

_____

_____

_____

Being all the directors of Profitable Corporation

APPENDIX B

Sample Corporate Minutes Establishing
a Section 1244 Stock Plan

Upon incorporation and at any time when stock is going to be issued, it is particularly valuable to ensure that this stock will qualify as Section 1244 stock. The benefit of 1244 stock is that upon the sale or disposition of the stock at a loss, the loss will qualify as an ordinary loss instead of as a capital loss. (A full discussion of the benefits of this particular section is found in Chapter 1, ¶105.4). It should be noted that the Tax Reform Act of 1986 has had a negative impact on the benefits of capital gains but has not removed the limitation of deduction of capital losses. Accordingly, this section can still be of benefit to the owner of a closely held corporation who suffers a loss on the sale or disposition of his stock.

WHEREAS, Section 1244 of the Internal Revenue Code and the Regulations issued thereunder require that only common and preferred stock of a corporation be issued during a period ending not later than two years after the date this plan is adopted; and

WHEREAS, Section 1244 and Regulations issued thereunder further require that the maximum amount to be received by the corporation in consideration of the stock to be issued pursuant thereto shall be $1 million and that such stock must be issued only for money or property (other than stock securities); and

WHEREAS, this corporation qualifies as a small business corporation as defined in Section 1244, and there is not unissued any portion of a prior offering of any of this corporation's stock, and

WHEREAS, pursuant to the requirements of Section 1244 and the Regulations issued thereunder, the following plan has been submitted to the corporation by the board of directors of the corporation.

PLAN TO ISSUE SECTION 1244 STOCK

WHEREAS, the following plan as herein set forth upon its adoption by the board of directors of the corporation shall become effective (initial issue date of stock of the corporation); and

WHEREAS, the corporation is authorized to offer and issue 44,000 shares of common stock, $1.00 par value,* and

WHEREAS, the corporation shall offer and issue such 44,000 shares of common stock from the date hereof to (two years less one day from initial date of issuance of stock) or to the date when the corporation shall make a subsequent offering of any stock, whichever shall sooner occur; and

WHEREAS, during such period as set forth above, the corporation shall offer and issue only such common stock; and

WHEREAS, the maximum amount to be received by the corporation in consideration of the stock to be issued pursuant to this plan shall be $1 million; and

WHEREAS, such common stock shall be issued only for money and other property (other than stock or securities); and

WHEREAS, such other action shall be taken by the corporation as shall qualify the stock offered and issued under this plan as "Section 1244 stock," as such term is defined in the Internal Revenue Code and the Regulations issued thereunder.

Upon motion duly made, seconded, and unanimously carried it was

> RESOLVED: That the foregoing plan to issue Section 1244 stock be and the same hereby is adopted by the corporation.
> FURTHER RESOLVED: That the proper officers of the corporation be and they hereby are authorized, empowered, and directed to do and perform any and all acts and deeds necessary to carry out such plan.

---

* Under the Tax Reform Act of 1984, it is now possible to issue preferred stock as well as common and have it qualify under Section 1244.

APPENDIX C

Sample of Minutes Establishing
a Discriminatory Medical
Reimbursement Plan

As noted in Chapter 2, ¶202.1, the whole game plan for medical reimbursement plans has been altered by the Revenue Act of 1978. The following is a sample of a discriminatory medical reimbursement plan. If this plan is utilized, a portion of the payments made to the higher compensated employees will have to be reported as ordinary income. A complete discussion of the taxation and impact of the act is set forth in the aforementioned section. The impact of the Tax Reform Act of 1986 and the regulations to be issued thereunder is not yet known. However, it would appear that the tax treatment of a plan such as this will remain unchanged.

The meeting was called to order by the president who stated that the purpose of the meeting was to consider the adoption by the corporation of a so-called medical expense reimbursement plan for the medical expenses of the officer/ employees of the corporation, their spouses, and other dependents. The board discussed the feasibility of such a plan. In the discussion, it developed that the consensus of the board was that the adoption of such a plan would provide incentive to the covered employees and encourage them and their dependents to get medical and dental checkups and treatment. The board felt this in turn would relieve the covered employees of concern regarding the health care of themselves and their dependents, thereby resulting in more attentive, productive employees.

The board intended then to benefit the covered employees and make them better employees. The board determined that the employees to be covered (namely, the full-time employees who are officers) constitute the only executive and managerial employees of the corporation. They are, therefore, a unique group within the corporation, both as to their duties and as to their remuneration. Therefore, the following resolution (being a medical expense reimbursement plan) was unanimously adopted:

RESOLVED that this corporation does hereby adopt the following medical expense reimbursement plan effective _____ .
                        (Date)

I

During the continuance of this plan, the company will reimburse any officer/employee of this company for all expenses incurred by that officer/employee for the medical care of such officer/employee, his spouse, and his dependents; provided, however, that reimbursement shall be made only in the event and to the extent that payment of such expenses is not provided for under any insurance policy or policies, whether owned by the company or the officer/employee, or under any other health and accident plan, wage continuation plan, any amounts recoverable under workmen's compensation, medicare, medicaid, or other similar programs. In the event that there is such a policy, plan, or other program, as defined in the preceding sentence, in effect providing for reimbursement or payment in whole or in part, then to the extent of the coverage under such policy, plan, or program, the company shall be relieved of any and all liability hereunder. The amount to be paid on account of such expenses for each officer/employee (and his spouse and other dependents) shall not exceed the sum of $_____ in any calendar year.

[*Alternative clause:* The amount to be paid on account of such expenses for any one officer/employee or for any one dependent of any officer/employee shall not exceed the sum of $_____ in any calendar year.]

II

A. "Officer/employee" shall mean those corporate officers duly elected by the board of directors of the company as corporate officers during the time that they remain corporate officers and full-time employees of the corporation. They shall be considered full-time employees of the corporation in any calendar year in which they work more than one thousand hours. The masculine pronoun shall be intended to refer to all officers whether masculine or feminine.

B. "Expenses for medical care" shall mean amounts paid for the diagnosis, cure, mitigation, treatment, or prevention of disease, or for the purpose of affecting any structure or function of the body, including but not limited to dental expenses, together with amounts paid for transportation primarily for and essential to the medical or dental care defined in the first clause of this sentence, and amounts paid for drugs, prescriptions, and prosthetic devices, all as defined in Section 213(e)(1) of the Internal Revenue Code.

C. "Dependent" shall mean dependents as defined in Section 152 of the Internal Revenue Code of 1954 as that section may be amended, to include generally any member of the officer/employee's family over one-half of whose support is furnished by the officer/employee.

III

The company may, in its discretion, pay directly any or all of the above defined expenses in lieu of making reimbursement therefore. In that event, the company shall be relieved of all further responsibility for that particular medical expense.

IV

Any officer/employee applying for reimbursement under this plan shall submit to the company with the application all hospitalization, doctor, dental, or other medical bills for verification by the company prior to payment. A failure to comply with this requirement may, at the discretion of the Board of Directors, terminate such officer/employee's right to reimbursement.

V

It is the intention of the company that benefits payable under this plan shall be eligible for exclusion from the gross income of the officer/employees covered by this plan as provided by Section 105 of the Internal Revenue Code of 1954, as amended or as may be amended hereafter, and that the benefits shall be deductible by the corporation under Section 162(a) of the Internal Revenue Code.

VI

Any person hereafter becoming an officer/employee of this company shall be eligible for the benefits provided under this plan.

VII

A copy of this plan shall be given to all present and future officer/employees of this company.

VIII

This plan shall be subject to termination or amendment at any time hereafter by affirmative vote of the board of directors of the company, reduced to writing and incorporated in the minutes of the company; provided, however, that such termination or amendment shall not affect any right to claim reimbursement for medical expenses under the provisions of Article I hereof, that arises prior to termination.

IX

The named fiduciary of this plan shall be _____
[Name of the corporation/employer]

X

In the event any claim for benefits hereunder is wholly or partially denied, notice of the decision shall be furnished to the claimant within a reasonable period of time after receipt of the claim by the named fiduciary. If notice of the denial of a claim is not furnished in accordance with the provisions of this article, and the claim has not been granted within a reasonable period of time, the claim shall be deemed denied.

The notice required hereunder shall be in writing, shall be set forth in a manner calculated to be understood by the claimant, and shall set forth the following:

1. The specific reason or reasons for the denial;
2. Special reference to the pertinent plan provisions upon which the denial is based;
3. A description of any additional material or information necessary for the claimant to perfect the claim and an explanation of why such material or information is necessary;
4. An explanation of the plan's claim review procedure.

XI

Every claimant or his duly authorized representative shall have the right to appeal a denial of a claim under this plan to the named fiduciary. Such appeal may be accomplished by a written notice of appeal filed with the named fiduciary within seventy-five (75) days after receipt by the claimant of written notification of denial of a claim. After notice of appeal has been filed, the claimant or his duly authorized representative may review all pertinent documents and may submit issues and comments in writing.

A decision by the named fiduciary shall be made promptly, and not later than sixty (60) days after the receipt of the notice of appeal, unless special circumstances (such as the need for a hearing if the named fiduciary determines that a hearing is required) require any extension of time for processing, in which case a decision shall be rendered as soon as possible, but not later than one hundred twenty (120) days after receipt of a notice of appeal. The decision on review shall be in writing, written in a manner calculated to be understood by the claimant, and shall include specific reasons for the decision and specific references to the pertinent plan provisions upon which the decision is based.

The meeting thereupon concluded, there being no further business.

_____

Secretary

APPENDIX D

Sample of Minutes Establishing Payment
for Medical and Health Insurance

As noted in Chapter 2, ¶202.1, it is no longer possible to discriminate in reimbursement of unpaid medical expenses to employees. However, it is still possible to purchase health and medical insurance on a discriminatory basis. The Tax Reform Act of 1986 and the regulations which are to be issued thereunder will have a profound impact on plans such as this. Thus, before establishing this plan, the law and the regulations should be carefully reviewed. It would appear that a discriminatory plan such as this will not provide substantial benefits after the implementation of the regulations under the Tax Reform Act of 1986.

The following is a sample of a plan which pays for medical insurance only for officers of the corporation.

ACTION BY UNANIMOUS WRITTEN CONSENT
OF THE BOARD OF DIRECTORS OF
XYZ CORPORATION

We, the undersigned, being all the directors of XYZ Corporation, hereby take the following action by unanimous written consent, without a meeting:

WHEREAS, the health and well-being of the corporation's employees are vital concerns for the corporation since such individuals are engaged in matters productive to the continued growth of the corporation; and

WHEREAS, it is in the best interest of the corporation to purchase health insurance for the benefit of its covered employees subject to the following limitation;

IT IS THEREFORE RESOLVED AS FOLLOWS:

1. Covered employee shall mean a present or future officer of the corporation:
   (a) whose customary employment exceeds twenty hours per week, and,
   (b) for whom health and hospitalization insurance can be purchased.
2. The president and secretary are authorized and directed to purchase either a group hospitalization and medical expense insurance or individual hospitalization and medical insurance with or without provisions for dental coverage as it deems appropriate for said covered employees.
3. While it is the intent to cover all covered employees with the same or similar insurance coverage, nothing contained herein shall make this mandatory.
4. The officers are authorized and empowered to consult with the covered employees as to the proper insurance coverage under this plan.

This action taken this _____ day of _____, 1985, at Appleton, Wisconsin.

_____

_____

_____

Being all the directors of said corporation

APPENDIX E

Sample Minutes Establishing
a Nondiscriminatory Medical Reimbursement Plan

As noted in Chapter 2, ¶202.1, the whole game plan for medical reimbursement plans had been altered by the Revenue Act of 1978. The following is a sample of a nondiscriminatory medical reimbursement plan. The final regulations have had an impact on the institution of plans such as these, and the following should be utilized solely as a guide rather than as a definitive plan which may be utilized in all cases. In this instance, I have drafted the plan to exclude all employees who do not work twenty-five hours per week, who have not attained the age of 25, and who have not completed three years of service. According to the final regulations, these would appear to be the maximum exclusions that can be safely utilized. In addition, this plan does provide for reimbursement up to $1,000 per individual. This, of course, can be altered to fit the corporate needs. Furthermore, it appears to be appropriate to have each covered employee acknowledge that he has received a copy of the plan and is aware of its terms and conditions. A draft of said letter to the corporation is also included.

It should be noted that upon the implementation of the regulations under the Tax Reform Act of 1986, there will be additional restrictions. It will at that time be impossible to deal only with discrimination on an individual plan basis. It will also be necessary to deal with it on the basis of the entire benefit package. All plans will of necessity need to be revised to deal with the law and the regulations once they have been enacted.

ACTION BY UNANIMOUS WRITTEN
CONSENT OF THE BOARD OF DIRECTORS
OF XYZ CORPORATION

We, the undersigned, being all the directors of XYZ Corporation, hereby take the following action, without a meeting:

WHEREAS, it is in the best interest of the corporation to establish a nondiscriminatory medical reimbursement plan; and

WHEREAS, it is the intent of the board of directors to comply with the Revenue Act of 1978 and that said plan is considered to be a nondiscriminatory plan within the meaning of said act and any terms to the contrary shall be disregarded.

The board of directors hereby adopts the medical reimbursement plan which will hereinafter be designated:

XYZ CORPORATION
MEDICAL EXPENSE REIMBURSEMENT PLAN

1. *Purpose:* The purpose of this plan is to encourage and help provide full and complete medical care for each participating employee and his or her spouse and dependents. It is the intention of the company that this plan qualify as an accident and health plan within the meaning of Section 105(e) of the Internal Revenue Code of 1954, as amended (the Code), and that the benefits payable under the plan be eligible for exclusion from gross income under Section 105(b) of the Code.

2. *Effective date:* The effective date of this plan shall be January 1, 198_. The records of the plan shall be kept on a fiscal year basis.

3. *Eligibility:* All full-time employees of the company shall be eligible to participate in this plan. For the purpose of this plan, full-time employees shall be considered as all employees who customarily work at least twenty-five hours per week and are employed at least nine (9) months during each and every fiscal year.

4. *Participation:* Each employee who is eligible to participate in the plan under Section 3 (an "Eligible Employee") shall become a participant in the Plan (a "Participant") on the effective date of the plan, if on the effective date he or she is at least

25 years old and has completed at least three (3) years of employment with the company. Each other eligible employee shall become a participant on the first day of the month after he or she has attained age 25 and has completed at least three (3) years of employment with the company. Three (3) years of employment shall mean one or more periods of employment aggregating three years. A participant who is discharged from employment with the company for cause shall forfeit all rights to reimbursement under this plan.

5. *Benefits:* The company shall pay to each participant such amounts as he or she has expended while a participant for medical care for himself or herself and his or her spouse and dependents. "Dependent" means a dependent as defined in Section 152 of the Code. Amounts expended for medical care means amounts paid for:

    (a) hospitalization, medical and dental bills, prescription drugs and eyeglasses; and

    (b) transportation primarily for and essential to medical care.

6. *Limitation:* No participant shall be entitled to receive more than $1,000 in reimbursements under this plan for any calendar year. Amounts payable or reimbursable under insurance or any other plan shall not be reimbursed hereunder.

7. *Claims procedure:* Claims for benefits under this Plan shall be made on forms maintained by the company. Each participant shall submit within thirty days after the end of each calendar quarter a request for reimbursement for medical expenses incurred by the covered employee, his or her spouse, and his or her dependents during the preceding quarter, together with such evidence of payment of such expenses as shall be required by the company in accordance with rules uniformly applied.

8. *Review procedure:* If any claim for benefits under this plan is denied, in whole or in part, the claimant shall be furnished promptly by the company with a written notice:

    (a) setting forth the reason for the denial;

    (b) making reference to pertinent plan provisions;

    (c) describing any additional material or information from the claimant which is necessary and why; and

(d) explaining the claim review procedure set forth herein.

Within sixty days after denial of any claim for benefits under this plan, the claimant may request in writing a review of the denial by the president of XYZ Corporation. Any claimant seeking review hereunder is entitled to examine all pertinent documents and to submit issues and comments in writing. XYZ Corporation shall render a decision on review of a claim not later than sixty days after receipt of a request for review hereunder. The decision of XYZ Corporation on review shall be in writing and shall state the reason for the decision, referring to the plan provisions upon which it is based.

9. *Administration:* The board of directors of the company shall have authority and responsibility to control and manage the operation and administration of this plan.

10. *Amendment; Termination:* This plan may be amended or terminated at any time by the board of directors of the company; *provided,* that termination shall not affect the right of any participant to claim reimbursement for amounts expended for medical care prior to the termination.

This action taken this first day of January, 198_, at Appleton, Wisconsin.

_____

_____

_____

Being all the directors of the corporation

LETTER

Dear Employee:

You are hereby notified that as of January 1, 198_, your employer, XYZ Corporation, has adopted a medical expense reimbursement plan.

This plan, a copy of which is attached hereto, provides that for all full-time employees as defined in said plan who are 25 years and older and have been employed by the company for at least three years, the company will pay up to $1,000 for amounts expended for medical care in any calendar year.

If you have any questions or comments regarding either the terms or the implementation of this plan, please do not hesitate to ask me.

Sincerely,

XYZ CORPORATION

_____

John Doe, President

RECEIVED:

_____   _____
Employee   Date

APPENDIX F

Regulation 1.79-3
of the Internal Revenue Code

The following regulations explain how to calculate the tax impact if insurance is provided for an employee in excess of the group term limitations. From time to time, the insurance agent establishing the group term plan may suggest that insurance in excess of $50,000 be purchased for certain employees. If the corporation purchases this additional insurance, it will result in income taxation to the employees as set forth in the Regulations 1.79-3(d)(2). The question then becomes, "On how much of the insurance premium cost is the individual employee being taxed?" If an additional $50,000 is purchased for the employee who is age 33, a premium of approximately $13.50 per month would be required. While this is the actual cost to the corporation, the tax impact would be only $4.50 per month pursuant to the rates set forth in the schedule. Thus, the corporation would get a deduction of $13.50, and the individual would only have to report $4.50 per month as income. The Tax Reform Act of 1986 will have an impact on group term insurance once the regulations have been promulgated under this act. Thus, current law should be reviewed when dealing with a plan which is supposed to provide the benefits contemplated by Section 79 prior to the implementation of the Tax Reform Act of 1986.

Reg. §1.79-3. Determination of amount equal to cost of group term life insurance. (TD 6888, filed 7-5-66; amended by TD 7623, filed 5-14-79; TD 7924, filed 12-1-83.)

(a) In general. This section prescribes the rules for determining the amount equal to the cost of group term life insurance on an employee's life which is to be included in his gross income pursuant to the rule of inclusion set forth in section 79(a). Such amount is determined by—

(1) Computing the cost of the portion of the group term life insurance on the employee's life to be taken into account (determined in accordance with the rules set forth in paragraph (b) of this section) for each "period of coverage" (as defined in paragraph (c) of this section) and aggregating the costs so determined, then

(2) Reducing the amount determined under subparagraph (1) of this paragraph by the amount determined in accordance with the rules set forth in paragraph (e) of this section, relating to the amount paid by the employee toward the purchase of group term life insurance.

(b) Determination of the portion of the group term life insurance on the employee's life to be taken into account. (1) For each "period of coverage" (as defined in paragraph (c) of this section), the portion of the group term life insurance to be taken into account in computing the amount includable in an employee's gross income for purposes of paragraph (a)(1) of this section is the sum of the proceeds payable upon the death of the employee under each policy, or portion of a policy, of group term life insurance on such employee's life to which the rule of inclusion set forth in section 79(a) applies, less $50,000 of such insurance. Thus, the amount of any proceeds payable under a policy, or portion of a policy, which qualifies for one of the exceptions to the rule of inclusion provided by section 79(b) is not taken into account. For the regulations relating to such exceptions to the rule of inclusion, see §1.79-2.

(2) For purposes of making the computation required by subparagraph (1) of this paragraph in any case in which the amount payable under policy, or portion thereof, varies during the period of coverage, the amount payable under such policy during such period is considered to be the average of the amount payable under such policy at the beginning and the end of such period.

(3) (i) For the purposes of making the computation required by subparagraph (1) of this paragraph in any case in which the amount payable under the policy is not payable as a specific amount upon the death of the employee in full discharge of the liability of the insurer, and such form of payment

is not one of alternative methods of payment, the amount payable under such policy is the present value of the agreement by the insurer under the policy to make the payments to the beneficiary or beneficiaries entitled to such amounts upon the employee's death. For each period of coverage, such present value is to be determined as if the first and last day of such period is the date of death of the employee.

(ii) The present value of the agreement by the insurer under the policy to make payments shall be determined by the use of the mortality tables and interest rate employed by the insurer with respect to such a policy in calculating the amount held by the insurer (as defined in section 101(d)(2)), unless the commissioner otherwise determines that a particular mortality table and interest rate, representative of the mortality table and interest rate used by commercial insurance companies with respect to such policies, shall be used to determine the present value of the policy for purposes of this subdivision.

(iii) For purposes of making the computation required by subdivision (i) of this subparagraph in any case in which it is necessary to determine the age of an employee's beneficiary and such beneficiary remains the same (under the policy, or the portion of the policy, with respect to which the determination of the present value of the agreement of the insurer to pay benefits is being made) for the entire period during the employee's taxable year for which such policy is in effect, the age of such beneficiary is such beneficiary's age at his nearest birthday on June 30 of the calendar year.

(iv) If the policy of group term life insurance on the employee's life is such that the present value of the agreement by the insurer under the policy to pay benefits cannot be determined by the rules prescribed in this subparagraph, the taxpayer may submit with his return a computation of such present value, consistent with the actuarial and other assumptions set forth in this subparagraph, showing the appropriate factors applied in his case. Such computation shall be subject to the approval of the commissioner upon examination of such return.

(c) Period of coverage. For purposes of this section, the phrase "period of coverage" means any one calendar month period, or part thereof, during the employee's taxable year during which the employee is provided group term life insurance on his life to which the rule of inclusion set forth in section 79(a) applies. The phrase "part thereof" as used in the preceding sentence means any continuous period which is less than the one calendar month period referred to in the preceding sentence for which premiums are charged by the insurer.

(d) The cost of the portion of the group term life insurance of an employee's life. (1) This paragraph sets forth the rules for determining the cost, for each period of coverage, of the portion of the group term life insurance of the employee's life to be taken into account in computing the amount includable in the employee's gross income for purposes of paragraph (a)(1) of this section. The portion of the group term life insurance on the employee's life to be taken into account is determined in accordance with the provisions of paragraph (b) of this section. Table I, which is set forth in subparagraph (2) of this paragraph, determines the cost for each $1,000 of such portion of the group term life insurance on the employee's life for each one-month period. The cost of the portion of the group term life insurance on the employee's life for each period of coverage of one month is obtained by multiplying the number of thousand dollars of such insurance computed to the nearest tenth which is provided during such period by the appropriate amount set forth in Table I. In any case in which group term life insurance is provided for a period of coverage of less than one month, the amount set forth in Table I is prorated over such period of coverage.

Table I.—Uniform premiums for $1,000 of group term life insurance protection

5-Year Age Bracket	Cost per $1,000 of protection for 1-month period
Under 30	$0.08
30 to 34	.09
35 to 39	.11
40 to 44	.17
45 to 49	.29
50 to 54	.48
55 to 59	.75
60 to 64	1.17

(2) The preceding table sets forth the cost of $1,000 of group term life insurance *provided after December 31, 1982*, for one month computed on the basis of 5-year age brackets. *See 26 CFR 1.79-3(d)(2) (revised as of April 1, 1983) for a table setting forth the cost of group term life insurance provided before January 1, 1983.* For purposes of Table I, the age of the employee is his attained age on the last day of his taxable year. However, if an employee has attained an age greater than age 64, he shall be treated as if he were in the 5-year age bracket 60 to 64.

(3) The net premium cost of group term life insurance as provided in Table I of subparagraph (2) of this paragraph applies only to the cost of group term life insurance subject to the rule of inclusion set forth in section 79(a). Therefore, such net premium cost is not applicable to the determination of the cost of group term life insurance provided under a policy which is not subject to such rule of inclusion.

APPENDIX G

Sample Minutes of Corporation Establishing
a Group Prepaid Legal Expense Plan

An employer may provide legal services to its employees through a group prepaid legal services plan. If such a plan is a qualified plan that conforms to the requirements of §120 of the Internal Revenue Code, benefits received are not included in the employee's gross income. This plan is designed to comply with the requirements of the Code. However, it is a sample form and has not been approved by the Internal Revenue Service. Note that unless extended by Congress, this fringe benefit will no longer be available for any corporate tax year ending after 1987 (see ¶202.3).

I. PURPOSE AND OBJECTIVES

_____ ("The Company") has established this Group Legal Services Plan for the exclusive benefit of its eligible employees, their spouses, and their dependents. The purpose of the plan is to provide such employees, spouses, or dependents with specified benefits consisting of personal legal services through prepayment of, or provision in advance for, legal fees in whole or in part by the company.

This Plan is intended to conform with the requirements of Section 120 of the Internal Revenue Code. Not more than 25% of the amount contributed in any year may be provided for shareholders or owners of an interest in Company stock, capital or profits, or their spouses or dependents.

■ *To qualify under §120, the plan must file an Application for Determination (Form 1024) and Schedule L with the IRS.*

418

II. DEFINITIONS

(1) *Administrator:* The administrator of this plan shall be the company or such officer or employee of the company as shall be designated by the board of directors of the company.

(2) *Dependent:* For purposes of this plan, an employee's dependents shall include only his or her spouse and unmarried children who are less than 21 years of age and are wholly dependent upon the employee for support and maintenance.

■ *Eligibility may be limited to salaried employees only or to any class that does not discriminate in favor of shareholders, officers, self-employed individuals, or highly compensated employees. Union-represented employees may be excluded if the plan was the subject of good faith collective bargaining.*

(3) *Eligible employee:* All employees who are 21 years of age or older and who are employed by the company on a regular basis for _____ hours or more a week are eligible to participate in the plan.

(4) *Plan year:* The plan year shall mean the 12-month period that ends on December 31 of each year.

III. PARTICIPATION

■ *Participation can be immediate or delayed. No waiting period is required or prohibited.*

Each eligible employee and his or her spouse and dependents shall become participants in the plan on the first day of the plan year after the employee commences employment with the company.

IV. CONTRIBUTIONS

(1) Employees are not required or permitted to contribute to the plan.

(2) All contributions to provide benefits under the plan will be made by the company.

■ *Plan may be funded by payments to insurance companies, a §501(c)(20) organization, a §501(c) trust, or a law firm; or by a combination of any of these.*

(3) Company contributions will be made in the form of premiums on policies issued by the _____ Insurance Company.

(4) Subject to the provisions of Article VII, the company will contribute from time to time such sums as are necessary to pay all benefits and expenses of the plan.

(5) If, at any time, an organization or person receiving contributions fails to satisfy the requirements of §120(c) of the Internal Revenue Code of 1954, the plan administrator shall reallocate the contributions to a qualified organization or person, or to several such organizations and persons, before the end of the plan year.

V. SERVICES PROVIDED

■ *The sample clause is for an "open panel" plan. A "closed panel" plan limits the provider of services to specified lawyers.*

1. A participant may employ any attorney of his choice. The participant will be reimbursed for covered services in accordance with the Schedule of Reimbursement appended to this plan.

2. The following legal services are covered by this plan to the extent provided in the schedule appended to the Plan:

(a) Drafting of wills and trust instruments for employees, their spouses, and dependents;

(b) Representation of employees and their spouses in real estate transactions;

(c) Representation of employees in civil litigation;

(d) Representation of employees, their spouses, and dependents accused of crimes or infractions.

3. Notwithstanding the provisions of paragraph (2) of this Article V, no legal services will be provided under this plan in any matter to which the company is a party.

VI. ADMINISTRATION

(a) The plan shall be administered by the plan administrator who is authorized and empowered to issue uniform rules and adopt forms to be used in carrying out the purposes of the plan. The plan administrator shall be the sole interpreter of the terms and conditions of the plan.

(b) The plan administrator may allocate fiduciary responsibilities among agents, including fiduciaries having investment responsibilities. Directions from the administrator to any fiduciary or agent shall be in writing.

(c) Claims for benefits under the plan shall be filed with the administrator on forms to be provided to all participants on request. The administrator shall provide notice in writing to any participant whose claim has been denied, setting forth the specific reasons for such denial. A participant whose claim has been denied shall have the right to appeal within ten days after receiving the written notice of denial, and the administrator shall afford the claimant an opportunity for a hearing within thirty days thereafter to review the decision to deny the claim.

(d) The administrator shall serve without compensation. The reasonable expenses of administering the plan shall be paid by the plan unless otherwise paid by the company.

VII. AMENDMENT OR TERMINATION

The company intends to continue this plan as a permanent plan. However, the company reserves the right to amend, suspend, or terminate the plan at any time and for any reason. No amendment, suspension, or termination of the plan shall effect benefits previously granted to participants, and in no event shall any funds contributed to the plan by the company be used for or diverted to purposes other than for the exclusive benefit of the participants.

VIII. NOTIFICATION OF EMPLOYEES

The company shall communicate in writing to all employees the terms and conditions of the plan and shall provide each eligible employee with a copy of the plan.

APPENDIX H

Sample of Minutes Establishing
a Death Benefit Plan

A corporation can pay a death benefit to an individual not to exceed $5,000 and have said death benefit excluded from the taxable income of the individual (see ¶204). There are certain restrictions upon this, all of which are incorporated in the minutes establishing this death benefit.

ACTION BY UNANIMOUS WRITTEN CONSENT
OF THE BOARD OF DIRECTORS
OF PROFITABLE CORPORATION

We, the undersigned, comprising all the directors of Profitable Corporation, hereby take the following action, without a meeting:

WHEREAS, it is in the best interest of the corporation to enact a plan to provide for a death benefit payable to the estate of any officer who shall die while in the employ of the corporation:

IT IS THEREFORE RESOLVED AS FOLLOWS:

DEATH BENEFIT PLAN

1. *Persons covered:* All officers who are employed on a full-time basis with the corporation who die while in the employ of the corporation shall be entitled to this benefit.

2. *Amount of benefit:* Five Thousand and No/100 Dollars, ($5,000.00), shall be paid by the corporation to the beneficiaries or the estate of an employee by reason of his death during his

full-time employment with the employer. This payment shall be in addition to any and all amounts which the employee during his lifetime would have been entitled to as compensation for his services, such as bonuses or payments for unused leave or uncollected salary or to any other amounts with respect to which said employee possessed, immediately prior to his death, a nonforfeitable right to receive the amounts while living.

3. *Methods of payment:* The payments to be made hereunder shall be made either in a lump sum or in installments, as is decided by the corporation.

This action taken this _____ day of _____, 19__, at Appleton, Wisconsin.

_____

_____

_____

Being all the directors of the corporation

APPENDIX I

Sample Employment Contract
Establishing Nonqualified Deferred
Compensation at Retirement

From time to time, as we discussed in Chapter 2, ¶205.4 it becomes necessary to compensate an employee at retirement other than through the qualified pension and profit-sharing plans that may be applicable to the general employees of the corporation. The following employment contract sets forth retirement benefits which will be taxable to the employee upon his retirement. There is no current benefit to the corporation nor current taxation to the employee. It is intended that the entire tax impact will occur upon retirement.

EMPLOYMENT CONTRACT

This employment contract entered into this first day of August, 198_, by and between Deferred Corporation, hereinafter referred to as "Company," and Faithful Employee, hereinafter referred to as "Employee."

WHEREAS, the Employee has been employed by the Company as its president since the date of incorporation upon the terms from time to time mutually agreed upon by the Company and the Employee, and has rendered valuable services to the Company; and

WHEREAS, the Company does not have a qualified deferred compensation plan which will produce sufficient benefits to all the older employees of the Company to retire with sufficient benefits to maintain a comfortable life-style; and

WHEREAS, the Company considers it in the best interest of the Employee and the Company to defer part of the Employee's salary until after retirement; and

WHEREAS, the Company has elected to have Employee defer a part of his salary until retirement to ensure that Employee's retirement income is sufficient to maintain his lifestyle; and

WHEREAS, the Employee is willing to enter into this Employment Contract and Deferred Compensation Agreement upon the following terms:

NOW, THEREFORE, in consideration of the services performed in the past and to be rendered in the future of said Employee, the parties agree as follows:

1. The Company hereby employs the Employee as the president of the Company and as one of the directors of the Company, his powers and duties in that capacity to be such as may be determined by the board of directors.

2. As the current compensation for his services to the Company, during the term of this agreement, in whatever capacity rendered, the Company shall pay to the Employee Three Thousand Dollars ($3,000.00) per month payable as is mutually agreed, however, no more infrequently than once a month. The term of this agreement shall commence on the date of its execution and shall terminate on November 1, 19__, unless the parties mutually agree to extend it.

3. At any time after November 1, 19__, which is hereafter referred to as "Retirement Date," said Employee may retire from the active and daily services of the Company. Upon such retirement, the Company shall pay to said Employee a monthly pension of One Thousand Eight Hundred Seventy-Five Dollars ($1,875.00) per month payable on the first business day of each calendar month beginning the month after his retirement. The Company shall make such monthly payments to Employee for a total of sixty (60) months.

   (a) If said Employee shall die after retirement before the expiration of sixty (60) months from the date hereof, the Company will continue to make the

monthly payments in the amount of One Thousand
Five Hundred Dollars ($1,500.00) to his widow for
the balance of sixty (60) months. If neither of them
is alive, then any and all payments due under this
paragraph shall cease, and neither the estate nor the
beneficiaries of the estate shall have any rights
thereunder.

(b) If the Employee shall die while still in the active
employment of the Company, but prior to his retirement date, the Company will pay to his widow sixty
(60) monthly payments or until she dies, whichever
occurs first, the sum of One Thousand Five Hundred Dollars ($1,500.00) per month. At her death,
the payment hereunder shall cease, and neither the
estate nor the beneficiaries of the estate shall have
any rights hereunder.

(c) If the Employee, prior to the retirement date,
   (i) becomes permanently and totally disabled, or,
   (ii) voluntarily terminates his employment with the
        Company after the completion of at least one
        year under this contract, or
   (iii) is discharged by the Company, the Company
        shall, upon receipt of satisfactory proof of the
        Employee obtaining the age sixty-five (65) pay
        to him beginning on the first day of the month
        following receipt of said proof of age, or to his
        widow upon satisfactory proof of his death af-
        ter having attained the age of sixty-five (65), a
        pension of One Thousand Five Hundred Dol-
        lars ($1,500.00) per month for a total of sixty
        (60) months.

   In the event that the Employee shall die prior
to receiving the sixty (60) payments, his widow shall
receive the sum of One Thousand Dollars
($1,000.00) for the remainder of the term or her
death, whichever occurs first. If neither survives the
entire term, the Company shall not be under any
further obligation to make any payments to the estate or any other beneficiaries of the Employee or
his widow.

4. This agreement shall commence on the 1st day of August, 198_, and shall terminate on the 1st day of November, 19__.

5. Notwithstanding anything herein contained to the contrary, no payment of any then unpaid installments of deferred compensation shall be made, and all rights under the agreement of the Employee, as designated beneficiary, personal representative, or any other person, to receive payment thereof shall be forfeited if either or both of the following events shall occur:

   (a) The Employee shall engage in any activity or conduct which in the opinion of the board is inimical to the best interest of the Company.

   (b) After the Employee ceases to be employed by the Company, he becomes employed by another person, corporation, or other entity which is in competition to the business of the Company.

6. If the board shall find that any person to whom the payment is payable under this agreement is unable to care for his affairs because of illness or accident, or is a minor, any payment (unless a prior claim therefore shall have been made by a duly appointed guardian, committee, or other legal representative) may be paid to the spouse, child, a parent, or a brother or sister, or to any person deemed by the board to have incurred expenses for such person otherwise entitled to payment, in such manner and in such proportions as the board may determine. Any such payments shall be a complete discharge of the liabilities of the Company under this agreement.

7. Nothing contained herein shall be construed as conferring upon the Employee, the right to continue in the employ of the Company as an executive or in any other capacity.

8. Any deferred compensation paragraph under this agreement shall not be deemed salary or other compensation to the Employee for the purpose of computing benefits to which he may be entitled under any profit-sharing or other arrangement of the Company for the benefit of the Employees.

9. Neither the Employee, his wife, nor any other beneficiary

under this agreement shall have any power to transfer, assign, anticipate, hypothecate, or otherwise encumber or advance any of the benefits payable hereunder, nor shall said benefits be subject to seizure for the payment of any debts or judgments, or be transferable by operation of law in the event of bankruptcy, insolvency, or otherwise.

10. Nothing in this agreement shall affect any right which the Employee may otherwise have to participate in, or under, any other retirement plan or agreement which the Company may now or hereinafter may have established.

11. Notwithstanding the provisions of paragraph 3, the Employee may, with the consent of the Company, continue in active employment after the retirement date. In such event, the Company may defer the start of the payments provided for in paragraph 3 until the date of actual retirement.

12. This agreement shall be binding upon the parties hereto, their executors, their heirs, personal representatives, administrators, or successors.

13. This agreement may be amended or revoked at any time by mutual written agreement of the parties.

IN WITNESS WHEREOF, the Company has caused this document to be executed by its president and its corporate seal affixed, duly attested by its secretary, and the Employee has hereunder set his hand and seal the day and year first above written.

_____

Faithful Employee

Deferred Corporation

BY: _____

APPENDIX J

Sample Annuity Tables—Payments to Be
Obtained by a Purchase of a Lump Sum
Annuity Upon Retirement

At retirement, it may become necessary to purchase an annuity with the amount in the qualified deferred compensation plan. For example, Joe Daley, D.D.S., in the example shown in Chapter 3, ¶300.1, had accumulated $947,471.00. He was 60 years old upon retirement. Thus, he could use this $947,471.00 to purchase a single payment annuity, ten-year certain, which would yield him monthly benefits of $7,835.58 ($8.27 per thousand, or $8.27 × 947.471) with a total annual benefit of $94,026.98. The concept of a ten-year certain annuity is that even if he dies prior to that date, at least 120 monthly payments will be made. He, in lieu thereof, could have purchased a fifteen-year certain annuity, which would have yielded him a monthly benefit of $8.04 per $1,000 ($8.04 × 947.471 equals $7,617.66 per month), or $91,399.92. If he wished to purchase a joint and survivor annuity, and if his wife was two years younger than he, then he could have received $7.42 a month per thousand for a total yearly benefit during their joint lives of $84,362.76. I have also been informed that these are standard tables and that the insurance companies will negotiate the rates when substantial sums of money are involved. (See following pages for tables.)

ANNUITY PAYOUT PER $1,000 NET AMOUNT JOINT
ANNUITY WITH 100% TO THE SURVIVOR*

Male Age	10 yrs. Less	8 yrs. Less	6 yrs. Less	FEMALE AGE 4 yrs. Less	2 yrs. Less	Same Age	2 yrs. More	4 yrs. More
50	6.98	7.00	7.02	7.05	7.07	7.10	7.13	7.16
51	6.99	7.02	7.04	7.07	7.10	7.13	7.16	7.20
52	7.01	7.04	7.06	7.09	7.12	7.16	7.19	7.23
53	7.03	7.05	7.08	7.12	7.15	7.19	7.23	7.27
54	7.05	7.08	7.11	7.14	7.18	7.22	7.26	7.31
55	7.07	7.10	7.13	7.17	7.21	7.26	7.30	7.35
56	7.09	7.13	7.16	7.20	7.25	7.30	7.34	7.40
57	7.11	7.15	7.19	7.24	7.29	7.34	7.39	7.45
58	7.14	7.18	7.23	7.28	7.33	7.38	7.44	7.50
59	7.17	7.22	7.26	7.32	7.37	7.43	7.50	7.56
60	7.20	7.25	7.30	7.36	7.42	7.49	7.56	7.63
61	7.24	7.29	7.35	7.41	7.48	7.55	7.62	7.70
62	7.27	7.33	7.39	7.46	7.53	7.61	7.69	7.78
63	7.31	7.38	7.44	7.52	7.60	7.68	7.77	7.86
64	7.36	7.42	7.50	7.58	7.67	7.76	7.86	7.96
65	7.40	7.48	7.56	7.65	7.74	7.84	7.95	8.06
66	7.45	7.54	7.63	7.72	7.83	7.93	8.05	8.17
67	7.51	7.60	7.70	7.80	7.91	8.03	8.16	8.29
68	7.57	7.67	7.77	7.89	8.01	8.14	8.28	8.42
69	7.64	7.74	7.86	7.98	8.12	8.26	8.41	8.56
70	7.71	7.82	7.95	8.08	8.23	8.39	8.55	8.72
71	7.78	7.91	7.05	8.20	8.36	8.53	8.70	8.89
72	7.87	8.01	8.15	8.32	8.49	8.68	8.87	9.07
73	7.96	8.11	8.27	8.45	8.64	8.84	9.06	9.27
74	8.06	8.22	8.40	8.59	8.80	9.02	9.25	9.49

* For unisex rates assume that the youngest age is female.

ANNUITY PAYOUT PER $1,000 NET AMOUNT JOINT ANNUITY
WITH ⅔ TO THE SURVIVOR*

Male Age	10 yrs. Less	8 yrs. Less	6 yrs. Less	FEMALE AGE 4 yrs. Less	2 yrs. Less	Same Age	2 yrs. More	4 yrs. More
50	7.24	7.27	7.29	7.32	7.35	7.39	7.43	7.47
51	7.27	7.30	7.33	7.36	7.39	7.43	7.47	7.52
52	7.30	7.33	7.36	7.40	7.43	7.48	7.52	7.58
53	7.34	7.37	7.40	7.44	7.48	7.52	7.57	7.63
54	7.38	7.41	7.44	7.48	7.53	7.58	7.63	7.69
55	7.42	7.45	7.49	7.53	7.58	7.63	7.69	7.76
56	7.46	7.50	7.54	7.58	7.63	7.69	7.76	7.83
57	7.50	7.54	7.59	7.64	7.69	7.76	7.82	7.90
58	7.55	7.60	7.64	7.70	7.76	7.83	7.90	7.98
59	7.61	7.65	7.70	7.76	7.83	7.90	7.98	8.07
60	7.66	7.71	7.77	7.83	7.90	7.98	8.07	8.17
61	7.72	7.78	7.84	7.91	7.99	8.07	8.17	8.27
62	7.79	7.85	7.92	7.99	8.07	8.17	8.27	8.39
63	7.86	7.93	8.00	8.08	8.17	8.27	8.38	8.51
64	7.94	8.01	8.09	8.18	8.27	8.38	8.51	8.64
65	8.02	8.10	8.18	8.28	8.39	8.51	8.64	8.78
66	8.11	8.19	8.29	8.39	8.51	8.64	8.78	8.94
67	8.20	8.29	8.40	8.51	8.64	8.78	8.93	9.11
68	8.31	8.40	8.52	8.64	8.78	8.93	9.10	9.29
69	8.41	8.52	8.64	8.78	8.93	9.10	9.28	9.49
70	8.53	8.65	8.78	8.93	9.09	9.28	9.47	9.71
71	8.66	8.78	8.93	9.09	9.27	9.47	9.69	9.94
72	8.79	8.93	9.09	9.26	9.46	9.68	9.92	10.19
73	8.93	9.09	9.26	9.45	9.67	9.91	10.17	10.46
74	9.09	9.25	9.44	9.65	9.89	10.15	10.44	10.76

* For unisex rates assume that the youngest age is female.

ANNUITY PAYOUT PER $1,000 NET AMOUNT
JOINT ANNUITY WITH 10 YEARS CERTAIN
WITH 100% TO THE SURVIVOR*

Male Age	10 yrs. Less	8 yrs. Less	6 yrs. Less	FEMALE AGE 4 yrs. Less	2 yrs. Less	Same Age	2 yrs. More	4 yrs. More
50	6.98	7.00	7.02	7.05	7.07	7.10	7.13	7.16
51	6.99	7.02	7.04	7.07	7.10	7.13	7.16	7.20
52	7.01	7.04	7.06	7.09	7.12	7.16	7.19	7.23
53	7.03	7.05	7.08	7.12	7.15	7.19	7.23	7.27
54	7.05	7.08	7.11	7.14	7.18	7.22	7.26	7.31
55	7.07	7.10	7.13	7.17	7.21	7.26	7.30	7.35
56	7.09	7.13	7.16	7.20	7.25	7.29	7.34	7.39
57	7.11	7.15	7.19	7.24	7.29	7.34	7.39	7.44
58	7.14	7.18	7.23	7.28	7.33	7.38	7.44	7.50
59	7.17	7.21	7.26	7.32	7.37	7.43	7.49	7.56
60	7.20	7.25	7.30	7.36	7.42	7.48	7.55	7.62
61	7.23	7.29	7.34	7.41	7.48	7.54	7.61	7.69
62	7.27	7.33	7.39	7.46	7.53	7.60	7.68	7.76
63	7.31	7.37	7.44	7.51	7.59	7.67	7.76	7.85
64	7.35	7.42	7.49	7.57	7.66	7.75	7.84	7.93
65	7.40	7.47	7.55	7.64	7.73	7.82	7.92	8.03
66	7.45	7.53	7.62	7.71	7.81	7.91	8.02	8.13
67	7.50	7.59	7.68	7.78	7.89	8.00	8.02	8.13
68	7.56	7.65	7.75	7.86	7.98	8.10	8.23	8.36
69	7.62	7.72	7.83	7.95	8.08	8.21	8.35	8.48
70	7.69	7.80	7.92	8.05	8.18	8.32	8.47	8.62
71	7.76	7.88	8.01	8.15	8.29	8.45	8.60	8.76
72	7.84	7.97	8.11	8.26	8.42	8.58	8.74	8.90
73	7.92	8.06	8.21	8.37	8.54	8.72	8.89	9.06
74	8.01	8.16	8.33	8.50	8.68	8.86	9.05	9.22

* For unisex rates assume that the youngest age is female.

ANNUITY PAYOUT PER $1,000 NET AMOUNT
JOINT ANNUITY WITH 10 YEARS CERTAIN
WITH 2/3 TO THE SURVIVOR*

Male Age	10 yrs. Less	8 yrs. Less	6 yrs. Less	FEMALE AGE 4 yrs. Less	2 yrs. Less	Same Age	2 yrs. More	4 yrs. More
50	7.21	7.23	7.25	7.28	7.31	7.34	7.38	7.42
51	7.24	7.26	7.28	7.31	7.35	7.38	7.42	7.47
52	7.26	7.29	7.32	7.35	7.38	7.42	7.46	7.51
53	7.30	7.32	7.35	7.39	7.42	7.46	7.51	7.56
54	7.33	7.36	7.39	7.43	7.47	7.51	7.56	7.61
55	7.36	7.39	7.43	7.47	7.51	7.56	7.61	7.67
56	7.40	7.43	7.47	7.51	7.56	7.61	7.67	7.73
57	7.44	7.48	7.52	7.56	7.61	7.67	7.73	7.80
58	7.48	7.52	7.57	7.62	7.67	7.73	7.80	7.87
59	7.53	7.57	7.62	7.67	7.73	7.79	7.87	7.94
60	7.58	7.62	7.68	7.73	7.79	7.86	7.94	8.02
61	7.63	7.68	7.73	7.80	7.86	7.94	8.02	8.11
62	7.69	7.74	7.80	7.86	7.94	8.02	8.10	8.20
63	7.74	7.80	7.87	7.94	8.02	8.10	8.20	8.30
64	7.81	7.87	7.94	8.01	8.10	8.19	8.29	8.40
65	7.87	7.94	8.01	8.10	8.19	8.29	8.39	8.51
66	7.94	8.01	8.10	8.18	8.28	8.39	8.50	8.62
67	8.02	8.09	8.18	8.28	8.38	8.50	8.62	8.75
68	8.09	8.18	8.27	8.37	8.49	8.61	8.74	8.87
69	8.17	8.27	8.37	8.48	8.60	8.73	8.87	9.01
70	8.26	8.36	8.47	8.59	8.71	8.85	9.00	9.15
71	8.35	8.46	8.57	8.70	8.84	8.98	9.14	9.29
72	8.44	8.56	8.68	8.82	8.97	9.12	9.28	9.44
73	8.54	8.67	8.80	8.95	9.10	9.26	9.43	9.59
74	8.65	8.78	8.92	9.08	9.24	9.41	9.58	9.75

* For unisex rates assume that the youngest age is female.

PAYOUTS PER $1,000 NET AMOUNT SINGLE LIFE ANNUITY RATES

Age	Life Only Male	Female	Life 5 Y.C.† Male	Female	Life 10 Y.C. Male	Female	Life 15 Y.C. Male	Female	Life 20 Y.C. Male	Female	Cash Refund Male	Female
50	7.70	7.39	7.67	7.38	7.60	7.34	7.51	7.30	7.41	7.25	7.54	7.31
51	7.76	7.43	7.73	7.42	7.65	7.38	7.55	7.33	7.44	7.28	7.59	7.35
52	7.82	7.48	7.79	7.46	7.70	7.42	7.59	7.37	7.47	7.31	7.64	7.39
53	7.89	7.53	7.85	7.51	7.76	7.47	7.64	7.41	7.51	7.34	7.69	7.43
54	7.96	7.58	7.92	7.56	7.82	7.51	7.69	7.45	7.54	7.37	7.75	7.47
55	8.04	7.64	8.00	7.62	7.89	7.57	7.74	7.49	7.58	7.40	7.81	7.52
56	8.12	7.70	8.07	7.68	7.95	7.62	7.80	7.54	7.62	7.44	7.88	7.57
57	8.21	7.77	8.16	7.74	8.03	7.68	7.85	7.59	7.66	7.48	7.95	7.63
58	8.31	7.84	8.25	7.81	8.10	7.74	7.91	7.64	7.70	7.52	8.02	7.68
59	8.41	7.92	8.35	7.89	8.19	7.80	7.97	7.69	7.74	7.56	8.10	7.75
60	8.53	8.00	8.46	7.97	8.27	7.87	8.04	7.75	7.78	7.60	8.19	7.81
61	8.65	8.09	8.57	8.05	8.37	7.95	8.10	7.81	7.82	7.64	8.28	7.88

62	8.79	8.19	8.69	8.14	8.47	8.03	8.17	7.87	7.86	7.69	8.38	7.96
63	8.93	8.29	8.83	8.24	8.57	8.11	8.24	7.94	7.90	7.73	8.48	8.04
64	9.09	8.41	8.97	8.35	8.68	8.20	8.31	8.01	7.93	7.78	8.59	8.13
65	9.26	8.53	9.12	8.47	8.79	8.30	8.38	8.08	7.97	7.82	8.70	8.23
66	9.44	8.66	9.28	8.59	8.92	8.40	8.45	8.15	8.01	7.87	8.82	8.33
67	9.64	8.81	9.46	8.73	9.03	8.51	8.52	8.23	8.04	7.91	8.95	8.44
68	9.85	8.97	9.64	8.87	9.16	8.63	8.59	8.31	8.07	7.95	9.09	8.55
69	10.07	9.14	9.84	9.03	9.29	8.75	8.66	8.38	8.10	7.99	9.23	8.68
70	10.32	9.32	10.04	9.20	9.42	8.88	8.73	8.46	8.13	8.03	9.39	8.81
71	10.58	9.53	10.26	9.38	9.56	9.02	8.80	8.55	8.15	8.07	9.55	8.95
72	10.86	9.75	10.49	9.58	9.70	9.16	8.86	8.63	8.17	8.10	9.72	9.11
73	11.16	9.99	10.73	9.79	9.83	9.31	8.92	8.70	8.19	8.13	9.89	9.27
74	11.83	10.55	11.26	10.27	10.11	9.61	9.03	8.85	8.22	8.18	10.28	9.63
75	11.83	10.55	11.26	10.27	10.11	9.61	9.03	8.85	8.22	8.18	10.28	9.63

* For unisex rates use the female rates.
† Y.C. = Years certain

APPENDIX K

IRS Form 2553 Election
By a Small Business Corporation

Form 2553 should be sent to the Internal Revenue Service Center in which the corporation will file its Form 1120S. It is suggested, because timeliness is extremely important, that this letter be sent certified mail, return receipt requested, so that the corporation has individual documentation that it has been timely filed. For operating corporations, the filing can take place at any time prior to the fiscal year or by the fifteenth day of the third month of the new fiscal year. If the filing is not effective for the current year, it will be considered effective for the following year. It is also suggested that a covering letter be sent with the form stating that the sender should be contacted if the form is not properly completed.

Form **2553**	**Election by a Small Business Corporation**	OMB No. 1545-0146
(Rev. February 1987)	(Under section 1362 of the Internal Revenue Code)	Expires 1-31-89
Department of the Treasury Internal Revenue Service	▶ For Paperwork Reduction Act Notice, see page 1 of instructions. ▶ See separate instructions.	

Note: *This election, to be treated as an "S corporation," can be approved only if all the tests in Instruction B are met.*

Part I Election Information

Name of corporation (see instructions) JOHN SMITH, INC.	Employer identification number (see instructions) 39-1234567	Principal business activity and principal product or service (see instructions) Manufacturing
Number and street 331 East Washington Street		Election is to be effective for tax year beginning (month, day, year) January 1, 1988
City or town, state and ZIP code Appleton, WI 54911		Number of shares issued and outstanding (see instructions) 100,000

Is the corporation the outgrowth or continuation of any form of predecessor? . . . ☐ Yes ☒ No | Date and place of incorporation

If "Yes," state name of predecessor, type of organization, and period of its existence ▶ . . . .   1/1/70 Wisconsin

A   If this election takes effect for the first tax year the corporation exists, enter the earliest of the following: (1) date the corporation first had shareholders, (2) date the corporation first had assets, or (3) date the corporation began doing business. ▶

B   Selected tax year: Annual return will be filed for tax year ending (month and day) ▶ . . . . 12-31 . . . .

See instructions before entering your tax year. If the tax year ends any date other than December 31, you must complete Part II or Part IV on back. You may want to complete Part III to make a back-up request.

C Name of each shareholder, person having a community property interest in the corporation's stock, and each tenant in common, joint tenant, and tenant by the entirety. (A husband and wife (and their estates) are counted as one shareholder in determining the number of shareholders without regard to the manner in which the stock is owned.)	**D** Shareholders' Consent Statement. We, the undersigned shareholders, consent to the corporation's election to be treated as an "S corporation" under section 1362(a). (Shareholders sign and date below.)*	**E** Stock owned		**F** Social security number (employer identification number for estates or trust)	**G** Tax year ends (month and day)
		Number of shares	Dates acquired		
John Smith	12/15/84 /s/ John Smith	20,000	2/1/79	233-34-9867	12/31
Emily Smith	12/15/84 /s/ Emily Smith	50,000	2/1/79	432-16-0408	12/31
Sam Brown	12/15/84 /s/ Sam Brown	20,000	1/1/70	302-64-1234	12/31
James Jones	12/15/84 /s/ James Jones	10,000	4/10/76	278-10-5678	12/31

*For this election to be valid, the consent of each shareholder, person having a community property interest in the corporation's stock, and each tenant in common, joint tenant, and tenant by the entirety must either appear above or be attached to this form. (See instructions for Column D, if continuation sheet or a separate consent statement is needed.)

Under penalties of perjury, I declare that I have examined this election, including accompanying schedules, and statements, and to the best of my knowledge and belief, it is true, correct, and complete.

Signature and Title of Officer ▶ /s/ John Smith President	Date ▶ 1/1/88

See Parts II, III, and IV on back.   Form **2553** (Rev. 2-87)

Part II   Selection of Tax Year Under Revenue Procedure 83-25 *

H   Check the applicable box below to indicate whether the corporation is:
☒ Adopting the tax year entered in item B, Part I.
☐ Retaining the tax year entered in item B, Part I.
☐ Changing to the tax year entered in item B, Part I.

I   Check the applicable box below to indicate the representation statement the corporation is making as required under section 7.01 (item 4) of Revenue Procedure 83-25, 1983-1 C.B. 689 (or comparable section of the Revenue Procedure to be issued in 1987).

☑ Under penalties of perjury, I represent that shareholders holding more than half of the shares of the stock (as of the first day of the tax year to which the request relates) of the corporation have the same tax year or are concurrently changing to the tax year that the corporation adopts, retains, or changes to per item B, Part I.

☐ Under penalties of perjury, I represent that the corporation is adopting, retaining, or changing to a tax year that coincides with its natural business year as verified by its satisfaction of the requirements of section 4.042(a), (b), (c), and (d) of Revenue Procedure 83-25 (or comparable section of the Revenue Procedure to be issued in 1987).

J   Check here ☐ if the tax year entered in item B, Part I, is requested under the provisions of section 8 of Revenue Procedure 83-25 (or comparable section of the Revenue Procedure to be issued in 1987). Attach to Form 2553 a statement and other necessary information pursuant to the ruling request requirements of Revenue Procedure 87-1. The statement must include the business purpose for the desired tax year. See instructions.

*At the time the Form 2553 and Instructions were printed, Revenue Procedure 83-25 was in the process of being revised.

Part III   Back-Up Request by Certain Corporations Initially Selecting a Fiscal Year (See Instructions.)

Check here ☐ if the corporation agrees to adopt or to change to a tax year ending December 31 if necessary for IRS to accept this election for S corporation status (temporary regulations section 18.1378-1(b)(2)(ii)(A)). This back-up request does not apply if the fiscal tax year request is approved by IRS or if the election to be an S corporation is not accepted.

Part IV   Request by Corporation for Tax Year Determination by IRS (See Instructions.)

Check here ☐ if the corporation requests the IRS to determine the permitted tax year for the corporation based on information submitted in Part I (and attached schedules). This request is made under provisions of temporary regulations section 18.1378-1(d).

☆ U.S. Government Printing Office: 1987—181-447/40083

**Department of the Treasury
Internal Revenue Service**

Instructions for Form 2553

(Revised February 1987)

Election by a Small Business Corporation

(Section references are to the Internal Revenue Code, unless otherwise specified.)

Paperwork Reduction Act Notice.—We ask for this information to carry out the Internal Revenue laws of the United States. We need it to insure that you are complying with these laws and to allow us to figure and collect the right amount of tax. You are required to give us this information.

A. Purpose.—To elect to be treated as an "S Corporation," a corporation must file Form 2553. The election permits the income of the S corporation to be taxed to the shareholders of the corporation except as provided in Subchapter S of the code. (See section 1363.)

B. Who May Elect.—Your corporation may make the election only if it meets the following tests:

1. It is a domestic corporation.
2. It has no more than 35 shareholders. A husband and wife (and their estates) are treated as one shareholder for this requirement. All other persons are treated as separate shareholders.
3. It has only individuals, estates, or certain trusts as shareholders. See instruction I for details regarding qualified subchapter S trusts.
4. It has no nonresident alien shareholders.
5. It has only one class of stock. See sections 1361(c)(4) and (5) for additional details.
6. It is not an ineligible corporation as defined in section 1361(b)(2). See section 6(c) of Public Law 97-354 for additional details.
7. It has a calendar tax year or other permitted tax year as explained in instruction G.
8. Each shareholder consents as explained in the instructions for Column D.

See sections 1361, 1362 and 1378 for additional information on the above tests.

C. Where to File.—File this election with the Internal Revenue Service Center where the corporation will file **Form 1120S**, U.S. Income Tax Return for an S Corporation. See the Instructions for Form 1120S for Service Center addresses.

D. When to Make the Election.—Complete Form 2553 and file it either: (1) at any time during that portion of the first tax year the election is to take effect which occurs before the 16th day of the third month of that year (or at any time during that year, if that year does not extend beyond the period described above) or (2) in the tax year before the first tax year it is to take effect. An election made by a small business corporation after the 15th day of the third month but before the end of the tax year is treated as made for the next year. For example, if a calendar tax year

corporation makes the election in April 1987, it is effective for the corporation's 1988 calendar tax year.

For purposes of this election, a newly formed corporation's tax year starts when it has shareholders, acquires assets, or begins doing business, whichever happens first.

E. Acceptance or Non-acceptance of Election.—IRS will notify you if your election is accepted and when it will take effect. You should generally receive determination on your election within 60 days after you have filed Form 2553. Do not file Form 1120S until you are notified that your election is accepted. If you are now required to file **Form 1120**, U.S. Corporation Income Tax Return, or any other applicable tax return, continue filing it until your election takes effect.

You will also be notified if your election is not accepted.

Care should be exercised to ensure the election is received by Internal Revenue Service. If you are not notified of acceptance or non-acceptance of your election within 3 months of date of filing (date mailed), you should take follow-up action by corresponding with the service center where the election was filed. If filing of Form 2553 is questioned, an acceptable proof of filing is: (1) Certified receipt (timely filed); (2) Form 2553 with accepted stamp; (3) Form 2553 with stamped IRS received date; or (4) IRS letter stating that Form 2553 had been accepted.

F. End of Election.—Once the election is made, it stays in effect for all years until it is terminated. During the 5 years after the election has been terminated under section 1362(d), the corporation can make another election on Form 2553 only if the Commissioner consents. See section 1362(g) and Revenue Ruling 86-141, IRB 1986-49 page 6, for more information. See sections 1362(d), (e), and (f) for rules regarding termination of election.

G. Permitted Tax Year.—Section 1378 provides that no corporation may make an election to be an S corporation for any tax year unless the tax year is a permitted tax year. A permitted tax year is a tax year ending December 31 or any other tax year for which the corporation establishes a business purpose to the satisfaction of IRS.

H. Investment Credit Property.—Although the corporation has elected to be an S corporation under section 1362, the tax imposed by section 47 in the case of early disposition of investment credit property will be imposed on the corporation for credits allowed for tax years for which the corporation was not an S corporation. The election will not be treated as a disposition of the property by the corporation. See section 1371(d).

I. Qualified Subchapter S Trusts.—When a qualified subchapter S trust consents to the election on Form 2553, an additional election must be made by the trust beneficiary in accordance with section 1361(d)(2) and temporary regulations section 18.1361-1(a). Failure to make and file the section 1361(d)(2) election in a timely manner will invalidate the election under section 1362 (Form 2553 election). See section 1361(d) and temporary regulations section 18.1361-1(a) for other details.

Specific Instructions

Part I.—Part I must be completed by all corporations.

Name and Address of Corporation.—If the corporation's mailing address is the same as someone else's such as a shareholder's, please enter this person's name below the corporation's name.

Employer Identification Number.—If you have applied for an employer identification number (EIN) but have not received it, enter "applied for." If the corporation does not have an EIN, you should apply for one on **Form SS-4**, Application for Employer Identification Number, available from most IRS or Social Security Administration offices. Send Form SS-4 to the IRS Service Center where Form 1120S will be filed.

Principal Business Activity and Principal Product or Service.—Use the Codes for Principal Business Activity contained in the Instructions for Form 1120S. Your principal business activity is the one that accounts for the largest percentage of total receipts. Total receipts are gross receipts plus all other income.

Also state the principal product or service. For example, if the principal business activity is "grain mill products," the principal product or service may be "cereal preparation."

Number of Shares Issued and Outstanding.—Enter only one figure. This figure will be the number of shares of stock that have been issued to shareholders and have not been reacquired by the corporation. This is the number of shares all shareholders own, as reported in column E, Part I.

Item B.—The selected tax year must be a permitted tax year as defined in instruction G.

A newly formed corporation may automatically adopt a tax year ending December 31.

Generally, an existing corporation may automatically change to a tax year ending December 31, if all of its principal shareholders have tax years ending. December 31, or if all of its principal shareholders are concurrently changing to such tax year. If a corporation is automatically changing to a tax year ending December 31, it is not necessary for the corporation to file **Form 1128**, Application for Change in Accounting Period. A shareholder may not change his or her tax year without securing prior approval from IRS. For purposes of the automatic change, a principal shareholder is a shareholder who owns 5% or more of the issued and outstanding stock of the corporation. See temporary regulations section 18.1378-1 for additional details.

If a corporation wants to change to a tax year ending December 31, but does not qualify for an automatic change as explained above, it may want to complete Part IV and indicate in an attached statement that it wants to change to a tax year ending December 31.

If a corporation selects a tax year ending other than December 31, it must complete Part II or IV in addition to Part I.

Column D.—Shareholders' Consent Statement.—Each person who is a shareholder at the time the election is made must consent to the election. If the election is made during the corporation's first tax year for which it is effective, any person who held stock at any time during that portion of that year which occurs before the time the election is made must consent to the election although the person may have sold or transferred his or her stock before the election is made. Each shareholder consents by signing in column D or signing a separate consent statement, described below.

The election by a small business corporation is considered made for the following tax year if one or more of the persons who held stock at any time during that portion of that year which occurs before the time the election is made did not consent to the election. See section 1362(b)(2).

If a husband and wife have a community interest in the stock or in the income from it, both must consent. Each tenant in common, joint tenant, and tenant by the entirety also must consent.

A minor's consent is made by the minor or the legal guardian. If no legal guardian has been appointed, the natural guardian makes the consent (even if a custodian holds the minor's stock under a law patterned after the Uniform Gifts to Minors Act).

Continuation Sheet or Separate Consent Statement.—If you need a continuation sheet or use a separate consent statement, attach it to Form 2553. The separate consent statement must contain the name, address, and employer identification number of the corporation and the shareholder information requested in columns C through G of Part I.

If you wish, you may combine all the shareholders' consents in one statement.

Column E.—Enter the number of shares of stock each shareholder owns and the dates the stock was acquired. If the election is made during the corporation's first tax year for which it is effective, do not list the shares of stock for those shareholders who sold or transferred all of their stock before the election was made but who still must consent to the election for it to be effective for the tax year.

Column G.—Enter the month and day that each shareholder's tax year ends. If a shareholder is changing his or her tax year, enter the tax year the shareholder is changing to. If the election is made during the corporation's first tax year for which it is effective, you do not have to enter the tax year of shareholders who sold or transferred all of their stock before the election was made but who still must consent to the election for it to be effective for the tax year.

Signature.—Form 2553 must be signed by the president, treasurer, assistant treasurer, chief accounting officer, or other corporate officer (such as tax officer) authorized to sign.

Part II.—Items H and I of Part II are to be completed by a corporation that selects a tax year ending other than December 31, and that qualifies under section 4.02, or 4.04 of Revenue Procedure 83-25, 1983-1 C.B. 689. (**Note:** Section 4.03 of Rev. Proc. 83-25 was suspended for S corporation elections made after November 5, 1986. See Announcement 86-113, IRB 1986-47 page 46, for details.) Items H and I are completed in place of the additional statement asked for in section 7.01 of the procedure. Sections 4.02, and 4.04 provide for expeditious approval of certain corporations' requests to adopt, retain, or change to a tax year ending other than December 31. The representation statements in Part II of Form 2553 highlight the requests provided for in sections 4.02 and 4.03 of the revenue procedure. A corporation adopting, retaining, or changing its accounting period under the procedure must comply with or satisfy all applicable conditions of the procedure.

The revenue procedure applies only to the tax years of corporations which are electing S corporation status by filing Form 2553. A corporation is permitted to adopt, retain, or change its tax year only once under the procedure. It is not necessary for the corporation to file Form 1128 when adopting or changing its tax year under the procedure.

Items H and J of Part II are to be completed by a corporation that is making a request as specified in section 8 of the procedure. Section 8 provides that if a corporation wants to adopt, retain, or change to a tax year not specified under section 4.02, or 4.04 of the procedure or certain paragraphs of temporary regulations section 18.1378-1, it should attach a statement to Form 2553 pursuant to the ruling request requirements of Revenue Procedure 87-1, IRB 1987-1 page 7. (Changes to this revenue procedure are usually incorporated annually into a new revenue procedure as the first revenue procedure of the year.) The statement must show the business purpose for the desired tax year.

Approval of tax year selections made under section 4.02, or 4.04 of Revenue Procedure 83-25 are generally automatic; however, a request under section 8 is not automatic. If a request is made under section 8, the corporation may want to make the back-up request under Part III. See section 8 of the procedure for details.

Part III.—Check the box in Part III to make the back-up request provided by temporary regulations section 18.1378-1(b)(2)(ii)(A). This section provides that corporations requesting to retain (or adopt) a tax year ending other than December 31, may make a back-up request to adopt or change to a tax year ending December 31, in case the initial request for a fiscal year is denied. In order to make the back-up request, a corporation requesting to retain its tax year ending other than December 31, must qualify for an automatic change of its tax year under temporary regulations section 18.1378-1(b)(1).

Part IV.—Check the box in Part IV to request the IRS to determine your permitted tax year under the provisions of temporary regulations section 18.1378-1(d). If you check the box in Part IV, enter "See Part IV" in the space in item B, Part I, for month and year.

You may attach a schedule to Form 2553 showing any additional information you want the IRS to consider in making the determination. IRS will notify you of the permitted tax year determination. The tax year determination by IRS is final.

☆ U.S. Government Printing Office: 1987—181-447/40084

APPENDIX L

Sample Form of Voluntary Revocation
of Election Under Subchapter S

For all taxable years beginning after 1982, a voluntary revocation is effective for the year in which it is made, but only if it is made by the fifteenth day of the third month of the fiscal year. If it is not made within that time, it is effective beginning in the next succeeding year. All of the following documentation should be signed by the proper persons and forwarded certified mail, return receipt requested.

L-1: COVERING LETTER

[Date]
Internal Revenue Service Center
[Applicable Service Center]
Re: Revocation of Election under
    Subchapter S for XYZ Corporation

Dear Sirs:

I am enclosing herein the following documents relative to the revocation of a Subchapter S election made for XYZ Corporation, Employer ID #00-0000000 on [date of original election]:

1. Statement of XYZ Corporation of Revocation of Election under Subchapter S of the Internal Revenue Code of 1954 duly executed by John Doe, President.

2. Statement of Consent of Shareholders to Revocation of Election under Subchapter S of the Internal Revenue Code of 1954 signed by the shareholders owning a majority [it could be all of the issued stock, if that is the case, but only a majority is necessary) of the issued stock of said corporation, namely, John Doe and Jane Doe.

If you require any additional information, or if I can be of any further assistance in this matter, please feel free to contact me.

Sincerely,

John Q. Attorney

Certified Mail
Return Receipt Requested

L-2: NOTIFICATION OF REVOCATION OF ELECTION
UNDER SUBCHAPTER S MADE BY CORPORATION

**Statement by XYZ Corporation of
Revocation of Election Under Subchapter S
of the Internal Revenue Code of 1954**

Internal Revenue Service Center
[Applicable Service Center]
Subject: Notification of Revocation
              of Election under Subchapter
              S Made by XYZ Corporation

Dear Sirs:

Please be advised that XYZ Corporation, 100 Main Street, City, State, Zip Code, hereby revokes the election to be subject to Subchapter S of the Internal Revenue Code of 1954 made by it on Form 2553 filed with the Internal Revenue Service Center on [date of election]. It is intended that the first taxable year of the corporation for which this revocation shall be effective is the calendar year beginning [year of revocation]. Statements signed by all the shareholders consenting to the revocation of the corporation's election are attached hereto and made a part hereof.

The current shareholders of the corporation and the shares of stock which they own are as follows:

Name and Address of Shareholders	Number of Shares Owned
John Doe 100 Main Street City, State Zip Code	50
Jane Doe 100 Main Street City, State Zip Code	50
Kid Doe 300 Westfield Avenue City, State Zip Code	20

The consent of the shareholders owning a majority of the common stock of the corporation included with this letter are as follows:

Name of Shareholder	Number of Shares Owned
John Doe	50
Jane Doe	50

Percentage of stock voting to revoke Subchapter S election: 83 percent.

XYZ CORPORATION

BY: _____
John Doe, President

Dated: _____
Attachments

L-3: CONSENT SIGNED BY ALL SHAREHOLDERS OR BY SHAREHOLDERS HOLDING A MAJORITY OF THE STOCK

Statement of Consent of Shareholders to Revocation of Election under Subchapter S of the Internal Revenue Code of 1954

The undersigned, being a shareholder of XYZ Corporation, on the date on which the revocation is made, hereby consents to the statement of revocation of the election to be subject to Subchapter S of the Internal Revenue Code of 1954 to which this consent is attached.

Name and Address of Shareholders	Number of Shares Owned
John Doe 100 South Main Street City, State Zip Code	50

_____

John Doe

Dated: _____

APPENDIX M

Sample Notification of Termination of Election—Nonresident Alien Shareholder

Beginning in tax years after 1982, if a new shareholder does not qualify as a qualified shareholder for Subchapter S purposes, the election is terminated as of the date the terminating event occurs. A sample of the notification by the corporation that this event occurred is set forth in this appendix. Because of the changes implemented by the Subchapter S Revision Act of 1982, it is anticipated that the IRS will issue regulations that will specify even more clearly than in the past the exact requirements as to timeliness and content of said notification. Until the final regulations are promulgated, the following could be utilized.

[Date]
Internal Revenue Service Center
[Applicable Service Center]

Subject: Notification of Termination
        of Election under Subchapter
        S Made by XYZ Corporation

Dear Sirs:

In accordance with the requirements of Regulations 1.1372–4(b)(3), this is to notify you that the election to be subject to Subchapter S made by the XYZ Corporation, 200 South State Street, City, State, Zip Code on [Election date], was terminated by the transfer on February 5, 198_, of 50 shares of stock in such corporation to a nonresident alien, Mr. Frank Smith. The Subchapter S election will be terminated beginning February 6, 198_.

The following additional information is submitted in accordance with Regulations 1.1372-4(b)(3);

Name and Address of Transferer	Name and Address of Transferee
John Doe	Frank Smith
100 Fernmeadow Drive	2 Kings Way
City, State Zip Code	Ontario, Canada

XYZ CORPORATION

BY: _____
John Doe, President

APPENDIX N

Agreement Filed Pursuant to
Section 302(c)(2)(A)(iii)
of the Internal Revenue Code of 1954

If the corporation completely redeems the stock of a shareholder in a closely held corporation in which the redemption would be taxed as dividend income because of the family attribution rules, it is necessary for the redeemed shareholders to file an agreement with the Internal Revenue Service to have the attribution rules waived. This agreement states that if the shareholder acquires an interest in the corporation within ten years after the redemption, he will notify the commissioner. This agreement must be filed with the individual's tax return for the year in which the redemption took place.

AGREEMENT FILED PURSUANT TO
SECTION 302(c)(2)(A)(iii) OF THE
INTERNAL REVENUE CODE OF 1954

[Dated:] _____

This agreement is filed by the undersigned taxpayer pursuant to the provisions of Section 302(c)(2)(A)(iii) of the Internal Revenue Code and Paragraph 1.302(4)(a) of the Income Tax Regulations with respect to a distribution to him from Redemption Corporation, 123 South Main Street, City, State, Zip Code on **[date of redemption],** in redemption of all of his stock in the corporation. The amount of such distribution to the undersigned was [a description of the amount and method of payment].

The undersigned is a distributee required by the aforesaid provisions to file this agreement.

The undersigned has not acquired any interest [as described in Section 302(c)(2)(A)(i)] in Redemption Corporation since the above mentioned distribution.

The undersigned agrees to notify the district director of Internal Revenue for the district in which his income tax return (to which this agreement is attached) is filed, in the event that he acquires any interest in Redemption Corporation of the type described in Section 302(c)(2)(A)(i) and Paragraph 1.302-4 of the Income Tax Regulations if such acquisition occurs within ten years from the above date of the distribution. The undersigned agrees to notify the district director within thirty days of such acquisition.

_____

John Doe
1395 West Spring Street
City, State Zip Code
Social Security #123-45-6789

APPENDIX O

Valuation of the Closely Held Corporation

In drafting stock purchase agreements or stock redemption agreements, one area that constantly poses a problem is how to value the corporation upon the death of one of the parties. Usually each individual shareholder in the corporation has his own particular idea as to what the corporation is worth. This value is not only dictated by an actual determination of the individual shareholders but also from their perspective. The older shareholder who foresees that he will be the first to die will usually place a greater worth on the corporation than the younger person who sees himself as buying out the older shareholder's stock.

Therefore, there is a basic need to understand the methods of obtaining valuation for these corporations. There are, of course, many other times when the value of the corporation must be known. Therefore, a fundamental knowledge of the approaches and methods of being able to determine the value of the corporation in question is indispensable. (For a more comprehensive discussion of the methods of determining fair market value of the closely held corporation, see Chapter 3 of "How to Buy or Sell the Closely Held Corporation" by Lawrence C. Silton.)

The following article was written by the author and excerpted with permission by *Trusts and Estates* magazine.

There is no doubt that the value of the closely held corporation is an elusive quarry. The determination of the value of a corporation is at best an art and not a science and at worst pure conjecture. However, the determination of the value of the corporation, and therefore the value of the stock, plays a major role in numerous tax and non-tax-planning decisions. The combination of the need for a proper determination taken in conjunction with the fact that human nature dictates that the person who owns the stock of a closely held corporation has only a vague and often incorrect notion of what the stock is worth, makes the determination of value even more imperative. In most cases, the need is not for a definitive answer, which could only be obtained through an appraisal of the business by a professional, but for a value determination within a reasonable range.

Before analyzing the factors which determine the value of a closely held corporation, it is necessary to define what constitutes a closely held corporation. Depending on the context in which it is used, the term has various meanings. For the purpose of this article, the term "closely held corporations" will refer to those corporations where the value cannot be ascertained solely with reference to an established market.[1] Nothing contained herein should imply that because there is an established market, the valuation of the shares of the stockholder involves nothing more than the multiplication of the price per share by the number of shares owned by him, or that this is the sole definition of a closely held corporation.[2]

The valuation of the shares of the closely held corporation is affected by two distinct and separate factors—intrinsic and extrinsic. The intrinsic factors which affect the value of the closely held corporation are those which relate to the financial condition of the company, such as earnings capacity, book value, dividend paying capacity, goodwill, or other intangible values. These factors are usually considered in relationship to the background and history of the business, the general economic conditions of industry, and the economic outlook of a specific industry. These factors are contrasted to the extrinsic factors which involve conditions and situations outside of the corporation itself which help determine its value. These include, among other things, agreements which restrict the transferability of the shares of the corporation, or transactions in a

---

[1] For a discussion of other definitions, see *Valuation of Shares of Closely Held Corporations,* 221 T.M. 1.

[2] "Blockage"—Sale of large quantities may result in lower per share value. *Helvering v. Maytag,* 125 F(2d) 55. Cert. den. 316 U.S. 689; *Bull v. Smith,* 119 F(2d) 490(e).

market place. These extrinsic considerations, while they may determine the value of a particular business, are beyond the scope of this article wherein it will be assumed that there is neither a marketplace nor are the shares subject to any restrictions affecting transferability.

An appropriate starting point for the determination of the relevant factors which determine the intrinsic valuation of the corporation can be found in *Rev. Rul. 59–60*,[3] which outlines in considerable detail the factors which should be considered, among which are the following:

1. the nature of the business and the history of the enterprise from its inception;
2. the economic outlook in general and the condition and outlook of the specific industry in particular;
3. the book value of the stock and the financial condition of the business;
4. the earning capacity of the company;
5. the dividend paying capacity;
6. whether or not the enterprise has goodwill or other intangible value; and
7. market price of stocks or corporations engaged in a similar line of business having their stocks actively traded in a free and open market, either on an exchange or over the counter.

The IRS, through this Revenue Ruling and other pronouncements, realizes that this is not the definitive list of factors. The relevancy of a factor is, of course, dependent upon the particular fact situation. For example, the death of the founding father, president or chief operating officer will have differing effects on the worth of a company depending not only on the strength of the remaining management but also on the type of business. Consider the difference that said death would have in a personal service business such as an advertising agency with that of a basic manufacturing company.[4]

---

[3]*Rev. Rul. 59–60*, 1959-1 CB 237.
[4]Id. at para. 6.

The above factors must be considered in a specific time frame. For general purposes, the basic frame in determining the value is a period encompassing five years. This may or may not be indicative for the simple reason that there may be extraordinary circumstances within the five-year period that affect the company, i.e., depression, war, or long strike.[5]

Various Methods of Valuation

There are an infinite number of sophisticated methods for valuing a corporation, involving numerous economic and mathematical assumptions and approaches which require a background far beyond what is available to anyone but a professional appraiser. In the final analysis, these methods involve one or more of the classical approaches which have historically provided the basis for appraising real estate:[6] income, market, and cost. The income (also known as capitalization) approach capitalizes the net-after-tax earnings at a reasonable rate of return considering the investment and its relative risk. The market approach compares the price earnings ratio of the company under analysis with that of comparable companies in the same industry which are traded in the public marketplace. The cost approach revolves around a basic determination of the costs of the underlying assets depreciated to date. The income (capitalization) approach is both beyond the scope of discussion here and in many cases may be unnecessary because its impact and appropriateness are mitigated by use of the market approach if a comparable publicly held corporation is located.

The appropriateness of each of the remaining two valuation approaches, market or cost, depends on the basic character of the company. When valuing stock of companies which sell products or services, the Internal Revenue Service and the courts have taken the position that the primary consideration in valuing these companies is their earning capacity, or the market approach. On the other hand, the investment or hold-

---

[5]Id.

[6]Henry A. Babcock, *Appraisal Principles and Procedures* (Homewood, Illinois: Richard D. Irwin, Inc., 1968), page 96.

ing type company which has as its basic assets real estate, stock, bond, or the like, will use as its basic valuation tool the book value of the company, which is basically the cost approach. The weight accorded each of these factors will vary from company to company.[7]

Earnings (Market) Approach

The basic supposition in the earnings approach is that the future earnings of the company can be predicted from the prior history of the company. In other words, prior earnings are the most reliable guide as to the future earnings of the company. Once the expected future earnings of the company have been determined, this figure is multiplied by the price earnings ratio of a comparable company which is publicly traded. The price earnings ratio is defined as the market price of a share of stock divided by the per share earnings.

A determination of the future earning power of the company requires analysis of the prior year's earnings, earning trends, and special adjustments to the earnings of the company. There is no doubt that earning trends are extremely significant in determining the value of the corporate stock. An illustration of the effect of these trends can be seen by studying the following example:

Corporations A, B, and C have the
following per share earnings:

	1971	1972	1973	1974	1975
A	$1.00	1.20	1.44	1.73	2.08
B	$1.50	1.48	1.51	1.47	1.49
C	$2.10	1.75	1.42	1.20	.98

Each of the three corporations above have an average per-share earnings for the five-year period of about $1.49. Corporation A's earnings are growing at 20 percent compounded per year, while Corporation B's earnings are static, and Corporation C's earnings are declining. It would appear axiomatic that

---

[7]*Supra* 3, para 5.

the predicted per share earning power of a particular corporation would have to take these trends into account. The Internal
Revenue Service has acknowledged the fact that where increasing or decreasing net income is found, the greater weight will
be accorded to the most recent year's profits.[8]

The Court of Claims in *Central Trust Co. v. U.S.*[9] took into
account a favorable earnings trend by weighing the earnings on
a scale of five for the most recent year to one for the furthest
year. Other cases have not been quite as scientific, but have also
given greater emphasis to the more recent year's earnings.[10]

In addition to analyzing trends, modifications to the year's
earnings will have to be made for nonrecurring factors which
would distort the earning trend of the business.[11] In the closely
held corporation, where the major shareholders are frequently
the officers of the company, tax considerations and economic
needs of the officers will, in most cases, dictate the amount of
the salaries rather than the value of the actual services rendered by them to the corporation. Accordingly, adjustments
should be made either upward or downward to reflect the correct amount of earnings based upon the fact that salaries were
paid commensurate to the services rendered to the corporation
rather than being dictated by tax ramifications.[12] Adjustments
should also be made for nonrecurring factors which have a
material effect on earnings. This includes such things as capital
gains and losses, changing of inventory valuation, accounting
method changes, abnormal retirement plan payments, etc.

Once the appropriate earning power has been determined
for the corporation, the task remains to find an appropriate
multiplier.

The best guide to finding an appropriate price earning
multiplier is to determine the price earnings in a comparable
company whose shares are publicly traded.[13] The problem here

---

[8]*Supra* 3, 4.02 (d).

[9]305 F(2d) 393, 424 (Ct. Cls., 1962).

[10]*Est. of Synder v. U.S.*, 285 F(2d) 857, 862 (4th Cir. 1961) rev'g and rem'g 182F.
Supp 71 (D.C. N.C. 1960).

[11]See *Estate of Joseph E. Goar;* 9 T.C.M. 854 (1950); *George E. Bartol, Jr.,* 11 T.C.M.
527 (1952).

[12]I.R.C., Sec 162(a)(i); Regs. 1.162-7; Regs. 1.162-8.

[13]I.R.C. 2031(b); *Supra* 3, para. 4.02(h).

is to find a truly comparable company. Even if a company is found in the same type and kind of industry, it is doubtful that it would be of the same size. Its earnings record (trends) should also be analyzed to see if it is comparable to the subject corporation.

If such a comparable situation is not found, it will then be necessary to find a price earnings ratio or capitalization ratio which would be indicative of a similar investment. The classical thesis here is that a risky business should be acquired at a lower price earnings multiple than a nonrisky stable business. Two factors that could be taken into consideration are the nature of the business and the stability or irregularity of the earnings.[14] Bringing specifics out of the general theory, arriving at a capitalization multiple in the income approach is more difficult, and a proper capitalization rate many times more closely resembles speculation than a mathematical formula. Therefore, the necessity of finding a comparable company becomes even more apparent. If a comparable company is found, care must be taken to ensure that the price earning ratios of the comparable company is derived from the same period of time that is utilized in the average earnings of the closely held company. In other words, the appropriate comparison is the earning power of the closely held corporation for the same period as that of a publicly traded company.

Accordingly, if on January 1, 1976, the company was selling at $60 per share, and if it was determined that during the period of time from 1971 through 1975, the average earnings were $10 per share, and the earnings in the current year, 1975, were $12 per share, the appropriate price earnings ratio, if the proper frame of reference is a five-year period, is six and not five.

Book Value (Cost) Approach

Book value means the net assets of the company per its financial statement; in other words, the gross assets less the liabilities. The stated assets as reflected on the company's books will almost always be at cost, or sometimes in the case of inven-

---

[14]Dewing, "The Financial Policy of Corporations," 264 n.b. Crev. Ed. (1926).

tories, at the lower of cost or market. The book value per share, which is nothing more than the total book value of the company divided by the number of outstanding shares of stock, will, in all likelihood, have little relationship to the fair market value of the underlying assets in an operating company.[15] An example of this is land bought many years ago will ordinarily have a fair market value which exceeds its book value. Machinery and equipment and other depreciable assets may be depreciated at a greater rate for tax purposes, and the net value may exceed its depreciated value; inventory may be valued at LIFO, last in-first out, which would indicate a lower value than the inventory would actually bring; goodwill, if stated at all, will be at a nominal factor.

This fact, along with the consideration that earnings in an operating company are the primary factors in valuing said corporation, makes book value of questionable use for valuation purposes. However, in both a business review and in the cases decided by the courts, we find that book value has an inordinate role in valuing a corporation. At the risk of seeming unduly cynical, the reason that the decisions of both businesspeople and the courts rely on book value is not logical analysis, but that book value is a determinable peg upon which they can base their decisions. Accordingly, when all else fails, this is the starting point for determining the value. Even in this situation, to equate "real value" with book value per share, the values of the underlying assets should be adjusted to market value. The Revenue Service has taken the position that assets of the investment type should be revalued on the basis of their market value and that the book value should be adjusted accordingly.[16]

In addition to this adjustment, which is relatively easy, the IRS takes the position that when it becomes apparent that there are intangibles which have no book value at all that add to the total valuation of the corporation, a determination of this value must be made and is added to the book value figure for the tangible assets. It should be noted that in investment companies, goodwill should have no bearing at all. However, in operating companies, the method of determining valuation has

---

[15]*Supra* 3, 4.02(c).

[16]*Estate of Warren H. Poley,* 166 F(2d) 434 (3rd Cir. 1948) aff'g 6 T.C.M. 288, 1947.

been set forth for tax purposes in *Rev. Rul. 68-609*.[17] The formula here provides for first valuing the tangible assets and then finding a value for goodwill or other intangible assets by capitalizing the earnings in excess of reasonable return on tangible assets. The IRS sets forth in *Rev. Rul. 68-609* that a reasonable return on tangible assets would be either an industry average or 8 percent for lower risk businesses to 10 percent for high risk businesses. The capitalization rate on these intangibles would then be 15 percent in low risk business and 20 percent in high risk business.

An example will help clarify the Treasury's position. ABC Corporation has average earnings of $100,000 per year and $1,000,000 in value of tangible assets. Assuming that ABC Corporation is a low risk business and that the appropriate rate of return is 8 percent, then a fair return on the tangible assets would be $80,000 (8 percent times $1,000,000). The excess earnings of $20,000 ($100,000 less $80,000) would be attributable to the intangible assets which in all likelihood would be goodwill. Applying the 15 percent capitalization rate, the multiplier is 6⅔ (this factor is derived by dividing 100 percent by 15 percent); therefore, the value of the intangible assets is approximately $130,000, and the total value of the corporation would be $1,130,000.

Weighing the Various Factors

The weight given each of the factors will vary from case to case. The Internal Revenue Service in *Rev. Rul. 59-60*[18] states: "That because valuation cannot be made on the basis of prescribed formula, there is no means whereby the various applicable factors in a particular case can be assigned mathematical weights in deriving the fair market value."

The courts in reaching their decisions as to the valuation of various closely held corporations many times do not detail the reasoning giving rise to their determinations. However, in the case of *Central Trust Co.*,[19] the courts gave a weight of 50

---

[17]*Rev. Rul. 68-609*, 1968-2 C.B. 327 superseding 34 A.R.M. 68, and *Rev. Rul. 65-192*, 1965—2 C.B. 259.

[18]*Supra* 3.

[19]*Supra* 9, page 4.05.

percent to earnings, 20 percent to book value, and 30 percent to an approach which based its value on capitalizing dividends. In the case of *Bader*[20] again, the earnings were given a 50 percent weight, and the dividend and book valuations were each given 25 percent.

Accordingly, if these cases give us a trend, it can be seen that earnings provide the major valuation method and that book value provides a minor, secondary approach.

Discounting the Valuation

Once a value for the share has been derived by weighing the values obtained by the various approaches, it is necessary to analyze those additional factors which may discount this intrinsic valuation once obtained. The most common discounting factor is, for lack of any better term, the minority discount. In a small closely held corporation, there is no doubt that there is a disparity of worth for that which constitutes 51 percent of the voting control of the corporation to that which constitutes 49 percent. In the absence of corporate agreements, minority shares appear to be worth substantially less than the majority interest in the corporation. Any practitioner who has represented the holders of shares constituting a minority interest in an intracorporate dispute knows how little leverage the minority shares have in the absence of any corporate agreement giving the minority shares special rights.[21]

IRS and Court Views

The Internal Revenue Service does not dispute this fact, but its position in a case-by-case determination has been to minimize the discount it recognizes.[22] The courts, on the other hand, have been rather liberal in their granting of a minority discount in their decisions, and in several cases the discount has

---

[20]172 F Supp. 833 (D.C. Ill., 1959).
[21]See O'Neal, F. Hodge, "Squeeze-Outs of Minority Shareholders" (Callaghan & Company, 1975) and O'Neal, F. Hodge, "Expulsion or Oppression of Business Associates" (Seeman Printing, Inc., Durham N.C. 1961).
[22]Regs. 20.203 1-2(e); Regs 25.2512(e).

amounted to up to 50 percent of the value obtained by analysis of the other factors.[23]

Another consideration is that the shares of stock of a closely held corporation are not marketable in the sense that there is no ready market for their immediate disposition. The courts have stated in numerous instances that the inability to transfer these shares is appropriate ground for discount. The court in *Central Trust Co.*[24] stated: "It seems clear . . . that an unlisted closely held stock of a corporation such as Heekin, in which trading is infrequent and which therefore lacks market-ability, is less attractive than a similar stock which is listed on an exchange and has ready access to the investing public."

To reflect such lack of marketability, the courts allow a discount from the value otherwise determined for such shares. It is necessary to distinguish the concept of marketability and minority interests. These are often confused for the reason that the rationale in allowing the discount in valuing shares repre-senting a minority interest in a closely held corporation is es-sentially the same as that for the lack of marketability discount, mainly that it would be difficult to sell the shares for the price at which the publicly held shares with comparable earnings could be sold. The distinction between the lack of marketability and the minority interest is that the lack of marketability principle could apply to controlling as well as minority interest. Dis-counts granted by the courts for lack of marketability have ranged between 10 and 20 percent.[25]

The final discount which may be available is attributable to nonvoting stock. In a closely held corporation, the majority or voting control will, in all likelihood, dictate the distribution of a good percentage of the earnings through increased salaries and bonuses rather than dividends. Accordingly, nonvoting stock as well as a minority interest in the corporation should give rise to a discount. The recognition of the amount of said discount has not received much attention by either the Internal Revenue Service or the courts but is a factor to be considered.[26]

---

[23]*Whittemore v. Fitzpatrick*, 127 F Supp. 710 (D.C. Conn., 1954), remanded to enter judgment; per stipulation (2d Cir. 1955); *Drybrough v. U.S.*, 208 F Supp. 279 (D.C. Ky., 1962).

[24]*Supra* 9.

[25]*Inga Burdahl*, 24 T.C.M. 841, 846 (1965); *Supra* 9; *Est. of Gregg Marcy*, T.C.M. 1969-158.

[26]*Rev. Rul. 67-54*, CB 1967-1, 269, *Richard P. Makoff*, T.C.M. 1967-13.

Summary

A review of the law and of the experts on valuing corporations gives only one definitive answer; that the worth of a corporation is a case study and not an application of mathematical formulas. The Internal Revenue Service has given broad guidelines but few formulas and reserves for itself a great deal of latitude in applying its value to each corporation's worth. It is imperative to acknowledge the fact that because of the lack of hard answers and human proclivities, the value attached to the corporation will vary according to a client's frame of reference. The value attached for sale purposes will vary significantly from that attributed to the same shares for gift tax or estate tax purposes. It is also important to recognize that the practitioner will almost invariably have the first opportunity to arrive at a determination of the value for the shares. Accordingly, the onus is on the practitioner to do his homework and have a logical analysis well documented for the value determined. If a proper analysis has been done and a range of value can be ascertained, planning, utilizing this value, will proceed with a relative degree of certainty.

APPENDIX P

Stock Option Agreement

The shareholder's agreement below should be used when stock of the corporation is sold to an employee who will probably never own a significant percentage of the total stock. This "keep-them-interested agreement" allows the employee the opportunity to own "a piece of the action" and at the same time protects the corporation upon his termination of employment. It allows the corporation to buy back the stock that was originally sold at its value on the date of termination. This agreement provides benefits to both the employee and employer and should be used where a small percentage of the stock is going to be sold to the current and future employees of the corporation at or near its current fair market value. It should be noted that the agreement gives the corporation the "option" to purchase the shareholder's stock upon the occurrence of termination of employment. Many times it is "fair" to provide a mandatory obligation instead of an option to purchase the stock of the terminating shareholder. In these cases, an additional paragraph restricting the terminating employee's ability to compete with the corporation should be inserted. The last thing that the corporation wants to do is to have the terminating employee use the funds received from it to compete with its established business. While covenants not-to-compete are not favored in the law, agreements which are reasonable as to both the corporation and the terminating shareholder will normally be enforced.

This agreement, made this _____ day of _____, 19____, by and between _____, hereinafter referred to as the "Stockholder," and _____, hereinafter referred to as the "Corporation."

WHEREAS, the parties hereto have found it in the best interest of themselves to enter into this agreement.

For and in consideration of the original sale of stock of the Corporation to the Stockholder, it is hereby agreed between the parties as follows:

1. In the event of the first of the following to occur:
   - (a) the Stockholder wishes to sell, assign, or transfer any stock which he owns in the Corporation;
   - (b) the Stockholder's employment with the Corporation is terminated for any reason other than death;
   - (c) the Stockholder dies.

   The Corporation shall have the option to purchase all of the stock owned by the Stockholder or personal representative as hereinafter set forth. The option to purchase shall cover all stock now owned by the Stockholder or hereinafter acquired by him.

2. The corporation shall have sixty (60) days after any of the occurrences set forth in (1) above or the receipt of the notice prescribed in Paragraph (1), whichever occurs later, to notify the Stockholder or his personal representative, as the case may be, of its exercise of the right to purchase the shares of stock so offered. If it fails to notify the Stockholder or his personal representative, the appropriate party may sell, assign, or transfer the shares of stock covered by this agreement free and clear of any restrictions or may exercise its rights under Paragraph (5).

3. The purchase price for the shares of stock to be purchased pursuant to Paragraph (2) shall be set at a price as determined as follows:
   - (a) The independent accountant who is currently employed by the Corporation shall determine all the assets and all the liabilities of the Corporation as of the end of the fiscal year prior to the occurrence giving rise to this option. All determinations shall be in accord with generally accepted accounting principles. The financial statements shall be based upon accrual basis accounting principles. Accounts receivables, if any, shall be discounted 10 percent to represent uncollectible accounts.

(b) Said accountant shall determine the net assets by subtracting the liabilities from the assets. The net assets shall be divided by the number of common shares issued and outstanding to arrive at the value of each common share.

(c) The purchase price shall be the value of each share multiplied by the number of common shares issued and outstanding to arrive at the value of each common share.

(d) If the Stockholder wishes to sell, assign, or transfer his shares of stock, and the offering price is less than that which is determined in (c) above, then in that event, he shall offer to the Corporation the shares of stock upon the terms and conditions as set forth by the third party.

4. Within thirty (30) days of the acceptance of the offer by the Corporation, the Stockholder, or his personal representative, shall sell, assign and transfer all right, title, and interest in and to the shares of stock covered therein to the Corporation, and the Corporation shall pay the purchase price set forth above in cash if less than Five Thousand Dollars ($5,000.00). In the event that said purchase price is greater than Five Thousand Dollars ($5,000.00), Five Thousand Dollars ($5,000.00) shall be paid in cash, and the remaining shall be paid by the Corporation executing a promissory note for the remaining purchase price payable in installments over a period not in excess of five (5) years with interest thereon at the rate determined as the minimum interest rate that can be charged under Section 483 of the Internal Revenue Code of 1954 as amended, that will not give rise to imputed interest under said section.

5. In the event that the Corporation chooses not to exercise the option set forth in Paragraph (1), the Stockholder or his personal representative, as the case may be, may, within sixty (60) days after the Corporation's failure to exercise its option, give notice to the Corporation that the Corporation must redeem the shares of the Stockholder or the personal representative at the lesser of the book value of the shares of stock as determined in Paragraph

(3), or (price substantially less than book value) per share. In the event that the Stockholder or his personal representative exercises the rights set forth herein, the payment of said shares will be in conformity with the provisions contained in Paragraph (4).

6. Any notice required to be given by the terms of this agreement shall be deemed to be validly given if made by certified mail addressed to the parties hereto at the following respective addresses:

[List addresses of shareholder and corporation]

Prompt notice of any change in the above addresses must be given by the Stockholder by written notice by certified mail to the president of the Corporation. The Stockholder shall be deemed to have received notice of any change in the principal office of the Corporation.

7. This agreement shall bind the parties hereto and their respective heirs, executors, administraters, and assigns.

8. Upon the execution of this agreement, the certificates of stock subject hereto shall be surrendered to the Corporation for endorsement as follows:

> This certificate is transferable only upon compliance with the provisions of an agreement dated the _____ day of _____, 19__, by and between _____ and _____, a copy of which is on file in the office of the secretary of _____ .

IN WITNESS WHEREOF, this agreement has been executed on the day and year first above written.

BY: _____
Corporation

BY: _____
ATTEST:

BY: _____

APPENDIX Q

Agreement between Stockholders and Company to Purchase Stock

The agreement that follows is what is commonly known as a "stock redemption agreement." In this agreement, the corporation will, upon the death of one of the shareholders, redeem the stock. This particular agreement determines the fair market value as follows:

a. Sets a current value for the stock. This is usually a value that has been agreed upon at the time of entry into the agreement; and

b. Increases or decreases the value in relationship to the change in retained earnings.

This particular agreement also restricts the lifetime transfer of the stock by giving the corporation the right to purchase the stock of any shareholder who desires to sell this stock during the existence of the agreement. The purchase price is calculated as the same price that would be paid upon death. However, in order not to place an undue burden upon the corporation, it provides for an installment payout of this purchase price. It also provides that if the corporation does not buy the stock offered, the shareholders shall have the right to purchase, and if they do not purchase, then he can sell the stock to a third party without any further restrictions. Absolute restrictions upon sale during the lifetime of an individual are of doubtful enforceability.

Agreement, made this _____ day of _____, 19___, by and between _____ and _____, hereinafter collectively referred to as "Stockholders," of City, State, and _____, a corporation organized under the laws of the State of _____ , hereinafter referred to as the "Company."

WHEREAS, the Stockholders are the owners of all of the capital stock of the Company, each stockholder owning 100 shares in the Company; and

WHEREAS, the Stockholders believe it to be for their best interest and for the best interest of the Company that the stock of a decreased Stockholder be acquired by the Company; and

WHEREAS, the Company has arranged to provide funds to acquire the stock of a deceased Stockholder through life insurance;

IT IS THEREFORE AGREED:

1. Upon the execution of this agreement, the certificates of stock subject hereto shall be surrendered to the Company for endorsement as follows:

   This certificate is transferable only upon compliance with the provisions of an agreement dated the _____ day of _____ , 19__, between _____ and _____ , a copy of which is on file in the office of _____ .

   After endorsement the certificates shall be returned to the Stockholders. All stock hereafter issued to any Stockholder shall bear the same endorsement.

2. The Company shall take out insurance on the life of each Stockholder for $_____ and name itself as beneficiary of the policies. All policies are listed in Schedule A attached to and made a part of this agreement. The policies and any proceeds received thereunder shall be held by the Company in trust for the purposes of this agreement. The Company shall have the right to take out additional insurance on the life of any Stockholder whenever, in the opinion of the Company, additional insurance may be reasonably required to carry out its obligations under this agreement. Any additional policies shall be listed in Schedule A and shall otherwise be subject to the terms of this agreement.

3. The purchase price of the stock of a deceased Stockholder shall be set at a price determined as follows:
    (a) During the period commencing on January 1. 1985, and ending December 31, 1985, the purchase price for one-half of the authorized and issued common stock of the Company shall be [set price].
    (b) For the period commencing January 1, 1986, and ending upon the termination of this agreement, the purchase price for one-half of the authorized and issued stock of the Company shall be [set price] plus one-half of the increase or minus one-half of the decrease by which the retained earnings as reflected on the U.S. Corporation Income Tax Return filed for the Company have varied from those reported for the year ended December 31, 1985, to the end of the year prior to occurrence giving rise to transfer of shares as contemplated in this agreement.

4. Upon the death of any Stockholder, the Company shall purchase the decedent's stock from his estate, and the estate shall sell such stock to the Company. The personal representative of the deceased Stockholder shall proceed with the probate of the estate and shall promptly transfer title to the decedent's stock to the Company.

    The Company shall collect the proceeds of the insurance policies on the life of the deceased Stockholder, and upon receipt of title to decedent's stock, shall pay such proceeds, or so much thereof as may be necessary, to the deceased Stockholder's personal representative in payment for the decedent's stock. In the event the purchase price exceeds the insurance proceeds, the Company shall pay to the decedent's personal representative any additional amount necessary to pay the purchase price by the Company executing a promissory note guaranteed by the survivor, payable in sixty equal monthly installments of principal and interest, commencing six months after the end of the calendar month in which the decedent's death occurred. Said note shall bear interest at the rate of __ percent per annum.

5. In the event any Stockholder desires to sell all or part of his stock, he shall give written notice of such election to the Company, which shall then have the right, exercisable within thirty days, to purchase such stock. The purchase price shall be the value determined in paragraph (3). Said purchase price shall be paid by the Company executing a promissory note guaranteed by the survivor, payable in sixty equal monthly installments, commencing six months after notification by the selling shareholder. The promissory note shall bear interest at __ percent per annum. If the Company declines to purchase the stock on the terms and conditions set forth above, the selling Stockholder shall offer said stock on the same terms and conditions to the other Stockholder. If the Company and Stockholder decline to purchase such offered stock, said offering Stockholder may sell said stock to any third party at a price no less than and upon terms no more favorable to the purchaser than those offered to the Company and other Stockholder. If and when all of the stock of a Stockholder shall have been transferred, he shall cease to be a party to this agreement.

6. If by operation of Section 5, any Stockholder's participation in this agreement shall terminate, then for thirty days thereafter he shall have the right to purchase the policies on his own life owned by the Company. The purchase price of the policies shall be the interpolated terminal reserve as of the date the retiring Stockholder ceased to be a party to this agreement, plus the proportional part of the gross premiums last paid before said date which covers the period extending beyond that date. In the event any permanent form policy to be transferred shall not have been in force for a period sufficient to obtain a value, as stated above, then the purchase price shall be an amount equal to all net premiums paid.

7. This agreement shall terminate in the event of the bankruptcy, receivership, or dissolution of the Company.

8. No insurance company shall be under any obligation in respect to the performance of the terms and conditions of this agreement. Payment by the insurance company pursuant to the terms of any policy shall be a complete dis-

charge of the said insurance company from all claims, suits, and demands of all persons whatsoever.

9. This agreement shall bind the Stockholders and their respective heirs, personal representatives, and assigns, but nothing herein shall be construed as an authorization to any Stockholder to assign his rights or obligations hereunder. Each Stockholder in furtherance hereof shall execute a will directing his personal representative to perform this agreement and to execute all documents necessary to effectuate the purposes of this agreement, but the failure to execute such will shall not affect the rights of any of the Stockholders or the obligations of any estate as provided in this agreement.

IN WITNESS WHEREOF, the parties have signed and sealed this agreement.

Corporation

BY: _____

President

ATTEST:

_____

Secretary

_____

Shareholder

_____

Shareholder

APPENDIX R

Stock Transfer Agreement

This stock purchase agreement is between the shareholders, although the corporation is also a party to the agreement. The reason for this is that the corporation has a contingent right and obligation to purchase the stock of a deceased or selling shareholder if for some reason the other shareholder does not deem this purchase in his best interest. The determination of the purchase price in this particular example is 150 percent of book value after a 25 percent discount for uncollectible accounts receivables. (For a discussion as to which type of plan (cross-purchase or stock redemption) is best suited for the corporation, see Chapter 6, ¶601.4.)

Agreement, made this _____ day of _____, 19__, by and between _____, _____, and _____, hereinafter collectively referred to as "Shareholders."

WHEREAS, the Shareholders are the owners of all the authorized and issued shares of stock of _____, a Wisconsin corporation, hereinafter referred to as the "Company," each shareholder owning the number of shares of outstanding stock set forth next to his name as follows:

_____   ____ shares of common stock
_____   ____ shares of common stock
_____   ____ shares of common stock

WHEREAS, the Shareholders believe that it is in their best interests and in the best interest of the Company that restrictions be placed on the sale or transfer of the stock.

IT IS THEREFORE, AGREED:

1. *Insurance:* Each Shareholder may, but is not obligated under the terms and conditions of this agreement, to take out insurance on the lives of the others, naming himself as beneficiary, in an amount not to exceed the purchase price. All such policies, if purchased, shall be listed in a schedule which shall be attached to this agreement and marked as "Schedule A." In the event that a Shareholder purchases said policies, he shall bear the premiums due on said policy or policies.

2. *Rights of ownership and policies:* In the event that a Shareholder purchases a policy or policies on the lives of the others, he shall be the sole owner of the policies taken out by him and may exercise all rights under such policies, provided, however, that before any right is exercised, thirty days' written notice shall be given to the other Shareholders.

3. *Right to purchase in the event of sale during life:* In the event that any Shareholder desires to sell all or part of his stock, he shall give written notice of such election to the company and other Shareholders. The company shall have the right, exercisable within thirty days, to purchase all or a portion of such stock as is offered for sale. In the event that it does not purchase all of the stock, the remaining Shareholders shall have the right, exercisable within thirty days after the company has notified that it will not exercise its election, to purchase such stock in the same proportion that their shareholdings bear to each other at the date of the given notice at the lesser of (1) that price and those terms which a bona fide party has offered or (2) the purchase price and payment terms set forth in paragraphs 6 and 7 of this agreement.

   Notwithstanding anything to the contrary, the right to purchase of the Company and the Shareholders must be exercised in its entirety or not at all, and all shares offered must be purchased by the company and remaining Shareholders.

4. *Freedom from transfer restrictions:* All shares of stock offered pursuant to paragraph 3 of this agreement not purchased

by the other Shareholders within the time provided therein shall be free from the terms of this agreement (and new certificates representing such shares shall be issued without the endorsement set forth in paragraph 11) if, within an additional ten days, such shares shall have been transferred on the books of the Company to a third person. If and when all stock of the Shareholders have been transferred, he shall cease to be a party to this agreement.

5. *Purchase of shares at death:* Upon the death of any Shareholder, the remaining Shareholders shall have the right to purchase all of the shares of stock from the Shareholder's estate, and the estate shall sell such stock. In the event that the remaining Shareholders do not purchase all of the shares owned by the estate of the deceased Shareholder, the Company shall purchase the remaining decedent's stock from his estate, and the estate shall sell the remaining shares to the Company. The personal representative of the deceased Shareholder shall proceed with the probate of the estate and shall promptly transfer title to surviving Shareholders, or Company, as the case may be. All stock purchased by the surviving Shareholders shall be in the same proportion that their shareholdings bear to each other at the date of the death of the deceased Shareholder.

6. *Purchase price:* The purchase price of the stock of the deceased Shareholder shall be set at the price determined as follows:

   (a) An accountant shall determine all the assets and all the liabilities of the Company as of the end of the month during which the death of the Shareholder shall have occurred. All determinations shall be in accord with generally accepted accounting principles. Financial statements shall be based upon accrual basis of accounting principles. Accounts receivables, if any, shall be discounted 25 percent to represent uncollectible accounts.

   (b) The accountant shall determine net assets by subtracting the liabilities from the assets. The net assets shall be divided by the number of common shares issued and outstanding to arrive at the value of each common share.

(c) The purchase price shall be the value of each share multiplied by the number of shares which are to be transferred pursuant to this agreement, multiplied by 150 percent to arrive at the purchase price.

7. *Payment of purchase price:* The purchase price of deceased Shareholder's stock shall be paid as follows:

(a) Whether the purchase of stock is by the Company or surviving Shareholders, the total amount of the policies of life insurance listed in Schedule A attached hereto and made a part hereof shall be paid to the estate of the decedent within thirty days after the appointment and qualification of the personal representative of such estate.

(b) The total purchase price, in the event that no insurance policies have been purchased, or the amount arrived at by subtracting the insurance proceeds from the purchase price arrived at in paragraph 6 of this agreement, shall be paid by the execution of a promissory note payable in equal monthly installments over a period not to exceed eight years, with interest thereon at the minimum amount that can be charged pursuant to the provisions of Section 483 of the Internal Revenue Code of 1954, as amended, which will not give rise to imputed interest.

8. *Delivery of shares:* Upon receipt by the estate of the deceased Shareholder of the purchase price in cash, or in cash and promissory notes, the legal representative of the estate shall endorse and deliver the shares of the decedent to the surviving Shareholders or the Company, whichever is applicable.

9. *Purchase of insurance policies by survivors:* Upon the death of a Shareholder, the surviving Shareholders shall have the right to purchase from the estate of the decedent any or all of the policies insuring the lives of the surviving Shareholders for a price equal to the interpolated terminal reserve as of the date of death of the shareholder, less any indebtedness against such policies, plus the proportionate

part of the gross premium last paid before the date of death which covers the period extending beyond that date. This right may be exercised at any time within sixty days after the qualification of the legal representative of the deceased Shareholder by the payment of the purchase price to such representative, and, if the right is not so exercised within the time allowed, it shall lapse. Upon receipt of the purchase price, the legal representative of the deceased Shareholder shall deliver the insurance policies to the surviving Shareholders and shall also execute and deliver to them all instruments necessary to transfer the policies to them.

10. *Purchase of insurance upon withdrawal from agreement:* If by operation of paragraph 3, any Shareholder's participation in this agreement shall terminate, then for thirty days thereafter, the policies owned by the terminated Shareholder and the policies owned by the remaining Shareholders on the life of the terminated Shareholder shall each be subject to purchase by the respective insureds. The purchase price shall be determined as set forth in paragraph 9 of this agreement, substituting date of withdrawal for date of death.

11. *Endorsement on share certificates:* Upon the execution of this agreement, the share certificates subject hereto shall be surrendered to the Company and endorsed as follows:

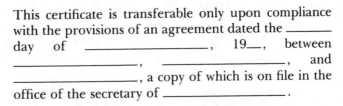

This certificate is transferable only upon compliance with the provisions of an agreement dated the _____ day of _____, 19__, between _____, _____, and _____, a copy of which is on file in the office of the secretary of _____.

After endorsement, the certificates shall be returned to the Shareholders, who shall be entitled to exercise all rights of ownership concerning such shares subject to the terms of this agreement. All shares hereafter issued shall bear the same endorsement.

12. *Term:* This agreement shall terminate upon the occurrence of any of the following events:
    (a) Cessation of the Company's business
    (b) Bankruptcy, receivership, or dissolution of the Company

(c) Bankruptcy or insolvency of any Shareholder

(d) Death of all Shareholders simultaneously or within a period of thirty days

Upon the termination of this agreement during the lives of the Shareholders, each Shareholder shall have the right to purchase from the other Shareholders any or all of the insurance policies on his life on the same terms provided in paragraph (9) for such purchase upon the death of a Shareholder. Upon the failure of any Shareholder to exercise this right within sixty days after termination, the right shall lapse. In the event that the agreement terminates under the provisions of subparagraph (d) of this paragraph, the respective legal representatives of the estates of the Shareholders shall be entitled to collect the proceeds of the policies held by them and to retain such proceeds free from the terms of this agreement.

13. *Benefit:* This agreement shall be binding upon the Shareholders, their heirs, legal representatives, successors, and assigns, and each Shareholder in furtherance thereof shall execute a will directing his personal representative to perform this agreement and to execute all documents necessary to effectuate the purposes of this agreement, but the failure to execute such will shall not affect the rights of any Shareholder or the obligations of any estate, as provided in this agreement.

IN WITNESS WHEREOF, the parties have signed this agreement as of the day and year first above written.

_____

Shareholder

_____

Shareholder

_____

Shareholder

Corporation

BY: _____

APPENDIX S

IRS Form 964 Election of Shareholder
under Section 333 Liquidation

When a corporation is being liquidated pursuant to Section 333, it is necessary that 80 percent of the total combined voting power of all classes of stock entitled to vote file an election to have their liquidation distribution taxed under Section 333. This election should be filed with the Internal Revenue Service Center where the corporation normally files its tax return and must be filed in duplicate thirty days after the adoption of the plan of liquidation. (See pages 478 through 481 for Form 964.)

Form **964**

(Rev. October 1987)

Department of the Treasury
Internal Revenue Service

Election of Shareholder under Section 333 Liquidation

(To be filed within 30 days after the adoption of the plan of liquidation. See instructions on page 4.)

▶ **For Paperwork Reduction Act Notice, see instructions on page 4.**

OMB No. 1545-0040

Expires 6-30-90

Name of shareholder	Identifying Number (See instruction F.)
John Smith	391-65-1910

Address of shareholder (Number, street, city, state, and ZIP code)
125 West South Street, Appleton, WI 54911

Name of corporation	Employer Identification Number
XYZ Corporation	39-8897764

Address of corporation (Number, street, city, state, and ZIP code)
123 South Main Street, Appleton, WI 54911

Time and date of adoption of plan of liquidation	Calendar month of transfer of all property
January 1, 1988	January, 1988

The above named shareholder elects to have recognized and taxed in accordance with section 333 of the Internal Revenue Code the gain on each and every share of the capital stock of the above named corporation owned by the shareholder at the time of the adoption of the plan of complete liquidation providing for a distribution in complete cancellation or redemption of all corporate stock and for the transfer of all corporate property under the liquidation entirely within the above stated calendar month of transfer of all property.

SCHEDULE A
Statement of Shares of Stock Owned at the Time and Date of Adoption of Plan of Liquidation

Class of stock	Certificate numbers	Number of shares	Total number of shares that are entitled to vote on adoption of plan of liquidation
common	#1	250	250

Form **964** (Rev. 10-87)

Form 964 (Rev.10-87)

SCHEDULE B

Statement of Shares of Stock Owned on Date of Execution of Election

Class of stock	Certificate numbers	Number of shares	Total number of shares that are entitled to vote on adoption of plan of liquidation
common	#1	250	250

SCHEDULE C

Statement of Shares of Stock Owned on January 1, 1954

(To be filled in only by corporate shareholders)

Class of stock	Certificate numbers	Number of shares	Total number of shares that are entitled to vote on adoption of plan of liquidation

Attach a statement showing all shares acquired or disposed of between January 1, 1954, and the time and date of adoption of plan of liquidation, both dates inclusive, giving date on which any share was acquired or disposed of, class of stock, the certificate numbers thereof, the number of shares involved in each transaction, the total number of shares that are entitled to vote on adoption of plan of liquidation, and the name of the person from whom acquired or to whom transferred.

SCHEDULE D

If any of the shares listed in any of the above schedules are not registered in the name of the person by whom this election is made, list below the name of the person in whose name such stock is registered giving the class of stock, the certificate numbers thereof, the number of shares, the total number of shares that are entitled to vote on adoption of plan of liquidation, and all facts pertinent to the claim of ownership.

(Use additional sheets if necessary.)

Under penalties of perjury, I declare that I have examined this return, including accompanying schedules and statements, and to the best of my knowledge and belief it is true, correct, and complete.

▶ /s/ John Smith _____ 1/15/88
Signature of electing shareholder   Date

If a corporation:

▶ _____ ▶ _____
Signature of officer   Date   Title

Instructions

(Section references are to the Internal Revenue Code unless otherwise noted.)

Paperwork Reduction Act Notice.—We ask for this information to carry out the Internal Revenue laws of the United States. We need it to ensure that taxpayers are complying with these laws and to allow us to figure and collect the right amount of tax. You are required to give us this information.

Section 333 Repealed.—The Tax Reform Act of 1986 repealed section 333 and revised section 337. However, transitional rules allow qualified corporations to liquidate with fewer tax consequences than others who liquidate. A qualified corporation is any corporation that on August 1, 1986, and at all times thereafter (ending with the date the corporation is completely liquidated) is 50% (by value) or more owned by 10 or fewer qualified persons, and the total value of all of its stock does not exceed $10,000,000. A qualified person is an individual, an estate, or any trust described in clause (ii) or (iii) of section 1361(c)(2)(A). Qualified corporations must use Form 964-A, Computation of Gain or Loss Recognized by Qualified Corporations on Complete Liquidation, to compute gain or loss on liquidation.

A. Purpose.—This form is to be used by qualified electing shareholders who elect the benefits of section 333.

B. Qualified Electing Shareholder.—No corporate shareholder may be a qualified electing shareholder if at any time between January 1, 1954, and the date of the adoption of the plan of liquidation, both dates inclusive, it was the owner of stock of the liquidating corporation possessing 50% or more of the total combined voting power of all classes of stock entitled to vote upon the adoption of the plan of liquidation. All other shareholders are divided into two groups for the purpose of determining whether they are qualified electing shareholders: (1) shareholders other than corporations, and (2) corporate shareholders.

Any shareholder of either group is a qualified electing shareholder if—

(1) The written election to be governed by the provisions of section 333 has been filed as prescribed by the regulations; and

(2) Like elections have been made and filed by owners of stock possessing at least 80% of the total combined voting power of all classes of stock owned by shareholders of the same group at the time of, and entitled to vote upon, the adoption of the plan of liquidation.

C. Election.—An election to be governed by the provisions of section 333 can be made only by or on behalf of the person by whom gains, if any, will be realized. Thus the shareholder who may make the election must be the actual owner of stock.

A shareholder is entitled to make an election for gain only on stock owned by him or her at the time of the adoption of the plan of liquidation. The election applies only to the shareholder.

D. Election.—Two or more electing shareholders may authorize an attorney or agent, by power of attorney, to file a consolidated election on Form 964 on their behalf. The attorney or agent must file the Form 964, together with the power of attorney and a list of those shareholders who consent to be qualified electing shareholders.

A shareholder may, however, individually file Form 964. In either case, a copy of the election must be attached to the shareholder's income tax return for the tax year in which the transfer of all the property under the liquidation occurs.

E. Time and Place for Filing.—Form 964 must be filed by the shareholder with the Internal Revenue Service Center where the final income tax return of the corporation will be filed. The election must be filed within 30 days after the adopton of the plan of liquidation.

Under no circumstances shall section 333 be applicable to any shareholder who fails to file an election within the 30-day period.

F. Identifying Number.—Individuals must enter their social security number; all others must enter their employer identification number.

G. Liquidating Corporation Filing on Behalf of the Shareholder.— A corporation liquidated under section 333 may provide certain information on behalf of the shareholder. The requirements will be satisfied if:

(1) The shareholder, prior to the designated date of the shareholders' meeting to consider the adoption of a plan of liquidation, has been advised of all material aspects of the plan;

(2) The shareholder (or the shareholder's duly authorized representative), by proxy, indicates approval of the plan; provides all information required by the form, except the unknown information relating to the time and date of the adoption of the plan and the calendar month of the transfer of the corporate property; signs the form; and forwards it to the corporation;

(3) The shareholder (or authorized representative) has been advised by the corporation that by signing the proxy and the Form 964 and returning them to the corporation, the shareholder will have authorized the corporation to insert on the form the time and date of the adoption of the plan of liquidation and the calendar month of the transfer of the corporate property (if known), and to file the form on behalf of the taxpayer;

(4) The corporation properly completes the Form 964 that it has received from the shareholder, and files the form within 30 days after the adoption of the plan of liquidation at the Internal Revenue Service Center specified above; and

(5) A fully completed Form 964 is attached to the shareholder's income tax return for the year in which the transfer of all the corporation's property occurred.

H. Calendar Month of Transfer of all Property.—If the calendar month of transfer of all property under the·liquidation is unknown when this election is filed, enter "unknown" and state the month on the copy of the election required to be attached to the shareholder's income tax return for the tax year in which the transfer of all property under the liquidation occurs.

If an electing shareholder has designated a particular month on a timely filed Form 964 as the transfer month but the property is transferred in a different calendar month, the shareholder's election will not be invalidated, if the shareholder files a copy of the Form 964 indicating the actual transfer month with his or her income tax return for the tax year of liquidation.

I. Supplemental Statement.—Each qualifying electing shareholder receiving distributions is required to file with his or her income tax return for the tax year in which the liquidation occurs a supplemental statement that must include the following information:

(1) A statement of stock ownership in the liquidating corporation, as of the record date of the distribution, showing the number of shares of each class owned on such date, the cost or other basis of each such share, and the date of acquisition of each share;

(2) A list of all the property, including money, received upon the distribution showing the fair market value of each item of such property other than money on the date distributed and stating what items, if any, consist of stock or securities acquired by the liquidating corporation after December 31, 1953;

(3) A statement of the stockholder's ratable share of the earnings and profits of the liquidating corporation accumulated after February 28, 1913, computed without reduction for distributions made during the month of liquidation (other than designated dividends under section 316(b)(2)(B)); and

(4) A copy of the shareholder's written election to be governed by the provisions of section 333. See Regulation section 1.333-3.

J. Signature.—If the shareholder making the election is a corporation, the election must be signed either by the president, vice president, treasurer, assistant treasurer, chief accounting officer, or by any other corporate officer (such as tax officer) who is authorized to sign.

A receiver, trustee, or assignee must sign any election which is required to be filed on behalf of a corporation.

This election may be executed by the shareholder's attorney or agent, provided such action is authorized by a power of attorney, which, if not previously filed, must accompany the election.

APPENDIX T

Minutes of Meeting of Shareholders and Directors Adopting a Plan of Liquidation under Section 337

> The following is a sample of the action taken by the shareholders and directors of a corporation in adopting a plan to liquidate the corporation pursuant to Section 337. Because time becomes extremely crucial, these minutes should be signed and sent along with the Form 966, certified mail, return receipt requested, within thirty days of adoption of the plan.

ACTION BY UNANIMOUS WRITTEN CONSENT OF ALL THE SHAREHOLDERS AND DIRECTORS OF LIQUIDATING, INC.

We, the undersigned, being the owners of all the authorized and issued common stock of the corporation and also being all of the directors, hereby take the following action, by unanimous written consent, without a meeting:

WHEREAS, it is in the best interest of the corporation to sell its assets and dissolve.

IT IS THEREFORE RESOLVED AS FOLLOWS:

1. *Plan of liquidation:* This plan is intended to accomplish the complete liquidation of Liquidating, Inc., a Wisconsin corporation, hereinafter referred to as "Liquidating," through the sale of all of its assets and distribution of the cash and remaining assets in complete liquidation in accordance with Section 337 of the Internal Revenue Code of

1954. Such liquidation shall be accomplished in the manner stated in this plan.

2. *Approval:* This plan shall be considered adopted by the shareholders and directors of Liquidating on the first day of _____, 19____.

3. *Authorization of terms of sale:* The officers of the corporation are authorized to accomplish the liquidation of Liquidating by a sale of all its properties and assets of every description, real and personal, for such consideration upon such terms and conditions as may be determined in the best interest of Liquidating and its shareholders. The proposed terms and conditions of such sale shall be considered approved upon execution of these minutes by the shareholders owning at least 67 percent of the outstanding shares of stock of Liquidating.

4. *Abandonment:* If a sale of all the properties and assets of Liquidating is not consummated before the end of the twelve-month period beginning on the date of the adoption of the plan, _____, its board of directors may abandon the plan and any action contemplated hereby. On such abandonment, the plan shall be void.

5. *Cessation of business:* Liquidating shall cease doing business immediately upon closing of such sale, and as soon thereafter as practicable shall file any and all papers with the State of Wisconsin which may be necessary to indicate such cessation of business.

6. *Dissolution:* As soon as practicable, after the closing of such sale, and in any event before the end of the twelve-month period, beginning on the date of the adoption of the plan, _____, Liquidating shall be formally dissolved in accordance with the laws of the State of Wisconsin, and the balance of the proceeds of the sale and any and all of its remaining assets (less any amount required to meet claims) shall be distributed pro rata to or for the account of each shareholder.

7. *Authorization to execute and file documents:* The officers and directors of Liquidating are authorized, empowered, and directed to execute and file all documents which they deem necessary or advisable to carry out the purposes and

intentions of this plan, including any Intent to Dissolve and Certificate of Dissolution under the laws of the State of Wisconsin and information returns on Treasury Department Forms 966, 1096, and 1099L, together with the income tax returns and the information required by the applicable regulations.

8. *Authorization of necessary acts:* The officers and directors of Liquidating are authorized, empowered, and directed to do any and all other things in its name on its behalf which they may deem necessary or advisable in order to carry out the purposes and intentions of this plan. They shall be held harmless by the company for any action under this plan taken in good faith, and any expense or liability so incurred by them shall be that of the company.

This action taken this first day of _____,
19__.

_____

_____

_____

Being all the directors of said corporation

_____

_____

_____

Being the owners of all the authorized and issued common stock of the corporation

APPENDIX U

Bardahl Formula Worksheet

The working capital needs of the business, at least from the perspective of the judicial decisions and the Internal Revenue Service, are subject to calculation under what is considered the Bardahl Formula. There are many variations of this formula, so a precise method is not available. An example of this is a seasonable business which may require high inventories and high receivables during the same period of time. Thus, a calculation utilizing the average working capital needs is not applicable. However, to approach the general needs of the business, the following will be illustrated by the Bardahl Formula Worksheet, hereinafter set forth, which is reproduced from the Internal Revenue Manual, MT 4 (12) 10-10 (1-22-74). (See ¶801.3.)

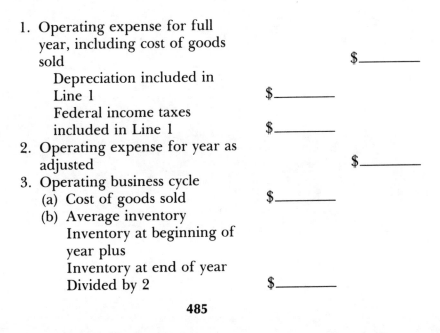

1. Operating expense for full
   year, including cost of goods
   sold $_____
       Depreciation included in
       Line 1 $_____
       Federal income taxes
       included in Line 1 $_____
2. Operating expense for year as
   adjusted $_____
3. Operating business cycle
   (a) Cost of goods sold $_____
   (b) Average inventory
       Inventory at beginning of
       year plus
       Inventory at end of year
       Divided by 2 $_____

    (c) Line (b) divided by Line (a)
multiplied by 365 =
Inventory Turnover   _____

    (d) Net sales for year $_____

    (e) Average accounts
receivables
Receivables at beginning of
year plus
Receivables at end of year
Divided by 2 $_____

    (f) Line (e) divided by Line (d)
multiplied by 365 =
Accounts Receivable
     Turnover   _____

    (g) Add Lines (c) and (f) =
days in Operating Cycle   _____

    (h) Divide Line (g) by 365 =
Operating Cycle expressed
as percentage of year   _____

4. Multiply Line 2 by Line
3(h)—Amount of working
capital needs for one cycle $_____

Form **966** (Rev. June 1987) Department of the Treasury Internal Revenue Service	**Corporate Dissolution or Liquidation** (Required under Section 6043(a) of the Internal Revenue Code)	OMB No. 1545-0041 Expires 6-30-90

Name of corporation	Employer identification number
Liquidating, Inc.	39-1197789

Address (Number and street)

123 South Main Street

City or town, state, and ZIP code

Appleton, WI 54911

Check type of return

☒ 1120 ☐ 1120L
☐ 1120-IC-DISC ☐ 1120S
☐ Other ▶

1 Date incorporated **1975**	2 Place incorporated **Wisconsin**	3 Type of liquidation ☒ Complete ☐ Partial

4 Internal Revenue Service Center where last income tax return was filed and tax year covered	Service Center **Kansas City, Missouri**	Tax year ending

Month **March**   Year **1985**

5 Date of adoption of resolution or plan of dissolution, or complete or partial liquidation **4-15-85**	6 Tax year of final return . . . . Was final return filed with a parent corporation (consolidated return)? . . ☐ Yes ☒ No

If "Yes," enter:

Name of parent corporation ▶ ------------------------------

Employer identification number ▶ ------------------------------
IRS Center where consolidated return was filed ▶

	Common	Preferred
7 Total number of shares outstanding at time of adoption of plan or liquidation	250	0
8 Dates of any amendments to plan of dissolution.	n/a	
9 Section of the Code under which the corporation is to be dissolved or liquidated.	Section 337	
10 If this return concerns an amendment or supplement to a resolution or plan for which a return was filed, give the date filed.	n/a	

Attach a certified copy of the resolution or plan, together with all amendments or supplements not previously filed.

Under penalties of perjury, I declare that I have examined this return, including accompanying schedules and statements, and to the best of my knowledge and belief it is true, correct, and complete.

/s/ John Smith	4/15/85	President
Signature of officer	Date	Title

Instructions

Paperwork Reduction Act Notice.—We ask for this information to carry out the Internal Revenue laws of the United States. We need it to ensure that taxpayers are complying with these laws and to allow us to figure and collect the right amount of tax. You are required to give us this information.

Who Must File.—A corporation files Form 966 if it is to be dissolved or if any of its stock is to be liquidated. Exempt organizations are not required to file Form 966. These organizations should see the instructions for Form 990 or 990-PF.

When To File.—File Form 966 within 30 days after the resolution or plan is adopted to dissolve the corporation or liquidate any of its stock. If the resolution or plan is amended or supplemented after Form 966 is filed, file an additional Form 966 within 30 days after the amendment or supplement is adopted. The additional form will be sufficient if you show the date the earlier form was filed and attach a certified copy of the amendment or supplement and all other information required by Form 966 and not given in the earlier form.

Where To File.—File Form 966 with the Internal Revenue Service Center where the corporation is required to file its income tax return.

Section 333 Repealed

Section 333 has been repealed by the Tax Reform Act of 1986. Transitional rules, however, allow small businesses to liquidate under section 333. In addition, corporations will have to include a portion of the gain from the liquidation in income. For more information, see sections 631(e) and 633 of the Tax Reform Act of 1986, and **Form 964-A,** Computation of Gain or Loss Recognized by Corporations on Section 333 Liquidations.

Signature.—The return must be signed and dated by the president, vice president, treasurer, assistant treasurer, chief accounting officer, or any other corporate officer (such as tax officer) authorized to sign. A receiver, trustee, or assignee must sign and date any return required to be filed on behalf of a corporation.

APPENDIX V

Flexible Benefits—A Guide to the Practitioner and a Program Booklet

Appendix V is composed of two parts.* The first is an article which sets forth the considerations that go into and the decisions that must be made before implementing a flexible benefit or cafeteria plan under Section 125 of the Internal Revenue Code. The second part sets forth a summary of the plan which was adopted by one company prior to the enactment of the Tax Reform Act of 1984. You should be aware that this act has had a significant impact on plans such as this, and before adopting such a plan, the Tax Reform Act of 1984, the Tax Reform Act of 1986, and the latest regulations and revenue rulings should be reviewed. This plan does, however, provide an approach for implementing a cafeteria plan. This is a rapidly changing area, and care should be exercised at all stages of implementation. In particular, the full impact of the Tax Reform Act of 1986 is as yet unknown. All indications are that plans such as these will be increasingly important in the area of fringe benefits for closely held corporations.

PART ONE: IS YOUR COMPANY READY FOR FLEXIBLE BENEFITS?

Has the time come for flexible benefits at your organization? It's a question only you can answer. For some firms, the answer

---

*The material contained in this appendix was written by James G. Waters, Vice President, Towers, Perrin, Forster & Crosby, New York, N.Y., and is reprinted with his permission. Part of this material previously appeared in Prentice-Hall's *Personnel Management: Compensation Service*, copyright Prentice-Hall, Inc., Englewood Cliffs, N.J. 07632.

is yes; for others, the right time for flexible benefits may be far off, or even never.

One thing is certain: The appropriateness of flexible benefits for your organization depends upon whether it meets a *business need*. Setting up such a program takes both time and money. Before you adopt a plan of flexible benefits, you will want to be sure that this investment of time and money can pay real dividends.

This article will help you weigh the merits of flexible benefits. It's written from the point of view of a benefits practitioner. It won't answer all your questions, but it will serve as a useful guide to a new and exciting way of employee benefits planning.

What a Flexible Benefit Program Is: Many conventional benefit programs already have some degree of flexibility built into them. Often they allow employees to choose such benefits as additional life insurance, dependent medical and dental coverage, and long-term disability income protection. Profit-sharing and savings plans options also provide employees a way of varying the amount and timing of the receipt of benefits. However, the type of benefit program discussed in this article has at least two other characteristics:

1. It permits employees to use *pretax* rather than after-tax dollars to "buy" benefit coverage.
2. It allows employees a trade-off among two or more benefit plans, not just options within a single plan.

These characteristics are not found in conventional benefit programs, even those with flexible elements.

Only a handful of true flexible benefit programs presently exist. There are, however, two basic types. The first is sometimes called the "add on" plan. Under this approach, the employer provides a "core" of benefits on a noncontributory basis. Employees may add additional benefit coverages to this core by applying "flexible credits"—amounts of employer money set aside for them as a consequence of cutting back the conventional benefit program to the core level.

A second type of plan might be termed the "mix and match" approach. Under this alternative, the prior benefit program is left essentially intact, but employees are given the choice of reducing some benefits in exchange for credits that allow them to increase other benefits—or to receive cash instead.

Note: In either case, employees are sometimes allowed to add their own after-tax contributions to the flexible credits to purchase even higher benefit levels.

Both types of flexible benefit programs have proved workable. What they have in common is a core level of benefits that may be modified by employees to suit their individual needs.

How to Set Up a Flexible Benefit Program: You will need to follow three basic steps in establishing a flexible benefit program:

1. Determine if it's feasible—that is, if it makes sense for your organization.
2. Design the program in detail.
3. Adapt your administrative and communications systems to the needs of the new program.

> *Important:* Undertaking a feasibility study—Step 1— need not commit your firm to the other two steps. Many employers, having studied the matter carefully, have decided not to proceed further. Still, it's a good idea to involve top management from the outset. Their support will be vital if you recommend moving to Steps 2 and 3.

Step I: The Feasibility Study

Human Resource Objectives: In conducting a feasibility study, you should begin by analyzing how a flexible benefits plan will support your organization's business objectives. Ask yourself these questions:

☐ What purpose will be served by flexible benefits?

☐ Will flexible benefits enhance your overall human resource program? Specifically, will such a plan enable you to attract and retain employees more effectively than your current benefit program?

☐ Will it respond more effectively to employee needs and therefore increase employee satisfaction?

☐ Will flexible benefits increase employees' interest in their benefits and make them more aware of the extent of their coverage?

Our experience tells us that very often flexible benefits *will* enhance an existing benefit program's attractiveness. However, in your organization, other factors may be important. For example, salaries or other cash payments may be the principal tool for attracting and retaining the kinds of employees that you need. Or, if your benefits are already modest, improving their liberality may be much more important than introducing flexibility.

Liberality of Benefits: Benefit liberality is almost a prerequisite for a successful flexible benefits program. In general, you should be able to answer yes to the following questions:

☐ Can the existing benefit program be reduced to a core level of coverages?

☐ Or, are your current benefits attractive and strong enough to permit benefit trade-offs?

☐ Are your life insurance or disability benefits (for example) generous enough so that employees might take less of one or both of them and use the value associated with those benefits to purchase another type of coverage? If your organization's benefits currently are at a minimal-needs level, you *may* not be able to provide alternative benefit choices.

> ***Exception:*** Educational Testing Services (ETS), one of the pioneers of flexible benefits, had a modest conventional program at the outset. It decided to let employees enhance their coverage selectively by using flexible credits with a value of up to 5 percent of pay. The old plan became the "core," and no benefits were reduced either by ETS or by employee option.

Complexity of Operations: The feasibility of a flexible benefit program will also be affected by the complexity of your business. You should consider the size and location of your facili-

ties, the types of employees you have, and the variety of your
business operations. Having numerous payroll and personnel
data systems can make it difficult to implement and administer
a flexible program effectively.

If your operations involve employees with widely varying
benefits patterns, flexible benefits may prove appropriate only
for some but not for others. This is especially likely if many of
your employee groups are unionized. To date, most unions
seem uninterested in flexible benefits. Presumably they fear
that such programs will undercut their role in making decisions
on behalf of their members.

Administrative Capabilities: Related to the issue of complexity
of operations is the strength of both your administrative staff
and administrative systems. You will need to consider whether
your existing staff could handle a flexible benefit program or
whether new or additional skills will be required. Flexible programs involve many more transactions and contacts between
benefits and personnel staff members on the one hand and
employees on the other than you are accustomed to.

Another major consideration is your human resource information or personnel records system. In fact, we believe that
an effective computerized human resource system is a prerequisite for a flexible benefit program. Substantial amounts of
information on employees and their benefit choices must be
maintained.

As to employee information, the data base must include at
least the following:

☐ Date of birth
☐ Date of employment
☐ Annual pay
☐ Sex
☐ Dependent status
☐ Plan entry date

Data on employee benefit choices are even more important. Here's an example of the variations in coverage available
to employees under the program adopted by one of TPF&C's
client companies:

Plan	*Employee Choices*
Medical	Four different options, including an HMO
Long-term disability	Two options
Life insurance	Six options
Dental	Two options
Vision/hearing care	Two options
Accidental death insurance	Over 20 levels of coverage available

For all but the long-term disability plan, coverages can also be elected on a single or family basis.

Finally, the human resource system must be able to calculate and display benefit plan costs and credits separately for each individual employee. In the program cited above, certain choices cost the employee money, while others produced flexible credits to determine if the employee's pay should be decreased or increased. This, in turn, required coordination with the company's payroll system. Such an interface is vital if your flexible benefit program is to run smoothly.

Capabilities and Interest of Employees: Finally, you must attempt to discern the interest employees will have in making benefit decisions, and their ability to do so. Here are some questions to ask:

☐ What are the personal characteristics of our employees? Are they well or poorly educated?

☐ How aware are they of benefit levels and costs under the current program?

☐ Will they be interested in making their own choices, rather than having the firm make them?

> ***Important:*** Some employees do not want to get involved in benefit choices. They resent the effort involved, or they may be fearful of making the wrong choice. That's why most flexible benefit plans allow employees the option of keeping their *former* coverage without any change.

Once you've satisfied yourself that the flexible benefit approach is feasible, you're ready to take the second step: to begin to consider what the new program might look like.

Step II: Detailed Program Design

Analysis of Employee Demographics: Designing a flexible benefit program begins with a careful analysis of the characteristics of the employees you plan to cover. You should have a very good knowledge of their average age, pay, and length of service, as well as their family situations. Knowing these things will help you anticipate employee needs and, in turn, what kinds of benefit choices might be of interest to employees in response to those needs.

> *Example:* If your analysis shows that you have a large number of young, single employees and a significant number of divorced or separated employees with dependent children, it's likely that offering life insurance choices would prove to be popular. The first group may want to choose less life insurance; the second, more.

Another factor that you should consider is the prevalence of working spouses. (If you do not have these data, now is a good time to gather them.) The chances are that a majority of your married employees have working spouses. These employees might well be interested in reducing their medical coverage because of the duplicate coverage provided by their spouses' employers. They may be interested, too, in additional vacation opportunities or plans that offer the facility to save and invest.

Market Test with Employees: At this point, it's time to find out firsthand how interested your employees are in a flexible program. You should seek information on *general areas* of interest, not specific benefit options. Developing specific benefit provisions comes later in the process.

The company referred to earlier did a good job of "market testing." Based on their experience, we suggest you do the following:

1. Select about 5 to 10 percent of your employees to help you. Ideally, they should represent a good cross-section of

the overall employee group in terms of age, length of service, job types, and other characteristics.

2. Break down this sample of employees into groups of about ten or twelve employees. A member of your personnel or benefits staff should meet with each group to lead a discussion on flexible benefits.

3. To guide the discussion during the meeting, prepare index cards that have the names of current and possible new benefit plans. Distribute these cards and ask employees to rank the individual benefit plans in terms of preference or importance to them. The ranking should first apply only to current benefits, then to new benefits only, and finally to a combination of current and new benefits.

4. Discuss the benefit rankings with the employees present and try to find out why the rankings differ. You may find that some employees have identified the pension plan as being very important and life insurance as being relatively unimportant. Other employees may have a completely opposite ranking. By getting the employees in the group to talk about their rankings and the reasons for them, you will become more sensitive to variations in the kinds of benefit needs that exist.

5. Following the meeting, analyze the results of the benefit rankings among the different employee groups. By recording the selections made in each meeting and relating them to the characteristics of the employees at each meeting, you will begin to have a sense of the direction your flexible benefit program should take.

Analysis of Existing Benefit Program: Before going further, you will need to take a fresh look at your organization's current benefit program. Review what benefit flexibility already exists and analyze where benefit choices can most easily be made. Note which specific benefits are more liberal than others and might provide a source of benefit reduction to produce credits for application to other benefits.

Example: Suppose your life insurance program presently provides three times pay on a noncontributory basis. By reducing this level of coverage to a core of, say, one times annual pay, you could pass the savings on to employees in the form of credits. Employees, in turn, could restore the original three times pay or—if reduced coverage suited their current needs—apply the credits to buy other forms of coverage.

Alternatives for Profit Sharing: If your firm presently has a cash-and-deferred profit-sharing plan, that plan could serve as the foundation of your flexible program. Very simply, in addition to the traditional choice between cash and a deferred profit-sharing contribution, employees may now be offered a third option: welfare benefits. Such a plan would permit a pretax replacement of some or all of the after-tax contributions paid by employees for group insurance coverages.

Develop the Core and Benefit Options: Based on the preceding analysis, your next job is to outline a benefits core and options. The core, remember, is the coverage that's automatic for everyone. This could be a minimal level of benefits—one that provides adequate but not superior coverage in each of the areas of employee needs. If the core is less generous than your present benefit program, you will be granting credits to individual employees based upon their age, pay, and other factors affecting cost.

Alternatively, your core program may be set at a more than minimal level. Employees will then be able to choose both benefit reductions and benefit additions. You could, of course, maintain your firm's current program intact, as the core of the flexible program. That may be the best approach if benefits are generally modest and, like ETS, you plan to meld the flexible approach with some overdue program liberalizations.

Review with Group Insurance Carrier and Pension Plan Actuary: The benefit options you have now developed must be reviewed with your group insurer for underwriting acceptability. The carrier will also help you determine the costs and credits associated with each of the benefit choices.

In the client company plan noted earlier, one of the employee choices was to elect a high deductible medical plan. The insurance company underwriting this plan helped establish how much money it was worth to the employee—in the form of flexible credits—to elect the high deductible coverage. Another planned choice was the election of either more or less life insurance than was provided previously. The group insurer not only suggested certain refinements in how the election should be made available but also assisted in developing the costs and credits involved.

The actuary for your pension plan should be involved if the plan is subject to employee choices under the flexible program. For example, employees might be given the option to take a lesser benefit accrual than provided under the basic plan. Or, they could have the right to elect more attractive early retirement benefits. The assistance of your pension plan actuary in pricing these choices is vital.

> ***Caution:*** Income tax law and regulations are both confusing and contradictory on the subject of including qualified pension plans in a flexible program. The advice of tax counsel should be sought before offering any options that involve the amount or timing of pension plan benefit payments.

Adverse Selection: The pricing of benefit options leads us to the problem of adverse selection—the tendency of employees to choose the coverages that will maximize their dollar return. Unchecked, adverse selection can wreak havoc with actuarially-determined benefit cost estimates. What can you do about it? Here's a list of techniques designed to minimize the problem:

1. Limit the frequency of benefit elections. In most flexcomp programs, benefit coverages cannot be changed, once elected, until the next annual election date. (An exception is sometimes made for changed personal circumstances, such as marriage, divorce, or the birth of a child.) If you are introducing a wholly new plan into your flexible program—e.g., one that provides vision and hearing care— you might be well advised that it be elected for a minimum of two years.

2. Benefit choices may be "bundled." For example, you might provide a combined medical, dental, vision, and hearing care benefit, making it available only as a single package. This would avoid employees' electing just one or another of these benefits, with the possible result of unacceptable claims experience.

3. Require evidence of good health for various of the choices. For example, where increased life insurance is an option, you could limit the election of additional coverage after the effective date of the new plan by requiring medical evidence of insurability.

4. Plan for some degree of adverse selection in setting the dollar value of contributions and credits. In general, that means pricing the options a bit high and reducing somewhat the credits attached to coverages waived by employees—in both cases as compared to the values that would apply on a purely actuarial basis.

Another area you'll want to explore with your insurer (and your legal counsel) is that of state insurance law. Certain states have minimum benefit laws and restrictions of benefit choices that could affect the design of your program. To avoid these restrictions, you may need to have the insurance contract underlying your flexible program written outside your "home" state. For example, New York State's minimum benefit laws required one program we worked on to be underwritten outside of that state.

Step III: Administration and Communication

Plan Administration: Before launching the new flexible program, you will need to modify your human resource information system to maintain the required employee data as well as a record of employees' benefit choices. The key to recording optional choices is a simple benefit election/authorization form, filled in by each employee and returned to your data processing unit. After these data are entered, the computer should prepare a printed "confirmation card" that verifies the employee's benefit elections. The confirmation card may then be sent to the employee for his or her review before the elections are deemed to be final.

The ongoing administration of flexible benefit programs is one of its major pitfalls, according to the popular literature. However, our experience suggests that this need not be so. Adding staff or greatly expanding computer systems is evidence of a flexible program that's overly complex. All you really need to do is capitalize upon your existing administrative strengths and tailor a flexible program to that. In other words, don't assume that you can administer anything the benefit design team can dream up. It's better to be realistic and aim for a program that is less flexible than you might wish, but one that can be administered—and communicated—without undue strain.

Communicating the flexible benefit program is absolutely critical to its success. The effort you'll need to make is undoubtedly greater than any you have made before. And it should spread over a significantly longer time span than is customary for new plans, even contributory ones.

Initial Announcement: The first step, we believe, should be a brief written announcement of the establishment of a flexible program, accompanied by a benefit election worksheet. The announcement folder or booklet should briefly describe the available benefit elections. (See Part Two of this appendix for a sample booklet.) The benefit election worksheet should be designed almost like a simplified income tax form, providing a step-by-step guide to the available benefit elections and the contributions and credits that will result from each choices.

Employee Meetings: Three to four weeks following the initial announcement, employee meetings should be held. The ideal group is no more than twenty to thirty at each meeting. These meetings should be led by a trained personnel or benefits staff member, using a slide or videotape presentation that describes in detail the flexible benefit program, its rationale and its operational characteristics. Use of a slide program or a videotape serves not only to heighten employee's interest and understanding but also to ensure that all of them receive the same message, regardless of location.

Employee Elections: At the meetings, employee election cards should be handed out. Employees may fill in the card at the meeting; some, having received the worksheet in advance, may be prepared to make their choices. However, most employees will not be ready to make their choices. Therefore, they should be instructed to return the authorization card within another two weeks, or whatever time period will enable you to process the benefit elections on a timely basis. They will generally want to discuss their choices with a spouse or other family member.

Confirmation of Elections: As mentioned earlier, after the employee elections have been recorded by the human resource information system, confirmation cards should be sent back to the employees. Properly designed, the confirmation card can serve as a communication tool as well as an essential administrative step. The confirmation brings employees in contact with their benefit program one more time and reinforces the flexible aspects of the program.

Annual Benefit Statement: An annual benefit statement is another effective way of keeping employees abreast of the choices they have made. Just prior to each year's resolicitation of employee elections, individualized benefit statements should be sent out. These give employees a status report of their existing benefit coverages. The statement will not only refresh their memories but will help them decide whether their choices should be changed for the coming twelve-month period.

A Key Reminder: The most powerful communications tool of all is the flexible benefit program itself. Such a program demands employee involvement. It requires employees to participate actively in shaping their benefit coverages. Doing so will make them more aware of the depth and breadth of their benefits than any conventional communications approach. In fact, the effectiveness of a flexible program as a communications tool may be the most important reason of all for having one.

Concluding Comments: There are many forces in our society that support the trend toward flexible benefits. These forces include the growing prevalence of working couples, the greater degree of education and sophistication of employees, and the increasing concern of employers about the cost of employee benefits. Clearly, too, most employees want to be involved in decisions affecting their jobs and their pay—including their benefit coverages.

As significant as these forces may be, they do not mean that flexible benefits are necessarily right for your organization. It is important, however, to look at the flexible alternative when next you undertake a review of your own benefit program. If you do conclude that flexible benefits respond to your business needs, remember that these programs *can* be designed to be relatively easy to administer and operate. What really counts is the planning you do *before* the program is set up—planning that capitalizes on the existing strengths of your benefit program and its supporting administrative systems.

PART TWO: A SAMPLE SUMMARY
FLEXIBLE BENEFIT PROGRAM BOOKLET

The material that follows is a reprint of the actual summary description of a cafeteria plan utilized by one company when it introduced its plan. Only references to the company's name have been deleted.

An Introduction to the Flexible Benefit Program

It is _____ tradition to provide its employees with an outstanding program of benefits . . . one that is more than competitive with our industry. Now we've taken a step that will move us even further ahead: the introduction of a Flexible Benefit Program. The new Program will become effective on April 1, 19__ . Here's what it will mean to you and your family:

☐ Comprehensive Financial Protection
☐ Design Flexibility
☐ Annual Selections

Comprehensive Financial Protection

Under the _____ Flexible Benefit Program, you will *automatically* and *without cost* participate in what are called *core* benefits, unless you elect to modify them by exercising certain options that are available to you. Following are highlights of the various plans that make up the core.

Medical Plan: Your Medical Plan is designed to protect you and your family against the financial consequences of both normal and catastrophic medical expenses. The Plan pays benefits for a broad range of medical services and supplies—in or out of a hospital. It is designed in two parts: Basic Medical—which pays 100% of most in-hospital services, and Major Medical—which picks up where Basic stops and pays 80% of covered expenses after you pay a small deductible amount. When you retire, you will continue to be covered by the Medical Plan, although benefits will then be coordinated with those of Medicare.

Life Insurance Plan: As an active employee, the amount of your life insurance will equal three times your base salary—to a maximum of $50,000 of coverage. When you retire, you will be covered by $5,000 of insurance for life. The Life Insurance Plan pays benefits to your beneficiary regardless of the cause of death.

Business Travel Accident Insurance (BTA) Plan: Your BTA Insurance protects you while you are traveling on Firm business anywhere in the world. The plan pays benefits to *you* for the loss of sight or limb and to your *beneficiary* in the event of your death. Basic coverage is equal to two times your base salary—with a minimum of $100,000 and a maximum of $400,000 of insurance.

Disability Plan: Disability protection is made up by two parts: Short and Long Term. The Short-Term Disability Plan covers you for the first 26 weeks of a disabling injury or illness by continuing your salary. Then the Long-Term Disability Plan takes over and pays you a total (including other disability benefits) of 60% of your salary—to a maximum benefit of $10,000 a month.

Deferred Profit-Sharing Plan: The Deferred Profit-Sharing Plan is one of the ways you participate in the Firm's success. Each year, _____ intends to make a contribution to the Plan. These contributions reflect the Firm's profits from year to year. A portion of the contributions made on your behalf may be taken in cash—if you choose—while the balance is deferred and invested at your discretion until you leave _____. There is flexibility in the amount you may take in cash by virtue of three optional percentages from which you may choose. In addition, *you* may contribute to the Profit-Sharing Plan—from 2% to 10% of your total compensation—and use the Plan's investment choices to build an even greater fund for your future.

Pension Plan: The _____ Pension Plan is built around a specific goal. It is designed so that an employee who spends a full career with us (35 or more years) retires with income—from the Pension Plan and Social Security—of from 60% (for higher paid people) to 80% (for lower paid people) of his or her base earnings near retirement. Other features of the Pension Plan include an early retirement provision and a spouse's benefit if you should die before retiring but after age 55. You may also be eligible for a pension even if you leave the Firm before retirement.

Now that we've briefly described the *core* to you, let's move on to the exciting new component of our Flexible Benefit Program.

Design Flexibility

One of the disadvantages of a conventional program of benefits is that it is often designed around a misimpression of who the average employee is. Since a large group of employees is to be covered by the identical program, some of the coverages will be more or less responsive to individual circumstances. Flexibility changes all that. Under the new _____ Flexible Benefit Program, *you* decide on the program that best fits your needs and those of your family. Here, briefly, is how it works:

☐ Three of your *core* plans have flexible provisions.

Under the Medical Plan, you may choose one of two *higher* deductible amounts. Because these choices would result in a greater out-of-pocket expense to you, you would receive a *credit* (stated as a dollar amount) for such an election.

Under the Life Insurance Plan, you may elect from one to five times your base salary as the amount of coverage. If your selection results in more than core coverage, you must *contribute* for the difference. If it results in less, you will receive a *credit*.

Under the Long-Term Disability Plan, you have the option of paying the cost of coverage. You might elect to do this because under current IRS rules, disability benefits would be tax free under those circumstances. If you did elect to pay for LTD, you would receive a *credit* equal to your contribution.

☐ There are three benefit plans that are in addition to the *core* and may be elected and paid for by you.

A Dental Plan which pays from 50% to 80% of reasonable and customary charges (depending on type of service), with a deductible applicable to some services may be elected. For example, expenses for most procedures related to diagnostic and preventive dentistry would be reimbursed at 80%, while orthodontic and prosthodontic services would be reimbursed at the 50% rate. Your election of this Plan would, of course, result in a *contribution* by you. However, in this instance, the Firm pays half the required premium.

A Vision Care and Hearing Aid Plan which pays the reasonable and customary expenses of an examination, lenses, and frames every two years, a $250 allowance for contact lenses, and an allowance for a hearing aid may also be elected, if you choose to *contribute* for it.

A Voluntary Accident Plan which pays benefits to *you* if you should lose your sight or suffer dismemberment, or to your *beneficiary* if you should die from an accidental cause. This Plan is elective, with *contributions* payable by you, based in part on a flexible schedule of coverage which starts at $10,000 and extends to $250,000. Family coverage is also available.

Those flexible items which you elect and which require contributions may be paid either from credits that you accrue from other elections, by payroll deductions, or by a combination of the two. If your Program should result in a *net credit,* you will receive that credit as an addition to your regular paycheck.

A schedule of credits and contributions, by plan, is included on the enclosed worksheet.

It will be up to you to select the options you want and thereby design the program that best meets your needs.

Annual Elections

Of course, circumstances change. The single individual who elects a lesser amount of life insurance coverage this year may be married next year and require additional protection. Or perhaps the birth of a child may prompt a decision to have the smallest deductible possible under the Medical Plan.

Therefore, our Program will permit the design of benefit coverages *annually.* The single exception to this is that the Vision Care and Hearing Aid Plan must be selected for two-year periods. You should know, as well, that if you elect to *increase* your Life Insurance amount, you must submit evidence of good health to the satisfaction of the insurer.

Let's Sum It Up

On April 1, 1981 _____ will be in the vanguard of U.S. companies by offering its employees the ability to design their own benefits under the new Flexible Benefit Program.

In February, you will attend one of a series of meetings during which you will view a presentation about the new Program and have the opportunity to have all your questions answered. At those meetings you will be given descriptive materials that will detail the provisions of each of the plans—core and optional—as well as the mechanics of the program itself.

Meanwhile, please use the enclosed worksheet to begin to think through your selections. Your choice—whether it is to accept the core or to customize your benefits—will have to be made during February of 1981.

Index